# FLASHING STEEL

# FLASHING STEEL

## Mastering Eishin-Ryū Swordsmanship

**25th Anniversary Edition**

*with entirely new material and a
memorial to Shimabukuro Hanshi*

Masayuki Shimabukuro
& Leonard J. Pellman

BLUE SNAKE BOOKS
BERKELEY, CALIFORNIA

Published by Blue Snake Books,
an imprint of North Atlantic Books
Berkeley, California

Cover photo by Robert Morris
Cover design by Jasmine Hromjak
Book design by Happenstance Type-O-Rama

Printed in the United States of America

*Flashing Steel: Mastering Eishin-Ryū Swordsmanship, 25th Anniversary Edition* is sponsored and published by the Society for the Study of Native Arts and Sciences (dba North Atlantic Books), an educational nonprofit based in Berkeley, California, that collaborates with partners to develop cross-cultural perspectives, nurture holistic views of art, science, the humanities, and healing, and seed personal and global transformation by publishing work on the relationship of body, spirit, and nature.

North Atlantic Books' publications are available through most bookstores. For further information, call 800-733-3000 or visit our websites at www.northatlanticbooks.com and www.bluesnakebooks.com.

PLEASE NOTE: The creators and publishers of this book are not and will not be responsible, in any way whatsoever, for any improper use made by anyone of the information contained in this book. All use of the information herein must be made in accordance with what is permitted by law, and any damage liable to be caused as a result thereof will be the exclusive responsibility of the user. In addition, he or she must adhere strictly to the safety rules contained in the book, both in training and in actual implementation of the information presented herein. This book is intended for use in conjunction with ongoing lessons and personal training with an authorized expert. It is not a substitute for formal training. It is the sole responsibility of every person planning to train in the techniques described in this book to consult a licensed physician in order to obtain complete medical information on his or her personal ability and limitations. The instructions and advice printed in this book are not in any way intended as a substitute for medical, mental, or emotional counseling with a licensed physician or health-care provider.

Library of Congress Cataloging-in-Publication Data
Names: Shimabukuro, Masayuki, 1948- author. | Pellman, Leonard J., author.
Title: Flashing steel : mastering Eishin-ryū swordsmanship / Masayuki
    Shimabukuro & Leonard J. Pellman.
Description: 25th anniversary memorial edition, with entirely new material
    and a memorial to Shimabukuro Hanshi. | Berkeley, California : Blue
    Snake Books, 2020. | Summary: "Revised and updated, the classic guide to
    the techniques, philosophy, and applications of iaijutsu—the art of
    self-defense with the Japanese sword"— Provided by publisher.
Identifiers: LCCN 2019059727 | ISBN 9781623175030 (trade paperback)
Subjects: LCSH: Iaido.
Classification: LCC GV1150.2 .S55 2020 | DDC 796.86—dc23
LC record available at https://lccn.loc.gov/2019059727

1 2 3 4 5 6 7 8 9 KPC 25 24 23 22 21 20

This book includes recycled material and material from well-managed forests. North Atlantic Books is committed to the protection of our environment. We print on recycled paper whenever possible and partner with printers who strive to use environmentally responsible practices.

This book is dedicated to

# Ko-Sōshihan Miura Takeyuki Hidefusa
## The Late Headmaster Miura

The late Miura Takeyuki Hidefusa was born January 5, 1922, in Shimane-ken, Japan. At the age of eleven he entered the Budō Senmon Gakkō, the martial arts training school operated by the Dai Nippon Butoku-Kai, where he began as a student of *kendō*, the sword-fighting sport based upon samurai swordsmanship.

Although it is probable that he studied aspects of *iaijutsu* during his *kendō* training, as well as during his many other martial arts studies, Miura Hanshi began his training in Musō Jikiden Eishin-Ryū in 1959 under Narise Sakahiro, who would later become the nineteenth *sōshihan* (headmaster) of the style, at the Dai Nippon Iaidō Yaegaki-Kai in Ōsaka. He also received instruction directly from the eighteenth headmaster, Masaoka Kasumi, while training at the Yaegaki-Kai. Only a year later, Miura Hanshi began his training in Shindō Musō-Ryū *jōjutsu* under Nakajima Asakichi, who was the most senior disciple of the twenty-fifth headmaster of Shindō Musō-Ryū, Shimizu Takatsugu, under whom he also occasionally trained.

Following this, Miura Hanshi began studying Koryū Kakushu Bujutsu, a system that includes a wide variety of traditional samurai weapons, in 1965, under the third headmaster of Enshin-Ryū, Kobashi Nikkan. In May 1970, Miura Hanshi undertook the study of Kukishin-Ryū *bōjutsu* under the instruction of Kanō Takehiko, the eleventh headmaster of Yanagi-Ryū.

Culminating more than forty years of diligent training in *budō*, including over fifteen years of *iaijutsu* and other samurai weapons, Miura Hanshi founded the Nippon Kobudō Jikishin-Kai in May 1975. He established its *hombu dōjō* (headquarters) on the grounds of Yasaka Jinja, in the Yasaka District of Neyagawa City in Ōsaka.

Among the rankings and titles bestowed on Miura Hanshi during his lifetime are eighth *dan* in Koryū Kakushu Bujutsu from the Zen Nippon Kobudō Sōgō Renmei (1975) and eighth *dan* in Toyama-Ryū Battō-jutsu (1977). In 2004 he was elevated to tenth *dan* Hanshi in *iaijutsu* by the Dai Nippon Butoku-Kai, the highest rank of any living member of that association.

During his life of service to the Dai Nippon Butoku-Kai as a member of its Board of Directors since 1990, and as *i-inchō* (executive director) for *kobudō shinsa* (promotion testing in weapons arts), *kobudō kenshō* (weapons seminars), and *taikai* (championships), Miura Hanshi received numerous awards, commendations, and honors, including Yōshūsho (Most Valuable Member) in 1984.

His selfless service extended well beyond just the *budō* community, and Miura Hanshi was also repeatedly recognized for his contributions to the betterment of his community, city, and region. He was named Honorary Mayor of Kyōto City in 1988, then Honorary Governor of Kyōto City later the same year, and in 1993 was named Honorary Governor of Kyōto-Fu (Prefecture) for his service to the Kansai region.

Despite his many honors and accolades, Miura Hanshi demonstrated tremendous humility in every aspect of life. His gracious and humble attitude is probably best remembered by those who knew him by his penchant for being the first to bow when greeting someone—even children or his lowest-ranking students, who knew of his habit and tried earnestly to be the first to bow. To some Westerners this desire to "out-respect" his students may seem trivial, but it made a powerful impression on all who ever met him, especially those knowledgeable of Japanese culture and customs.

He was frequently asked what the guiding principle of his life had been, and his answer was always the same: "*shisei*" (sincerity). He was certain that sincerity was the highest expression of a pure heart and mind, and the secret to success in every facet of life.

For the first edition of *Flashing Steel*, Miura Hanshi inscribed the word *shisei* in masterful *shodō* (brush calligraphy) for inclusion in the book's illustrations and signed it with his *kenshi* (sword master) name, Hidefusa, to emphasize the importance of sincerity to mastery of *iaijutsu*. For the second edition, he provided an updated rendition of the image, this time signing with only his first name, Takeyuki, to symbolize his personal imprint on the content of the book. And now that the passing of both Miura Hanshi and Shimabukuro Hanshi has brought their work and contributions to *iaijutsu* to its culmination in this volume, it seems most fitting to conclude this dedication to Miura Hanshi's memory with that same expression of his life's guiding principle.

Shisei

# *Shaji* 謝辞
## Acknowledgments

So many people have contributed to this book and its two previous editions in numerous ways that it would be impossible to thank them all individually here. We greatly appreciate all of the people who have provided assistance, support, and encouragement to the completion of this project who we are unable to mention by name.

We especially want to acknowledge and thank the following people for their essential contributions to the 25th Anniversary Edition of *Flashing Steel*.

## PHOTOGRAPHY AND ILLUSTRATIONS

The photographs for the major instructional portions of this book in chapters 6–12, 15, and 19 were taken by Mr. Robert Morris. Additional photography for chapter 20 was provided by Mr. John DeLuca. Additional photographs for chapters 13–18 were taken by Mr. Bill Villareal. Drawings and illustrations were provided by Mr. Chuck Arnold.

## MODELS

We wish to thank those who, in addition to the authors, modeled for the instructional portions of this book, particularly Mr. Jason Mizuno, who appears in chapter 15, and Mr. William E. "Ed" Ganz, who appears in chapters 16–18.

## SPECIAL APPRECIATION

Mr. Carl E. Long Hanshi, twenty-second *sōshihan* of Masaoka-Ha Musō Jikiden Eishin-Ryū *iaijutsu* and chairman of its official governing body, the Kokusai Nippon Budō Kai, has been of immeasurable inspiration and encouragement in the completion of this 25th Anniversary edition.

# *Mokuji* 目次

## Contents

# *Kinen* 記念
## In Memoriam

# A MEMORIAL TRIBUTE
## to Ko-Sōshihan Shimabukuro Masayuki Hidenobu, the Late Headmaster Shimabukuro Masayuki Hidenobu

The late Shimabukuro Masayuki Hidenobu, who would become the twenty-first *sōshihan* (headmaster) of Masaoka-Ha Musō Jikiden Eishin-Ryū *iaijutsu*, was born on March 27, 1948, in Ōsaka, Japan. Although he played the sports of *jūdō* and *kendō* in middle school and high school, he considered the true beginning of his training in *budō* (the Japanese arts of peace-making) when he undertook instruction in Shōrinji Kempō at the age of fifteen under the founder of that system, Sō Dōshin. Two years later he began his study of Hayashi-Ha Shitō-Ryū Karate-Dō under its founder, Hayashi Teruō.

He originally intended to become a lawyer and was admitted to law school after graduating high school, but he soon realized that his first love was *budō*. After dropping out of law school, he worked in a variety of jobs while concentrating on his training in *karate-dō*. In 1975, at the age of twenty-seven, he began training in Musō Jikiden Eishin-Ryū *iaijutsu* under the tutelage of its twentieth *sōshihan* (headmaster), Miura Takeyuki Hidefusa.

After moving to Escondido, California, in 1978, he began teaching *karate-dō*, *iaijutsu*, and other forms of Japanese and Okinawan *budō* at schools and law enforcement agencies there. He also gained local notoriety for his *budō* demonstrations at the San Diego County Fair and other public events. Once or twice each year he returned to Ōsaka to visit his family and continue his training. By 1990 Shimabukuro Hanshi had established *iaijutsu* programs at the University of California, San Diego, and several *dōjō* throughout Southern California. His growing reputation began to attract attention from other parts of the United States and Mexico, so Miura Sōshihan established an International Division of the Nippon Kobudō Jikishin-Kai and appointed Shimabukuro Hanshi as its chairman.

In 1993 Shimabukuro Hanshi opened his own *dōjō* in San Diego, California. By that time the majority of his American students knew him simply as "Shima." The following year, he was promoted to *nanadan* (seventh degree) and awarded the prestigious title of Kyōshi by Miura Sōshihan. Upon his return from training in Japan, he began working with his senior student, Leonard Pellman, to write a comprehensive textbook on the art and philosophy of Musō Jikiden Eishin-Ryū *iaijutsu*. The following year, with the approval and encouragement of Miura Sōshihan, he established the Jikishin-Kai International (JKI). Later that year, *Flashing Steel: Mastering Eishin-Ryū Swordsmanship* was published by North Atlantic Books and quickly became the best-selling book on *iaijutsu* in the English language.

With the publication of *Flashing Steel* came global recognition of Shima's mastery of *iaijutsu* and other forms of Japanese *budō*. *Flashing Steel* was a major factor in the sudden rise in popularity of *iaijutsu* throughout the world. Within ten years, *iaijutsu* went from an art rarely taught outside Japan to having more practitioners outside Japan than in its native land. In 2000, Shima was promoted to *hachidan* (eighth degree) and awarded the title of Hanshi—the highest accolade accorded to practitioners of *budō*. The second edition of *Flashing Steel* was published in 2008, the same year the Dai Nippon Butoku Kai, Japan's oldest and most prestigious governing body, selected Shima as its International Division representative for the art of *iaijutsu*.

In 2009, Miura Takeyuki was forced to retire from public life due to Parkinson's disease, and Shima was announced as his successor as the twenty-first *sōshihan* of Musō Jikiden Eishin-Ryū *iaijutsu*. This was an unprecedented act, because Shima was then a naturalized American citizen and thus became the first foreigner to lead a classical style of Japanese *budō*. The following year, Shima was diagnosed with cancer of the gall bladder. During surgery it was discovered that the cancer had spread to his liver and lymphatic system. True to his training, he fought valiantly against the disease for two years while continuing his grueling schedule of world travel to spread the art of *iaijutsu*. During that period, he and Leonard Pellman rushed to complete about two-thirds of a second book on *karate-dō*. On September 7, 2012, Shimabukuro Masayuki Hidenobu succumbed to his illness, having lived his final days still teaching and spreading the art of *iaijutsu* and expressing his love, devotion, and compassion through his acts of service to others.

In chapter 2, "Jinseikan," of *Flashing Steel*, in our presentation of the concept of *hei-jōshin*, we ask the reader the question, "If you were given only one week to live, what would you do?" After outlining some possible answers, we conclude with, "or would you do nothing different than you had done the previous week, or the week before that? That would indicate that your lifestyle had produced *heijōshin!*"

Right up until just days before being admitted to hospice care, Shima Sensei was doing exactly what he had done the week before, and the week prior to that—traveling and teaching the arts he loved to the people he loved. He didn't just write and lecture about the life and principles of a samurai, he *lived* the life and principles of a samurai.

In 2013, the Dai Nippon Butoku Kai posthumously inducted Shimabukuro Masayuki Hidenobu into their Hall of Fame for his lifetime of contributions to the arts and people he loved. Deservedly so. His life and his achievements stand as an inspiration to all who would strive to live by the highest principles and values of *budō*—a life that was imbued with the spirit and actions of *bushidō*, producing a legacy that lives on in his body of work and the hearts of the thousands of students worldwide whom he trained.

When describing Shima's accomplishments, the tendency is to focus on the many awards, accolades, honors, rankings, and titles that were bestowed on him, and the number and importance of his achievements. But the real measure of Shima's life is the impact he had on the lives of others. Everyone who came in contact with Shima walked away better for having met or known him. His life—his words of wisdom and encouragement, his acts of kindness and compassion toward others—improved the lives of thousands of people around the world. And *that* is the hallmark of a life of genuine importance. A life truly well lived.

You now hold in your hands a book that explains all the character traits, principles, ideals, and wisdom to live such a remarkable and meaningful life yourself, if you wish to do so, together with a detailed program of training and personal growth by which you, too, can acquire those traits—all presented in the words of a man who actually *did* it.

So, read on....

# Maegaki 前書

## Preface

A quarter-century has passed since the publication of the original edition of *Flashing Steel*. In the preface to the second edition in 2008 we noted that tremendous growth had occurred in the popularity and practice of Musō Jikiden Eishin-Ryū *iaijutsu* since the release of the first edition in 1995. That growth has continued unabated in the twelve years since the second edition went to press. There are now Eishin-Ryū *dōjō* scattered all across the globe with strong, growing, and highly dedicated followings. Even more rewarding is the personal growth that so many readers of *Flashing Steel* have reported experiencing during that time. It is deeply gratifying to know that the book has been serving the purpose for which it was written.

This is likely to be the final edition of *Flashing Steel*.

It was an emotional shock even to type those words just now! But the logic behind them seems inescapable. Shimabukuro Hanshi passed away in 2012, so he can contribute nothing further to the *Flashing Steel* legacy. His coauthor, Len Pellman Shihan, is now sixty-eight years old, and his health and stamina are fading. By the time another edition is due, he may no longer be living either. And beyond the matter of authorship is the growth and direction of Eishin-Ryū itself. Shimabukuro Hanshi was succeeded as *sōshihan* of Masaoka-Ha Musō Jikiden Eishin-Ryū *iaijutsu* by Carl E. Long Hanshi in 2012. It is now his responsibility and privilege to determine the future direction of the art. He and his successors are the future. The authors of *Flashing Steel* are now the past.

Which brings us to the purpose of this 25th Anniversary Edition of *Flashing Steel*.

Some of the most significant changes to the Masaoka-Ha Musō Jikiden Eishin-Ryū *iaijutsu* style and traditions occurred in the years immediately following the publication of the second edition, and it seems entirely fitting to record those changes for posterity and to create a lasting tribute to the life, work, and memory of the man primarily responsible for them: Shimabukuro Masayuki Hidenobu Hanshi.

Readers of the second edition may recall that we said, "in some respects, little has changed in the body of this work. The history, philosophy, and techniques of *iaijutsu*, after all, have changed little in the past ten years." While substantial truth remains in that statement, much has, in fact, changed since the second edition was published. The history of our *ryū* (style), for example, has advanced another twenty-five years since the first publication of *Flashing Steel*, and many events during that time have been of significance to the art of *iaijutsu* and to our *ryū* in particular. While the curriculum of Eishin-Ryū has not changed in the past twenty-five years, two aspects of the curriculum have changed: (1) the depth of our technical understanding of it, and (2) the training emphasis we place on various portions of the curriculum. Similarly, the philosophy of *iaijutsu* and Eishin-Ryū have not changed, but our understanding and ability to explain that philosophy have changed substantially with time. All of this is reflected in the addition of five entirely new chapters of curricular material in this edition, plus updates, revisions, and even a few corrections to nearly every other chapter of the book.

Although several more English language books on *iaijutsu* in general and Eishin-Ryū in particular have been published since 1995, *Flashing Steel* is still generally considered to be the most comprehensive and authoritative of the books on *iaijutsu* currently in print. Since it remains in continued use and demand—still informing and influencing new generations of *iaidōka*—updating its content to maintain its relevancy seems almost obligatory.

In the preface to the second edition we lamented the apparent increase in violence across the globe—acts of terrorism, school shootings, and the like. Tragically, this trend does not appear to have changed, but we continue to hope that as increasing numbers of people worldwide engage in classical *budō*, such as *iaijutsu*, that the spirit of peace-making central to these arts will begin to pervade more cultures and serve as a balm in this troubled world.

We also observed that mass media continue to portray martial arts in exaggerated and implausible ways that often create unrealistic expectations in the minds of the potential students inquiring about training in *budō*. This, too, has only gotten worse in the past decade. Between imaginative fight choreography, the use of harnesses and special effects to enhance action sequences, and CGI animation, the public is now inundated with movie and television depictions of martial arts that are pure fantasy. By comparison, traditional *budō* appears tame and even lame. If they were not real and written in earnest, many of the comments on social media in response to exhibitions of classical *budō* would be hilarious, as in: "That guy wouldn't stand a chance against my favorite fictional action hero in a real fight." Do people actually think about what they say on social media? A *real* fight against a *fictional* character? And yet this is a mentality and perception with which we must now contend in our social media– and video game–saturated world of comic book heroes.

Perhaps the solution is simply to stay true to our arts and trust that if we persevere, those who yearn for something more than fantasy or cosplay will eventually find their way to us to begin training. And perhaps the problem in the past has been that we in traditional *budō* have tried to compare ourselves with and compete against sports (mixed martial arts, *jūdō*, tournament karate, etc.) and entertainment (movies, television, and video games), rather than presenting our arts and our *ryū-ha* as something entirely different. Something to ponder as you read further....

In the preface to the second edition we also addressed a controversy that we had inadvertently fomented with our use of the term *iaijutsu* for Musō Jikiden Eishin-Ryū, rather than *iaidō*, which was the more widely known term at the time. It was not so much the term itself that incited the controversy as our somewhat clumsy attempt to explain it. We tried to clarify matters in the second edition and were apparently reasonably successful, but we still receive occasional feedback and questions, so we have once again addressed the issue in the *naiyō shōkai* (introduction) that follows.

The goals and limitations of this 25th Anniversary Edition of *Flashing Steel* are still basically the same as those of the first two editions. We want it to serve you well, to improve your life, to guide you to a fuller understanding of yourself, other people, and the art of *iaijutsu*. We still wish to remind you that *iaijutsu* cannot be learned from this or any other book. That is not its purpose. Its purpose is to serve as a reference, a primer of the fundamental concepts of the art and its culture, traditions, and philosophy, a study guide, a handy resource to use when you are not in the *dōjō*, and a stimulus for your memory. To learn an art as complex and profound as *iaijutsu* requires regular training under the supervision of a competent *sensei*.

In preparing this edition it was a constant temptation to try to improve every sentence on every page, to find a more compelling way of stating everything presented in the previous editions. After all, it is the nature of both the author and the *budōka* to try to improve one's performance with every iteration. At the same time, the primary goal of this 25th Anniversary Edition of *Flashing Steel* was to complete and preserve the legacy of Shimabukuro Hanshi, and an integral part of that legacy is the way he expressed his ideas. So, in the end we tried to strike the right balance between clarifying, supplementing, and improving the wording where it was needed, while leaving intact those portions that were already well phrased and cogently explained in previous editions.

We must also caution you not to attempt any of the techniques described in this book without the benefit of supervision by a qualified instructor. Whether you are training with a *bokken* (wooden sword), *iaitō* (unsharpened steel sword), or a *shinken* (live sword), you are wielding a potentially lethal weapon. The authors and publishers therefore accept no responsibility for any injuries or damages you may sustain as a result of attempting any of the techniques described or illustrated in this text.

It remains our fervent and sincerest hope that you will gain a kernel of wisdom or inspiration from this updated 25th Anniversary Edition of *Flashing Steel*, and that you will long treasure it as a tribute to the life, work, accomplishments, and legacy of the late *sōshihan*, Shimabukuro Masayuki Hanshi.

*"Kokoro tadashi karazareba, ken mata tadashi karazu."*
*"If your heart is not true, your sword will also not be true."*

May your heart and sword always remain true.

# Naiyō Shōkai
## Introduction

When the original edition of *Flashing Steel* was published in 1995, very few people outside Japan had ever heard of *iaidō* or *iaijutsu*, and fewer still were actively training in the art. In order to appeal to an audience that was largely unaware of *iaijutsu*, we limited our use of Japanese terminology and framed most of our description and explanation—with the exception of those essential terms we believed even beginners should know—in English, speaking of "swords," "scabbards," "blades," and "martial arts" instead of *katana*, *saya*, *ha*, and *budō*. We completely avoided terms like *ryū-ha*, *koryū*, and *gendai-ryū* out of the belief that most of our readers would not understand them.

The publication of *Flashing Steel* and the tireless efforts of Shimabukuro Masayuki Hanshi to spread *iaijutsu* globally had much to do with changing that. Now there are more *iaidōka* outside Japan than within its nation of origin, and there are vastly more people today who have at least a cursory knowledge of the vocabulary of *budō*. As a result, in this edition we have included considerably more Japanese terminology in the expectation that most of our readers are knowledgeable enough to handle it. In addition, with the ease of accessibility to the internet with computers, tablet PCs, and smart phones, definitions of Japanese words are just a few taps away.

Nevertheless, in this brief introduction we have included some of the key terms readers will encounter in the early chapters as they delve into this edition.

## BUDŌ AND BUJUTSU

In the first edition, we spoke often of "martial arts," but what we truly meant by that was *budō* or *bujutsu* instead. We recognize a significant difference in meaning between "*budō*" and "martial arts," so in this edition we have made greater efforts to distinguish between the two.

As explained in greater detail in chapter 2, true *martial* arts are the arts of warfare—*martial* meaning "military"—whereas *bujutsu* means "arts of peace-making," and *budō* means "Ways of Life of peace-making." With their purpose and intent of peace-making, *budō* and *bujutsu* seek first to avoid or prevent conflict or war, and only engage in physical combat if forced to do so—and then strive to bring peace as quickly and with as little harm to others as possible. Thus, true *budō* and *bujutsu* are entirely defensive and protective in nature, whereas martial arts, in the strictest sense, can be either aggressive or defensive.

*Iaijutsu* is *budō*, and we have endeavored in this edition to identify it as such, and we have tried to limit our use of the term "martial arts" to those situations in which it is common parlance or in reference to a combination of both offensive and defensive combat styles.

## RYŪ, HA, AND RYŪ-HA

The Japanese word, *ryū* literally means "flow" or "current," as in the flow of a river or stream. It denotes the passage of something—water, electricity, or knowledge—and when appended to another word is taken to mean "style," "school," "type," or "system." A *ha* is a word closely related to *ryū* that originally referred to a "tributary" or "branch" of a stream, but now means "faction" or "sect." So in the context of *budō* a *ryū* is a style or school, such as Eishin-Ryū (the style, school, or system of Eishin). A *ha* is a branch, sect, or derivative of a *ryū*. Masaoka-Ha Eishin-Ryū is a branch or sect of Eishin-Ryū, for example. And the word *ryū-ha* combines the two words for use as a general and collective term for schools and their branches, as in "all the *ryū-ha* [schools and their branches] of *iaijutsu*." In this edition we speak of *ryū* and *ryū-ha* quite extensively.

## KORYŪ AND GENDAI-RYŪ

*Koryū* means "ancient *ryū*" and *gendai-ryū* means "modern *ryū*." To our knowledge there is no authoritative definition of "ancient" and "modern" with respect to the *ryū* of *budō*, but in general parlance, *koryū* are those *ryū* that were established prior to the beginning of the Meiji Era (1868–1912) and *gendai-ryū* are those *ryū* that were established during or after the Meiji Era.

In our opinion, the distinction between *koryū* and *gendai-ryū* is purely a matter of dating, and recognition of the fact that *koryū* were established during the age of the samurai, whereas *gendai-ryū* were established during the post-samurai era.

This has nothing to do with the efficacy of either one; it is the equivalent of distinguishing between "prewar" or "postwar" regarding events before or after World War II.

# *IAIJUTSU* AND *IAIDŌ*

These are the terms that unintentionally sparked a controversy following the publication of the first edition of *Flashing Steel* in 1995. Hopefully, with this further clarification of the authors' use of these terms, that controversy—together with any question of our intentions—will be forever settled.

For the entire duration of his tenure as *sōshihan* (see the definition below), Miura Takeyuki Hanshi preferred the term *iaijutsu* to *iaidō* to describe Masaoka-Ha Eishin-Ryū. He also frequently used the term *iai-heihō* (*iai* strategy) to describe the art.

Miura Hanshi's use of *iaijutsu* simply reflected identical widespread uses at that time (the 1970s) of "-*jutsu*" versus "-*dō*" as a naming convention—such as the art of *kenjutsu* versus the sport of *kendō*, the art of *jūjutsu* versus the sport of *jūdō*, and others. It was common parlance, then and now, to identify systems of *koryū budō* as "-*jutsu*" and *gendai-ryū* arts (like *jukendō*) or sports derived from *budō* as "-*dō*." In particular, the Zen Nippon Kendō Renmei (the "KenRen") was actively promoting competitions in the performance of its Seitei Iaidō *kata*, so making a distinction between the sporting applications of KenRen *iaidō* and the *koryū iaijutsu* of Eishin-Ryū seemed both justified and wholly consistent with similar distinctions being made in other *budō* disciplines.

Unfortunately, in describing this distinction and the differences between judging the performance of sporting applications of *iai*, and judging the performance of *koryū iai* in the first edition of *Flashing Steel*, some readers received the impression that we considered *iaidō* inferior to *iaijutsu*, which was certainly not our intent.

For the reasons explained above, we still refer to the *koryū* art of Eishin-Ryū as *iaijutsu* throughout *Flashing Steel*. However, we find it perfectly acceptable to use *iaidō* instead, if that is the reader's preference. The two terms are, for all intents and purposes, interchangeable, and you will note that we most often refer to practitioners of Eishin-Ryū as "*iaidōka*" rather than "*iaijutsuka*."

# *IAIDŌKA* AND *BUDŌKA*

*Iaidōka* and *budōka* are common terms used to identify the practitioners (*ka*) of *iaijutsu* and *budō* or *bujutsu*. *Ka* means "household," so an *iaidōka* is a member of the household—or family—of *iaidō*, and a *budōka* is a member of the household of *budō*. In previous editions we tended to use the general term "martial artist," but in this edition we have replaced it, where appropriate, with either *iaidōka* or *budōka*.

## EISHIN-RYŪ

Eishin-Ryū is a convenient shorthand for Musō Jikiden Eishin-Ryū or Masaoka-Ha Musō Jikiden Eishin-Ryū. For the sake of brevity and to maintain a brisk pace for our readers, we have used Eishin-Ryū in this manner extensively throughout the book, substituting the full name or specifying Masaoka-Ha only where it seemed necessary for clarity.

## *WAZA, KATA, KUMITACHI,* AND *KATACHI*

These are four closely related terms. A *waza* is a technique. A *kata* is an example. *Kumitachi* means to "cross swords," and refers to a training activity in which two people practice attack and defense using *bokken* (wooden swords). And a *katachi* is a pattern.

In *Flashing Steel*, the term *waza* is used to designate the techniques of the Eishin-Ryū curriculum that are performed by an individual, usually with an *iaitō*. The only time we use the word *kata* is to identify the solo practice patterns of Zen Nippon Kendō Renmei Seitei Iaidō presented in chapter 19. *Kumitachi* is a generic term for any form of mock combat between two or more *iaidōka*. The Tachiuchi no Kurai (chapter 15) and Tsumeai no Kurai (chapter 17) are examples of *kumitachi*. Another term we use as shorthand for the Tachiuchi no Kurai is *katachi*, since they are clearly defined and choreographed patterns of movement.

## BOKKEN AND *BOKUTŌ*

*Bokken* means "wooden sword." *Bokutō* also means "wooden sword." Other than the words themselves there is no difference between the two. The *ken* in *bokken* is the *ken* from *kenjutsu*, and the *tō* in *bokutō* is the *tō* from *iaitō*. It is essentially the difference between a bush and a shrub. Nevertheless, there are some who express a strong preference for one term over the other. We consider them interchangeable, but if your *sensei* has a preference, use that one to maintain harmony and discipline in the *dōjō*.

## *SŌKE* AND *SŌSHIHAN*

These are terms for the leaders of a *ryū*. A literal reading of *sōke* is "family origin," but in normal usage a *sōke* is the leader of a religious or philosophical sect. Technically, it should be—as "family origin" suggests—a hereditary position passed down within a family, but in practice there are many *ryū* that use the term *sōke* for an appointed or elected leader.

Since the successive leaders of Eishin-Ryū have historically been appointed, it has been the custom within Masaoka-Ha to call the leader of the style *sōshihan*. *Sōshihan* means "supreme teacher" and is the equivalent of the English words "headmaster" (leader of a school) or "grandmaster" (leader of an order of knighthood). For an English equivalent, "grandmaster" sounded too pretentious for the leader of a *ryū* steeped in a tradition and culture of personal humility, so we have used "headmaster" in *Flashing Steel* as the English term for *sōshihan*.

## OTHER TERMS

A few other basic Japanese words that will help the reader quickly adjust to our frequent use of Japanese terminology in this edition are:

*katana:* a Japanese (samurai) sword

*iaitō:* an unsharpened steel practice sword

*dōjō:* the place in which *budō* training is conducted

*sensei:* a teacher of *budō*

*sempai:* a senior student

*kōhai:* a junior student

*shihan:* a senior teacher

*seito:* a student

*deshi:* a disciple (implying a strongly committed student)

## PRONUNCIATION GUIDE

For the benefit of those readers with a limited knowledge of the Japanese language, here is a brief guide to the pronunciation of Japanese words; they are written in *rōmaji* (the Roman alphabet) in *Flashing Steel*.

The vowels in Japanese are always pronounced the same way, as follows:

| | | |
|---|---|---|
| *a* "ah" as in *father* | *u* "oo" as in *tool* | *o* "oh" as in *hole* |
| *i* "ee" as in *bee* | *e* "eh" as in *red* | |

Doubled vowels (*aa, ii, uu, ee, oo*) or vowels written with a bar above them (usually *ū* and *ō*) are simply voiced twice as long as single vowels, like a half note instead of a quarter note in music.

Diphthongs (*ai, ao, au, ae, ao, ia, iu, ie, io, ua, ui, ue, uo, oa, oi, ou,* and *oe*) are pronounced by pronouncing both vowels in normal fashion, so that *ai* sounds like "eye," *ao* sound like the "ow" in cow, and so on. Although they are technically different sounds, *ō* and *ou* are so similar that they usually sound alike.

Most Japanese consonants, as written in *rōmaji*, are also pronounced like their English equivalents:

| | | |
|---|---|---|
| *k* "k" in *kick* | *ts* "ts" in *nuts* | *w* "w" in *way* |
| *s* "s" in *see* | *n* "n" in *no* | *g* "g" in *go* |
| *sh* "sh" in *she* | *h* "h" in *hot* | *z* "z" in *zoo* |
| *t* "t" in *toe* | *m* "m" in *me* | *d* "d" in *day* |
| *ch* "ch" in *chair* | *y* "y" in *you* | *j* "j" in *jar* |

The two consonants that give English speakers the most difficulty are *f* and *r*. The *f* in Japanese is pronounced as a cross between an English *h* and *f*, like the sound made when blowing out a candle. The *r* in Japanese is like a cross between an English *r* and *l* and is made by pressing the tip of the tongue against the roof of the mouth—not the back of the incisors, like an English *l*—and trying to say an *r*, so *ren* should sound halfway between "ren" and "len."

Also troublesome for English speakers are the digraphs, *ky, ny, my, hy, ry, gy, by,* and *py*. These should be pronounced with its accompanying vowel as one syllable, so *kya* is pronounced "kyah" rather than "key-ah." The capital of Japan is Tōkyō, two syllables, "toh-kyoh," not "toh-key-oh."

Now that you are fluent in Japanese, you are ready to delve deep into the history, philosophy, culture, traditions, techniques, and mysteries of Masaoka-Ha Musō Jikiden Eishin-Ryū *iaijutsu*.

# Chapter 1

# *Rekishi*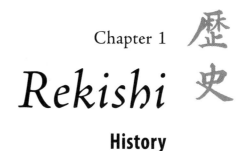

## History

*Iaijutsu* is the art of swordsmanship in face-to-face combat, as practiced by the samurai of feudal Japan. It is impossible to fully understand the history of *iaijutsu* without at least a cursory knowledge of the history of the samurai warrior class and their fabled swords.

The earliest forms of what we now call the samurai sword seem to have made their appearance around the beginning of the Heian Period, which began in AD 782. Technically, swords of this period were not truly "samurai" swords, since the samurai caste itself did not actually arise until the twelfth century. These swords were generally much longer and more deeply curved than the type now used in *iaijutsu* practice. Because of their length and shape, these early swords are usually referred to as *tachi* (large sword).

For the first 250 years of the Heian Period (794–1185), the Fujiwara clan wielded the true power behind Japan's imperial government, acting as regents to the figurehead emperors. As centuries passed, however, other factions steadily grew in economic and military power, among which the famed Taira and Minamoto families were the most prominent by the middle of the twelfth century. As the power of the Fujiwara declined in the late Heian Period, disorder quickly arose. By the early eleventh century, it was not uncommon for armed priests and bands of mercenaries to battle in the very streets of Kyōto, Japan's capital city.

In an attempt to restore order, the imperial family wrested control away from the Fujiwara regents for a brief time. But in 1156, the Taira family defeated its chief rival, the Minamoto, and seized power. Another horrendous battle between the two clans followed in 1160, but the Taira remained in control until they were ultimately defeated by the Minamoto in 1185.

This half-century of continual military conflict between the Taira and Minamoto families and their respective vassals gave rise to the samurai as a distinct class in Japanese society. This period also witnessed the development of the warrior's code of conduct, which eventually came to be called *bushidō*, the "Way of the Warrior." Two of Japan's most famous literary epics, the *Genji Monogatari* (Tale of Genji) and the *Heike Monogatari* (Tale of Heike) depicted this monumental struggle and the emergence of the samurai as the leading social caste. In these and similar works of the period, the heroic deeds of the samurai were romanticized, and the samurai sword itself was elevated to so sacred and mystical a position that it was said to embody the very soul of its owner. It was sometimes even said to possess a soul of its own.

Much of the credit for the excellence of these swords must go to Minamoto Mitsunaka, who not only developed large-scale iron mining on his lands in western Japan, but also cultivated the art of swordsmithing to such a degree that its artisans attained a status akin to priesthood. No sword created before or since can match the strength and cutting edge of those forged by the master swordsmiths of feudal Japan. Not surprisingly, such weapons were revered almost as objects of worship by their owners, who perceived their unsurpassed cutting ability as resulting from each sword being imbued with a spirit of its own. The long, deeply curved *tachi* slung edge-down at the left hip remained the tangible symbol of samurai spirit and power for the next four centuries.

*Tachi*, late Ashikaga Period

As the subsequent Ashikaga Period (1338-1500) came to a close, Japan was once again embroiled in widespread warfare. Skirmishes had periodically arisen throughout the country since 1400, culminating in the Ōnin Civil War in 1467. Although the Ōnin War ended after ten years, the Ashikaga Shōgunate was bankrupt. The country continued in turmoil and anarchy for the next three decades, leading into the Sengoku (Warring States) Period. A full century of incessant warfare was obviously a propitious time for the samurai caste, and this period gave rise to numerous schools and styles of swordsmanship.

At the height of this tumultuous period, Hayashizaki Jinsuke Minamoto no Shigenobu (usually referred to as Hayashizaki Jinsuke or occasionally as Hayashizaki Shigenobu) was born in Hayashizaki Village in Okushū Dewa (near modern-day Murayama City, Yamagata Prefecture). He was born in the year 1549 (various sources also give dates between 1542 and 1546) to a samurai family under the ruling Minamoto clan. After his father was killed in a duel, young Hayashizaki was determined to avenge his father's death. Being only thirteen or fourteen years of age, Hayashizaki knew he would need a significant advantage to defeat his father's killer, so he entered the local Shintō shrine, Hayashizaki Jinja, seeking inspiration. There he spent a hundred days in prayer and practice to develop the techniques of drawing and cutting in a single motion that we now call *iaijutsu* or *iaidō*. Hayashizaki prevailed in avenging his father's death, and his style of swordsmanship came to be known as Shinmei Musō-Ryū (Divine Vision Style).

Less than forty years later, the most significant development in the history of *iaijutsu* occurred. Along with the introduction of firearms into Japan by the Portuguese, the Sengoku Period also witnessed a significant change in sword design. Blades were now made shorter and a little straighter in shape than the *tachi*, and were worn with their cutting edge upward. These newer swords, called *katana* or *daitō*, are the weapon most people think of as the "samurai sword" today.

*Katana*, Tokugawa Era

A typical *tachi* had a blade ranging from twenty-nine to thirty-one inches in length and a handle (*tsuka*) ten to eleven inches long. As illustrated in the photograph on page 8, the *saya* (scabbard) of *tachi* were fitted with a set of mountings (*ashi*) so that they were slung at the wearer's hip with the sharp edge downward. From this position it was impractical to draw the *tachi* in any manner other than by swinging the blade in an upward arc.

The blade of a typical *daitō* was twenty-six or twenty-seven inches long with less curvature, and its handle about nine inches. With a blade three to four inches shorter and a handle an inch or two shorter than a *tachi*, and worn edge-upward in the wearer's belt, the *daitō* could be drawn more rapidly than the *tachi* and deployed at a greater variety of angles. Naturally, with the advent of this newer, shorter sword improved techniques of swordsmanship were required to make the best use of this radical change in blade design.

Hasegawa Chikara-no-Suke Hidenobu (better known today as Hasegawa Eishin), the seventh-generation successor to Shinmei Musō-Ryū and widely considered to be nearly equal in skill with the *tachi* to the style's founder, adapted *iaijutsu* techniques to the shorter *katana*. Since the *katana* is worn with its edge upward, Hasegawa literally turned the art of *iaijutsu* upside down by changing the manner in which the sword is drawn to make its initial cut.

Because of his reputation for great skill and his modification of sword techniques for the newer design, Toyotomi Hideyoshi, the supreme military commander who ruled a recently unified Japan as Daijō-daijin (Chancellor) from 1586 to 1598, invited Hasegawa to his recently completed palace near Kyōto to demonstrate his modified form of *iaijutsu* around 1590. Toyotomi was so impressed with Hasegawa's skill that he bestowed on him the title Musō Ken, "Sword without Equal."

Upon the death of Manno Danemon-no-Jo in 1610, Hasegawa succeeded him as leader of Shinmei Musō-Ryū. However, there were other disciples of Hayashizaki Jinsuke who did not adopt the *katana*, and instead carried on the original *tachi*-based curriculum of Shinmei Musō-Ryū. This resulted in two highly dissimilar systems briefly coexisting. Eventually Shinmei Musō-Ryū became known as Hayashizaki Shin Musō-Ryū (Hayashizaki New Vision Style) and Hasegawa's system was renamed Hasegawa-Ryū or Eishin-Ryū to distinguish them.

Eishin-Ryū has now been passed down for over four hundred years to the present time through an unbroken succession of leaders. This has been accomplished through personal instruction that imparts not only the technical expertise but also the strategy and philosophy of the style. This process is called *jikiden* in Japanese, and is a term that has no simple English equivalent. *Jiki* means "straight," "direct," "pure," "true," or "honest." *Den* is an equally nuanced word that includes concepts like communication, tradition, heritage, commentary, biography, promulgation, transmission, and connection. *Jikiden* thus describes an intimate personal connection through which the teachings, traditions, and heritage of Eishin-Ryū are transmitted from one person or generation to the next.

The highly personal nature of this transfer of knowledge and skill from one instructor to the next generation students is also reflected in the Japanese word *ryū*, which is typically translated as "style" or "school." A *ryū* is actually a stream, a flow, a current, or the passage of time, meaning that it is the continual accumulation of wisdom of all those who have shared this personal connection for more than four hundred years.

If we speak of Eishin-Ryū with a sense of reverence, it is because the authors recognize and deeply appreciate that we have been gifted with more than just knowledge and skills in *iaijutsu;* we have been assimilated into this centuries long flow of wisdom, compassion, and personal mentoring and nurture to become an integral part of the tradition and heritage that will continue flowing to countless future generations.

This principle is illustrated by the history of our style. Hasegawa Eishin passed his skill and knowledge to his successor, Arai Seitetsu, who in turn conveyed it to Hayashi Rokudayū. Hayashi, however, did more than simply impart to his successor what he had been taught. He added to the body of knowledge of *Eishin-Ryū* to reflect another major change in the lives and purpose of the samurai that occurred in the early Tokugawa Era.

The defeat and suicide of Toyotomi Hideyori at the Siege of Ōsaka in 1615 began 250 years of continual peace under the rule of the Tokugawa clan. The samurai, who had seldom known a time of peace during the preceding four hundred years, no longer had wars to fight. Instead, they were now guardians of the peace and government administrators, whose duties often involved meetings and negotiations to conduct the affairs of government and settle disputes and grievances, placing them in formal settings in which their conduct, demeanor, etiquette, and strategy were usually more important than their swordsmanship. In these settings, the samurai were required to sit on their knees in *seiza* (literally, "correct sitting") under conditions that could turn unexpectedly violent if negotiations went badly. This created a need for techniques and tactics to deal with a surprise attack while seated in the *seiza* posture. Hayashi Rokudayū developed a collection of techniques to address these situations and incorporated them into Eishin-Ryū as what are now called the Ōmori-Ryū Seiza *waza* and are described in more detail in chapter 8.

To varying degrees, each successive leader of Eishin-Ryū has not only transmitted the knowledge of his predecessors to the next generation, but also added the wisdom gained from his own analysis and experiences to the art. In this way, the body of knowledge inherited by each successive generation has been both broadened and deepened by those who preceded them.

Eishin-Ryū—as the term *ryū* implies—is not stagnant. It is growing and constantly improving.

It is this continuum of expanding knowledge and nurture that makes a *ryū* so important. A *ryū* is more than just a prescribed method of sword combat or a collection of techniques that can be memorized and performed by rote. It is more than merely curriculum, rituals, traditions, and standards of performance. A *ryū* is a family—a living organism whose purpose is to enhance the lives of its members and perpetuate its "DNA" through their descendants—by personal interaction and mentoring.

This is why training in any classical *ryū* is always face-to-face, hands-on, *sensei* to *deshi*, by direct contact—sometimes painful and embarrassing contact—and not merely by books or videos. The intricacies and profundities of a classical *ryū* cannot be fully understood from explanation and observation alone, but must be personally experienced to be fully learned.

Through this personal *jikiden* mentoring process, Eishin-Ryū has been passed down through the centuries in an unbroken line of succession to the present day, and has survived and overcome many difficulties in that course. Although the line—or more correctly, lines—of succession remain unbroken, disputes and divisions have occurred over the years, with prominent adherents leaving to found their own *ryū* or *ha* (branches) and historical events forcing change on both the art of *iaijutsu* and Eishin-Ryū.

The first such division occurred within a few years of the style's founding, when Tamiya Heibei, who was the direct successor to Hayashizaki Jinsuke and considered the second headmaster of Shinmei Musō-Ryū, broke away to found his own style, called Tamiya-Ryū. Not long thereafter, Tamiya's successor, Nagano Murakusai Kinrō, also split away and formed Muraku-Ryū. In fact, the lineages of most styles of *iaijutsu* still practiced have some direct connection with Hayashizaki Jinsuke. It is a tribute to the strength of the bond between the *sensei* and *deshi*, and the commitment *iaidōka* have for centuries made to the perpetuation of their art, that Eishin-Ryū has thrived despite the occasional conflict or crisis.

Perhaps the greatest internal schism within Eishin-Ryū occurred in the late eighteenth century, when its tenth headmaster, Hayashi Yasudayū, and the eleventh headmaster, Ōguro Motoemon, both died shortly after one another in 1776 without having appointed a successor. As a result, two branches (*ha*) of Eishin-Ryū arose, each of which considered its leader to be the legitimate twelfth successor to the Eishin-Ryū lineage. One of these branches, Shimomura-ha, evolved into Musō Shinden-Ryū (Visionary Divine Tradition Style) prior to World War II, while Tanimura-ha has survived to the present.

Below is a chart depicting the lines of succession following the death of eleventh headmaster Ōguro Motoemon and the Tanimura-ha and Shimomura-ha lineages of Eishin-Ryū, which may help in following their roles in developments that occurred in the Meiji and Taishō eras.

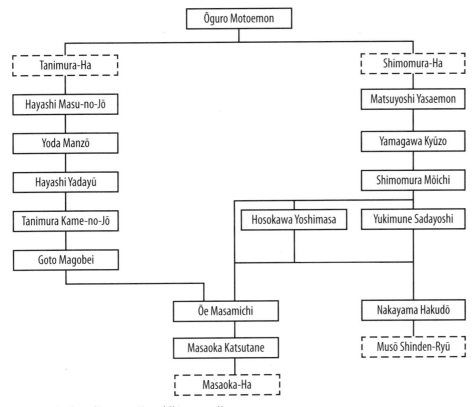

Successive leaders of Tanimura-Ha and Shimomura-Ha

One of the greatest historical events to imperil Eishin-Ryū was the Meiji Restoration, which began in 1868. With the fall of the Tokugawa Shōgunate that year, rule over Japan was restored to the imperial family for the first time in some seven hundred years. Having ascended to the throne at the age of 15, Emperor Meiji soon introduced a series of edicts intended to diminish the power of the samurai and prevent them from regaining control of Japan.

Gotō Magobei Masasuke was the leader of Tanimura-Ha Eishin-Ryū at the time of the Meiji Restoration. Gotō was closely associated with Itagaki Taisuke, a samurai from Tosa Province (now Kōchi Prefecture) on the island of Shikoku, who served as one of the commanders of the forces supporting the imperial family during the Boshin War that defeated the Tokugawa Shōgunate in 1869. Itagaki was appointed a Councilor of State (*sangi*) by Emperor Meiji in 1871 and was the leading advocate of many of the early Meiji reforms, including the abolition of the *han* (*daimyō*) system in 1871. Gotō and Itagaki were both advocates of a national education system for Japan.

It was in this tumultuous time that one of the most important leaders of Eishin-Ryū arose in Tosa. Ōe Masamichi was born in 1852 in Tosa Province. He first trained in *iaijutsu* as a youth under Shimomura Sadamasa, the fourteenth headmaster of the Shimomura-Ha line, mentioned previously. At the age of fifteen, together with many other students of both Shimomura and Gotō, Ōe fought under the command of Itagaki Taisuke in the four-day Battle of Toba-Fushimi in late January 1868—the first battle of the Boshin War. He returned to Tosa and continued his training under Shimomura, eventually receiving a *menkyō kaiden* (License of Complete Transmission) of the Shimomura-Ha curriculum. He also studied *bōjutsu* (six-foot staff) under Itagaki Taisuke. Upon Shimomura's death in 1877, a dispute arose over the leadership of Shimomura-Ha. Rather than assert a claim to leadership as a holder of a *menkyō kaiden*, Ōe began training under the sixteenth headmaster of the Tanimura-Ha line, Gotō Magobei, eventually succeeding him as the seventeenth headmaster of Tanimura-Ha Eishin-Ryū.

In 1873, Emperor Meiji issued the Haitō Rei (Sword Revocation Decree), forbidding the ownership of a sword by anyone other than those serving in the military or police, or former *daimyō*. Initially, the edict was not rigidly enforced, and *katana-gari* (sword confiscation raids) did not begin until 1877. Nevertheless, this could easily have ended training in *iaijutsu* and *kenjutsu* forever and relegated both arts to the dustbin of history. However, by this time *gekiken* (an old name for *kendō*) was already a popular sport. Furthermore, *sensei* were still needed to teach *iaijutsu* and *kenjutsu* to the police and military personnel still permitted to possess and carry swords, so many styles, including Eishin-Ryū, were able to continue after the Haitō Rei.

At the urging of Itagaki, Gotō, and other influential former samurai in the imperial court, Emperor Meiji later recognized the historical and cultural importance of the samurai to Japan and to sustaining the spirit of the Japanese people, and in 1895 authorized the establishment of the Dai Nippon Butoku-Kai (Greater Japan Institute of Martial Virtues) as a means to preserve and govern the instruction of traditional Japanese *budō*, and the Butokuden (Hall of Martial Virtues) was constructed on a site near the Heian Jingu in Kyōto, which was built that same year for a cultural and industrial festival.

Between having the support of the Japanese imperial family, rising nationalistic pride in Japan's growing prosperity and international stature, and its strong affiliation with the Ministry of Education, the Butoku-Kai soon became the single greatest influence on traditional *budō* in the twentieth century. One of its major accomplishments during the latter part of the Meiji Era (1868–1912) and early Taishō Era

(1912–1925) was persuading most classical *ryū-ha* (styles) of *budō* to establish an organized curriculum and explicit standards of practice and ranking.

In 1911 the Butoku-Kai established its own school for the preparation of teachers of *budō*, called the Budō Senmon Gakkō (Budō Specialty School), nicknamed the Busen. By 1920, in order to teach practically any classical *budō* in Japan, especially in a quasi-official setting like the Japanese school system, or to law enforcement or military personnel, it was necessary to be properly accredited by the Dai Nippon Butoku-Kai, preferably after studying at the Busen.

Gotō Magobei died in 1898 and was succeeded by Ōe Masamichi, who had also received a *menkyō kaiden* from Gotō in Tanimura-Ha Eishin-Ryū. This placed Ōe at a pivotal moment in time with a unique set of qualifications. He was a former samurai with battlefield experience, yet he had supported the dissolution of the samurai caste. He held a *menkyō kaiden* in both Shimomura-Ha and Tanimura-Ha Eishin-Ryū and had decades of teaching experience. So, shortly after assuming the role of seventeenth headmaster of Eishin-Ryū, the Dai Nippon Butoku-Kai asked him to establish a branch *dōjō* in Kōchi, which he did.

Early in the twentieth century, the Meiji government's Ministry of Education asked Ōe to restructure and formalize the curriculum of Eishin-Ryū. The result was the curriculum essentially as it is practiced today, with the *waza* grouped into categories reflecting their tactical and methodological similarities to facilitate systematic instruction. These are listed in chapter 20, "Eishin-Ryū no Yōten."

In addition, it was Ōe who renamed the style Musō Jikiden Eishin-Ryū to properly reflect its character as an art that was unequaled (*musō*) in the opinion of Toyotomi Hideyoshi, passed down by direct instruction from *sensei* to *deshi* for generations (*jikiden*), from the adaptation of its techniques to the *daitō* by Hasegawa Eishin (Eishin-Ryū). He also created the Hayanuki (fast draw) exercise from the Chūden *waza*, as described in chapter 10. In 1924, Ōe became only the second person to be awarded the title of Hanshi (Exemplary Warrior) by the Dai Nippon Butoku-Kai as a fitting tribute to his remarkable achievements.

Another controversy—one which has lost much of its significance and divisiveness over the past twenty-five years—arose when Ōe Masamichi died of cancer in 1927. He had awarded at least fifteen of his disciples *kongen no kan* (origin books, also known as *kongen no maki*), which are documents equivalent to *menkyō kaiden*, but had not designated any of them as his chosen successor. It is further tribute to Ōe's teaching ability and diligence that so many of his students were fully qualified to succeed him, but when several claimed to be his rightful successor, it led to the creation of several *ha* (branches) that did not initially acknowledge each other's legitimacy.

Two of Ōe's disciplines who rose to prominence prior to World War II were Hogiyama Namio and Masaoka Katsutane (better known by his nickname Kazumi). Hogiyama personally attended Ōe during the final stages of his illness and was given possession of Ōe's documents related to Eishin-Ryū, which served to establish his legitimacy as Ōe's successor. Hogiyama is therefore generally considered the eighteenth headmaster of the Seitō (orthodox) or main line of Eishin-Ryū, while others, including Masaoka, are considered leaders of *ha*, or branches.

Masaoka Katsutane was born in Kōchi Prefecture (formerly Tosa Province) in 1896. He attended middle school in Kōchi city, where the school's *kendō* instructor was Ōe Masamichi. After *kendō* class, a select group of students stayed for instruction in Eishin-Ryū *iaijutsu*, and Masaoka was soon invited to join this group. Thus, Masaoka began his training in Eishin-Ryū while Ōe was still in the process of reformatting and systematizing its curriculum. In addition to training with Ōe most of his five years in middle school, Masaoka also trained regularly at the Butoku-Kai *dōjō* in Kōchi. In 1917 Masaoka moved to Kyōto to attend the Butoku-Kai's Budō Senmon Gakkō (Budō Specialty School) to receive advanced training in classical *budō*. The rigorous training at the Busen is legendary: beginning before breakfast and ending after dinner, six days per week. After his graduation in 1919, Masaoka was asked to remain at the Busen as a *kendō* instructor. In 1921 the Butoku-Kai awarded Masaoka the title of Renshi (Warrior Trainer) in both *kendō* and *iaijutsu*, and in 1924 Masaoka received a *menkyō kaiden* in *iaijutsu* from Ōe. Two years later Ōe presented Masaoka with a *kongen no kan*, and the following year the Butoku-Kai awarded him the title of Kyōshi (Warrior Instructor). He was still only thirty-one years old.

About this time, Masaoka was transferred to Kanazawa in Ishikawa Prefecture to take a teaching position. He also began teaching *kendō* and *iaijutsu* at the Ishikawa branch of the Butoku-Kai, where he developed a close friendship with Nakayama Hakudō, who had briefly been a student of Itagaki Taisuke before becoming a disciple of Hosokawa Yorimasa of Shimomura-Ha Eishin-Ryū. He had also trained in Tanimura-Ha Eishin-Ryū under Morimoto Tokumi, who had been a student of Gotō Magobei. In 1925, at the request of the Ministry of the Army (Rikugun-shō), Nakayama devised the five *tachiwaza* (standing techniques) of Tōyama-Ryū Iaidō for use in training members of the Imperial Japanese Army. In 1933, at the height of his friendship with Masaoka, Nakayama established Muso Shinden-Ryu Iaidō as the successor to Shimomura-Ha, after which the remainder of Shimomura-Ha faded into oblivion.

In 1931, several holders of *menkyō kaiden* in Eishin-Ryū founded the Dai Nippon Yaegaki-Kai (Greater Japan Eight-Fold Fences Association) in Ōsaka in order to provide *iaijutsu* instruction in the largest metropolitan area of the Kansai region. Since Masaoka was living in Kanazawa at this time, it is doubtful that he was directly involved in the establishment of the Yaegaki-Kai, but his most senior student, Narise Sakahiro, would later become one of the most important leaders of that organization. The Yaegaki-Kai would later play a crucial role in the restoration of *budō* training in Japan after World War II.

Following the outbreak of the Sino-Japanese War in 1937, the Japanese Ministry of the Navy (Kaigun-shō) decided that its naval officers would benefit from training in an abridged set of *iaijutsu waza* similar to the Tōyama-Ryu Iaidō *waza* created for the Imperial Army in 1925, and requested that the Budō Senmon Gakkō develop an appropriate curriculum. So, in 1939 the Busen tasked Kōno Hyakuren, then one of its principal *iaijutsu* instructors, to devise a suitable set of *waza* for the Imperial Navy. The eleven *waza* that he devised for this purpose came to be known as the Dai Nippon Battō-Hō (described in chapter 13). Although the Battō-Hō were not widely taught in other *ha* of Eishin-Ryū for many years, since they were created to be separate from any orthodox curriculum, they are not exclusive to Kōno's lineage, either. In the ensuing years the Battō-Hō have been taught to *iaidōka* from a variety of styles through the Dai Nippon Butoku-Kai.

The Second Sino-Japanese War seemed to be greatly benefiting the Butoku-Kai and *budō* in general. Interest in classical *budō* was at an all-time high, and the Butoku-Kai had more than two million members nationwide, with a branch *dōjō* or Butokuden in every one of Japan's prefectures and more than five thousand instructors. In addition, many forms of *budō*—especially *jūdō* and *kendō*—were integral parts of the curriculum of Japanese schools under the auspices of the Butoku-Kai. *Budō* was viewed as a healthy, invigorating activity for people of all ages. Training instilled strong character, discipline, morality, dignity, cultural pride, and indomitable spirit in its practitioners, so it was encouraged by the Japanese government and media.

But that would all change just three and a half years after the attack on Pearl Harbor. The demise of the Butoku-Kai was unwittingly assured in March 1942 when Major General Tanaka Ryūkichi, former commander of the Rikugun Nakano Gakkō (Army Nakano School) military intelligence training center, placed the Butoku-Kai under the oversight of the Imperial Army and ordered it to shift its instructional focus from classical *budō* to modern military training in support of Japan's entry into World War II. This led to the Butoku-Kai being considered a military training facility following Japan's defeat three years later.

On December 2, 1945, the Supreme Commander for the Allied Powers (SCAP), General Douglas MacArthur, issued directives SCAPIN 548 and SCAPIN 550, ordering the closure of all military-related schools and training facilities and the removal from positions of authority of any individuals that had in any way supported the Japanese armed forces. Many have come to believe that these edicts constituted a ban on *budō* training in Japan, but this is not the case. In actuality the closure of the Butoku-Kai and numerous other organizations were the result of the Ministry of Education misinterpreting and overreacting to General MacArthur's directive. In fact, Ministry of Education Hatsutai (Notification) No. 80, abolishing the practice of *budō* (and specifically *kendō, kyūdō, jūdō,* and *naginatajutsu*) in all Japanese schools and extracurricular activities, was sent to all prefectural governors and teacher's schools on November 6, 1945—more than a month before SCAPIN 548 was issued. That same day, the Ministry of Education also sent a memorandum to all high schools, teacher's schools, and colleges instructing them to abolish all training in *budō*, listing specific sports to be taught, and stating that "special consideration should be given *budō* instructors, such as to enable them to teach other subjects if they are found to have the necessary qualifications and aptitude."

As a result of the Ministry of Education's zeal to eradicate all militaristic influences from Japanese education, and the direct intervention of Japanese military leaders in the affairs of the Butoku-Kai during World War II, it was officially disbanded on November 9, 1946.

Many of the former Butoku-Kai instructors suffered greatly in the postwar years. Jobs were scarce to begin with, and it was illegal to do the work for which they were most qualified. A fortunate few obtained positions in the government, guiding the reconstruction and reformation of Japan, but most were forced to take any employment available. Masaoka Katsutane, for example, returned to Shikoku and worked as a farmer in the years following the war.

Efforts began as early as 1947 to reinstate training in several forms of *budō*, particularly *jūdō, kendō,* and *kyūdō*. Several appeals were made to the Ministry of Education between 1946 and 1950; some were even supported by American physical education consultants, who encouraged the resumption of training in arts that had little or no modern practical application, but those appeals were denied. In several cases, memoranda from the Ministry of Education reveal that the basis for denial was the fear of involvement by former members or leaders of the Butoku-Kai, who were stigmatized by the imposition of military control over the organization in 1942. The Ministry went so far as to track down a large number of Butoku-Kai instructors it believed had been complicit in militarizing the Butoku-Kai and order the termination of their employment as teachers or government workers. It was not until late 1952 that the Ministry of Education finally relented in its persecution of the Butoku-Kai. Even then, the Ministry did not allow the reinstatement of the Butoku-Kai, but instead insisted that an entirely new organization with a completely revamped charter, philosophy, and objectives be established.

In 1953, the newly chartered Dai Nippon Butoku-Kai was created as a private organization not directly affiliated with Japan's Ministry of Education. By this time, however, many of the former Butoku-Kai instructors had formed private organizations of their own. The Dai Nippon Yaegaki-Kai, for example, had resumed operation in Ōsaka. The Zen Nippon Kendō Renmei (All-Japan Kendō Federation) and the Kokusai Budōin (International Budō Federation) had both been formed in 1952 and were building their own followings. The Zen Nippon Iaidō Renmei was founded in 1954 by Kōno Hyakuren, a student of Hogiyama Namio, and became the governing organization for the "main" lineage of Eishin-Ryū. So, the Butoku-Kai was now just one of many sources of legitimate training and certification in classical *budō*.

Unlike the original Butoku-Kai, which was supported by the Ministry of Education, each of these private organizations had to fund the costs of operating its own facilities, which meant they had to compete for members—a radical change from prewar times. To attract students, each organization and its instructors had to establish its legitimacy as a source of authentic instruction in traditional *budō*, which unfortunately led to claims, counterclaims, and disputes over the authenticity of the credentials of various instructors and organizations. Although the leaders of these fledgling organizations—men like Nakayama Hakudō, Kōno Hyakuren, Masaoka Katsutane, and many others—had known each other for decades and were fully aware of one another's eminent qualifications, such was not the case with their students, particularly as their organizations grew in size and scope. Rivalry between students sometimes devolved into accusations of illegitimacy of their lineage.

Fortunately, with the translation of hundreds more books, articles, and prewar documents into English and other languages, and diligent research by *iaidōka* from all parts of the globe, much of which is now instantly accessible on the internet, several legitimate lines of succession flowing from Ōe Masamichi through his many *menkyō kaiden* holders have been well established and thoroughly documented.

In the 1950s the largest of the *iaidō* organizations continued to be the Dai Nippon Yaegaki-Kai. The degree of involvement, if any, in the Yaegaki-Kai by Masaoka Katsutane is not well documented. By most accounts, he appears to have remained in Kanazawa for much of the decade, but his senior-most student, Narise Sakahiro, was elected to an unprecedented three terms of office as president of the organization during Masaoka's lifetime. In 1956 the Zen Nippon Kendō Renmei (Kenren) established an *iaidō* division and appointed Masaoka as its director. The following year the Kenren awarded Masaoka the rank of *nanadan* (seventh *dan*) in *kendō* and the organization's first *hachidan* (eighth *dan*) in *iaidō*, together with the formal title of Hanshi. Five years later the Kenren promoted Masaoka to the rank of *kyūdan* (ninth *dan*). In

1967 the Kenren formed a committee to develop an abridged set of *iaidō kata* collected from several major styles and appointed Masaoka to represent Eishin-Ryū. The result of that effort was the creation of the Kenren's original seven Seitei Iaidō *kata.*

Near the end of his life, Masaoka wrote a two-volume set of books in which he described in detail the history, techniques, strategy, and philosophy of Eishin-Ryū as taught to him by Ōe Masamichi. The first volume is titled *Musō Jikiden Eishin-Ryū Iai Heihō—Ten no Maki* and the second volume is *Musō Jikiden Eishin-Ryū Iai Heihō—Chi no Maki.* In these books, Masaoka documented and illustrated the teachings of both major lines of Eishin-Ryū, Shimomura-Ha, and Tanimura-Ha, which he had effectively synthesized into the consolidated system that now bears his name: Masaoka-Ha.

Unfortunately, Masaoka did not live to see his books in print. In 1973, after teaching a children's *kendō* class, he went to change his clothes, removed his *men* (headgear), sat down, and died still wearing his *bogu* (body armor) at the age of seventy-seven. His books were published in limited editions posthumously the following year.

Narise Sakahiro succeeded Masaoka only briefly, serving as *sōshihan* from 1973 until his death in 1975, at which time Miura Takeyuki assumed leadership of Masaoka-Ha Eishin-Ryū.

Miura Takeyuki was born on January 5, 1922, in Tsuwano-shi, Shimane-ken, Japan. He was a thirty-fifth-generation descendant of the bloodline of Fujiwara Mitsunaga (966–1028), who was Daijō-daijin (regent) to Emperor Go-Ichijō. In 1933, at the age of eleven, he entered the Budō Senmon Gakkō in Kyōto and began his formal training in *budō*. Although his primary focus was *kendō* as a youth, he received an introduction to several other forms of *budō*, including *iaidō*, at the *Busen.*

His introduction to Eishin-Ryū began in 1959, when he joined the Dai Nippon Iaidō Yaegaki-Kai in Ōsaka and began training under its president and chief instructor, Narise Sakahiro. He also met and received instruction directly from Masaoka Katsutane. The following year he began training in Shindō Musō-Ryū *jōjutsu* under Nakajima Asakichi, who was then the most senior student of the last acknowledged headmaster of Shindō Musō-Ryū, Shimizu Takatsugu. During the next ten years, he trained in other classical forms of *budō*, including Enshin-Ryū Koryū Kakushū Bujutsu, a system that incorporates numerous ancient weapons of the samurai, and Kukushin-Ryū Bōjutsu. It is a testament to his growing skill and reputation that in 1967, the Zen Nippon Kendō Renmei selected Miura to represent the Ōsaka region on the committee formulating the Seitei Iaidō *kata.* In 1970 the Zen Nippon Iaidō Renmei awarded Miura the rank of *nanadan* (seventh *dan*) and the title of Kyōshi (Warrior Instructor).

The following year, in February 1971, Miura embarked on a forty-day *musha shugyō* (training pilgrimage) in the mountains. While performing *misogi*—a Shintō purification ritual—he encountered a *sennin* (mystic) living alone in the mountains who helped guide him in his training, meditations, and prayers. He returned from his journey with a vision for eighteen extremely difficult *suemonogiri* (cutting techniques). On each of the eighteen days following his return he successfully completed these eighteen cuts. To this day no one has been able to duplicate that feat. When asked in a magazine interview in 2001 if there was some trick or secret—like a special way of sharpening his sword or a certain curvature of its blade—to making these apparently impossible cuts for which he was famous, Miura Hanshi answered, "Nothing other than perfect technique."

After serving as *sōshihan* for less than two years, Narise Sakahiro died in 1975. On June 8 of that year, Miura founded the Nippon Kobudō Jikishin-Kai, which can be translated as "Japanese Ancient Weapons Pure-Heart Association," and established its *hombu* (headquarters) *dōjō* on the grounds of Yasaka Jinja in Ōsaka, where he served as a priest.

*Jikishin* is a term of considerable importance to students of Masaoka-Ha Eishin-Ryū, so it warrants further explanation here. *Jiki*, as explained when defining the term *jikiden* earlier, is a nuanced word that means "straight," "direct," "pure," "true," or "honest," and it can means all of these simultaneously. *Shin* is an alternate pronunciation of *kokoro*, which means "heart" in all the same senses the word is typically used in English: the organ that pumps blood through the body as well as "mind," "spirit," "courage," "compassion," "strength," "stamina," "determination," "emotions," and more.

Miura Hanshi borrowed this word from an ancient Zen proverb: *Jikishin kore dōjō nari*, which is frequently translated as "A pure heart is the [true] *dōjō*." But that translation only scratches the surface of meaning that the adage is intended to convey. That obvious meaning—that the real training place (*dōjō*) is not the building in which we practice, but our character, spirit, mind, and emotions—is, of course, the foundation for all training in Masaoka-Ha Eishin-Ryū.

It should be apparent that in the modern world, skill with a sword is of little or no practical value. Even in the most capable hands, a sword is no match for a modern firearm. This was also the case when the Butoku-Kai was at its pinnacle in the 1930s. But even when swords and spears were the superior weapons of their time, training in *budō* was always more about developing character than fighting skill. And this fact is reflected in the concept of *jikishin kore dōjō nari*, and is embodied more directly in another ancient saying: *Kokoro tadashi karazareba, ken mata tadashi karazu*—"If your heart is not true, your sword will also not be true."

Fundamentally, both sayings are admonitions to make your mind *straight*; that is, focused and purposeful, not easily driven off course by the winds of change, the tides of adversity, or the currents of peer pressure and popular opinion. Your mind should not be swayed by your environment, but remain unyielding to all external pressures and temptations.

At the same time, your mind, heart, and spirit must be *pure*. The most obvious attributes of a traditional *dōjō* are that it is clean, uncluttered, and totally functional. Like a *dōjō*, your heart and mind should exude the pristine beauty that comes from simplicity and clarity of purpose. Your spirit should shine like a *dōjō* floor that has been polished by the years of sweat and effort that have gone into your training.

The *dōjō* often seems a harsh and punishing place that rewards diligent training only with bruises, aches, and calluses. Yet this apparent harshness disguises the true gentility and compassion of the *dōjō*, which smiles down from its rafters on your toil, pain, and disappointment, cherishing the knowledge that you are refining and purifying your mind, body, and spirit in the crucible of trial and perseverance. In the same way as the *dōjō*, your mind must be gentle and compassionate toward others, yet with the strength to allow them to endure hardship and pain when it is truly in their best interest.

The open, spacious feeling of a *dōjō* should also reflect the openness of your mind. Your mind should be "open" both in the sense of being uncluttered by unnecessary thoughts and feelings—especially destructive emotions like hate, jealousy, stress, doubt, anger, and fear—and in the sense of being open and eager to learn. In this way, your mind will continue to expand as you learn, experience, and grow. For the disciples of Masaoka-Ha, this is the true meaning of *ku no kokoro* or *mushin* (empty mind). There is no benefit to having a small but empty mind, so the *budōka* must strive to develop a mind with ever-increasing room for greater knowledge, wisdom, and compassion—a mind so spacious that regardless of how much it now contains, there is always room for more. For the *budōka*, this is the true meaning of *mushin*.

One of the first students to join the newly formed Jikishin-Kai in 1975 was Shimabukuro Masayuki, who, after more than a dozen years of training in the modern sports of *jūdō*, *kendō*, and *karate-dō*, was longing for a deeper connection to the samurai origins and traditions of classical *budō*. Shimabukuro found what he was looking for at the Jikishin-Kai and earnestly devoted himself to his training under Miura Hanshi. In the late 1970s Shimabukuro moved to Southern California, where he began training law enforcement officers in *karate-dō* and Ryūkyū *kobudō*, returning to Japan two or three times a year to visit his family and further his training in *budō*. Despite his irregular visits to *hombu dōjō*, Shimabukuro steadily advanced in the arts of *iaijutsu* and *jōjutsu*, remaining one of Miura Hanshi's senior students as a result of his diligent training. In late 1988, he began teaching *iaijutsu* as a guest instructor at a *dōjō* in El Cajon, California, a suburb of San Diego. Shortly thereafter, he established an *iaidō* club at the University of California at San Diego (UCSD), and soon he was traveling to a half-dozen *dōjō* in southern California regularly teaching *iaijutsu* as a guest instructor, and had as many students in total as the *hombu dōjō* in Ōsaka.

As one of the first native Japanese people to teach a classical style of *iaijutsu* in the United States, Shimabukuro's reputation spread rapidly. In 1990, Miura Hanshi approved the creation of an international division of the Jikishin-Kai and appointed Shimabukuro as its chairman, tasking him with spreading Masaoka-Ha Eishin-Ryū worldwide. In 1993, Shimabukuro opened a *dōjō* in San Diego, which also served as the *hombu* (headquarters) of the Jikishin-Kai International (JKI).

While Shimabukuro was industriously promoting Eishin-Ryū in America, Miura Hanshi was increasing his involvement in the reconstituted Dai Nippon Butoku-Kai, which by the 1970s had overcome the stigma of its wartime affiliation with the Imperial Army and was regaining its reputation as Japan's leading institution for the promotion of classical *budō*. In 1984, the Butoku-Kai awarded Miura the rank of *hachidan* (eighth *dan*) and the title of Hanshi (Exemplary Warrior). Throughout the 1980s he received numerous awards and was appointed to positions of increasing importance in the Butoku-Kai. In 1993 the Butoku-Kai promoted Miura Hanshi to *kyūdan* (ninth *dan*), making him the highest ranking living member of the organization at that time.

By 1994, *dōjō* were affiliating with the Jikishin-Kai International in increasing numbers and included *dōjō* in Nevada, Colorado, Mexico, and Venezuela. In that year, Shimabukuro was promoted to *nanadan* (seventh *dan*) in *iaijutsu* and awarded the title of Kyōshi by Miura Hanshi. With interest in *Eishin-Ryū* rapidly growing worldwide, Shimabukuro realized that a textbook in the English language would facilitate transmission of the history, culture, traditions, and philosophy that are the essence of the *ryū* to a wider audience than he could possibly reach through personal instruction alone. Together with one of his senior students, Shimabukuro began writing the book that would be published the following year as *Flashing Steel*.

The publication of *Flashing Steel* and the release of a set of seven instructional videos in 1995 brought worldwide attention to Eishin-Ryū. People called and wrote to the JKI *hombu* from Europe, Africa, and South America, in addition to all parts of the United States. Soon afterward, Shimabukuro was traveling extensively to teach seminars and establish affiliations with local *dōjō*. By the year 2000 the JKI had affiliated *dōjō* in at least twenty states and a dozen foreign countries on three continents.

Miura Hanshi promoted Shimabukuro to *hachidan* (eighth *dan*) in 2000, and in 2002 bestowed the title of Hanshi on him in recognition of his accomplishments in spreading Eishin-Ryū to the world. In 2004 the Butoku-Kai elevated Miura to *jūdan* (tenth *dan*), the highest ranking possible in traditional *budō*. Now eighty-two years old and having reached the pinnacle of his accomplishments, Miura Hanshi began to consider the issue of appointing a successor. Shimabukuro Hanshi was clearly the most qualified to become the next *sōshihan* of Masaoka-Ha, particularly considering his achievements in spreading Eishin-Ryū globally and developing an enormous following of students worldwide. But Shimabukuro was now a naturalized U.S. citizen, living with his family in California, and it seemed unthinkable for the leader of a 450-year-old uniquely Japanese traditional *ryū* of *budō* to be headquartered anywhere but in Japan. Several times, Miura Hanshi urged Shimabukuro to return to Japan and succeed him as *sōshihan*, but Shimabukuro declined.

In 2007 Shimabukuro and his coauthor began updating and revising *Flashing Steel* in preparation for the publication of its second edition. Not long after the final draft was submitted and the cover design approved, Miura Hanshi began showing symptoms of Parkinson's disease and realized that he could not long continue to actively teach at *hombu dōjō* and lead the Jikishin-Kai. This prompted him to suggest that Shimabukuro Hanshi form a separate organization from the Jikishin-Kai in order to maintain his leadership of the affiliated *dōjō* outside Japan. Taking this suggestion, Shimabukuro Hanshi founded the Kokusai Nippon Budō Kai (International Japanese Budō Association) or KNBK to succeed the Jikishin-Kai International. To demonstrate his explicit approval of the KNBK as the governing body for Masaoka-Ha Eishin-Ryū outside Japan, Miura Hanshi accepted the position of Chairman Emeritus of the new association, and Shimabukuro Hanshi was elected its Chairman. Under this arrangement, a Japanese national junior to Shimabukuro could be appointed the next titular *sōshihan* of Masaoka-Ha and provide leadership in Japan.

A few months after the publication of *Flashing Steel's* second edition in January 2008, the Butoku-Kai awarded Shimabukuro *hachidan* (eighth *dan*) ranking, the title of Hanshi, and appointed him as its international representative for *iaijutsu*. This appointment solidified Shimabukuro's standing as the leader of Masaoka-Ha outside Japan, and appeared to provide a resolution to any problem that might arise over his successorship. It also galvanized him into action. Now that he was clearly the international authority on Masaoka-Ha Eishin-Ryū, he was determined to ensure that it upheld world-class standards of technical proficiency, personal conduct, completeness of curriculum, and teaching methods. So he began systematically reviewing every *waza* in the system and ensuring that his understanding was not only correct and complete in the context of Eishin-Ryū but also embodied the highest principles found of all related forms of classical Japanese *budō*, particularly *kenjutsu*.

Parkinson's disease continued to ravage Miura Hanshi's health, forcing him to retire from active teaching in 2010 and return to his hometown near Tsuwano, where he could be cared for in his final years of life. In November of that year, Shimabukuro Hanshi flew to Japan to pay what he believed would be his final visit to Miura Hanshi, so that he could personally show his appreciation for all the years of instruction and nurture he had received from Miura and thank him for entrusting him with the dissemination of Masaoka-Ha Eishin-Ryū throughout the world. During that visit, Miura Hanshi formally announced that Shimabukuro Hanshi would be his successor as *sōshihan* upon his death.

The enormity of that appointment and the gravity with which Shimabukuro Hanshi accepted it was immediately evident in his accelerated travel and teaching schedule in 2011. What few knew, however, was that he was diagnosed with gallbladder cancer late in the year. Despite his illness he maintained a hectic travel and teaching schedule throughout the year. In March 2012 he underwent surgery for removal of his gallbladder and other affected tissues, and it was discovered that the cancer had spread to his liver. He kept this information to himself and resumed his teaching shortly after his release from the hospital.

On June 19, 2012, Miura Hanshi succumbed to Parkinson's and died. Shimabukuro Hanshi succeeded him as the twenty-first *sōshihan* of Masaoka-Ha Eishin-Ryū the following day. Tragically, his tenure as leader of the style would last only eighty days. On September 7, 2012, just days after conducting an *iaijutsu* seminar in Los Angeles, Shimabukuro Hanshi lost his battle with liver cancer.

Having been the first leader of a traditional *ryū* of *budō* to live outside Japan, Shimabukuro Hanshi took one final action that made Masaoka-Ha Eishin-Ryū the first truly international style of authentic Japanese *budō* and appointed an American, Carl E. Long Hanshi, as his successor. Immediately after Shimabukuro's death, Long Hanshi became chairman of the Kokusai Nippon Budō Kai and twenty-second *sōshihan* of the Masaoka-Ha line.

Carl E. Long was born in Hunlock Creek, Pennsylvania, on July 28, 1955. He began his study of Japanese *budō* at the age of thirteen by training in Shōrin-Ryū *karate-dō*, receiving an instructor's license ten years later. By 1986 he had also received *dan* ranking in *aikidō* and opened his own *dōjō*, the Sakura Budōkan, in Kingston, Pennsylvania, in 1989. In 1994, he learned that Shimabukuro Hanshi was teaching *iaijutsu* in the United States and traveled to San Diego to meet and train with him. In 1995, after making several training visits to San Diego, Long was appointed as

Eastern USA Representative of the recently formed Jikishin-Kai International. Two years later, the Sakura Budōkan was officially designated as the East Coast *hombu* of the Jikishin-Kai International. In 2000, Long was promoted to *godan* (fifth *dan*) in Eishin-Ryū *iaijutsu*. Four years later, he received his *rokudan* (sixth *dan*) ranking and Renshi (Warrior Trainer) title from both the Jikishin-Kai International and the Dai Nippon Butoku-Kai.

In 2006 Long was appointed Vice Chairman of the Jikishin-Kai International, and he began traveling extensively, both with Shimabukuro Hanshi, as well as independently, to conduct seminars throughout North and South America and Europe. The following year, when the Kokusai Nippon Budō Kai was formed, he was appointed its Vice Chairman. He was promoted to *nanadan* (seventh *dan*) and awarded the title of Kyōshi by the Butoku-Kai in 2009, and received the same rank and title from the Jikishin-Kai shortly thereafter. And he received *godan* (fifth *dan*) rank in *jōjutsu* in 2010.

On August 15, 2012, Shimabukuro Hanshi made the official announcement that Carl Long was to be his successor as *sōshihan* of Masaoka-Ha Eishin-Ryū and Chairman of the KNBK. Just three weeks later, a broken-hearted Long Hanshi assumed both offices, but his duties in those roles left him little time to fully mourn the loss of his *sensei*.

Since taking office, Long Hanshi has maintained an exhausting teaching and travel schedule in order to continue the legacy of Miura Hanshi and Shimabukuro Hanshi. He was promoted to *hachidan* (eighth *dan*) in *iaijutsu* in 2014 and elevated to the title of Hanshi in 2015 by the Butoku-Kai. The following year he was appointed the USA Representative of the Dai Nippon Butoku-Kai International Division. In 2017 he received *nanadan* (seventh *dan*) ranking and the title of Kyōshi in *jōjutsu* from the Butoku-Kai.

Although the foregoing history of *iaijutsu* and the Masaoka-Ha Eishin-Ryū lineage omits mention of many of the *sōshihan* who maintained the continuity (*jikiden*) of our art, it is mostly because their lives and contributions are not well documented, not because they were insignificant. Every leader of our style has had an important impact on its evolution.

In fact, that is the purpose of devoting such a large portion of this work to detailing the history of our *ryū*. Every leader and every student becomes part of the "flow" that is embodied in the word *ryū*. Every person who joins the *ryū* leaves the imprint of his or her personality and thus contributes to its "DNA," keeping the *ryū* alive and growing generation after generation, making it vital that we continue to document that flow so that future generations can absorb that "DNA" and sustain the vitality and viability of the *ryū*.

(A complete listing of the genealogy of Musō Jikiden Eishin-Ryū *iaijutsu* is presented below.)

# GENEALOGY OF MASAOKA-HA MUSŌ JIKIDEN EISHIN-RYŪ *IAIJUTSU*

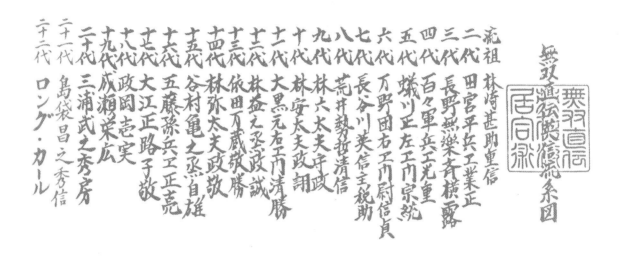

**Genealogy of Masaoka-Ha Musō Jikiden Eishin-Ryū Iaijutsu**

| | |
|---|---|
| *Ryūsō:* | Hayashizaki Jinsuke Shigenobu |
| *Ni-dai:* | Tamiya Heibei Shigemasa |
| *San-dai:* | Nagano Murakusai Kinrō |
| *Yon-dai:* | Momo Gumbei Mitsushige |
| *Go-dai:* | Arikawa Shōzaemon Munetsugu |
| *Roku-dai:* | Manno Danemon no Jō Nobusada |
| *Nana-dai:* | Hasegawa Shigenobu (Eishin) Shūzei no Suke |
| *Hachi-dai:* | Arai Seitetsu Kiyonobu |
| *Kyū-dai:* | Hayashi Rokudayū Morimasa |
| *Jū-dai:* | Hayashi Yasudayū Seishō |
| *Jūichi-dai:* | Ōguro Motoemon Kiyokatsu |

**Genealogy of Masaoka-Ha Musō Jikiden Eishin-Ryū Iaijutsu** *(continued)*

| | |
|---|---|
| *Jūni-dai:* | Hayashi Masu no Jō Masanari |
| *Jūsan-dai:* | Yoda Manzō Yorikatsu |
| *Jūyon-dai:* | Hayashi Yadayū Masayori |
| *Jūgo-dai:* | Tanimura Kame no Jō Yorikatsu |
| *Jūroku-dai:* | Gotō Magobei Masasuke |
| *Jūnana-dai:* | Ōe Masamichi Shikei |
| *Jūhachi-dai:* | Masaoka Katsutane (Kazumi) |
| *Jūkyū-dai:* | Narise Sakahiro |
| *Nijū-dai:* | Miura Takeyuki Hidefusa |
| *Nijūichi-dai:* | Shimabukuro Masayuki Hidenobu |
| *Nijūni-dai:* | Carl E. Long |

If the postwar history of *iaijutsu* has taught us nothing else, it should be that as our art becomes more widely practiced worldwide, it will continue to produce an increasing number of exceptional leaders who will create even more *ha* with the passage of time, and that as the number of practitioners outside Japan continues to grow, a greater number of those leaders will be non-Japanese.

# Chapter 2

# *Jinseikan* 人生観

## Iaijutsu Philosophy

It is highly unlikely that you will ever slip into your *hakama*, sling your *katana* at your side, and saunter down the street prepared to use your *iaijutsu* skills to defend yourself or take up the cause of your lord like the samurai of old. If you do, you are likely to be arrested. So what benefit is there in *iaijutsu* training?

The fact that you will probably never engage in a real sword battle may, paradoxically, be the greatest benefit of sword training. Those who train in *budō* that have obvious practical application in current times, such as *karate-dō* or *jūjutsu*, too often find themselves so involved in developing skill in the physical self-defense applications of their art that they overlook or minimize their mental and spiritual training. Especially in the West, *budō* training often merely gives lip-service to these vital elements of mental and spiritual training. In recent years, far greater emphasis seems to be placed on the street-fighting applications of so-called mixed martial arts, and the benefits of traditional *budō* training have been minimized and even ridiculed. The opposite is true of *iaijutsu*.

By its very nature, as an activity that is highly ritualized, moderately paced, and without obvious "street" application, *iaijutsu* provides an ideal environment in which to refine mental and spiritual discipline. All forms of traditional *budō* are supposed to develop these qualities, but few seem to adequately emphasize them in modern practice.

This is not to say that *iaijutsu* has no practical or beneficial applications. Far from it: *iaijutsu* develops qualities and skills that are not only useful for self-defense, if needed, but also improve one's experience of daily life. For this reason, training in this seemingly "impractical" art is far more practical than learning street-fighting techniques for anyone but a thug.

# BUDŌ NO ARIKATA
## Purpose of Martial Arts

To understand the purpose of *budō* training, we need only understand the goal of *budō*: to win. It is that simple.

At the same time, it is far more complex. Obviously, we train in *budō* in order to prevail in an encounter. We certainly don't spend years training in order to be defeated. However, *budō* training involves much more than merely learning how to injure or kill another person in battle.

A Japanese legend relates that, centuries ago, there were two samurai who were closer than brothers. As they matured and prepared to embark on their *musha shugyō*—the customary travels to perfect their skills—it was apparent that their paths would separate for many years. So, before departing, they met by a quiet stream and vowed to meet again on that very spot twelve years later to share tales of their training and heroic exploits. Just as they had vowed, they returned to the bank of the stream on the very day twelve years later, but found that a recent storm had swollen the gentle stream into a raging torrent, barring their way to the exact spot of their last meeting.

Determined to live up to the letter and spirit of his vow, and to demonstrate the incredible skills he had mastered during their twelve-year separation, one samurai dashed to the river and made a spectacular leap that carried him over the deadly current and safely to the other side. The jump far exceeded today's Olympic records, and should have amazed his friend. Instead, the other samurai calmly walked a few paces upstream and hired a boatman to row him across for five *mon* (about 50 cents).

The skills one man spent a lifetime of sacrifice and dedication to develop could be duplicated effortlessly for a few pennies. Similarly, if our goal is merely to kill people, we can simply purchase a gun, rather than invest years of training. So, the first lesson of *iaijutsu* is to be certain that your training goals are worthwhile.

Next, we must realize that "winning" is not merely defeating an opponent; it is perfecting yourself—your personal character as well as your skills—to the degree that an opponent cannot prevail against you. Yet, winning is still more than this.

In *iaijutsu*, there is a saying: *Kachi wa saya no naka ni ari* ("Victory comes while the sword is [still] in the scabbard"). Physical skills alone, no matter how highly perfected, are simply not enough. There is always someone more skillful, or someone with a dirty trick for which you are unprepared. But attitude is more important than aptitude in real combat. We have all seen encounters reminiscent of that between David and Goliath, where the underdog defeated a far mightier opponent through sheer determination and faith.

Without the courage or determination to use it, a high degree of skill is useless. It would be like painting a great masterpiece, then storing it away where no one can ever see it. This is not only a waste of time, talent, and effort, but a loss of something valuable to humankind.

So, the higher purpose of *iaijutsu* is to develop the mind and spirit of a *bushi*, an attitude and strength of character that wins the battle before it begins. This is no simple matter to achieve. It takes years of daily training to cultivate these attributes and to rid oneself of attitudes and reactions, such as anger, fear, selfishness, jealousy, and hate, that are counterproductive or self-destructive.

Furthermore, winning must be accomplished without trying to win. Once again, this concept at first seems self-contradictory. After all, how can you be victorious if you don't even try to win? The answer is that the key to winning a battle is a steadfast determination to not lose.

This is more than just a semantic difference; it requires a fundamental shift of focus and commitment. When you are trying to win, you will be inclined to take unnecessary risks in your determination to defeat your opponent. But when you are instead resolved to not losing the encounter, you have the luxury of waiting for your opponent to make a mistake or expose a vulnerability that you can then exploit to achieve victory.

However, *iaijutsu* training demands a still higher and nobler purpose than merely winning (or not losing) battles. The great Chinese tactician Sun Tsu said that the highest principle in the *Art of War* is to win without a battle. This is the true ideal of *iaijutsu*, as embodied in the Chinese ideograms for "martial art":

Bujutsu: "martial" "art"

The symbol on the left above (the *bu* in *bujutsu* and *budō*), typically translated as "martial," was formed from the two *kanji* (characters) below:

Tomeru hoko: "prevent" "conflict"

Thus, in the strict or literal sense, the word *bujutsu* does not mean "martial arts," but instead from the earliest of times has truly meant "the art of conflict prevention," or perhaps more artfully, "the art of peace-making." The way *iaijutsu* training accomplishes this goal can only be discovered by understanding the underlying ideals of *budō*.

# SHUGYŌ NO MOKUTEKI
## Ideals of Training

Japan's most famous and revered samurai, Miyamoto Musashi, once asked his young disciple, Jōtarō, what his goal in life was. Without hesitation, the teenager replied, "To be like you."

"Your goal is too small," Musashi scolded him. He went on to admonish his student to "aspire to be like Mount Fuji, with such a broad and solid foundation that the strongest earthquake cannot move you, and so tall that the greatest enterprises of common men seem insignificant from your lofty perspective. With your mind as high as Mount Fuji," he explained, "you can see all things clearly. And you can see all the forces which shape events; not just the things happening near you."

Walking together along a twisting mountain path, Musashi and Jōtarō soon came to a bend at which an enormous overhanging boulder loomed above the path. At first glance, the boulder seemed precariously suspended above them, as if the slightest jar would break it loose and send it crashing down to annihilate them. Yet, a closer look showed it to be so firmly embedded in the mountainside that it would take the forces of nature eons to work it free. Nevertheless, Jōtarō scuttled nervously along the path beneath it, anxious to be out from under it. As Musashi calmly followed, he noticed his disciple's natural reaction to the threatening presence of the massive rock, and used it to reinforce his lesson.

"You should train to become like this boulder," Musashi told Jōtarō, "with most of your strength hidden, and so deeply rooted that you are immovable, yet so powerful that what can be seen will make men cringe to walk in your shadow."

This, Musashi felt, was the ultimate goal of training, to be so highly skilled and mentally developed that your mere presence was intimidating, and no man would dare challenge you. And, indeed, Musashi reached, even exceeded, this level of personal development during his colorful life. Clearly, someone this highly trained will have to fight few, if any, battles to achieve life's victories.

Later in life, it was this very quality that Musashi looked for in selecting a student to train. After he had retired to refine his character through the arts of painting, sculpting, and calligraphy, Musashi accepted an invitation by the Kumamoto *daimyō* to come to his castle and train an elite corps of samurai to become the *daimyō's* personal retainers. So great was the *daimyō's* respect for Musashi that he had all of his samurai—several hundred of them—form a processional line on both sides of the street, extending from the castle gates to the town. As Musashi strode between the two columns of men, each bowed reverently at his passage. But, as Musashi's keen eye detected, even these elite samurai averted their gaze from his bold stare. Only one among them seemed not to be intimated by Musashi's mere countenance.

When Musashi finally reached the *daimyō* and his counselors, the *daimyō* asked if any of his samurai had particularly impressed Musashi, perhaps testing to see if Musashi could discern his most skillful swordsmen at just a passing glance. Musashi led the *daimyō* back to the one man who had not cast his eyes down as Musashi passed.

"This man," Musashi announced.

"I don't understand," the *daimyō* blustered. "He has little training and only modest rank. In fact, he is an *ashigaru* (foot soldier) whose main duty is stonecutting for the castle."

"This may be so," Musashi answered, "But he is your best-trained samurai." Turning to the man, Musashi asked him, "Tell me, how do you train that you have no fear of death?"

"I hardly train at all," the samurai admitted humbly, "When I go to bed each night, I simply unsheathe my sword and hang it above my face by a slender thread. Then I lie down beneath it and gaze up at its point until I fall asleep."

"This is indeed your best trained samurai," Musashi told the *daimyō*, with a knowing smile. "He alone of all your men faces death every day, for he knows that it would take little for that tiny thread to break and end his life. I will train this man to be your personal bodyguard."

However, as Musashi continued to mature, he found—to his great dismay—that even such an incredible level of personal development was not enough. Despite the fact that even the bravest samurai could not bear to gaze upon Musashi in awe of him, he was still challenged many times and forced to kill more than sixty opponents in sword duels. He found that his reputation and his aura of power and invincibility attracted fame-seekers like moths to a flame. Obviously, anyone who could defeat the legendary Miyamoto Musashi would be instantly famous, able to found his own school of swordsmanship, and command riches, position, and prestige as a high-ranking retainer to any *daimyō*, or perhaps even the Shōgun. So, throughout most of his life, Musashi found himself beleaguered by challengers betting their lives against a chance at such fame and fortune.

Several years after his encounter with the Kumamoto *daimyō*, Musashi was once again in the mountains seeking to perfect his character. Together with his lifelong friend and mentor, the priest Sōhō Takuan, he was seated beside a gentle stream with a small tranquil waterfall, engaged in *zazen* meditation. As they meditated, Musashi's keen senses alerted him to another presence nearby. Without disturbing the serenity of his meditation, Musashi allowed his gaze to fall upon a deadly *mamushi* (viper) slithering into the clearing from some shrubbery near Takuan.

Knowing that the slightest movement might frighten the venomous snake into attacking his friend, Musashi carefully controlled his spirit, watching the serpent in utter stillness. He was surprised to see a faint smile appear on Takuan's lips as he, too, became aware of the snake's approach and calmly watched it crawl across his own thighs. Even more amazing than the priest's complete tranquility in the face of mortal danger was the snake's casual acceptance of Takuan as a natural part of its surroundings.

After slithering across the priest, the lethal serpent continued on its winding course toward Musashi. But, several feet away, the snake sensed Musashi's presence and recoiled, preparing to attack the seated samurai. Musashi gave no reaction. Even though his spirit was undisturbed by the ominous bared fangs of the viper, Musashi's power, skill, and menace were so palpable to the snake that it scurried away into the bushes like a terrified rabbit. Most men would have been proud to possess such an intimidating aura, but Musashi felt only shame as he suddenly understood his own greatest shortcoming.

"What troubles you so?" asked Takuan, sensing his friend's mood change.

"All my life," Musashi lamented, "I have trained myself to develop such skill that no man would ever dare attack me. And now that I have reached my goal, all living things instinctively fear me. You saw how the snake fled from me."

"I saw it," the priest said. "Since it dared not attack you, you defeated it without striking a blow. And because of your great skill, both you and the snake are alive now." Although he already knew the answer, Takuan asked, "Why does that sadden you?"

"Because I am so strong that no one can ever grow close to me. I can never have true peace." Musashi pointed a finger at the priest. "Not like you," he said with admiration, "You did not fear the snake, nor did the snake fear you. Your spirit is so calm, so natural, that the snake treated you no differently than the rocks, the trees, or the wind. People accept you that way, too."

Takuan only smiled, pleased that his friend had made such an important self-discovery.

Musashi spent the rest of his days training to perfect a spirit like that of his friend Takuan. This mental state, the ideal to which all martial artists aspire, is called *heijōshin*. Literally translated, it means "constant stable spirit," but such a translation hardly does it justice. The nuances of the Japanese language help greatly in understanding the full nature of *heijōshin*, a word comprised of three *kanji* (characters):

*Hei jō shin*

*Hei* has numerous related meanings in Japanese: "peaceful," "calm," "steady," and so on. The closest English equivalent, however, may be "level" or "even," since these terms can be used in such ways as "level-headed" and "even-handed" in English. *Jō* has a more precise meaning, at least in terms of its English translations: "always," "constant," or "continually."

*Shin* translates both literally and figuratively as "heart," with almost all the same nuances. Thus, to Asians and Westerners alike, *shin* is understood as more than simply the internal organ that pumps blood, but connotes the mind, the spirit, the emotions, the character—the whole inner essence of the individual.

Thus, *heijōshin* is a concept of the whole inner being of a person being continually at peace. For lack of a more effective translation, we will simply call it "peace of mind." However, the fullness of *heijōshin* warrants a more detailed explanation.

# HEIJŌSHIN
## Peace of Mind

*Heijōshin*, true peace of mind, is probably best understood not as a single attribute but as a combination—or rather the culmination—of several character traits. Each of the aspects that together create *heijōshin* may take years of effort, experience, and disappointment to develop, making *heijōshin* the product of a lifetime of patient training. To achieve genuine peace of mind requires a high degree of mental development in three key areas: (1) the intellect, (2) the emotions, and (3) that indefinable element we usually call "character" or "integrity." And these three areas must be developed in balance.

Why is *heijōshin* so important?

As we age, our physical prowess, no matter how great, will eventually lessen. This is especially evident in professional sports, where few athletes enjoy a career longer than ten years. But, with diligence, our character and our mental prowess will constantly improve. And we can never be certain that ill health or a serious accident might not leave us with drastically impaired physical ability, while our mental faculties remain strong. The key to lifelong fruitfulness and happiness, then, is not in our physical skills, but in our mental development.

This is why cultivating *heijōshin* is far more important to the *budōka* than merely perfecting skill with a sword. Furthermore, *heijōshin* is an unlimited quality. There is always room for more knowledge, greater compassion, stronger love, and a higher level of character development.

How do you obtain *heijōshin*?

*Heijōshin* is not only difficult to attain, but there is no simple, precise method to develop it. This is a stumbling block to many Westerners, especially in the United States, where people have become culturally conditioned to a "quick-fix" approach to nearly everything. If something cannot be achieved with a wonder drug, an overnight miracle, or a three-step, five-day program, it seems too difficult and time-consuming to attempt.

So, to begin with, you might as well understand that *heijōshin* demands a lifestyle change: a life of discipline, effort, sacrifice, and commitment. Such a commitment to developing excellence of character sets the *budōka*—particularly the *iaijutsu* practitioner—apart from most people in a confused and unhappy society.

Not only is there no easy way to develop *heijōshin*, but for each of us the path will be different, because of our different personality, experiences, and circumstances. To further complicate matters, *heijōshin* is rife with paradoxes. The first of these is the nature of *heijōshin* itself: it is the product of diligent training and continual effort to reshape the mind, yet in the end it must be completely natural and unforced. So, how do we practice something that must occur spontaneously?

The tales of Miyamoto Musashi told earlier in this chapter contain some clues that may help answer this question. If you read them again now, you may notice that Musashi did not train himself in the "art" of *heijōshin* itself, but rather in the elements that lead to its development. In effect, in another of its paradoxes, while *heijōshin* is the true goal of martial arts training, it is achieved as a by-product of training.

If *heijōshin* was merely a single attribute, it could be practiced and learned, like the alphabet or multiplication tables. But, since it is itself the by-product of a person's complete inner being, it can only be achieved by refining that whole inner essence. And this can only be accomplished if one's intellect, emotions, and character are developed in balance.

Why is *budō* training the best method for developing *heijōshin*?

When a person realizes the true nature of *budō* training, and practices accordingly, it leads to a fuller understanding of the nature of life itself. *Budō* is concerned essentially with life and death. This is most apparent, perhaps, in *iaijutsu* training, since the outcome of a sword battle is clearly that one opponent lives and the other dies. This is not the case with *karate-dō* or several other forms of *budō*, in which the "loser" might merely be rendered incapable of continuing the fight.

So, if the *iaijutsu* student is serious about his or her training, each *waza* represents far more than simply swinging a sword around. It is a symbolic battle in which your opponent will most certainly die. Will you end his life without good cause? Will you throw his family into turmoil and perhaps ruin over some triviality? Will you risk or sacrifice your own life over a minor disagreement or offense? When you have developed true compassion for others, then train in a life-or-death context, you gain a whole new appreciation of life—both your own and the lives of others.

Isn't "life-or-death" training unrealistic in modern society?

The irony of a comfortable modern life is that few people, other than the best-trained *budōka*, truly understand how tenuous life is. The samurai understood this, because he was trained to realize that each new day might bring death. The pioneers of the Old West understood it, because of the tremendous hardships and uncertainties they faced. But, in an age in which hunger, disease, and most of our mortal enemies have been all but vanquished, we seem to have become blinded to the precariousness of our existence. Even when we read of a celebrity succumbing to cancer, or a terrible plane crash, or a terrorist bombing, or a drive-by gang shooting, most of us believe that "it won't happen to me."

The life-or-death awareness of *iaijutsu* training allows us to clearly see that death is, quite literally, only one heartbeat away. Part of *heijōshin* is coming to grips with the inevitability of death. That it will eventually claim the "high" and "low" alike—celebrities, drug addicts, politicians, bank robbers, aristocrats, business executives, and even ourselves.

Once we understand how fragile our lives are, we have a vital choice to make. We can either live in seclusion, like Howard Hughes in his later years, cowering in paranoid fear of everything from germs to fatal accidents, or we can determine to live each moment we are given to the utmost and die with no regrets. Yet it is only after deciding to live life to its fullest that we have the most difficult choices to make. It is then that we must come to grips with what brings true and lasting happiness and fulfillment to life.

If you were given only one week to live, what would you do? Would you live out your final days in a wild, uninhibited bacchanalia of sensual pleasures? Many would. Would you sell all that you had accumulated and spend your last week donating to every worthy cause you could think of? That would be nobler. Would you feverishly attend to every detail of settling your estate, so your loved ones would be provided for after your death? That would demonstrate a high degree of responsibility and integrity. Would you spend every moment possible with your family and closest friends? That would probably give your final hours the greatest comfort. Or would you do nothing different than you had done the previous week, or the week before that? That would indicate that your lifestyle has produced *heijōshin*.

This brings us to another paradox: If you have achieved *heijōshin*, you will live every day as if it was your last. But just because you live every day as if it was your last does not mean you have attained *heijōshin*. It is not simply "living like there's no tomorrow" that demonstrates *heijōshin*, but *how* you live your last day that is the barometer of your character. It is the quality and purpose of your life that gives it value.

How should I live my life to have *heijōshin*?

The highest principle of *heijōshin* is to develop your mind (the combination of intellect, emotions, and character) to such an elevated state that you are unaffected by your environment. This is what Musashi was trying to impress upon Jōtarō by admonishing him to train himself to be like Mount Fuji. It means not allowing circumstances to control your emotions, nor emotions to confuse your judgment.

If your happiness and security are based primarily upon your financial status, then you will only be comfortable when things are going well. If you lose your job and begin to have difficulty paying your bills, soon you will find yourself constantly under stress, doubting your own abilities and value, and angered by the loss of the material freedom you once had. In the end, you will likely find yourself taking a job that is not right for you, just to regain your self-esteem and recover your lost financial status. This is an example of your circumstances controlling your emotions, and your emotions in turn confusing your judgment.

But, if your contentment is derived from knowing the type of person that you are inside, then you will more readily understand that life has its ups and downs. You will realize that the sun rises upon the evil and the good, and the rain falls upon the righteous and the unrighteous alike. Everyone experiences an occasional windfall, and no one is exempt from times of hardship, so it is foolish to allow these circumstances to dictate your emotions. What is more, the rich and famous are often the unhappiest people in the world, while those who eschew material wealth and comfort, like Mother Teresa, enjoy a rich and fulfilling life. Once you understand that it is what you *are*, not what you *have*, that is important, you are able to rise above your circumstances.

The second key tenet of *heijōshin* is to understand that you are part of your environment; that what you are and what you do has an effect on other people. Even your emotions affect others. If you are discouraged, you will drop a cloud of gloom on the people with whom you come in contact. If you are joyful, just the sight of you will gladden them. If you behave rudely, you will anger people or hurt their feelings. If you are pleasant and respectful, you will brighten their day and make them feel important. People who look up to you will follow your example, whether it is good or bad.

This presents another of *heijōshin*'s paradoxes: How can we be unaffected by our environment when we are *part* of our environment?

Obviously, our environment will affect us to some degree. The state of the economy will affect us, our health will affect us, the actions of friends and loved ones will affect us. *Heijōshin* is not a condition in which we insulate ourselves from our surroundings, nor deny that our problems exist, nor deaden our minds and senses to our feelings. *Heijōshin* is not a means of escape, like drugs, which allows you to ignore or be unaware of your emotions. Quite the opposite, to possess *heijōshin* demands that you be deeply in touch with your emotions. It is perfectly natural to feel anger, joy, disappointment, love, and the full range of emotions. *Heijōshin*, however, allows us not to be controlled by these emotions, so that our actions are not determined by a fleeting impulse, but are the product of a consistent, balanced, and focused mind.

How can I experience my emotions, yet not let them affect my actions?

The answer comes from developing two essential character traits: understanding and compassion. First, you must understand yourself; understand why you feel the way you do, why certain events or situations evoke particular emotions in you. Then, you must have compassion for yourself. Accept yourself for who you are, and why you are who you are. You cannot change who you are now. You have already become that person. You can only change who you will be in the future. If you berate yourself for your faults and failures, it is only a waste of your emotional energy and destructive to your self-esteem. But, if you can compassionately accept yourself as you are now and understand the process and influences that shaped you into that person, then you have a positive starting point from which to begin developing into the person you want to become.

Second, you must have the same understanding and compassion for others. Once you have thoroughly understood yourself, you can appreciate that other people have become who they are for a reason. There have been influences, circumstances, and events that have shaped them into the people they have become. By compassionately accepting others with both their strengths and weaknesses, you will be able to distinguish between your feelings toward the person and your feelings about their behavior. This separation is vital to human relationships.

If someone behaves rudely, for example, I can either become offended by the *person* or by the person's *behavior*. If I become offended by the person, my natural reaction will be to avoid that offensive person. If, instead, I look beyond the person and see the behavior as offensive, then my natural reaction will be to try to understand what caused it, because I am now viewing the situation as an offensive action committed by an acceptable person. Rather than shunning the person, I will try to communicate with him or her, and my reaction will be motivated by concern for their well-being rather than anger or resentment over their actions.

Westerners reflect an understanding of this aspect of *heijōshin* in this commonly quoted prayer: "God grant me the serenity to accept the things I cannot change, the courage to change the things I can, and the wisdom to know the difference."

When should I use *heijōshin*?

*Heijōshin* is not something you turn on and off like a politician's smile. Once *heijōshin* is rooted in you, it is with you at all times everywhere you go, from the time you wake up to the time you go to bed—even while you are sleeping. It becomes your natural state of mind, not something you summon only when you "need" it.

What are the benefits of *heijōshin*?

By developing a constant, peaceful state of mind, you, as an individual, will lead a happier, more serene life, liberated from the emotional roller coaster of forces beyond your control. But the benefits of *heijōshin* cannot remain exclusively personal. By its nature, *heijōshin* cannot exist in a vacuum, so its benefits will spread from you to society as a whole.

Society is simply a collection of individuals. Social ills, like crime and drug abuse, are merely the reflection of the combined failings of the individuals who make up that society. Laws cannot reform society and cure its ills; they can only punish violators. Society is like our collective shadow. If the shadow is bent and twisted, no amount of effort can straighten it. Only by straightening ourselves does our shadow also straighten, and then it does so effortlessly and automatically. So it is that reform must start with individuals and spread through society. It is a grassroots process in which each of us either remains part of the disease or is part of the cure.

If our behavior is controlled by our circumstances and emotions, rather than by our strength of character and ideals, then we are part of the disease. If, instead, our *heijōshin* lifts us above our circumstances and helps us live with greater purpose and meaning, our example will inspire others to become part of the cure. The cure for social ills works the same way as the disease: virally.

Thus, the ultimate objective of *heijōshin* is the same as the ultimate objective of *budō*: to help each individual reach his or her full potential, and thereby improve society as a whole.

# SHUGYŌ NO HAJIME
## The Journey's Beginning

Having determined to set out on this journey of self-discovery and perfection of character through *budō* training, you need to know where to start. As good as any book or video may be, you cannot learn *budō* from it alone. *Budō* instruction is personal and requires human contact. It is nothing like learning spelling or arithmetic in school.

True *budō* instruction—the development, maturation, and shaping of a good *budōka*—is not a process; it is a relationship. For that reason, it requires a good instructor and a good *dōjō*. The depth of understanding of both the technical and philosophical aspects of *iaijutsu* can only be passed on through a mentoring relationship. As mentioned in chapter 1, *budō* training is more than just learning techniques and skills; it is becoming part of a *ryū*—a continuum of history, culture, philosophy, traditions, and relationships that has been growing and flowing for centuries. This is why the Japanese place such importance—bordering on reverence—on the close, personal connection between a student (*seito* or *deshi*) and *sensei* (teacher), and in the relationship between *sempai* (senior students) and *kōhai* (junior students).

A *sensei* is more than merely a *budō* instructor; he or she is the living example of technical and philosophical excellence to which students aspire. The *sempai*, or senior student, is a partner in the training process who acts like a nurturing older brother or sister, guiding and encouraging the student on the often difficult and discouraging road toward his or her objectives and ideals.

*Dōjō* literally means "Place of the Way." It is not just a building in which to practice *budō*; it is a laboratory in which to study, experiment, and refine a complete and fulfilling way of life. You should select your *dōjō* with the utmost care, as though your life, or at least the quality of your life, depended upon it. To be blunt, if all you want to do is engage in samurai cosplay, a *dōjō* is no place for you. If you just want to learn some impressive moves with a sword, watch some videos on the internet. A *dōjō* is a place you go to change your life—to improve your character, discipline, attitudes, intentions, and ideals—and to become an integral part of a living and growing *ryū*.

The first step, therefore, in reaching your full potential is to find a good *sensei* teaching in a good *dōjō*. Remember that a good player is not always a good coach, so you must look not only at the instructor's technical expertise, but also at his ability to lead, instruct, and inspire his students. Some good measures of these abilities are the degree of respect shown by his students, whether the senior students show a nurturing attitude toward their juniors, and whether the students are able to acquire the skills and—more importantly—the attitudes the instructor is trying to impart.

The best way to do this is to visit those *dōjō* in your area that have the highest reputation among respected *budōka*. Visit each one in which you are interested several times to observe classes and discuss your training goals with the instructor. You should not only determine if the instructor's teaching style is suited to your personality and the way you best learn, but pay particular attention to the *sensei*'s attitude and demeanor. Does the *sensei* exhibit the highest ideals of *budō* in his or her conduct? Does he or she lose interest in you if you don't join the *dōjō* right away? Does he or she show more concern for you as a potential student, or in your ability to pay for the lessons? The bottom-line question to ask yourself is: "Is this *sensei* the kind of role model I want to emulate?"

Once you have selected a *dōjō*, it is important for you to seek and maintain a close relationship with your *sensei*. After all, *iaijutsu* training is training for everyday life, so in order for it to take root, your training must be part of your everyday life, and your daily life must be part of your training. The Japanese have a saying, *shi-tei fu ni* ("Master and disciple are not two"), meaning that your *sensei* should be like a wise, patient parent to you. Seek the counsel of your *sensei* concerning the opportunities, issues, and problems you are facing, so that he or she can show you how to apply sound *budō* principles to the important decisions you make.

Lastly, train seriously. Use your imagination to "feel" your opponent and face death through your training. The more vividly and realistically you face death while you practice *iaijutsu*, the more your eyes will be opened to what life is really about.

## IKA NI SHINU KA
### How to Die Well

An extremely significant part of a samurai's training was learning and deciding to die well. As we have emphasized repeatedly, facing death—either vicariously in the *dōjō*, or literally on the battlefield—was a daily routine for the samurai. Part of a samurai's training included instruction in the proprieties of ritualistic suicide (*seppuku*), accomplished by slitting open his own abdomen. A samurai was also trained and prepared to act as *kaishakunin*, or assistant, in the event one of his peers was called upon to commit *seppuku*, and was well-versed in both the technique and etiquette of this crucial role. Even the women of samurai rank were prepared to perform ritual suicide, albeit by the more genteel method of slitting their own throat.

One of the hallmarks of a samurai was his avowed purpose: *shinu kikai o motomeru* ("Seeking the opportunity to die"). In the West, this has often been portrayed and interpreted as an exaggerated sense of fatalism among the samurai—a view that reduces them to little more than half-crazed warriors throwing themselves wantonly into battle as if their lives were worthless. Exactly the opposite is true.

While applying the principle of *shinu kikai o motomeru* did free the samurai to face his enemy with fearless disregard for his own life, it was not for the reason suggested by this shallow interpretation. Instead, the samurai held his life to be of extreme value. It was therefore only to be lost—or even risked—if the cause was worthy of such a supreme and noble sacrifice.

Thus, in searching for the opportunity to die, the samurai actually sought the reason to *live*. As modern samurai we should do no less. People die every day from senseless and careless causes: drug overdoses, texting while driving, or taking foolish risks. The samurai would consider dying for such a reason shameful. Facing death in our training helps us to focus on those things that are truly important to our lives, such as family, personal relationships, strength of character, and so forth. In this way, *shinu kikai o motomeru* leads us to decide what is really worth living for.

When we begin to focus our thoughts, ideals, and desires on the things we are willing to die for, most of the ambiguities, gray areas, and dilemmas of life are removed from our path. We no longer allow the trivialities and distractions that so complicate most people's lives to be a factor in ours.

By becoming a complete *budōka*—a person who understands Budō no Arikata and Shugyō no Mokuteki, who possesses *heijōshin* and has determined their *shinu kikai*—we will know what truly victorious living is. When we live only for the things worth dying for, we will live a life truly worth living: a life of purpose and meaning, filled with rich, intimate relationships and significant accomplishments. And when we reach the end of our appointed days, we will be able to look back on our lives without regrets.

This is the true purpose of *iaijutsu* training.

Chapter 3

# *Bushi no Me*

## Eyes of a Samurai

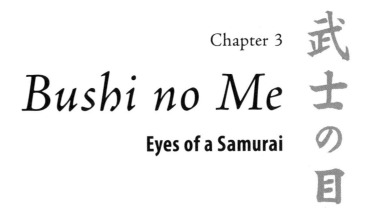

A samurai does not see things in an ordinary way. He has trained his mind and spirit to process the impulses from his optic nerves in a highly refined manner.

Just as in Western culture, samurai concepts of "eye" and "sight" include both physical vision (to see an object) and mental insight (to "see" someone's point of view). In fact, to the samurai, there is probably less distinction between these two concepts than in the West. For most Westerners, vision seldom rises above the first or second levels described below, but the samurai recognizes five distinct levels of eyesight and tries to "see" at the highest of these levels in a way that combines physical sight with deep insight.

## NIKUGEN

### "Naked Eye"

*Nikugen* is no more than the plain image received on the retina, devoid of any mental or emotional process. Obviously, it is the lowest of the five levels of vision, and it has three major limitations. First, *nikugen* is completely superficial. A person using *nikugen* sees nothing beyond the existence of the objects within his or her field of vision. *Nikugen* does not involve any deeper comprehension of these objects, such as how they came to be where they are, how they might interact, what direction they might be heading, how they might affect the observer or others, or any other implications.

Secondly, *nikugen* is limited by the observer's point of view. Someone using *nikugen* can see only that side of things that is facing his direction. In this sense, *nikugen* is almost two-dimensional. Staring at a circular object, a person using *nikugen* would not know if he sees a true circle, the bottom of a cone, the bottom of a cylinder, or the visible outline of a sphere.

Thirdly, *nikugen* is easily obstructed. By simply placing something in front of the observer's eyes, he would be rendered effectively sightless.

These qualities not only apply to physical sight, but also to the "insight" sense of *nikugen*. A person trying to "see" a problem using only *nikugen* can see only its superficial aspects. He also sees the problem only from his own point of view, and his vision is easily obscured by his circumstances, preconceived ideas, and emotions. For example, using only *nikugen*, a person with no money in his pockets would see himself as penniless. If he wants a sandwich, then he would view purchasing the sandwich as a hopeless impossibility.

With this two-dimensional view, the hungry man is blind to other possibilities, such as bartering work for the sandwich, selling another possession to raise money for the sandwich, or seeking food from another source.

## TENGEN
### "Neutral Perspective"

The next developmental step in vision is *tengen*, translated literally as "heavenly eye." This type of sight is described as heavenly not in a divine sense but in terms of the observer's point of view—as if looking down from high above to gain a wider perspective.

With *tengen*, the observer is no longer bound by his own point of view, but has a neutral perspective in which he is better able to see the relationships between the objects or problems being observed, as well as more of the environment in which they exist. Quite literally, *tengen* is being able to "see the forest for the trees." In this way, not only can one clearly see the true nature and shape of objects, as in the first example of *nikugen*, but also all aspects of a problem from a detached and broad perspective. Furthermore, with the less self-centered perspective of *tengen*, the observer's viewpoint is not as susceptible to the distortions of his own preconceived ideas, emotional reactions, or living conditions as it would be with *nikugen*. *Tengen* cannot be easily obstructed, because a clear view of the situation is not dependent on the observer's point of view.

Using the previous examples, a person with *tengen* is more likely to perceive what the unseen surfaces of the circular object are. By applying knowledge and experience, his or her mind will be able to conclude whether what is seen is just a circle, or an outline of a sphere, or the bottom of a cylinder or cone. Similarly, someone with *tengen* will have the ability to "see" more sides to a problem. Rather than narrowly perceiving a lack of money for a sandwich, a person with *tengen* would view the situation in the broader sense of a need for sustenance, which offers more options for a solution than merely the desire for purchase of a sandwich.

However, even with this elevated perspective, the observer's emotions, preconceptions, and life circumstances can interfere to some degree with true understanding, and his or her view is still limited to what the eyes alone can see.

# EGEN
## "Interpretive Sight"

*Egen* (literally "thinking sight") is a higher level, at which the image received by the brain is enhanced by an understanding of the implications of the things being observed. It is important, however, not to confuse *egen* with analytical thought. *Egen* is not the product of consciously thinking about what you see; it is an automatic, subconscious process in which the eye and mind work together to interpret the images received by the brain, thus producing a deeper level of vision than mere physical eyesight. It is the product of knowledge and experience enhancing and informing what the eyes behold.

To use a simple example that many of us may have experienced, a person observing two cars approaching a blind intersection at right angles sees a collision about to occur. Most people would not have to stop and think to realize this. By experience, realizing that neither driver can see the other's oncoming vehicle, we automatically and subconsciously know they are about to collide. With only *nikugen* or *tengen*, however, we would only see two cars moving independently of each other, much as a child who had never witnessed a traffic accident might perceive them.

Unfortunately, while most mature adults have *egen* with respect to common physical events, many lack the same insight with respect to human interactions. But with true *egen*, we would recognize when a clash of personalities or wills was about to occur just as readily as we can see an accident about to happen. *Egen* is the ability to comprehend an event not just in its visible form, but also the forces that led to it and the effects it will have.

Thus, the main benefit of *egen* is that the observer now naturally and subconsciously perceives and understands the cause-and-effect relationship of the things he or she witnesses. *Egen* is not limited by the observer's point of view, nor is his or her vision or insight clouded by emotions, preconceptions, or life circumstances. However, *egen* remains impaired in a crucial way.

# SHINGEN/HŌGEN

## "Compassionate Eye"

For all its benefits, *egen* is still incomplete. Although the observer receives a complete, unobstructed, and undistorted view of situations and their causes and effects—including the reasons and motives underlying peoples' actions—the *egen* perspective is detached and dispassionate.

The next level of vision, *shingen*, adds the most vital ingredient of all: compassion. Compassion is the spark that motivates the samurai to take the correct action in a situation. He sees an event not merely from his own perspective and how it may affect him personally, but how the event will shape the lives of everyone involved—including society as a whole. Furthermore, he sees it with understanding and compassion for all those affected, so that his action will not be motivated solely on what is best for him, but what will be the best for all involved.

The samurai with *shingen* does not view the feelings, actions, or desires of others in terms of "right" or "wrong." Therefore, his judgment is not clouded by a need to prove himself right. Nor does the samurai have to overcome the natural hesitancy of another person to admit that he or she is wrong. Instead, the samurai is only concerned with what has greater *value*. Thus, in a disagreement, the samurai sees the views of others only as alternatives, and he is able to use *shingen* to see which of these alternatives has the most value to those affected, whether it is his own preference or not. With this approach, it is far easier to persuade others to accept the best choice as well.

A samurai's evaluation also takes into account the immutable laws of nature. He understands the principles of cause and effect, and that even wrongful actions are produced by these cause-and-effect forces. Because of this, *shingen* is often also referred to as *hōgen*. *Hōgen* translates literally as "Law Sight," but it does not refer to the laws of people. Instead, its nuance might be best understood as "Universal Perspective" in the sense of having equal compassion for each person in a world operating under a natural order that never changes, but in which a person can choose to intervene. It is from this neutral, compassionate point of view that the samurai tries to observe the world and take the most beneficial action.

Thus, as shown in the table below, a samurai is trained to "see from the heart." Training in the life-or-death art of *iaijutsu* develops a deep, abiding compassion for people, and the experiences of life teach an understanding of the unchanging forces that shape both people and events. As his training and experience continue, his sight evolves through these stages from *nikugen* to *shingen*.

**Nikugen ⟶ Tengen ⟶ Egen ⟶ Shingen/Hōgen**

**DEEPER INSIGHT
BROADER PERSPECTIVE
GREATER COMPASSION
MORE NATURAL**

The easiest way to compare the differences—and the effects of those differences—between *nikugen, tengen, egen,* and *shingen* may be an example from everyday life: You are running late for a very important business meeting, and when you get onto the freeway, the traffic is heavily congested and moving at a crawl.

With *nikugen,* all you can see is that you are going to be extremely late for the meeting and make a terrible impression. As a result, you will probably speed frantically through the traffic, swerving wildly from lane to lane, trying to gain a few precious minutes.

A person with *tengen,* however, can see that his wild driving might earn him a traffic ticket. He might slow down a little, but more likely he will just be more vigilant in watching in the mirror for police cars, since he still wants to save as much time as possible getting to the meeting.

The person with *egen,* on the other hand, does not allow his desire to make a good impression make him act rashly. Based on experience, he knows that driving recklessly not only could earn him a traffic ticket and an additional delay, but also endangers himself and other people on the road—people who have just as much right to safe use of the highway as he does. Furthermore, he is also aware that his business associates may be delayed by the same traffic jam, and that the minor consequences of being late do not justify the risks of driving negligently. Without having to think about it, he will understand the futility of speeding to make up lost time.

The samurai is already at the meeting, waiting for the others to arrive. With the benefit of *hōgen,* he understood that the freeways would be packed at rush hour, so he got up earlier than usual to be sure traffic would not be a problem. In this way, if traffic was terrible, he would still be on time; if traffic was not congested, he would arrive early. He also understood that by being early, his associates would feel obligated to "make it up" to him, so he would gain a psychological advantage at the meeting as well.

A true-life historical example of *shingen* comes from the exploits of one of Japan's greatest military leaders, Takeda Shingen, whose life exemplifies many of the training goals of *iaijutsu*. In Takeda's time, there was a brilliant tactician and warrior named Yamamoto Kansuke. Yamamoto's prowess, however, was not apparent to the naked eye (*nikugen*), but his ugliness most certainly was. His battlefield experience left him with only one eye, a maimed leg, and a disfigured finger, in addition to his generally unattractive appearance. One of Takeda's rivals, Imagawa Yoshimoto, took one look at Yamamoto and turned him down flatly for a command position.

Takeda, possessed of *shingen*, quickly saw past the scarred and unpleasant surface appearance of Yamamoto to his strength of character and tactical knowledge. Takeda at once selected Yamamoto as one of his twenty-four *taishō* (generals). Not only did Yamamoto produce numerous victories for Takeda, but as a man who overcame severe physical handicaps, especially for his day, he was a tremendous inspiration to Takeda's other commanders and warriors, and thus doubly valuable.

## BUSHI NO ME NO RENSHŪ
### Training to Develop Eye of a Samurai

Understanding Bushi no Me is a good start, but developing Bushi no Me is quite another task altogether. This is especially true when you are trying to develop the Eye of a Samurai in both its literal and figurative sense.

You should also be aware that *iaijutsu* training does not really change the core of your personality. The essence of your personality was formed by the time you were five years old. Instead, *iaijutsu* training helps you develop your existing character strengths to greater levels and suppress or compensate for your weaknesses. Since "the eyes are the mirror of the soul," developing Bushi no Me allows you to see yourself clearly so you can make the greatest improvement possible in your attitude and character.

To develop Bushi no Me in the literal sense, gradually developing eyesight that is all-encompassing, compassionate, and deeply understanding requires concentrated effort in the *dōjō*. Your objective should be to both broaden and deepen your sight as well as your insight.

Broadening your sight means enhancing your use of peripheral vision and combining sight with your other senses to provide awareness of things and events your eyes alone cannot see. Deepening your sight involves developing an understanding that delves far below the surface. A simplified example is being able to see past the frown on a person's face (surface) to the emotion or problem that produced that frown. Of course, *shingen* is far more subtle, deep, and complex than this simplistic example, but it serves to convey the concept.

Whether you are training literally or figuratively to develop Bushi no Me, the first step, obviously, is to open your eyes. Of course, this means more than simply looking around—that would merely be *nikugen*. It means to practice being aware, to observe the "big picture" without missing the details, to be cognizant of the causes and effects of the events you witness, to strive to understand other people's point of view and why they hold to it, to notice the subtleties of people's behavior, and to refrain from being judgmental toward them. It equally implies making an effort to "stop and smell the roses," to realize that there are always positive influences in your life—even when you are beset by what appear to be insurmountable difficulties—and to give at least equal attention to them.

To train in the figurative sense of Bushi no Me and reach a point where you are naturally using *shingen* most of the time is a difficult, lifelong process. So it helps to find a good starting point, such as Shin ▪ Ku ▪ I, as a means to begin developing Bushi no Me.

# SHIN ▪ KU ▪ I
## Body ▪ Mouth ▪ Mind

Like most training concepts in *iaijutsu*, Shin ▪ Ku ▪ I will seem a bit paradoxical at first. Literally "Body ▪ Mouth ▪ Mind," Shin ▪ Ku ▪ I refers to action, speech, and thought. This order is stated in the reverse of causation, but is the proper order of training.

It is practically self-evident that the mind controls speech and action (with the exception, perhaps, of reflexive reactions), yet *budōka* through the centuries have found that in training it is more effective to begin at the surface and work back toward the source.

This approach may also recognize the fact that people readily notice our actions and immediately judge us by them. People also listen to our words, but in doing so they usually weigh them against our actions to test for hypocrisy. Our thoughts, of course, remain forever hidden from others. It doesn't matter to others what our thoughts or intentions are, if our actions are harmful or disrespectful. Similarly, if we speak negatively, no amount of good thoughts and intentions will alter the impression left by our words.

Therefore, when we train to improve our character, we begin with the outward manifestation—our behavior. We act with respect toward ourselves and others. We train with discipline and diligence. As we train with this focus, our actions begin to be reflected in the way we speak. The more we consciously act in a respectful and disciplined manner, the more our language becomes respectful and disciplined as well. Thus, by learning to exercise control over our actions, we also develop control over our speech.

Of course, the conscious effort to control our actions and speech requires that our mind exert that control, and this conscious effort eventually becomes habitual and unconscious, thereby reshaping and controlling our thought processes. Once we have developed thoughts and emotions reflective of our improving character, then our words and deeds will continue to demonstrate our increasing maturity. In this way, the process naturally reverses, so that at higher levels of training, the mental discipline produces change in our actions and speech.

Shin • Ku • I is a vital part of training for a samurai, for whom the slightest misstatement or misdeed could result in instantaneous lethal combat. It is therefore essential that a samurai exercise discretion in both words and actions. This can only be accomplished if his or her mind is thoroughly in control.

Even in modern Western cultures, Shin • Ku • I remains a valuable asset. Read the biographies of highly successful, inspirational people, and you will uniformly find that their lives are guided by principles (the mind), which find their way into every word they utter and every action they take. Those aspiring to any measure of greatness in life must follow this model, and Shin • Ku • I is an effective means of developing such a lifestyle.

## KEN SHIN ICHI NYO
### Body and Mind as One

The next stage of training to achieve Bushi no Me is known as Ken Shin Ichi Nyo (Body and Mind as One). In Shin • Ku • I, we train our bodies to respond to our minds, so that our actions become the result of our guiding principles and character. Ken Shin Ichi Nyo takes that process a step farther and makes our mind and body act in unison.

*Iaijutsu* is again an excellent training method to accomplish this unity of body and mind. Ken Shin Ichi Nyo is written like this:

This actually has the meaning "Sword and Mind as One," which is a training objective of samurai swordsmanship. Rather than the body swinging the sword—wielding it as a tool—which is a beginner's level, the master's sword is merely an extension of his own body. As we train toward mastery, we eventually reach a stage at which, rather than the mind instructing our arm to swing the sword, our mind merely instructs the sword to move. In actuality, our mental commands do not bypass our arm; instead, what we have accomplished is to train our mind and body to act as a single unit, which in turn controls the sword.

In Japanese poetry, the word *ken* (sword) often serves as an allusion to the body. Perhaps this has come about because diligent *iaijutsu* training causes the literal "Sword and Mind as One," Ken Shin Ichi Nyo, to steadily evolve into the more profound "Body and Mind as One."

An interesting paradox to consider while you are progressing through Shin ▪ Ku ▪ I to achieve Ken Shin Ichi Nyo is the Japanese proverb: *Kokoro no shito wa narutomo, kokoro o shito sezare.* "Your mind can't be your master; you must master your mind." How are we to understand this axiom when we are training so that our mind controls our speech and action (Shin ▪ Ku ▪ I), and our body and mind act as one (Ken Shin Ichi Nyo)?

The answer is found in the fact that your mind is a complex mechanism in which your intellect, emotions, character, ideals, and motivations continually interact to produce your speech and actions. Each of these areas of your mind has both strengths and weaknesses. And each of these elements is also constantly evolving, influenced not only by external forces and circumstances, but by the development of the other parts of your mind as well.

Not only are these elements continuously struggling to control your conduct, but you are relentlessly besieged by outside influences trying to shape your behavior. The most obvious of these are advertising, peer pressure, laws, social forces, financial pressures, and a variety of temptations. As if these were not enough, your own character adds stresses to this complex equation. For example, you might have a tendency toward laziness that is in constant conflict with your desire to succeed, or perhaps it is a sweet tooth at odds with your plans to go on a diet right after you finish the next doughnut … or the one after that. Each of our internal conflicts is different, both in nature and severity, but they plague every human being.

The point made by the proverb is that the sum total of all these forces will control your mind, unless you make a conscious determination that they will not. Your mind will either react to the inundation of these influences, or you must instead take proactive steps to ensure that it will stand against the combined effect of this bombardment.

It is not enough merely to ensure that your mind is in control of your speech and actions, and that your mind and body act as one; you must also ensure that it is you—meaning your character, ideals, principles, and highest aspirations—who is in charge of that mind.

# HEN DOKU I YAKU
## Change Poison to Medicine

Another way in which Bushi no Me serves to improve your quality of life is found in the adage *Hen doku i yaku* ("Change poison to medicine"). This is a deeper approach to adversity than simply learning to recognize that "Every cloud has a silver lining." It is more akin to the notion that "When life deals you a lemon, make lemonade."

Many of the medicines we use to cure illnesses are quite toxic. They work by killing bacteria or viruses in a small enough dosage that they do not seriously harm us. However, taken in greater quantity, many medicines can be lethal to humans. Recognizing this, the samurai have long known that, like certain poisons, adversities can often have a medicinal effect if taken in the right dosage. Once again, the proverb mandates a proactive approach by the samurai; not merely looking for the good that might come out of a negative event, but *creating* a positive outcome from it.

The comparison of difficulties to "medicine" is also quite deliberate in other respects. Most of the time we do not like the taste of medicine, but we take it to cure a malady. Some medicines even produce unpleasant side effects, but we take them because the disease is worse than the cure. Likewise, we seldom enjoy adversity, but we can use it as a means for self-improvement. With insight and effort, we can use life's setbacks to develop and improve such character traits as patience, endurance, determination, winning spirit, moral stamina, and perseverance.

Medicines are used to cure disease. Often, if we reflect honestly on the causes of our adversities, we find that they either resulted from, or were worsened by, our own shortcomings. By making a forthright self-analysis when we encounter a challenge, we can identify the area of our personality or character that requires a dose of "medicine."

Medicines are also frequently preventive. This is also the case with *Hen doku i yaku*. If we take our "medicine" every time the symptoms appear, we will find fewer and fewer instances in which it is needed. By maturing in our character and improving our Bushi no Me, the frequency and severity of our difficulties will be steadily reduced.

Takeda Shingen knew how to apply the lesson of *Hen doku i yaku* in dire circumstances. Itagaki Nobukata, one of his generals, plunged his troops into a battle that

Takeda's twenty-three other generals had strongly advised against and was soundly defeated. Upon Itagaki's return, he was harshly criticized by his peers, and he fully expected Takeda to strip him of all rank and honor—or possibly worse.

Takeda could have ordered Itagaki to commit suicide and made an example of him to impress on his other generals the importance of taking sound advice and never losing. Instead, Takeda wisely chose *Hen doku i yaku*, so instead of chastising Itagaki, he praised him as a brilliant commander for having minimized his losses under such a crushing defeat, and saying that he doubted any other general could have done so well under the same circumstances.

Instead of being shamed and disheartened by his overwhelming defeat, Itagaki's attitude was strengthened with a renewed determination to merit Takeda's lavish praise and faith in him. As a result, he went on to lead several victorious campaigns for Takeda.

## YUDAN NASHI
### Never Off-Guard

The last—and broadest—aspect of Bushi no Me is *yudan*, being "off-guard." The fighting skills of a samurai were so great that the best chance to defeat one was to catch him off-guard. A famous story about Miyamoto Musashi illustrates this point well.

According to the legend, one of Musashi's enemies brought a force of several men to his bathhouse while he was bathing. They heavily stoked the fire under his bathwater, lit the bathhouse on fire, then waited in ambush outside the tiny shed. They intended to leave him only three choices: to be boiled alive, burned to death, or run out naked and defenseless to be slaughtered by their superior forces. With the benefit of Bushi no Me, Musashi had anticipated the possibility of such an attack, and brought his swords with him to the bathhouse. As the treachery unfolded, Musashi broke out through a side of the shed weakened by the flames and killed the enemies who were lying in wait for him.

Even when relaxing in his bath, when a sense of fair play should have placed him off-limits to attack by any but the most craven coward, Musashi never permitted *yudan*. His mind and senses were always alert to danger, almost in the fashion of an animal subject to predation. By virtue of *hōgen* and without any conscious effort, his eyes were continually evaluating the cause and effect of all they surveyed, so that he could never be caught unaware.

An example of training to avoid *yudan* is the instruction given by the swordmaster Itō Ittōsai to one of his disciples. Rather than teach his young student the fine points of swordsmanship, as one might expect, Itō instead spent the first several years of the youth's training merely slapping him on the head at every opportunity. This was, of course, extremely annoying to the young trainee, but month after month—as his perception improved—he received fewer and fewer slaps. As the years passed, the great master had to become increasingly treacherous and inventive to catch his disciple off-guard, until at last he was no longer able to do so. After this, with only minimal instruction in the handling of a sword, the disciple quickly developed into a master swordsman, since no opponent was able to find an opening for attack.

If you have *hōgen* and remain constantly vigilant, you will never be caught off-guard. Nothing in life will catch you by surprise. This is not to say that your life will never be beset by adversity or trials, but that you will be prepared to meet these challenges when they arise. Thus, true Bushi no Me—the combination of *hōgen* with the complete avoidance of *yudan*—is essential to achieving *heijōshin*.

You should be aware that the most vulnerable time for *yudan* to overtake you is during your happiest times. In ancient days, it was well known that one of the best times to attack was when the enemy was celebrating a victory. When you are happy, you tend to relax and grow serenely oblivious to the events transpiring around you. It is also a state in which it seems pressing problems can be temporarily ignored. Typically, when you are unusually happy, your customary inhibitions are lessened, and it is easier for various pitfalls and temptations to slip unnoticed into your life.

On his deathbed, Takeda Shingen counseled his son Katsuyori to wait three years before leading an attack against any of his enemies. This period of engaging only in defensive battles would allow time for Takeda's army to adjust to Katsuyori's leadership, and for Katsuyori to mature and gain experience and credibility as their commander. Ignoring his father's advice, immediately after the mourning period for his father's death had ended, Katsuyori led his forces into a decisive battle against Oda Nobunaga at Nagashino, relying on the legacy of his father's reputation and countless past victories to motivate the troops and intimidate the opponents. Instead, because of the *yudan* of his overconfidence, Takeda's army was decimated. Soon thereafter, they were attacked again and utterly destroyed, forcing Katsuyori to commit seppuku. In a single act of *yudan*, Takeda Katsuyori lost everything his father had spent a lifetime building.

As we have seen throughout this chapter, the mind is the focal point of all *budō* training. The mind working in concert with the eyes is *shingen* or *hōgen*. The mind controlling words and actions is Shin • Ku • I. The mind working in inseparable harmony with the body is Ken Shin Ichi Nyo. The mind never dropping its guard is *yudan nashi*. The constant factor throughout these concepts—the hub around which they all revolve and the source of their fulfillment—is the *mind*.

The mind is the key to all of life, so the conclusion to be drawn is: Make up your mind! All other training will be pointless unless you do. You will never achieve *shingen*, you will never progress through Shin • Ku • I, you will never develop *heijōshin* without first having made up your mind. Once you have set your mind to something, and you believe in yourself strongly enough, nothing can prevent you from accomplishing that goal.

But this is not simply saying to yourself that you will do it. Nor is it merely writing some goals on paper. It means making an unshakable, steadfast determination that nothing short of death itself will stop you. This is the type of resolve that leads you to train even when you don't feel up to it—when you are bruised and blistered and aching and bone-weary, and you can't bear the thought of going back to the *dōjō*—but you go anyway because that is what you made up your mind to do.

The Japanese call this kind of strong spirit *shinnen*, meaning "unshakable faith or conviction." But *shinnen* is more than simply iron-willed determination or merely believing strongly in yourself. It implies a belief that you are part of something greater than just yourself; that you have a moral right and responsibility to do what you are doing. The moral imperative of *shinnen* was a powerful stimulus for self-discipline and noble deeds to the samurai, and it is an equally motivating force in our times for those whose character and conduct is righteous.

When you begin to apply this same determination outside the *dōjō*, you find that once you set goals for your life—goals that are worth living and dying for—no power on earth can deter you from achieving them.

# KIMARU

## Inevitability

Anyone who has watched a Noh or Kabuki play or a classic *chambara* (swordplay) movie has seen a visual depiction of the concept of *kimaru*. One of the best-known examples is the climactic duel in Kurosawa Akira's classic movie *Sanjurō*, between the protagonist, Tsubaki Sanjurō, played by Mifune Toshirō, and the antagonist, Muroto Hanbei, played by Nakadai Tatsuya. When these archenemies face off, Sanjurō reacts slightly faster and slays Muroto with a single cut. For several seconds the two remain motionless, as if frozen in time, Sanjurō with his sword uplifted at the peak of his cut and Muroto with his sword pointing earthward, having missed his cut. Finally, eyes wide with incredulity, Muroto topples to the ground, dying. That time-frozen pose of the two adversaries is used to visually express the concept of inevitability, called *kimaru* in Japanese.

The word *kimaru* is used to convey several similar ideas: "decisiveness," "certainty," "conclusiveness," and "predetermined" or "predestined." In classical Japanese cinema and drama it signifies that the outcome was inevitable, in the sense that it was the inescapable consequence of the collective decisions and actions of both men leading up to that confrontation. In the movie *Sanjurō* this display of *kimaru* symbolizes the inevitable triumph of good motives, good decisions, and good actions on the part of the victor over the selfish or evil motives, decisions, and actions of the defeated foe.

*Kimaru* is one of the best reasons to engage in *iaijutsu* training. Most events in our lives are the product of cause and effect, the consequences of innumerable decisions and actions previously made, and the motives underlying them. If we understand this, and train accordingly, we are creating better outcomes for ourselves and others in the future.

The duel between Sanjurō and Muroto serves as an example. Its outcome was predetermined by such factors as the time and effort each devoted to their training, their motives underlying the actions that led up to the final confrontation, and how determined each was to prevail. By applying that concept to our training, devoting the time and effort needed to ensure that we are better prepared and more capable than any opponent, unwavering in our determination, pure in our motives, and single-mindedly committed to victory, we have made the outcome inevitable.

By applying the same principles to our daily lives that we apply to our *iaijutsu* training, *kimaru* assures us that our work, family life, personal relationships, and all other endeavors will have inevitably favorable outcomes as well.

# Chapter 4

# *Katana no Meishō*

## Sword Nomenclature

刀の名称

Throughout this book, as well as in any traditional *dōjō* you might attend, the various parts of the sword are referred to by their Japanese names. The following two illustrations identify the most commonly used parts of the sword. Eventually, with continued practice and reference, you will learn the Japanese names for all parts of the sword that are frequently used in *iaijutsu*. A table follows the illustrations, giving the names of those parts of the sword that beginners should memorize as early as possible in their *iaijutsu* training.

The sword in its entirety is usually called a *katana*, which is a somewhat generic term for "sword." Another way of pronouncing the *kanji* for *katana* (刀) is *tō*. A more specific term for the *katana* we generally practice with is a *daitō* (long sword), to distinguish it from the *wakizashi* (side-carry) or *shōtō* (small sword), the shorter companion-sword often worn by samurai. The unsharpened sword used for *iaijutsu* practice is called an *iaitō* (iai sword), and the wooden swords used in *kumitachi*—combative training exercises like those described in chapters 15 through 18—are called either *bokken* or *bokutō*, both of which mean "wooden sword."

You may also occasionally hear reference to *chūtō* (middle sword), which in modern times denotes a mid-length sword typically used by children for *iaijutsu* or *kenjutsu* training, or *tantō* (short sword), which is a dagger often worn instead of a *wakizashi*. Another generic term for sword is *ken*. This term is most commonly found in such terms as *kendō* (the sport of swordsmanship), *kenjutsu* (the art of sword battle), *bokken* (wooden sword), or in such phrases as *Ken shin ichi nyō*, discussed in Chapter 3.

The parts of a *katana* fall into two major categories: the *koshirae* (mountings), and the *tōshin* (body of the sword, meaning the blade only), consisting of the individual components identified in the illustrations and chart that follow.

# KOSHIRAE
## Mountings

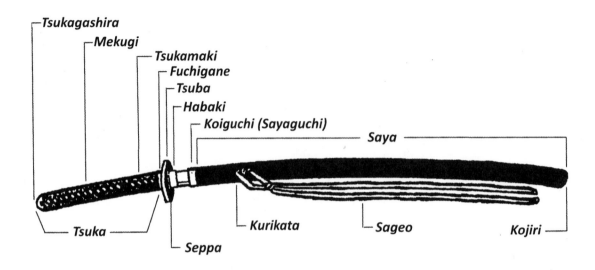

The major parts of the *koshirae* (sword mountings) for beginning students to remember are:

| Japanese Term | English Equivalent |
|---|---|
| *tsuka* | handle |
| *tsukagashira* | end (cap) of the handle |
| *mekugi* | retaining peg |
| *tsukamaki* | handle wrappings |
| *fuchigane* | metal flange on handle side of *tsuba* |
| *tsuba* | guard |
| *seppa* | spacer/washer between *tsuba* and *habaki* |
| *habaki* | brass collar on blade |
| *saya* | scabbard |
| *koiguchi* or *sayaguchi* | mouth of the scabbard |
| *kurikata* | mounting for the *sageo* |
| *sageo* | strings attached to *saya* |
| *kojiri* | end (butt) of the *saya* |

# TŌSHIN
## Bare Blade

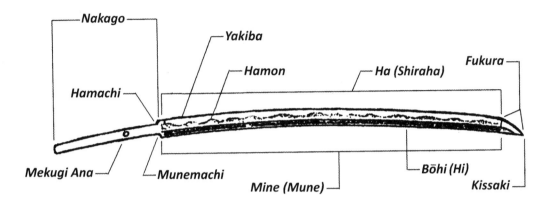

The most important parts of the *tōshin* (bare sword blade) for beginning students to remember are:

| Japanese Term | English Equivalent |
| --- | --- |
| *nakago* | tang |
| *ha* or *shiraha* | blade (as a whole) |
| *hasaki* | sharpened edge of the blade |
| *mine* or *mune* | ridge (*mine*) or spine (*mune*) of the blade |
| *kissaki* | point of the blade |
| *hi* or *bōhi* | groove or fuller |
| *fukura* | curved tip of the blade |
| *habaki* | brass collar on blade |
| *yakiba* | tempered portion of the blade nearest the edge |
| *hamon* | temper line (line between *yakiba* and untempered portion) |
| *hamachi* | notch separating blade and tang—edge side |
| *munemachi* | notch separating blade and tang—*mine* side |
| *mekugi ana* | hole in tang for *mekugi* (peg) |

Less frequently used in typical training sessions are the names of the different surfaces of the side of the blade. The two areas most often mentioned during training are the *hi* or *bōhi*, which is the fuller or groove used to lighten and strengthen the sword, and the *shinogi*, which is the bevel that delineates the upper and lower portions of the blade. The area above the *shinogi* is called the *shinogi-ji*, and the section beneath the *shinogi* is called the *hiraji*, as shown in the illustration below depicting a cross-section of a *katana*.

## SWORD CROSS SECTION

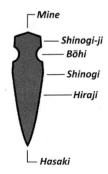

Mine
Shinogi-ji
Bōhi
Shinogi
Hiraji
Hasaki

The foregoing are the parts of the sword and its furnishings that are most frequently discussed throughout the instructional portions of this book, as well as the most often referred to during *dōjō* instruction. Some additional nomenclature students can expect to encounter during training or when researching Japanese swords and sword-making include:

| Japanese Term | English Equivalent |
| --- | --- |
| *nagasa* | length (of blade or handle) |
| *sori* | curvature (of blade), a key design factor |
| *yokote* | boundary line between the *hōshi* and the rest of the blade |
| *hōshi* | temper line from *yokote* to *kissaki* |
| *same* or *samehada* | ray skin beneath the *tsukamaki* |
| *menuki* | metal ornaments beneath the *tsukamaki* |
| *makidome* | fitting to which the *tsukamaki* are attached |
| *shitodo-me* | metal bushings sometimes used inside the *kurikata* |

# MONOUCHI
## Cutting Area

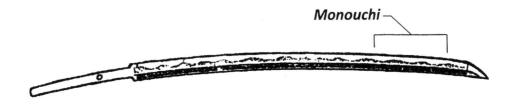

**Monouchi**

Of all the parts of a *katana*, the single most important one for *iadōka* to know is the *monouchi*. The *monouchi* (striking part) is the portion of the blade that is actually used to cut. Knowing which section of the blade is the *monouchi* and training yourself to consistently align the *monouchi* with your intended target is the key to proficiency in *iaijutsu*. Unlike most of the other areas of the *katana*, there is no precise way to identify the *monouchi*—no lines, notches, or curves to mark its boundaries. As indicated in the illustration below, the *monouchi* is approximately a ten-inch section of the blade that begins about four inches to the rear of the *kissaki*. This portion of the blade is where the optimal combination of blade strength, speed at impact, and reach occur.

Chapter 5

# *Shugyō no Junjō*
## Progression of Training

修行の順序

As you train in *iaijutsu*, you will pass through several stages of development in your progression from beginner to expert to master of the art. You may also reach physical and emotional plateaus, at which your progress may appear to slow or stop—or even decline. Understanding that such plateaus are a normal part of the training process will help you avoid allowing a setback or plateau to discourage you.

## KETSUI O SURU
### Make Up Your Mind

The first step in your journey is to make up your mind. You must decide to make your training a high priority in your life, not merely something you do for entertainment or a diversion whenever you lack something more interesting to do.

*Budō* training, especially in a serious art like *iaijutsu*, is a lifestyle, not just a pastime, hobby, or extracurricular activity. As you progress, the discipline and dedication of your training will set you apart. You will begin to approach all of life with the outlook of a *budōka*. Over time, your entire attitude and personality will evolve. But this kind of fundamental improvement of your character cannot occur without a strong determination to train, even when you don't feel like it—especially when you don't feel like it.

In chapter 3 we explained extensively the importance of making up your mind and of having *shinnen*—an unwavering determination—as the foundation for all your endeavors. Applying this knowledge now is the first step in your *iaijutsu* training.

## KIHON O MANABU
### Emphasize the Basics

There is always a great temptation, particularly for beginners, to learn the flashy, complex, or difficult techniques of any art. It is natural for you to feel this way, especially if you have a desire to excel at *iaijutsu* and truly master it. However, your primary emphasis must be on the fundamentals, which are described in chapter 7.

It is true with any form of *budō* that a practitioner who has truly mastered the basics will handily defeat one who has trained in advanced techniques after having only a cursory knowledge of the fundamentals. If you understand the nature of basic techniques, it is easy to see why this is universally true.

Basics are no more or less than the ideal technique, as it would be performed under ideal circumstances. Fundamentals demonstrate the perfect method of maximizing power, balance, self-protection, and effectiveness of technique. It is only after you have mastered performing under such ideal conditions that you can learn how to best adapt basic techniques to less-than-ideal circumstances.

It is also a mistake to assume that basics are only for beginners. Emphasis on fundamentals must be a lifelong habit. Anyone who has studied the lives of the renowned *budō* masters has observed that, without exception, they have shared a continuing passion for improving their basics.

In the final analysis, there really are no "advanced" techniques; only fundamentals that have been applied to less-than-ideal circumstances. Everything is fundamentals, and the fundamentals are everything.

## RIRON O SHIRU
### Understand the Principles

As you study the fundamentals, it is not sufficient merely to master the body mechanics necessary to perform them with precision and power. To progress beyond the basics, you must understand the underlying principles that make them effective—as well as the exigencies that can make them fail.

With such an understanding, you will then be able to apply the basics to intermediate and advanced techniques and make these techniques as effective and natural as your basics. Furthermore, with a deep understanding of the principles that make techniques effective, you can readily apply those same principles to the decisions, challenges, and conflicts you face in everyday life.

# KAISŪ O KASANERU
## Develop through Repetition

The objective of *iaijutsu* is to make the techniques natural—to make the sword simply another appendage of your body. Nothing becomes this natural without practice, which is another reason for *kihon o manabu*: emphasizing the basics. You must be certain you are developing good habits in your training; that you are reinforcing correct technique, not errors or sloppiness, through your countless repetition.

It can truly be said that the only difference between a novice and an expert is the number of repetitions of technique. A master is simply a novice who has practiced the techniques literally thousands, or in some cases, millions of times. His depth of character and his knowledge of the art came in the same fashion—endless repetition.

There is a well-known saying among Japanese *budōka* from many disciplines: *Manabu no tame ni hyakkai, jukuren no tame ni senkai, satori no tame ni manga okonau.* This adage translates as "One hundred repetitions to learn, a thousand repetitions for proficiency, ten thousand repetitions for enlightenment." To truly master the fundamentals requires countless repetitions—and not just mindless repetitions, but repetitions performed with conscious effort to improve your technique with each one. Consider this: if you attend class three times a week and repeat a technique ten times in each class, then it will take only a little over three weeks to learn the technique. However, to become proficient—meaning to be able to perform the technique correctly almost every time—will take seven and a half months of training. And to be able to execute the technique flawlessly and with complete understanding of all its intricacies, principles, and applications will take over six years. Just for one technique!

Repeated practice not only develops the physical skills of the art, but also develops the mental attributes needed for mastery. You simply will not be able to train frequently and regularly for a prolonged period without developing both the physical skills and the mental attitudes—patience, persistence, fighting spirit, Bushi no Me, compassion, and *heijōshin*—of a *budō* master.

# TAIRYOKU NI ŌJITE OKONAU
## Different Strengths—Different People

Different people have different strengths and weaknesses. Some people learn faster or slower than others, have more or less innate athletic ability, and are in different stages of physical condition. All these things must be taken into account, because they can significantly affect the pace at which one is able to learn new skills.

The only fair and true measure of progress is *your* progress. It is not fair to compare yourself to others, either to yourself or them. Your body structure, learning ability, athletic prowess, age, maturity, and motivation are all vastly different from anyone else's, and your comparative rate of progress in learning *iaijutsu* will likewise be different.

You must also keep in mind how deceptively simple *iaijutsu* appears. Even people with years of training in other forms of *budō* find *iaijutsu* movements and principles difficult to master, because the body mechanics are so different. Paradoxically, while *iaijutsu* stresses the natural posture and movement of the body, it feels extremely *unnatural* for the first several months of training. It is important to begin your training with realistic expectations, so plan on training at least a year before feeling comfortable with most techniques.

In keeping with such realistic expectations, you should start your training slowly, concentrating on correct movement and easy, natural swinging of the sword, and gradually build up your speed and power. This not only prevents injuries from overtraining and overexertion, but also allows your body to assimilate the correct sequence of muscle contractions and extensions before attempting to do them with power.

# JISHIN NI TSUITE
## Confidence

Just as there will be times during your training that you reach plateaus or encounter disappointments, there will also be times in which your performance really excels or you achieve significant triumphs. And, just as there is danger in allowing disappointment to cloud your perception of your progress, there is equal danger in becoming overconfident when your situation seems favorable.

Confidence is an important strength to possess. A samurai had to be confident, not only to face life-or-death battles, but also to achieve *saya no naka ni kachi* (victory while still in the scabbard) in all areas of life. But confidence must also be realistic, balanced, and tempered with humility.

One of ancient Japan's most famous leaders was Takeda Shingen, who was not only a great general but a great philosopher. He firmly believed that the best fight was no fight, and very seldom provoked a conflict. However, between the years 1553 and 1564, one of his most tenacious adversaries, Uesugi Kenshin, engaged his army in no less than five major battles. Takeda's forces were always victorious and could easily have crushed Uesugi's army on several occasions. But Takeda carefully engineered his victories so they appeared to come by only a narrow margin, because he understood the danger of overconfidence.

In Takeda's view, the best victory was by a 60-40 margin—wide enough to allow for unexpected events, yet narrow enough to keep his troops aware of the possibility of defeat and therefore intensely focused. He felt that the closer to an absolute 100-0 victory he achieved, the more likely his warriors would become overconfident, leading to recklessness, lack of discipline, and *yudan*. For his first forty years, Takeda's goal in battle was to win, but as he matured as a commander, his perspective shifted to *not losing*, as we explained in detail in "Budō no Arikata" in chapter 2.

The same reasoning applies to overconfidence at the personal level. If we allow ourselves to become overconfident because of a few triumphs, we are likely to lose our strength of concentration and self-discipline and we will begin to decline rather than progress in our training.

# JIGA NI TSUITE
## Control Your Ego

It was consistent with Takeda Shingen's philosophy that he selected a wide variety of trees to grow in his garden. He had cherry trees so he could admire their blossoms in the spring, weeping willows to provide spreading shade in the heat of summer, maples to set his garden ablaze with color in the fall, and pines to add bright spots of greenery to the stark winter landscape.

He selected his twenty-four subordinate generals (*taishō*) in a similar manner. These men not only reported to him and controlled his troops in battle, but acted as his trusted advisers. Having risen to such positions of power and prestige, many men would surround themselves with sniveling yes-men, but Takeda instead chose men of varied backgrounds, perspectives, and ideas in order to get the very best and most creative advice possible. In addition to their having the courage to speak their minds frankly even if they felt he would not like to hear it, Takeda had five key criteria for selecting each of his generals: (1) they had to be good *budōka*, (2) they had to possess deep compassion and understanding for people, (3) they had to exhibit extreme *reigi* (politeness and self-discipline), (4) they had to evidence *heijōshin* in their behavior, and (5) they had to have a resolute sense of loyalty.

In order to receive the best possible advice from this diverse group of leaders, Takeda had to be willing to accept blunt criticism of his own plans and ideas, even of his goals and motives. Furthermore, he was willing to listen to their suggestions because of their wisdom and sincerity, not necessarily because they were his friends or agreed with him. Few of us are truly willing to subject ourselves to this sort of scrutiny, especially when our egos have been enlarged by holding a position of any consequence or power. But to achieve our highest potential, we must set our egotism aside and willingly listen to the voice of sincere, constructive criticism, whether it be from our *iaijutsu sensei* in the *dōjō* or our close family members and friends.

In fact, one of the best ways to make significant improvement in areas of personal character is to surround yourself with loving, compassionate friends or family members who are willing to examine your actions and hold you unflaggingly accountable for your personal growth. While this is often a painful ordeal, for most of us it is the only way we can build the resolve needed to tackle the really deep-rooted integrity issues in our lives.

Like Takeda Shingen, you must be extremely careful in your selection of the people who will hold you accountable. They do not all have to be *budōka*, but they should all possess the compassion, discipline, *heijōshin*, and loyalty exemplified by Takeda's generals. And they must all love you enough to be willing to face you honestly and boldly, but with tenderness, and deal with your worst faults and failings, even though to do so will usually be as painful for them as it is for you.

# SHIN ▪ KI ▪ RYOKU
## Mind ▪ Spirit ▪ Technique

When we presented the concept of Shin ▪ Ku ▪ I in chapter 3, we explained how the mind is the key to self-control. The first topic in this chapter as well was making up your mind. There can be no question that the mind is the pivotal aspect of all martial arts training—all human endeavor, in fact. Once again, the concept of Shin ▪ Ki ▪ Ryoku points to mental focus as the core of *iaijutsu* technique.

Shin ▪ Ki ▪ Ryoku is used to signify that mind, spirit, and technique should be inseparable. But it is even more refined than the notion of the three simply working together in harmony; it is the recognition that technique is the product of the mind (conscious thoughts, strategy, mental focus) and spirit (emotions, attitudes, character, and subconscious) working together. For an analogy, think of your left hand as your mind and your right hand as your spirit. When the two hands slap together, the resulting clap is technique.

Thus, a goal of your training should be to so completely unite your mind and spirit that your body's movements are the instinctive and natural response to their combined workings.

# DAI ▪ KYŌ ▪ SOKU ▪ KEI
## Big ▪ Strong ▪ Fast ▪ Light

Dai ▪ Kyō ▪ Soku ▪ Kei (Big ▪ Strong ▪ Fast ▪ Light) best describes the proper sequence of training emphasis in *iaijutsu*. The progression from one to the next—from "big" to "strong" to "fast" to "light"—must not be forced. Instead, it must be the natural evolution of your skills, passing successively through each stage as you practice and improve.

**Big:** As a beginner, you should concentrate on the big features. This actually takes two forms. First, you should initially focus primarily on correctly performing the major (big) movements, rather than the finer details of technique. Later, as you become more proficient, you can emphasize the intricacies of the movements. This is much like the way a sculptor carves a statue: first shaping the general outline, then gradually refining it, and only later delicately adding the minute details. The second aspect is performing the movements in a "big" manner; that is, almost exaggerating the motions. This allows you to fully understand the mechanics of the techniques you are practicing. As your skill develops, you will later strive to make the movements more compact.

**Strong:** It is difficult to swing powerfully until you first learn to swing correctly. So you should wait until you have developed consistency in performing the larger movements before you attempt to develop power in the techniques. Once you are swinging the sword correctly, it is only a matter of repetition until you develop powerful technique.

**Fast:** The next stage is to increase the speed of your techniques. Once again, wait until you can perform the techniques properly and with power before trying to develop speed. Otherwise, you are likely to develop fast, sloppy, ineffective techniques instead.

**Light:** In this final stage, your techniques become light, meaning subtle, precise, and effortless. As you reach a point of exercising Shin ▪ Ki ▪ Ryoku in which your mind and spirit together produce technique, your movements will become light and subtle. At this phase, you will have more speed and power than ever before—not as a result of physical strength or additional effort, but due to the refinement of your technique—so that you will appear to be moving effortlessly. Again, do not attempt to perform light techniques immediately; they will only be weak. Instead, the lightness must be the product of countless repetitions and diligent training, resulting in speed and power that appear effortless.

Each stage must be taken in order. If you attempt to skip a stage—from "Big" to "Strong," for instance—you will only end up compounding your errors. The technical skills that produce power are learned during the "Big" phase, so if you try to develop power by some other means, you wind up using muscle strength rather than proper technique, and this only magnifies your errors. It helps to understand that if your body mechanics are correct, big is powerful. As we describe in more detail in chapter 7, a large, circular *kirioroshi* (downward cut) develops far greater *enshin ryoku* (centripetal force) than a compact motion. For the same reason, a large *kirioroshi* also produces more speed, and when performed applying Shin ▪ Ki ▪ Ryoku it even requires far less effort.

"Big" and "Strong" are the only levels at which you can practice to improve. You can mentally concentrate on the "Big" movements, correcting the errors you notice, and you can consciously apply correct technique to increase the power of your movements. But "Fast" and "Light"—although they are achieved through repetition—cannot be consciously practiced, or they will simply produce sloppy, weak technique. Instead, they are a by-product of repetitive practice: the natural evolution of your training in the "Big" and "Strong."

# SHU ▪ HA ▪ RI

## Obey ▪ Break ▪ Separate

Shu ▪ Ha ▪ Ri is a term the Japanese use to describe the overall progression of *budō* training, as well as the lifelong relationship the student will enjoy with his or her instructor.

### Shu

*Shu* can either mean "to protect" or "to obey." The dual meaning of the term is aptly descriptive of the relationship between a *budō* student and teacher in the student's early stages, which can be likened to the relationship of a parent and child. At this level, the student should absorb all the teacher imparts, and be eager to learn and willing to accept all correction and constructive criticism. The teacher must guard the student in the sense of watching out for his or her interests and nurturing and encouraging his or her progress, much as a parent guards a child through their growing years. *Shu* stresses basics in an uncompromising fashion so the student has a solid foundation for future learning, and all students perform techniques in identical fashion, even though their personalities, body structure, age, and abilities all differ.

## Ha

*Ha* is another term with an appropriate double meaning: "to break free" or "to frustrate." Sometime after the student reaches *dan* (black belt) level, he or she will begin to break free in two ways. In terms of technique, the student will break free of the fundamentals and begin to apply the principles acquired from the practice of basics in new, freer, and more imaginative ways. The student's individuality will begin to emerge in the way he or she performs techniques. At a deeper level, he or she will also break free of the rigid instruction of the teacher and begin to question and discover more through personal experience. This can be a time of frustration for the teacher, as the student's journey of discovery leads to countless questions beginning with "Why …" At the *Ha* stage, the relationship between student and teacher is similar to that of a parent and an adult child; the teacher is a master of the art, and the student may now be an instructor to others.

## Ri

*Ri* is the stage at which the student, now a *kōdansha* (high-ranking black belt), separates from the instructor, having absorbed all that he or she can learn from them. This is not to say that the student and teacher are no longer associated. Actually, quite the opposite should be true; they should now have a stronger bond than ever before, much as a grandparent does with their son or daughter who is now also a parent. Although the student is now fully independent, he treasures the wisdom and patient counsel of the teacher, and there is a richness to their relationship that comes through their shared experiences. But the student is now learning and progressing more through self-discovery than by instruction and can give outlet to his or her own creative impulses. The student's techniques will bear the imprint of his or her own personality, character, and decades of training. *Ri* too has a dual meaning, the second part of which is "to set free." As much as the student now seeks independence from the teacher, the instructor likewise must set the student free.

Shu ▪ Ha ▪ Ri is not a linear progression. It is more akin to concentric circles, so that there is *Shu* within *Ha* and both *Shu* and *Ha* within *Ri*. Thus, the fundamentals remain constant; only the application of them and the subtleties of their execution change as the student progresses and his or her own personality begins to flavor the techniques performed. Similarly, the student and teacher are always bound together by their close relationship and the knowledge, experience, culture, and tradition shared between them.

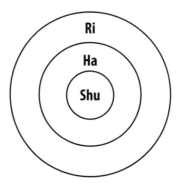

Ultimately, Shu ▪ Ha ▪ Ri should result in the student surpassing the master, both in knowledge and skill. This is the source of improvement for the art as a whole. If the student never surpasses his master, then the art will stagnate at best. If the student never achieves the master's ability, the art will deteriorate. But, if the student can assimilate all that the master can impart and then progress to even higher levels of advancement, the art will continually improve and flourish.

## SHINGI O OMONZURU
### Stand for Righteousness

True *budō* and true *budōka* are rooted in a tradition of righteousness. *Budō* are a means of preserving peace and overcoming ill intention. This foundation allows the *budōka* to develop *shinnen*, an unflagging strength of conviction that is a powerful motivation to prevail over adversity.

In battle, however, the *budōka* will often find himself pitted against *jadō* (literally, "the Way of Evil") embodied in those who hold to the belief that "all is fair in love and war." You may even encounter instructors whose teaching philosophy would condone underhanded tactics or inhumane acts for the sake of winning at any cost. While it is true that there are no rules on the battlefield, there is good and evil. To use the glare of the sun, kick sand in the face of the opponent, or use the terrain or obstacles to one's advantage are battle tactics, but they are not inherently evil. However, to harm or kill innocent people in order to distract or coerce an opponent would indeed be *jadō*.

The true *budōka* also realizes that *jadō* is more than just unscrupulous fighting techniques. It inevitably degenerates into a perverse approach to life. In effect, this approach applies Shin ▪ Ku ▪ I in the negative: misdeeds influence one's speech and ideals, leading to increasingly hostile behavior and an amoral, utterly self-centered attitude.

In addition to its degenerative effects, *jadō* is also inherently weak. There are few people so depraved that their conscience does not inhibit them—at least slightly—when they utilize some underhanded method to gain advantage. This restraining influence, however small, prevents them from employing *shinnen*, so they cannot put their whole body, mind, and soul into their actions. On the other hand, the *budōka* who is acting justly can wholeheartedly pursue any endeavor. *Shingi* (righteousness) is therefore an empowering influence, creating a moral imperative that lends not only mental and spiritual strength, but—through Ken Shin Ichi Nyo—physical power as well.

## SAIGO MADE EIZOKU SURU
### Persist to the End

This chapter began with an exhortation to make a strong commitment to training—a challenge to make up your mind to train as a lifestyle. It ends with a similar admonition to persist until the end. Commitment and persistence are the beginning and end of all worthwhile human endeavors. To state it simply and directly: do not quit!

To understand the importance of persistence, we need only to look at the common struggle to control bulging waistlines. The reason diets fail and people almost always gain back the weight they lost (usually with a little extra thrown in for good measure), is that a diet—by definition—is only a short-term commitment. Diets are designed to accomplish only one goal—a specific amount of weight loss, a change in waistline, a change in appearance, and so on—and once that goal is achieved (or abandoned), the diet ends—by design.

The only weight-loss programs that ever succeed in the long run are nutritional lifestyle changes. This may sound like merely a semantic distinction, but it is not. A diet is temporary, but a nutritional lifestyle is permanent. Lifestyle changes are not dependent upon reaching a predetermined goal; they are lifelong commitments to a different behavior pattern.

The same holds true for *iaijutsu* training. To succeed, you must make a lifelong commitment to continual growth and improvement. *Budō* training is not just for a certain time or until you achieve a certain goal; it is a lifestyle. Always remember that *iaijutsu* is a method for perfection of character, not a hobby or a fitness program.

If an accident or illness, or a drastic change in your life makes an interruption of your training necessary or unavoidable, simply resolve that you will resume as soon as you are able. And then do it! Even if you stop training for five years due to some circumstance, you will not have quit if you eventually resume.

Also remember that there is more to *iaijutsu* than just swinging a sword. If an injury leaves you temporarily or even permanently unable to practice your techniques, you can still continue your training by applying *iaijutsu* principles to other areas of your life. You will probably find that you recover faster if you apply *iaijutsu* principles to your recovery process, whether it is recovering from a physical, emotional, or even a financial setback.

*Iaijutsu* is training for life-or-death confrontation, so to quit means *death*. Once you have decided to be an *iaijutsu* practitioner, you cannot quit.

# Chapter 6

# Sahō to Reihō

## Preparation and Etiquette

作法と礼法

Sahō (preparation) and reihō (etiquette) are almost inseparable in any form of budō, including the art of iaijutsu, since it is nearly impossible to define where preparation ends and etiquette begins.

It is likely that much of the formal etiquette of iaijutsu evolved from the incorporation of the Ōmori-Ryū Seiza waza into the art by Hayashi Rokudayū in the seventeenth century. The descriptions in this chapter are given in the order in which they would normally be conducted while preparing to engage in iaijutsu training or a performance of waza.

The formalities of iaijutsu begin even before you enter the dōjō. Actions like the process of changing into your hakama should not only involve a transformation of your outer appearance but a concurrent transformation of your state of mind and are thus considered sahō. By the time you finish tying the bow on the front of your hakama, you should have set aside all the concerns of everyday life in order to concentrate exclusively and intently on your iaijutsu practice. When you pick up your sword, now clothed as a samurai, your training has already begun, and you perform the first formality of swordsmanship.

## 6A: TEITŌ

### Carrying the Sword

It will seem to the beginner that even the smallest detail of iaijutsu is rigidly controlled, starting with something as simple as carrying the sword. But when you consider that an *iaijutsu* battle is won in the blink of an eye, you will realize that such details often meant the difference between life and death to the samurai.

When standing or walking prior to, or following, *iaijutsu* practice, the sword is normally held in the left hand at the left hip as shown in figures 6A.1 (front view) and 6A.2 (side view). This position is called *teitō*, which means "controlled sword," and the purpose of holding the *katana* in this manner is to control its movement and avoid accidental contact with others.

Note that in figure 6A.1 that the sword is turned slightly outward from vertical (15 to 30 degrees), so the left hand is held in a natural position.

As shown in figure 6A.2, the *tsuka* is slightly higher than the *kojiri* to prevent the sword from falling from the scabbard.

Figure 6A.1. *Teitō* (front view)     Figure 6A.2. Teitō (side view)

To ensure that the sword remains in the scabbard, especially while moving, it is extremely important that the left thumb remain hooked over the *tsuba* while holding and carrying the sword. This also facilitates *koiguchi no kirikata*—separating the sword from its *saya*, as explained in chapter 7—to initiate drawing the sword, should it become necessary. It is also important to place the thumb slightly to the right of top-dead-center, at about the one-o'clock position if the *tsuba* was an analog clock, as shown in figures 6A.3 and 6A.4. This prevents the thumb from being cut by the *fukura* as the sword is drawn.

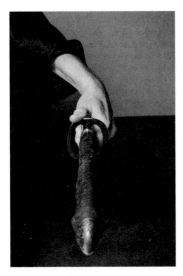

Figure 6A.3. Position of thumb on *tsuba* (front view)

Figure 6A.4. Position of thumb on *tsuba* (rear view)

During *koiguchi no kirikata* (see chapter 7 for description) the left thumb pushes the *tsuba* forward to release the sword from its scabbard and begin the process of cutting while drawing the sword (also described in chapter 7). If the thumb is placed to the side as shown in figure 6A.5, there is ample room for the *kissaki* to emerge without touching the thumb, but if the thumb is directly above the blade (fig. 6A.6) the *fukura* will split the tip of the thumb in half as it emerges from the *saya*.

Figure 6A.5. Correct position of thumb during *koiguchi no kirikata*

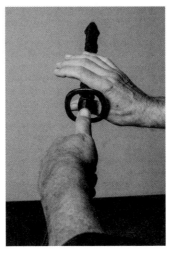

Figure 6A.6. Incorrect position of thumb during *koiguchi no kirikata*

Posture (also discussed in detail in chapter 7) should be erect but not stiff, with the shoulders relaxed. The head must be straight, but the chin not pulled in.

The left hand, gripping the *saya* just beneath the *tsuba*, should be resting against the body at the left hip with the elbow tucked in close to the body. The right hand is curled into a comfortably loose fist, and should rest along the right thigh.

The cords (*sageo*) are gripped between the index and middle fingers of the left hand (gripping the *sageo* in the right hand is done differently—see section 6B, "Hairei," below)—to keep them from dangling loosely where they might catch on objects while moving. By gripping them between the index and middle fingers, they can be held securely while holding the *saya*, allowing the thumb to be latched over the *tsuba*. In this way, you have secure control of the *katana* as implied by the word *teitō* (fixed [controlled] sword).

This is the position in which the sword should be held when entering the *dōjō* to begin *iaijutsu* practice, at any time the *katana* is not secured in the belt (see section 6E, "Taitō," below), and when leaving the *dōjō* after training.

# 6B: HAIREI
## Bowing to the Dōjō/Founder

Immediately upon entering the *dōjō*, an *iaijutsu* student must show respect for the training area and the founder or headmaster of the style (as represented by the founder's or headmaster's portrait on the wall) by bowing. This initial bow, called *hairei* (bow of veneration), shou ld be made in the direction of the founder or headmaster's portrait. If there is no portrait in the *dōjō*, then bow facing an appropriate symbol of the *dōjō* such as its emblem, flag, *dōjō* shrine, or similar focal point. It is also customary for the class to perform *hairei* together, at the command of the *sensei* or *sempai*, at the beginning and end of each training session or group performance.

The *hairei* bow begins from a standing position, with the sword held at the left hip (*teitō*) as shown in figures 6B.1 and 6B.9.

The sword is transferred from the left hand to the right hand, turning it so the *tsuka* is to the rear of the body, as shown in figures 6B.3 and 6B.11. During this transfer, care must be taken to handle the *sageo* properly, pinning the cords (still looped) against the *saya* with the palm of the right hand, so they can be readily retrieved by the left hand when the sword is switched back to the left hand after the *hairei* bow is completed.

Figures 6B.1–8. *Hairei* (front view)

Notice the direction of the curvature of the *saya* in the photographs of *hairei* in side view. In the proper position for *hairei*, the sharp edge of the sword (*hasaki*) is held rearward, opposite from the correct position for drawing the sword. In addition, the *tsuka* is behind the right elbow, also making it difficult to draw. Since an attack cannot readily be initiated from this position, it is a proper position for demonstrating the deepest sincerity, trust, and respect.

There is no prescribed duration for the *hairei* bow, but the forward tilt of the upper body should be crisp and quick, the bow held for an appropriate duration (meaning somewhat longer than a normal bow), then returning slowly to an erect posture. The important factor is that the length and character of the bow reflect the sincerity of your respect. Even a long bow will be disrespectful if your posture and demeanor betray it as insincere.

Figures 6B.9–16. *Hairei* (side view)

# 6C: SHIREI

## Bowing to the Instructor

At the beginning of class, the students will all assemble facing the instructor, usually seated in the *seiza* position as described under "Kamae" in chapter 7. If the class is assembled standing, then *shirei* would be performed in the manner described later for *tachirei*.

As students initially attain *seiza*, they will still be holding their swords (*teitō*) at their left hips, as shown in figure 6C.1. Prior to bowing, students will first transfer their swords to a position at their right sides, as depicted in figures 6C.2–6. Begin by using your left hand to push the sword diagonally from left to right across your body until the *tsuba* is past the center of the body (fig. 6C.2). Transfer the *sageo* to your right hand, taking them between the middle and ring-fingers so that the index finger is free to clasp over the edge of the *tsuba* (fig. 6C.3). Slide the left hand along the *saya* to the left hip and use the right hand to pull the sword diagonally forward (fig. 6C.4) until it slides free of the left hand. Then place it along your right side with the *tsuba* even with your right knee (fig. 6C.5) and the sword's *mine* (dull side) to the outside, then straighten to correct *seiza* posture (fig. 6C.6).

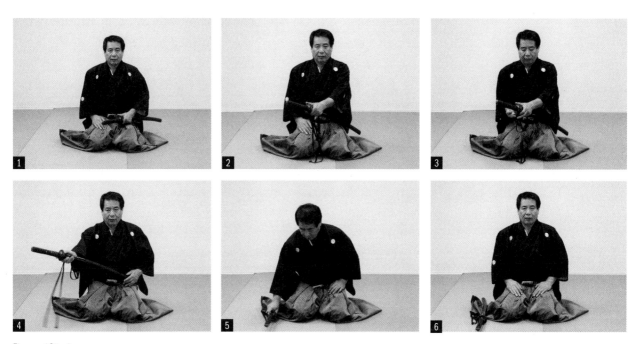

Figures 6C.1–6.

Once again, posture in *seiza* is erect, with the shoulders and arms relaxed. The head is straight, but the chin is not tucked in. The hands rest naturally on the tops of the thighs with the thumbs beneath the forefingers and aligned with the crease between the thigh and groin.

As seen in figure 6C.6, the sharp edge of the sword, revealed by the curvature of the *saya*, is facing toward the student. This would make the sword difficult to draw quickly and shows the student's respect and trust for the instructor. The *sageo* are neatly aligned along the outer curve of the *saya* and folded in half, so the ends rest close to the *kurikata* to which they are tied.

The *sensei* or *sempai* will give the command "*Rei*," and the students bow together toward the instructor *(shirei)*.

Ordinarily, when bowing in the *seiza* position, the left hand is placed on the floor first, followed by the right hand. However, when bowing to the instructor (*shirei*), students demonstrate their implicit trust and respect by moving both hands simultaneously, as shown in figures 6C.7–11. The tips of the index fingers come together, and the natural angle of the arms forms an "arrowhead" shape in the space between them (see fig. 6C.8). The bow is again made from the waist, keeping the back and head straight. Do not allow the hips to rise when bowing in the *seiza* position.

The forehead does not touch the floor, but remains four to six inches above the floor, with the nose centered above the "arrowhead" formed by the hands. At the deepest part of the bow, the spine should be parallel to the floor (see fig. 6C.9).

The longer the bow is held in this position, the more respect is shown to the instructor. It is always good manners for students to hold the bow until the instructor has bowed in return and begun to rise, then the students follow.

To rise, simply reverse the procedure for bowing. Straighten from the waist, being sure to keep the back and head straight, while pushing upward with the arms. Once the arms have nearly straightened, the hands will almost naturally rise from the floor and return to their original positions (shown in fig. 6C.11) simply by continuing to return to an erect posture.

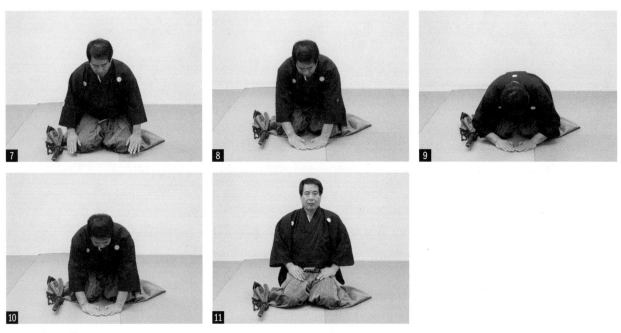

Figures 6C.7–11. *Shirei*

# 6D: TŌREI

## Bowing to the Sword

After bowing to the instructor, *iaijutsu* students show respect for their swords by bowing to them as well. The sword was the life of the samurai. Without it, he would surely perish in battle, and because of its grace, beauty, and strength, to many samurai the sword seemed to possess a spirit of its own. In addition, many swords were handed down from father to son for generations, so the sword was both a treasured heirloom and a symbol of the family's honor, status, traditions, and a heritage of loyal service to their lords, past and present. During the Tokugawa Era, only samurai were allowed to wear a *katana* in public. So, for all these reasons, it became an object of great respect, deserving of *tōrei*.

The samurai's respect for his sword goes beyond mere appreciation, however. In many respects, it resembles the respect the American cowboys of the late nineteenth century had for their horses. At the end of a hard workday, bone-weary and choking on trail dust, the cowboy would unsaddle, curry, feed, and water his horse even before preparing his own well-deserved meal and resting from his labors. That was an act of true respect.

There are many useful parallels between American cowboys and Japanese samurai. Without a stout horse, a cowboy might well find himself suffering a lonely, agonizing death by dehydration or starvation on the vast prairie, so he did well to accord his mount proper respect. He usually had a name for his horse, and treated it as a friend and partner. Similarly, a samurai depended upon his sword for his life and livelihood. Many named their swords and treated them as if they had a life of their own.

Perhaps one reason the cowboy and the samurai have come to hold such prominence in each of their respective cultures—and both continue to influence their cultures and philosophies to this day—is that both the samurai of feudal Japan and the Wild West cowboy developed such a similar appreciation for the fine line between life and death and how to cope with it. Those with an appreciation of western folklore, especially the famed "Code of the West," which had many similarities to the Code of *Bushidō*, may more readily understand the subtleties of samurai philosophy.

The samurai symbolizes his respect for his sword with the *tōrei* (Bow to the Sword). Since the *tōrei* is normally performed immediately after *shirei* at the beginning of a class or just prior to *shirei* at the end of class it will usually begin from the position shown in figure 6D.1.

To begin the *tōrei* from the position shown in figure 6D.1, catch up the *sageo* between the middle and ring fingers, using the index finger to hold the *tsuba*, and pick up the sword. Gently place the *kojiri* on the floor to the outside-front of the right knee, as shown in figure 6D.4, with the *saya* tilted back toward your face at about a 45-degree angle. From this point, carefully lay the sword down in front of you, perpendicular to the direction you are facing, as illustrated in figure 6D.5.

The *tsuba* should be aligned with the outside of the left knee, and the sharpened edge of the sword (*hasaki*) should be toward you, as evidenced by the curvature of the *saya*. Next, carefully arrange the *sageo* along the outer edge of the *saya*, so they extend to about three inches from the *kojiri*, allowing them to double back from that point and cross the *saya*, as shown in figure 6D.6. By draping the ends of the *sageo* over the *saya*, they can more easily be grasped when picking up the sword after the *tōrei* is completed. After arranging the *sageo*, straighten to *seiza* position with erect posture and hands resting on the thighs, looking straight ahead (fig. 6D.7).

The *tōrei* bow is then performed in a similar manner to the *shirei* bow. The first exception is that before moving the hands, look at the sword, then place the left hand on the floor in front of the sword (fig. 6D.8), followed by the right hand (fig. 6D.9), and bow from the waist, as shown in figure 6D.10.

Once again, the duration of the bow is a benchmark of the sincerity of your respect for the sword with which you are training, so be certain your demeanor reflects genuine respect from your heart.

As you rise from *tōrei*, continue looking at your sword (fig. 6D.11) while both hands are still touching the floor. As you draw your hands back to your thighs and straighten (fig. 6D.12), allow your gaze to rise with your head, so that you are looking straight ahead at the completion of the bow (fig. 6D.13).

It is also common to perform *tōrei* from a standing position. This is done, for example, when first picking up the sword to prepare for practice, or when removing the sword after *waza* practice in order to use a *bokken* or *jō* for a portion of class.

A standing *tōrei* begins at "attention," with the feet close together and erect posture, as in figure 6D.14. The *sageo* should be looped between the middle and ring finger of the right hand and the right index finger should be hooked over the *tsuba* to be sure the sword does not slide from its *saya*. Raise the sword to eye level, resting on the upturned palms of both hands. As depicted in figure 6D.17, the left hand should be positioned near the *kojiri* (end of the *saya*), with the eyes looking directly at the sword. From this position, bow from the waist, again keeping the back and neck straight, until your forehead is level with or lower than the sword, as shown in figure 6D.18.

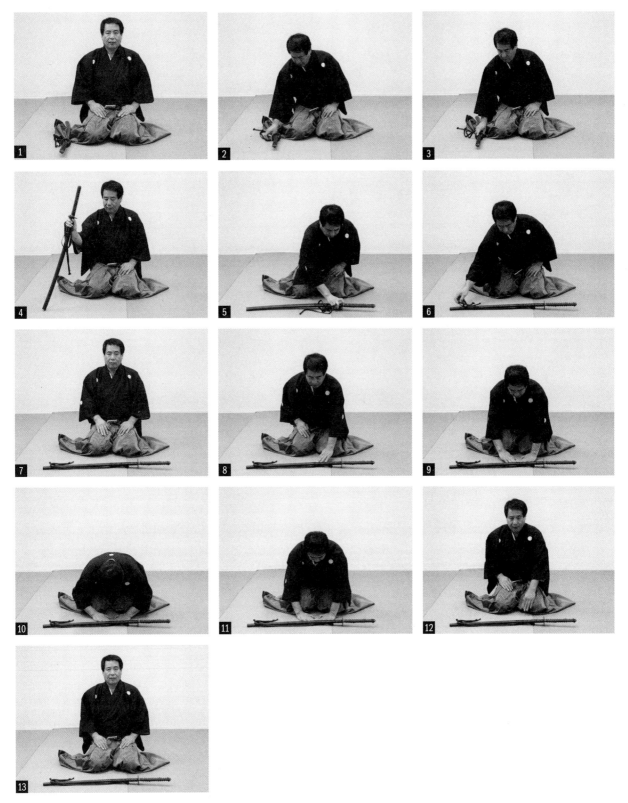

Figures 6D.1–13. *Tōrei*

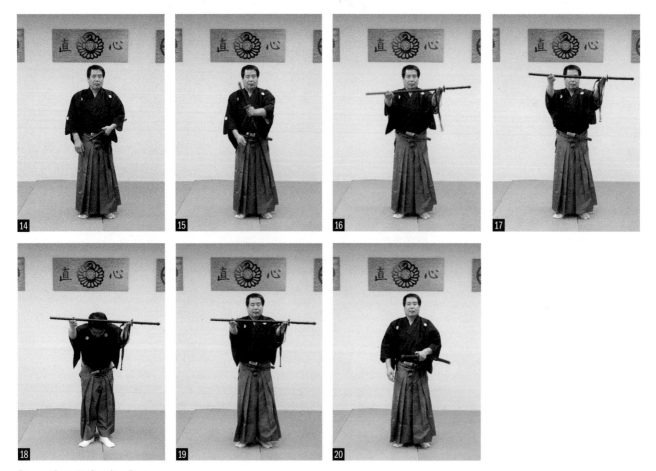

Figures 6D.14–20. Standing *Tōrei*

As before, the duration of your bow and your attitude while performing *tōrei* are an indication of the sincerity of your respect. It is disrespectful to treat this bow as a begrudging duty rather than an opportunity to express heartfelt appreciation.

## 6E: TAITŌ
### Wearing the Sword

In one way of thinking, the completion of *tōrei* and placing the sword in position for practice marks the delineation between *reihō* (etiquette) and *sahō* (preparation). However, this is only a superficial distinction. Proper etiquette is a vital part of preparation (*sahō*) for training. After all, in *iaijutsu*, as with every form of true *budō*, *Rei ni hajimari, rei ni owaru* ("Everything begins and ends with respect"). So, the outward manifestations of respect—bowing and formal courtesies—are simply an integral part of preparation (*sahō*). Similarly, proper preparation is an outward demonstration of respect for one's self, *dōjō*, *sensei*, sword, and colleagues. True *reihō*, however, as we shall see later in this chapter, is *internal*. Although we try to make a distinction between *sahō* and *reihō* for explanatory purposes, in practice the two are truly inseparable.

Once *tōrei* has been completed from the *seiza* position, you will be in the position shown in figure 6E.1, with your sword in front of you. Use the right hand to grasp the *sageo* between the middle and ring-fingers (fig. 6E.2) and run the hand along the *saya* to the *tsuba* (fig. 6E.3). Grasp the *saya*, hooking the right index finger over the *tsuba*. Pick up the sword and stand it straight up in front of you with the *kojiri* resting on the floor, centered between your knees (fig. 6E.4) at roughly arm's length from your body. The curve of the *saya* (denoting the sharp edge of the blade) should be facing toward you. Once in this position, you should be looking past the sword to your training partner, instructor, any other person who is facing you, or in *enzan no metsuke* (as if gazing at distant mountains). While still looking beyond the sword, reach forward with the left hand, touching the *saya* with your fingertips at a point about one-third the distance from the *kojiri* up the *saya* (fig. 6E.5) then run your left hand down to the *kojiri* (fig. 6E.6). Lift the *kojiri* slightly off the floor with your left hand, and pull it unhurriedly toward your waist, as you allow the *tsuka* to tilt forward in your right hand (fig. 6E.7).

Once the *kojiri* has reached your belt level, use your left hand to insert it into your *obi* about midway between your left hip and your navel (fig. 6E.8); not at the hip. Use the fingers of your left hand to separate the layers of your obi in order to insert the *kojiri* beneath the outermost winding of the *obi*, rather than between the *obi* and your *iaidō-gi*. It is very important not to "stir" the *tsuka* around while inserting the *saya* in the *obi*. Although it is entirely acceptable to move the *left* hand considerably while inserting the *kojiri*, the right hand should remain as still as possible.

Once the left hand has manipulated the *kojiri* between the layers of the *obi*, use the right hand to push the sword through, so it emerges at the left hip through the opening in the upper left side of the *hakama*, then pull the *saya* with the left hand (fig. 6E.9) until the sword is fully inserted with the *tsuba* directly in front of your navel, jutting about one foot in front of the body, as shown in figure 6E.10. Use the left hand to take the *sageo* from the right hand and drape them over the *saya* at the point where it emerges from the *obi* at the left hip (fig. 6E.11). Make any final adjustments needed (fig. 6E.12). When the sword is completely in place, lower the left hand first (fig. 6E.13), then the right hand (fig. 6E.14) to your thighs. You are now ready to begin *iaijutsu* practice.

Figures 6E.1–14. *Taitō*

Figures 6E.15 and 6E.16 show the correct position of the sword in a standing position.

Figures 6E.15–16. *Taitō* standing

# 6F: TACHI REI

## Standing Bow

Under less formal circumstances, such as when changing partners during practice, a standing bow (*tachi rei*) can be performed for expediency while simply holding the sword at the hip or while it is being worn (*taitō*). From a normal standing posture, whether holding the sword or wearing it, make sure your left thumb is hooked over the *tsuba* to prevent the sword from sliding out of the *saya* as you bow (fig. 6F.1), then simply bow from the hips, keeping the back and neck straightly aligned as depicted in figure 6F.2.

Figures 6F.1–2. *Tachi rei* (standing bow)

## 6G: DATTŌ

### Removing the Sword

Once you have completed *iaijutsu* practice, you will return to the formal *seiza* position. There are similar formalities at the conclusion of practice to those performed prior to practice, and these are of utmost importance, since they are again a reflection of the respect and dedication of the practitioner.

Removal of the sword at the conclusion of practice *(dattō)* is performed in nearly the exact reverse of the procedure for *taitō*, or wearing the sword. Beginning from the *seiza* posture, as shown in figure 6G.1, grasp the *sageo* between the index and middle fingers of the left hand and remove them from behind the *saya*. With a small circular motion of the left hand, form a loop with the *sageo* as you pass them to the right hand, gripping them between the middle and ring fingers of the right hand (fig. 6G.2). The right hand then grasps the *saya* near the *tsuba*, with the index finger hooked over the *tsuba* to secure it in place, and the left hand returns to the left hip.

While the left hand remains at the hip, as though preventing the *obi* from snagging on the *saya* while it is removed, the right hand pulls the *saya* toward the right-front of the body, as shown in figure 6G.3. The right hand then tilts the *tsuka* back toward the body, swinging the *kojiri* outward beyond the right knee, where it is carefully placed on the floor, as shown in figure 6G.4.

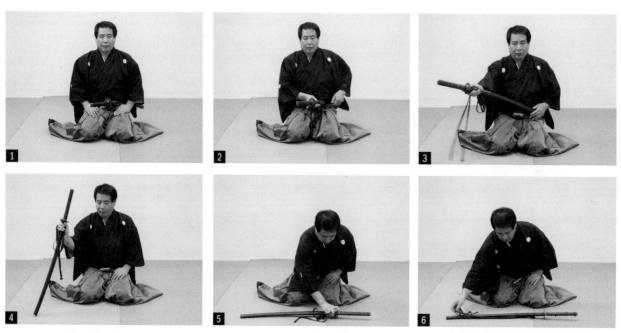

Figures 6G.1–6. *Dattō*

Gently lay the *saya* on its side in front of you, with the *tsuba* aligned with the outside of your left knee, as shown in figure 6G.5, and straighten the *sageo* along its outer edge, draping them across the *saya* about three-fourths the distance from the *tsuba* to the *kojiri* (fig. 6G.6).

Straighten, with your eyes looking straight ahead, not yet at the sword, then perform *tōrei* in the manner described previously in greater detail (figs. 6G.7–9).

Figures 6G.7–9. *Tōrei*

As always, the duration of your bow is a reflection of the sincerity and depth of your respect for your sword. This fact bears frequent repetition, as it is too often overlooked in *budō* today. The measure of your respect should not be based on the value or condition of your sword. Even if your sword is of low quality and minimal monetary value, it is *your* sword. It is the sword with which you train. It is the sword you are using to reshape your mind, your values, and your character—the sword that is creating the person you are striving to become. For that reason, if no other, it merits your deep and heartfelt respect regardless of its cost or condition.

Most often, this *tōrei* will be followed by bowing to the instructor *(shirei)*. In such cases, the instructor or *sempai* will clearly indicate that this is to be the case and it will only be necessary to follow his lead or directions. To transition from *tōrei* to *shirei*, use the right hand to grasp the *sageo* between the middle and ring fingers (as in fig. 6G.10), running the hand along the *saya* to the *tsuba*, then grasp the *saya*, with the index finger hooked over the *tsuba* (see fig. 6G.11), raise the sword, and place it at your right side with the *tsuba* aligned with your right knee (fig. 6G.12), then straighten in preparation for *shirei* (fig. 6G.13).

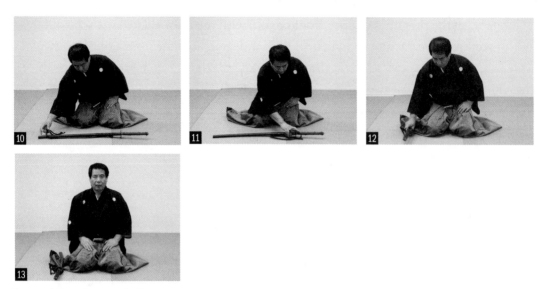

Figures 6G.10–13. Preparing for *shirei*

Refer to the preceding description of *shirei* for a detailed review of this bow to the instructor at the end of training, which is summarized in figures 6G.14–16.

Figures 6G.14–16. *Shirei*

Upon rising from *shirei*, use the right hand to grasp the *sageo* between the middle and ring fingers and run the hand along the *saya* to the *tsuba*, then grasp the *saya*, with the index finger hooked over the *tsuba* (see fig. 6G.17), and raise the sword, placing the *kojiri* on the floor, centered between your knees as shown in figure 6G.18. From this position, take the *sageo* in your left hand, between the index and middle fingers, as you grasp the *saya* with the thumb hooked over the *tsuba*, then hold the sword at your left hip (fig. 6G.19), just as if you were standing upright (see "Teitō," at the beginning of this chapter).

Figures 6G.17–19. *Teitō*

Rise to your feet by first raising the right foot, then use both legs to push yourself up to a standing position (fig. 6G.20). If necessary (but avoid this if possible), you may press your right hand against your right knee for assistance in rising. However, never use the sword as a crutch to assist you in rising. It is better to fall down than to disgrace your sword in this manner! As you rise, bring the feet together by drawing the left foot forward to the right foot. Although it may seem easier at first, do not step back with the right foot, as this can be taken as a sign of timidity unbecoming a samurai.

Figure 6G.20.

If you have been practicing with a partner, or if an observer or audience has been watching your practice, or if you were not instructed to perform *shirei* to your *sensei* at the close of class, it is customary to perform *hairei* to these individuals immediately upon standing.

You are now ready to leave the training area.

Turning your back on an observer would be disrespectful, and turning your back on your training partner is not only disrespectful but could be construed as an insult by implying that your partner's sword skills are not worthy of your concern. For this reason, even if you were training alone, walk backwards to the edge of the training area. Be certain to make your first backward step with your left foot, since a right-foot-forward stance facilitates drawing the sword and makes you less vulnerable to attack.

When you reach the edge of the training area, perform a standing bow with your sword held at the left hip, then walk to the *dōjō* exit. Before you leave the *dōjō*, turn and again bow in the direction of the *dōjō* emblem, shrine, or other suitable focal point as your final gesture of respect before exiting.

If, for any reason, you did not perform *tōrei* at the conclusion of your practice while in the *seiza* position, you should always give due respect to your sword before changing out of your *hakama* and leaving the *dōjō*. In such cases, before putting your sword away, raise it in your hands as described earlier in this chapter, and perform a standing *tōrei*.

The more you perform the formalities of *iaijutsu*, the more profoundly you will understand and appreciate the depth of respect that is inherent to the *sahō* and *reihō* of this art. In addition to the outward expressions of respect performed during *hairei*, *shirei*, and *tōrei*, the very actions of *sahō* themselves—the painstaking handling of the sword during *teitō*, *taitō*, and *dattō*—are suffused with respect. The time and attention we pay to these seemingly insignificant details of ritual, and the degree of sincere devotion we give these actions, are themselves gestures of respect, in much the same way that "quality time" with someone is an expression of our love or respect for them.

So avoid the temptation to rush through the *sahō* and *reihō* in order to begin the "fun" part of your training. Take the time to appreciate your sword, your *dōjō*, your teacher, and your fellow students. Take the time to fully prepare your garments, equipment, and body for training, and you will find this helps calm and prepare your mind as well. As you mature in your training, you will discover that *sahō* and *reihō* become some of the most enriching time you will spend in the *dōjō*. By learning the true meaning of respect and practicing it on a daily basis, you will find that the respect you develop for your sword, your *dōjō*, your teacher, and your colleagues will increase the amount of respect you have for yourself.

# REI NI TSUITE
## True Respect

We have devoted an entire chapter to preparation and respect, pointing out that the two are inseparable in *iaijutsu* training, but to this point we have explained only the outward manifestations of respect without discussing what is most important—the *inward* manifestation of respect.

The emphasis *iaijutsu* places on *sahō* and *reihō* is an application of the principle of Shin ▪ Ku ▪ I (see chapter 3). By constantly practicing the physical expressions of respect (*shin*, the body), we gradually develop a more respectful attitude that next shows in our speech (*ku*, the mouth), and eventually harnesses our mind (*i*). This is why we have described *sahō* and *reihō* in such painstaking detail. These physical actions themselves are not what is truly important. Their importance lies in the process our minds and spirits undergo as a result of these repetitive actions. As we mature as *budōka*, respect becomes so inherent to, and evident in, our spirit and demeanor that the depth or duration of a bow no longer expresses the depth and sincerity of our respect, but instead respect exudes from our inner being and overshadows our physical actions.

So respect is far more than courtesy and the rituals of proper etiquette. It must become an attitude that pervades every aspect of our character. In simplest terms, it is *caring* about people and things. Consider again the analogies between samurai and cowboys. Samurai cared about their swords, and cowboys cared about their horses, because their lives depended upon them. This care led to them *taking care* of their swords and horses—even to placing the well-being of their swords and horses before their personal comfort, and demonstrating their care by naming them and showing them outward courtesies.

A simple way of describing respect is treating others the way you want to be treated. Even the most loathsome criminals can be treated with respect by not abusing them, ensuring that their rights are not infringed, and giving them a fair trial presided over by an impartial judge, based on factual evidence, and decided by an impartial jury. Respect does not require admiration, agreement, or acceptance of misbehavior; it merely demands humane and considerate treatment of others, regardless of their attitude or conduct.

Respect also has two sides, like a coin: respect for the benefit and value of someone or something, and respect for the potential danger that person or object presents. The sword that protected the samurai's life, if mishandled could also injure or kill its owner. And every cowboy knew that to walk behind a horse without placing a hand on its haunch to let it know he was there could lead to a painful or even fatal kick. Even an enemy was to be respected for the danger he or she represented.

Viewed in this context, every aspect of our training derives from respect. The care we take in *sahō* shows our respect for the *dōjō*, our equipment, and colleagues. The courtesies we offer in *reihō* likewise demonstrate our respect. But also, the diligence and perseverance we exercise in perfecting our skills are derived from respect for our potential opponents. As you read chapter 7 and practice the fundamentals and principles of *iaijutsu*, consider how respect for the skill of your potential opponents is exemplified in posture and bearing (*shisei*), in correct stances that optimize balance and power (*kamae*), in maintaining eye contact (*chakugan*), controlling the distance between yourself and opponents (*maai*), the intensity of your spirit (*kihaku*), and maintaining a constant state of alertness and vigilance (*zanshin*).

Respect is not merely a matter of courtesy and politeness; it is a matter of life and death.

You will also find that the time you spend cultivating respect through the depth and sincerity of your *reihō* will reap great rewards by improving your personal relationships. As you learn to take the time to demonstrate your respect and appreciation, these attributes will carry over from the *dōjō* into your personal life. There it will reveal itself in your desire and ability to invest time in the people you care about, the way you treat customers and coworkers, and help solidify those relationships you hold most dear.

# Chapter 7

# Kihon 基本

## Fundamentals

*Kihon*, or Fundamentals, are those attributes that underlie all Eishin-Ryū techniques (*waza*). Once you have mastered the fundamentals, it will be far easier to apply them to the performance of *waza* (chapters 8–14). Each element of *kihon* is explained in detail in this chapter, so that such detail can be omitted from the subsequent chapters describing Eishin-Ryū *waza*. Thus, this chapter will be a source of continual reference as you begin practicing the *waza* presented later.

Generally, these fundamentals are grouped into categories of related items, but since their functions are all interrelated, it is impossible to completely separate them from each other. In this chapter we will first explain the major actions used in *iaijutsu*: *tsuka no nigiri kata* (gripping the sword), *nukitsuke* (drawing cut), *furikaburi* (raising), *kirioroshi* (downward cut), *chiburi* (shaking blood off), and *nōtō* (resheathing).

After describing the key elements of these major actions, we will review the general principles that maximize their effectiveness, such as *shisei* (posture), *kamae* (stance), *kokyū* (breathing), *chakugan* (eye contact), *maai* (distance), *kihaku* (focus and power), and *zanshin* (spirit), and relate how these principles affect the physical actions and techniques.

The importance of *kihon* cannot be overemphasized. Without sound fundamentals—all working together flawlessly—you will not be able to perform *iaijutsu* techniques or *waza* with grace and precision. Furthermore, from a practical standpoint, until you have truly mastered the fundamentals, you will not be unable to generate sufficient power, control, and accuracy to actually cut effectively.

# PART I.
## Major Actions

The major actions involved in *iaijutsu* techniques are presented here in the same order in which they would usually be performed in a *waza*.

# 7A: TSUKA NO NIGIRI KATA
## Gripping the Handle

Fundamentals begin with correctly gripping the sword. Without a proper grip, you will be unable to draw or swing the sword correctly, so the grip is the most fundamental aspect of *iaijutsu* basics.

The right hand is placed in front, gripping the *tsuka* just behind the *fuchigane* (the metal flange directly behind the *tsuba*). This leaves the thumb and index finger about three-quarters of an inch away from the *tsuba*—not pressed up against the *tsuba* as many beginners suppose—as shown in figure 7A.1.

The groove between the thumb and forefinger rests along the top of the *tsuka* and the middle knuckles of the fingers are aligned on the bottom of the *tsuka*. The top view in figure 7A.2 shows this alignment of the right hand.

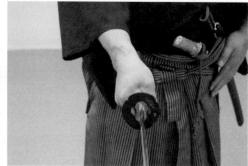

Figure 7A.1. Grip position right hand (side view)     Figure 7A.2. Grip position right hand (top view)

The left hand is aligned in identical fashion approximately the width of one finger behind the right hand. The correct grip with both hands is shown in figures 7A.3 (side view) and 7A.4 (top view). With the hands in position, the right hand should push forward and the left hand pull rearward on the *tsuka*, as if trying to stretch it a quarter inch—not a powerful, energy-wasting effort, but a steady opposing tension between the hands that keeps the sword straight, even if tapped by an opponent's sword to drive it off line.

Figures 7A.3. Correct grip with both hands (side view)     Figures 7A.4. Correct grip with both hands (top view)

As the sword is swung downward to cut, both hands squeeze together, twisting slightly inward toward the center as if wringing the last drops of water out of a twisted wet towel. This motion, called *tsuka no nigiri kata* (wringing the handle), tightens the grip while the blade is moving and helps ensure that it travels straight downward to make a clean, unwavering cut.

# 7B: NUKITSUKE

## Drawing Cut

The dominant characteristic of *iaijutsu*, the element which makes the art unique and distinctive, is that the first movement—drawing the sword from its scabbard—also simultaneously *cuts* the opponent. This technique, called *nukitsuke*, is referred to as "The Life of Iaidō" because, quite literally, life hangs in the balance. If this first cutting stroke is successful, the samurai has assured his victory; if not, the advantage will almost certainly shift to his opponent.

With some sixty *waza* (techniques performed individually) in the Eishin-Ryū system, plus twelve Seitei Kata, there are a large number of *nukitsuke* variations. Some are designed to cut level during the draw, others upward or downward, and still others block the opponent's first strike, then counterattack in a single, fluid motion that is all but unstoppable. All of these, however, work on the same basic principles, so only the most basic—the level drawing-cut—will be described in this chapter.

*Nukitsuke* begins from the preparatory posture, either kneeling seated (*seiza*), semi-seated (*tatehiza*), or standing (*tachi*), depending upon the technique being employed. Since it is the most fundamental posture, *seiza* will be used in this description of *nukitsuke*.

Both hands move simultaneously toward the *tsuka*. In *shoden* (initial level) techniques (chapter 8), the left hand encircles the *saya* with the thumb uppermost (see the warning in chapter 6), near the *koiguchi* slightly before the right hand touches the *tsuka*. Just as the right hand begins to grasp the *tsuka*, the left thumb presses almost imperceptibly forward against the edge of the *tsuba*, pushing it about a half inch forward. Since the *habaki* usually fits quite snugly into the *koiguchi*, this loosens the sword from the scabbard to ensure a smooth and fast draw. This subtle yet essential movement is called *koiguchi no kirikata* (opening the *koiguchi*). A close-up of the hands performing *koiguchi no kirikata* is shown in figure 7B.1.

Figure 7B.1. *Koiguchi no kirikata*

In addition to this basic method of *koiguchi no kirikata*, there are two variations. One alternative is to keep the tip of the thumb hidden behind the *tsuba*, pushing against the flat of the *tsuba*, rather than its outer edge. This hides the movement from the opponent and may delay his reaction a few precious tenths of a second. This stealth variation, called *uchi-giri*, is actually the preferred method in Eishin-Ryū, with the more noticeable version (*soto-giri*) being used only in the Shoden *waza* (chapter 8).

The second variation does not use the thumb at all. With the left hand wrapped around the *saya*, very close to the *koiguchi*, the hand is simply squeezed tight, which swells the hand sufficiently so that the sides of the thumb and index finger press the *tsuba* forward, resulting in *koiguchi no kirikata*. This variation would normally be employed in a situation in which you were uncertain of your opponent's intentions, but you want an advantage if they are found to be hostile. In this way, the left hand can open the *koiguchi* completely unnoticed, while the right hand remains away from the sword, thus giving no apparent signs of threat. Whenever a samurai made an overt *koiguchi no kirikata*, it signaled hostility to his opponent and nearly always resulted in a preemptive counterattack—an act which this disguised movement would not provoke.

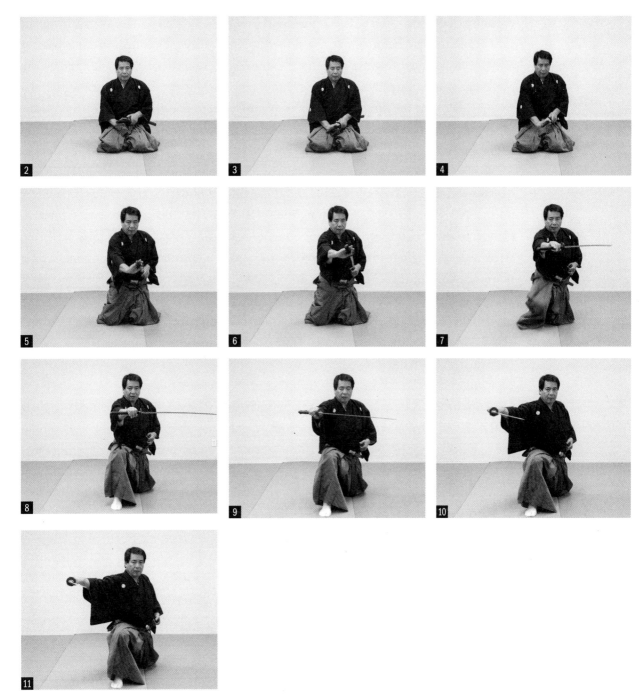

Figures 7B.2–11. *Nukitsuke* front view

Just as *koiguchi no kirikata* is completed, the right hand grasps the *tsuka*, with the middle knuckles aligned along the upturned ridge of the *tsuka*. Initially, the grip is loose, with only the fingers and thumb in contact with the *tsuka* as the drawing motion begins (fig. 7B.2). The right hand *pushes*—not pulls—the sword from the *saya* while the left hand draws the *saya* back (*saya-biki*). This dual motion has the effect of nearly doubling the speed of the draw. It is crucial that the right hand guides the *tsuka-gashira* directly toward the opponent's eyes (figs. 7B.5–6) during the first two-thirds of the drawing motion, preventing the opponent from seeing exactly how much of the sword has been drawn and thus throwing off his timing for a block or counterattack.

As the *kissaki* leaves the *saya*—an event called *saya-banari*—both hands twist 90 degrees counterclockwise (fig. 7B.6), and the fingers of the right hand tighten into a normal (one-handed) grip, snapping the sword free and causing it to swing forward parallel to the ground, cutting the opponent (figs. 7B.7–9) as you step forward. From *seiza*, a deep lunging step is taken with *nukitsuke* to ensure that the opponent does not evade the cut (figs. 7B.7–11). *Nukitsuke* finishes with the sword at armpit level, the *kissaki* just slightly lower than the *tsuba* and pointing at the opponent (fig. 7B.11).

Your feeling while performing *nukitsuke* is extremely important. Drawing and cutting should not feel like two separate but linked functions; instead, they should have the feeling of one movement, the sole purpose of which is cutting the opponent. Drawing the sword is merely a by-product of this cutting motion.

Some aspects of *nukitsuke* are perhaps best seen in the side view presented in figures 7B.12–20. In particular, note that the back remains as straight as possible throughout the *nukitsuke* process. Also essential for both speed and power of the cutting technique, notice that the rear foot does not remain flat on the floor, but that both feet are raised by the point depicted in figure 7B.17 and set on the balls of the feet. This provides greater stability and power for the lunging step completed in figure 7B.19.

At the completion of *nukitsuke*, the *tsukagashira* should be approximately one fist's width from the forearm, as shown in figure 7B.21, and the *kissaki* should be pointing toward the opponent's *seichūsen* (center line). Triangulating the final position of the sword in this manner is a simple way of assuring that you have made neither too narrow nor too wide a cut with *nukitsuke*.

The variation of *nukitsuke* described and illustrated here is Shimomura-ha *nukitsuke*, which is used primarily in Shoden *waza*. In the Shimomura-ha method, the hips and shoulders both rotate to the left—the opposite of the direction the blade swings—during *saya-banari*. In the Tanimura-ha variation of *nukitsuke*, which is used in most *chūden* and Okuden *waza*, the shoulders and hips rotate to the right—in the same direction as the blade travels—following *saya-banari*.

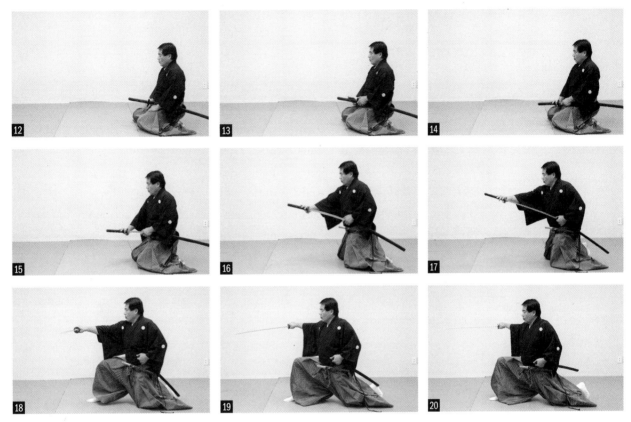

Figures 7B.12–20. *Nukitsuke* side view

Figure 7B.21. Gauging correct position of *tsuka*

## 7C: FURIKABURI

### Raising the Sword

Once the sword is drawn, and the first cutting motion is complete, the sword is raised overhead in preparation for the powerful, downward finishing cut. This raising of the sword, called *furikaburi*, is performed in a manner which affords the best combination of speed and protection against attack.

With the sword still level from *nukitsuke* (edge toward opponent, as shown in figure 7C.1), *furikaburi* is initiated by moving the sword slightly forward, then the *kissaki* is swung backward by first bending the right wrist. This action should feel as if you are trying to poke yourself in the left ear with the *kissaki* (figs. 7C.1–3). As your bent wrist reaches the limit of its range of flexibility, your elbow should then begin to bend, as shown in figure 7C.4. The motion must remain smooth and uninterrupted until the *tsuba* is directly in front of your nose (fig. 7C.5), at which point the sword is raised directly overhead.

Figures 7C.1–7. *Furikaburi* front view

The left hand raises at the same time, so that it grips the sword the instant it has reached the fully raised position shown in figure 7C.7.

Figures 7C.8–14 show *furikaburi* in side view. From this perspective it is easier to see that at the completion of *furikaburi*, the sword should be about level with the ground. It is permissible for the *kissaki* to be lower than the *tsuba*, but it should not be higher, since this will reduce swinging power and speed.

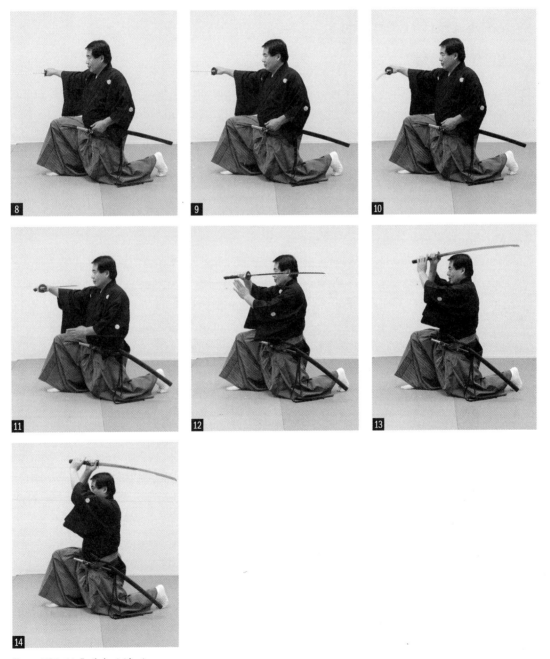

Figures 7C.8–14. *Furikaburi* side view

This is one of two primary types of *furikaburi* employed in Eishin-Ryū, typically referred to as Shimomura-ha *furikaburi*, and it is used exclusively in the *shoden* (beginning level) *waza*. A slightly different *furikaburi*—called Tanimura-ha *furikaburi*—is used in *chūden* (middle level) and most *okuden* (deep-level) *waza*. In the Tanimura-ha variation, once the *kissaki* reaches your *seichūsen* (center line), it travels directly rearward, making *furikaburi* more compact and slightly quicker.

## 7D: KIRIOROSHI
### Downward Cut

With the sword raised overhead, you are now poised for *kirioroshi*. Although *nukitsuke* is "The Life of Iaidō," it does not always inflict an immediately fatal wound but is often used to gain the extra few moments a samurai needed to execute a killing technique. Also, *nukitsuke* is only effective on the first opponent, so another technique is needed to deal with situations involving multiple opponents. This technique, *kirioroshi* (also called *kirikudashi* or *kiriotoshi* in alternate readings of the same *kanji*), is instantly fatal if performed correctly, since it slices from the top of the skull all the way down to the navel.

While this may conjure brutal images, it is not only necessary for self-defense, but—equally important to the samurai—it was also an act of respect and compassion for his enemy. The safest way to win a sword battle is to cut the adversary's right arm. Wounded, the opponent cannot wield his sword and will either bleed to death or succumb later to infection. However, to allow a foe to die in such an ignominious manner would be highly disrespectful. A samurai, after all, lived for *giri* (duty and honor). To lose his ability to serve his master or to die pitifully ravaged by gangrene would be the ultimate shame to himself and his family. On the other hand, to die at the hands of a master swordsman, serving his lord proudly and making the supreme sacrifice, would bring only honor to his memory. Thus, the samurai's goal in a sword battle was to dispatch his enemy as quickly and painlessly as possible, both as a matter of self-preservation and out of respect for an honorable foe. The surest way of accomplishing this is *kirioroshi*.

*Kirioroshi* begins with the sword raised at the completion of *furikaburi* (see fig. 7D.1).

The cut is initiated by squeezing the pinky fingers of both hands, which start the *kissaki* moving upward on a circular path. The forearms then swing up and forward, continuing this high arc until the arms and wrists straighten and reach full extension (fig. 7D.3). Until the arms reach this point, the elbows should not move. Only as the arms straighten do the elbows begin swinging downward toward the target, which is only six to eight inches below the point at which the *monouchi* is in figure 7D.3. At the point of impact the blade is still angled upward at about 30 to 45 degrees. From this point, it completes the cut by following the natural downward arc of your hands as they drop to waist level (figs. 7D.4–6).

The sword completes *kirioroshi* when the hands reach waist height. At this point, the sword is almost level, with the top of the *kissaki* at about the height of the bottom of the *habaki* and the *tsukagashira* pointing at your navel. When *kirioroshi* is performed kneeling (as shown in figure 7D.6), the *tsuba* is aligned with the front of the leading knee, and the *tsuka* is at thigh level. When standing, *kirioroshi* is completed at precisely the same point, but the knee and thigh are not available as handy reference points. The *tsukagashira* will be about six to nine inches in front of the body, depending upon your height and the length of your arms.

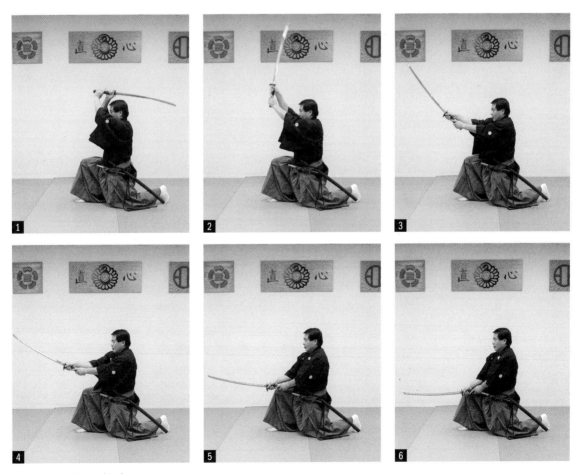

Figures 7D.1–6. *Kirioroshi* side view

Figures 7D.7–10. *Kirioroshi* front view

No muscle strength is involved in making the sword cut; it is entirely a matter of technique. In Japanese, all of the technical aspects of cutting are collectively referred to as *te no uchi* (inside the hands).

# 7E: TE NO UCHI
## Cutting Technique

The objective of *kirioroshi*, and all other cutting techniques, is to make the blade *slice*—not hit or chop—the target, so the blade must travel straight and cut completely through the target utilizing a circular motion. A samurai cannot afford to get his sword wedged in an opponent's body. The time it takes to work it free might easily cost him his life.

The first way to ensure a straight cut is to be certain the blade does not wiggle as it swings downward. This is called *hasuji o tōsu*. Proper *tsuka no nigiri kata* (wringing the *tsuka*) is one important way to keep the sword traveling straight. A correct grip (*mochi*), as previously described, with the hands close together and tightening inward as the sword swings downward, reduces the degree to which the blade can sway from side to side while in motion. To completely eliminate shimmy in the sword, be certain both hands swing in exactly the same line.

In addition to a proper grip and straight alignment of the hands while swinging the sword, the key to cutting technique is *enshin-ryoku*, or centripetal force. The Japanese *katana* is, without question, the finest sword ever produced by human hands. It was painstakingly designed to slice perfectly if swung correctly. The *sori* (curvature) of the blade ensures that it will slice if it is traveling in a circular path, so it is only necessary to guide the sword to the target and let it do the job for which it was designed.

By making a large, circular movement and snapping the arms and wrists forward so they reach full extension just above the target, the cutting section (*monouchi*) of the sword reaches a high velocity just before impact (fig. 7E.1). From there, the weight of the sword and its natural path of follow-through will cause it to slice effortlessly downward, finishing as shown in figure 7E.2.

Figure 7E.1. *Kirioroshi* at full arm extension (point of impact)

Figure 7E.2. *Kirioroshi* completed

A simple exercise for practicing correct cutting technique is to swing the sword in a half-cut, stopping at the point shown in figure 7E.4 without allowing your elbows to move forward or downward yet, then bring the sword back to *furikaburi* (fig. 7E.5) again and make a full cut, finishing as shown in figure 7E.6.

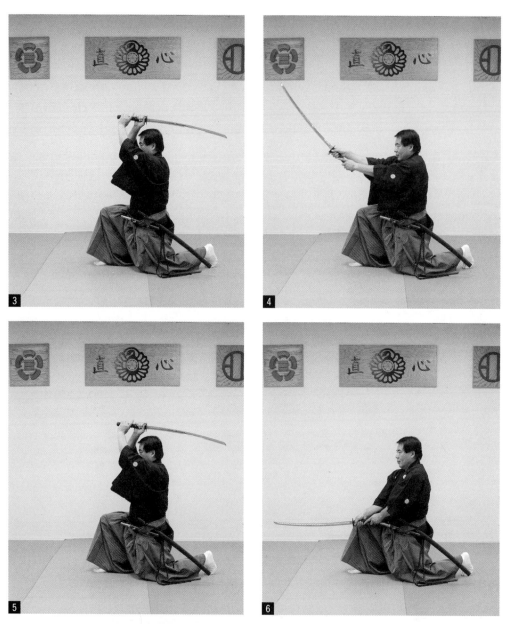

Figures 7E.3–6. Half swing–full swing practice exercise

By repeating this half swing–full swing, you will develop a habit of reaching full extension just above the target and allowing your arms to fall naturally to the finishing position. If your sword has a *bōhi* (groove), you will hear a loud and very satisfying *tachikaze* (swoosh) when you swing the blade correctly.

# 7F: CHIBURI

## Blood Removal

At the completion of each *iaijutsu* technique, a movement is performed that is designed to remove the opponent's blood from the blade before it is resheathed. This movement is called *chiburi*, and there are three basic types: "wet umbrella," "flicking," and "dripping." All three of these methods as used in Eishin-Ryū are largely symbolic, since none of them alone would clean the blade sufficiently of blood to be resheathed.

The type of *chiburi* most beginners will encounter first is the "wet umbrella" method (*kasa no shizuku o harao*), which gets this nickname from its resemblance to flinging the water from a wet umbrella. This style of *chiburi* is found in most of the Seiza *waza*, the first techniques usually taught to beginners, and is also often called "Ōmori-Ryū *chiburi*," since it is most commonly used in the Ōmori-Ryū *waza* taught to beginners. Another common term for this style of *chiburi* is ō-*chiburi* (big *chiburi*) due to its large, circular pattern.

After completing *kirioroshi* (fig. 7F.1), the right hand pushes the *tsuka* forward out of the left hand, then the sword is drawn slowly to the upper-right side as if the *kissaki* is dragging through *mochi* (compressed sticky rice, the consistency of taffy), keeping the arm relatively straight and rotating the blade clockwise as it rises. When the *kissaki* is pointing upward and outward at about a 45-degree angle (fig. 7F.4), it springs rearward as if it came unstuck from the *mochi*, following the path shown in figures 7F.5 and 7F.6 to the position shown in figure 7F.7. The left hand simultaneously returns to the left hip, cradling the *saya* across the palm and through the gap between the thumb and forefinger.

Following a brief pause with the *tsuka* is directly in front of the forehead (see fig. 7F.7) and the fingers gripping the *tsuka* loosely, allowing the sword to tilt down, away, and behind the body at about a 45-degree angle, the blade is swung counterclockwise, by powerfully clenching the right hand, which snaps it sharply downward, completing the motion, as shown in figures 7F.8–11. The *kissaki* should finish a little outside the line of the right foot. The right hand should be about a foot ahead of the body and no more than a foot to the right of the right hip. The *kissaki* should be pointing toward a spot directly in front of the center of the body, and there should again be one fist-width distance between the forearm and the *tsukagashira*.

Finally, in most cases (but there are exceptions), the right foot is drawn back in preparation for *nōtō* (fig. 7F.12).

Figures 7F.1–12. Ōmori-Ryū *chiburi* front view

In the side view presented below, the posture and the position of the sword and right hand relative to the body can be more clearly seen:

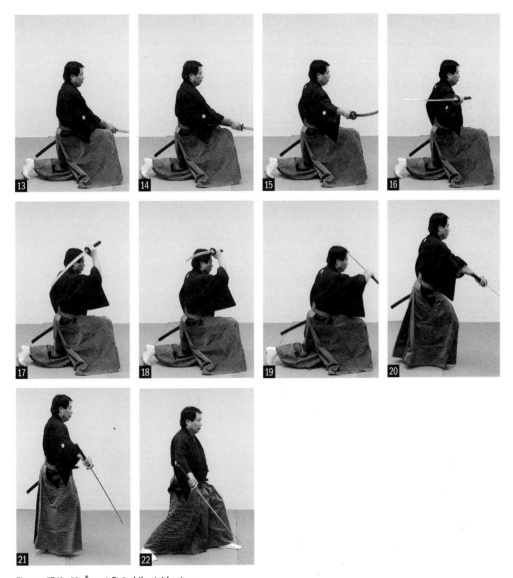

Figures 7F.13–22. Ōmori-Ryū *chiburi* side view

## 7G: YOKO-CHIBURI

The most common type of *chiburi* used in Eishin-Ryū is the "flicking" method (*katana o kaesu*). This method is used in most of the *tatehiza* and *tachiwaza*, which are normally taught to intermediate and advanced students. It is also frequently referred to as Eishin-Ryū *chiburi*, since it was originated by Hasegawa Eishin when he adapted *iaijutsu* to the shorter swords (*daitō*) of modern design. Another common term for this is *yoko-chiburi* (sideways *chiburi*) due to the sideward movement of the sword.

At the completion of *kirioroshi*, the fingers of the left hand are loosened, with the exception of the little finger, which remains hooked tightly around the *tsuka* (fig. 7G.1), while the right wrist begins to twist counterclockwise to create counterbalancing tension. With a snap of the wrist, the right hand twists the blade one-quarter turn counterclockwise on its longitudinal axis, while the hooked little finger of the left hand tugs in the opposite direction as the left hand pulls away (figs. 7G.2–5). The sudden release of tension between the right and left hands causes the blade to snap sharply outward, flinging the blood away.

At the completion of this motion (fig. 7G.5), the right hand has snapped outward a few inches and is still level with its starting point, with the blade outside and roughly parallel to the line of the right leg. Due to the curvature of the sword, the *kissaki* is still directed toward the opponent.

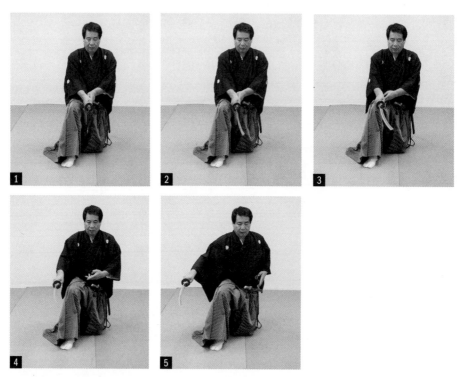

Figures 7G.1–5. Eishin-Ryū *chiburi*

The left hand has darted back to the left hip and cradles the *koiguchi* across the palm and through the web between the thumb and forefinger. Eishin-Ryū *chiburi* is performed in this identical manner when standing as well. A key factor in *yoko-chiburi* is that the *tsuba* should move directly sideways, so that it is in the same line laterally at the finish (fig. 7G.5) as it started in figure 7G.1.

# 7H: CHINUGUI

The "dripping" method of *chiburi*, *chi no shizuku o otosu*, is used occasionally in both *seiza* and *tachiwaza*, and it is most likely to be the third type encountered by most students. Another common term for this *chiburi* is *chinugui* (blood wiping), since it appears to wipe the blade against the *hakama*. In this method, after the completion of the final cut (fig. 7H.1), the *kissaki* is tilted down and to the right at about a 45-degree angle and the *mine* is rested against the right outer thigh, as shown in figures 7H.3–5. To prepare for *nōtō*, the right hand is then reversed (figs. 7H.5–6).

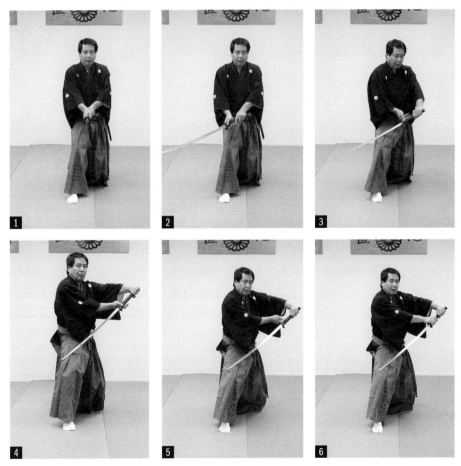

Figures 7H.1–6. "Drip" *chiburi*

## 71: *NŌTŌ*

### Resheathing

*Nōtō* is the act of returning the sword to its *saya* at the completion of a technique. Since *iaijutsu* always begins with the sword in its scabbard, no *waza* is truly completed until the sword has been resheathed so that another technique can be begun.

*Nōtō* begins at the point at which *chiburi* ends—regardless of which style of *chiburi* was used. There are three slight variations of *nōtō*: *shoden*, *chūden*, and *okuden*, which are used in the Shoden, Chūden and Okuden *waza*, respectively. When a *waza* concludes with either a "flicking" (as in figure 71.1) or "wet umbrella" (as in figure 71.2) *chiburi*, a Shoden, Chūden, or Okuden *nōtō* will follow, in accordance with the type of *waza* performed. However, the *nōtō* performed after a "drip" *chiburi* is a distinct variation.

**Shoden *nōtō*:** While the sword is still positioned as shown in either figures 71.1 or 71.2, the left hand envelopes the *sayaguchi* so that the *sayaguchi* itself is one finger-width inside the hand. Thus, the encircled thumb and forefinger form the actual *koiguchi*—the flexible "mouth" into which the sword is inserted during *nōtō*. The word *koiguchi* means "carp's mouth" because it is shaped like the mouth of a *koi* (carp) and is flexible. The *koiguchi* opening in the hand should be made as narrow as possible to ensure that the *kissaki* is guided by the flexible *koiguchi* into the inflexible *sayaguchi* during *nōtō*.

Once the left hand has formed the *koiguchi* in this fashion, the blade is swung to the left side in a broad motion—almost exaggerated in Shoden *nōtō*—and positioned edge-upward atop the left forearm (figs. 71.3–5), resting along the forearm from the crook of the elbow to the web between the thumb and index finger, as shown in figure 71.5.

The sword is then drawn forward with the *mine* sliding across the crease between the thumb and forefinger, while the left hand and left hip both pull simultaneously back, so that the right hand does not overextend in front of the body, causing an off-balanced posture. This motion should be timed so that just as the right arm reaches full extension, the *kissaki* passes the web between the thumb and forefinger and drops into the crook of the index finger, forming the lower lip of the *koiguchi* (see fig. 71.6). After a momentary pause, the motion of the two hands is reversed, so the left hand pushes the *saya* forward while the right hand pushes the sword into the *saya* and the hips return to their original position. This dual motion should be timed so that the *tsuba* meets the left hand directly in front of the navel about a foot away from the body, as shown in figure 71.10. During the entire forward and backward motion of the sword, it should be kept as level as possible, not dipping the *tsuka* below nor raising it above waist level. Once the *habaki* has been fully inserted into the *saya*, the left thumb hooks over the *tsuba* to secure it in place (fig. 71.11), then the right hand slides along the *tsuka* to the *tsuka-gashira*, where it remains until the very end of the *waza*.

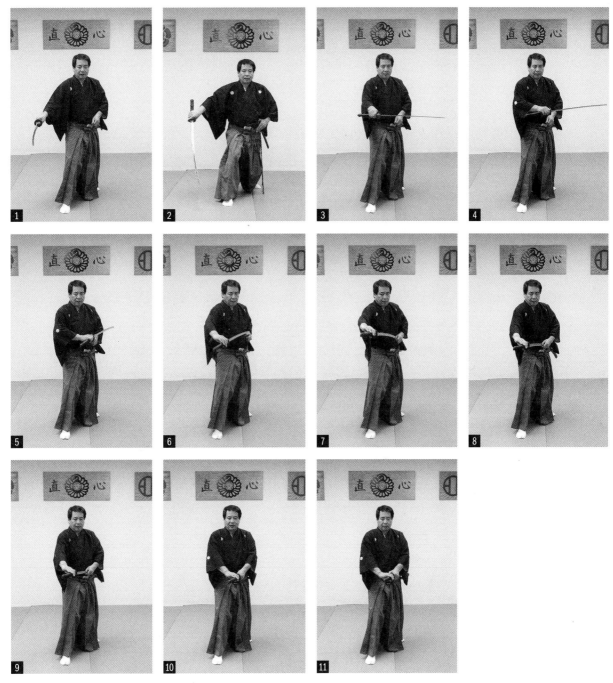

Figures 71.1–11. Shoden *nōtō*

An important facet of *nōtō* is *zanshin*. Neither *chiburi* nor *nōtō* are performed until the battle appears to be over. *Nōtō* is the most vulnerable portion of every *waza*, so you must remain alert to the possibility of further attack and use *nōtō* as the opportunity to calm your breathing, heart rate, and nerves using *fukushiki kokyū*. Hence, *nōtō* should never be rushed.

In most of the Shoden *waza*, the practitioner gradually lowers to one knee while performing Shoden *nōtō*, as depicted in figures 71.12–15. This is done gradually, so that the *tsuba* touches the left hand at the *koiguchi* at the same moment the lowering knee touches the floor (fig. 71.14).

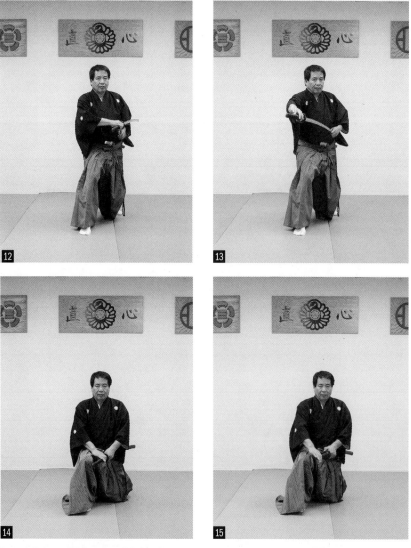

Figures 71.12–15. Shoden *nōtō* while kneeling

**Chūden** *nōtō:* The same sequence of motions is performed in Chūden *nōtō.* The key difference is that, instead of placing the blade along the full length of the left forearm, as in Shoden *nōtō* (fig. 71.5) and drawing nearly its full length forward, this portion of *nōtō* is foreshortened to reduce exposure to a secondary attack. Instead of taking the sword to the position shown in figure 71.5, it is taken to the position shown in figure 71.16, so that only about half the blade is drawn forward during *nōtō.* From there it is also drawn forward more rapidly than in Shoden *nōtō,* and with no pause when the *kissaki* enters the *koiguchi,* then slowly sheathed as before.

Figure 71.16. Intermediate position for Chūden *nōtō*

**Okuden** *nōtō:* The sheathing is foreshortened and sped up even more in Okuden *nōtō.* Instead of slowly taking the sword to the position previously shown in figure 71.5 for Shoden *nōtō* or figure 71.16 for Chūden *nōtō,* it is quickly taken to the position shown in figure 71.18, with only a few inches of the blade extending behind the *koiguchi* at first contact with the left hand. From there it is drawn quickly forward until the *kissaki* drops into the *koiguchi* (fig. 71.19), then about half the blade is quickly sheathed (reaching the position shown in figure 71.20) before slowly sheathing the remaining length of the blade. This action reduces exposure to secondary attack to an absolute minimum during *nōtō,* so it is most appropriate for advanced practitioners performing Okuden *waza.*

As noted in the preceding descriptions, Shoden *nōtō* is normally performed in Shoden *waza,* Chūden *nōtō* in Chūden *waza,* and *okuden nōtō* in Okuden *waza.* This fact has led some to mistakenly believe that one must make a conscious effort to learn the three types of *nōtō* in order to use them appropriately. Instead, the progression from Shoden to Chūden to Okuden *nōtō* should be a natural one—the product of years of repetition, rather than conscious effort. Years of training involving thousands of repetitions of Shoden *nōtō* will naturally lead to a smoother and somewhat abbreviated performance of *nōtō*. Without trying, your body will simply make the motions involved smoother and more compact, as is the case with any other action you repeatedly perform. Additional years of performing Chūden *nōtō* will likewise evolve into Okuden *nōtō*. In the end, you merely have to remind yourself which form of *nōtō* to perform with a given *waza*.

Figures 71.17–20. Okuden *nōtō*

# 7J: GYAKUTE NŌTŌ

***Gyakute nōtō:*** The final and most notable variation of *nōtō* is used in connection with the "drip" method of *chiburi* and is often called *gyakute* (reversed-hand) *nōtō*. This variation of *nōtō* begins after holding the position depicted in figure 7J.1 for several seconds to represent most of the blood having dribbled from the blade.

Figure 7J.1. "Drip" *chiburi (chinugui)*

The right hand is then inverted, so that it holds the *tsuka* palm-down, with the left and right thumbs in proximity to each other, as shown in figure 7J.2. The sword is then swung to the left side—again in an almost exaggerated motion, as depicted in figures 7J.3–7—and positioned edge-upward along the left forearm from the crook of the elbow to the web between the thumb and index finger, this time with the right hand inverted from its normal *nōtō* position (see fig. 7J.8).

This time, as the sword is drawn forward, with the *mine* sliding across the crease between the thumb and forefinger and the left hand pulling simultaneously back, the body turns about 45 degrees to the right. This motion should be timed so that the *kissaki* drops into the *koiguchi* just as the right arm reaches full forward extension and the body is again facing directly forward, as shown in figure 7J.10.

Again, the motion of the two hands is reversed at this point, although the right hand remains in an inverted position while the left hand pushes the *saya* forward and the right hand pushes the sword inside. This motion should also be timed so that the *tsuba* meets the left hand directly in front of the navel about a foot away from the body, as shown in figure 7J.15. After the *habaki* has been fully inserted into the *saya*, the left thumb hooks over the *tsuba* to secure it in place and the right hand slides along the *tsuka* to the *tsuka-gashira*, just as in the other types of *nōtō*, remaining there until the very end of the *waza*.

Figures 7J.2–15. *Gyakute nōtō*

# PART II.
## General Principles

Like any art, *iaijutsu* is experiential by nature. Many elements of it simply cannot be understood except through practice and actually feeling and experiencing what is meant. Therefore, most attempts at explanation often sound at first like a *koan*, one of those annoying, self-contradictory parables for which Zen monks became famous. If you find any of these explanations frustrating in that way, we suggest that you simply try what is stated and keep the paradox in mind while you practice. With time, we are certain that you will come to experience and understand what we mean.

It is impossible to present the general principles outlined in this section in order of importance, since they are all of equal importance in terms of their contribution to effective *iaijutsu* technique. Nor can they be explained in order of use, since they all occur simultaneously during the performance of *iaijutsu waza*. Instead, we have tried to present them in the order in which they might naturally become apparent to the beginning *iaijutsu* student.

# 7K: SHISEI
## Posture

Since each *iaijutsu* technique is begun by assuming a sitting, crouching, or standing posture, this subject is a logical starting point to review the general principles of *iaijutsu* technique.

The basic rule of posture is to remain erect and natural. For most of us, this is already a contradiction in terms, since slouching or slumping has become "natural" to us. The body must be held erect and alert, but this carriage must not be forced or artificial. The neck and back of the head should be in a straight line with the spinal column, but with the chin not tucked in. This is definitely a paradox, since the back of the head cannot be truly straight unless the chin is, in fact, tucked in. Again, what is meant by this admonition is that a happy medium must be found, so that the head is held high with the neck and back straightly aligned, yet the chin is not tucked so far in as to cause a double or triple chin.

In the simplest terms, it means to sit straight when sitting, and stand tall when standing. If you can do this and still remain relaxed, then you are on the right track. It is especially important for beginners to avoid muscle tension in the shoulders. In the awkwardness of trying to perform *iaijutsu* techniques the first several times, it is quite common to tense and raise the shoulders in an effort to maintain better control over the sword, which often seems to have developed a mind of its own. This tension will usually throw off the balance and cause the arms to swing unnaturally, robbing the body of power and causing the sword to waggle while moving.

Until the basic movements of *iaijutsu* begin to feel natural and comfortable, it often helps to make a conscious effort at the beginning of every technique to relax and lower the shoulders.

This upright yet relaxed bearing is maintained in every aspect of *iaijutsu*, from the time you assume a preparatory position for performing a technique until you rest after completing the technique. Figure 7K.1 depicts correct posture while seated in the *seiza* position; figure 7K.2 shows proper *tatehiza* (half-seated, half-kneeling, literally "upright-knee sitting"); and figure 7K.3 is standing posture.

Figure 7K.1. *Seiza*          Figure 7K.2. *Tatehiza*          Figure 7K.3. *Tachi*

As with nearly everything in *iaijutsu*, there is a prescribed method for taking a seated (*seiza*) or crouching (*tatehiza*) posture. These are presented in detail under the heading "Kamae," later in this chapter.

*Shisei* is of greatest importance while you are moving during *iaijutsu waza*. Much of your power and correct cutting technique rely upon proper posture. Your balance also stems predominantly from correct posture.

An essential element in maintaining posture and balance while moving is *iai-goshi*, or *iai*-hips. *Iaigoshi* involves keeping the hips—and thus, the body's center of gravity—low while moving; not allowing the body to bob up and down as you step forward or back. At first, this will require conscious effort, and it will feel like you are trying to balance a glass of water on your head while you are moving.

It is important to maintain this upright alignment of back, neck, and head regardless of your stance. Whether you are seated, kneeling, crouching, standing upright, or lunging in to attack, both *iaigoshi* and straight spinal alignment must be maintained for optimum balance, speed, and power.

Try to avoid training in *shisei* only while performing *iaijutsu* techniques. Instead, if practiced from the moment you enter the *dōjō* to the moment you leave, proper posture will soon become habitual. With sufficient time and training, it will simply become your natural state, no longer requiring any conscious effort. You will have correct posture whether you are practicing *iaijutsu*, driving your car, or relaxing at home.

# CHAKUGAN
## Eye Contact

The next element you will probably become aware of is eye contact, called either *chakugan* or *metsuke* in Japanese. As soon as you try to draw a sword for the first time, you will find yourself wondering where to look: Should you watch your sword? Should you stare at your target? When you are looking at your opponent, should you look at his eyes? His hands? His feet?

As you might imagine, *chakugan* is crucial to *iaijutsu*. If a samurai failed to notice an opponent's attack, he met a sudden and premature end. If he was fooled by a feint, the result was the same.

There are as many theories about eye contact as there are schools of swordsmanship, and each theory has much merit. Some say to watch the opponent's eyes, but the eyes can often be used to deceive with a fake glance. Others advocate watching the opponent's hands, because the hands cannot lie. But a swordsman's hands can move so swiftly that by the time you notice them moving, it may be too late for a parry. Another idea is to watch the opponent's hips, since he cannot move without betraying it in his hips. Still others believe the opponent's elbows should be the focal point for the same reason. How can we possibly know which theory is right?

Eishin-Ryū is not concerned with which of these theories is right, because it uses *enzan no metsuke* (eyes fixed on distant mountains). By viewing the opponent with the same slightly out-of-focus eyesight we use when viewing a panorama of distant scenery, with the eyes directed at about the level of the adversary's solar plexus, our vision encompasses the entire person. In this way, we can watch our adversary's eyes, hands, elbows, hips, and feet all at the same time. This method also prevents us from being duped by an eye-fake or a distracting hand movement, because the positions of the hips, elbows, and feet will betray any deception attempted by the rest of the body. The Eishin-Ryū *iaidōka* only reacts when the opponent's whole body reveals his true intentions.

When practicing without a partner, *enzan no metsuke* is performed by directing the line of sight toward a spot on the ground about fifteen to twenty feet away. This angle approximates the correct direction and focal length that would be used with an opponent.

# KOKYŪ
## Breath Control

The commencement of every *iaijutsu* technique is keyed to breathing, so *kokyū*, or breath control, will be another factor of immediate interest to anyone practicing the art.

At the beginning of each *waza*, after assuming the initial posture, take three breaths before moving. These three breaths should be natural but deep. The feeling should be as though the air is being drawn in through the nostrils up around the crown of the head, then down the spinal column to the *tanden*—the lower abdomen. Exhaling is done normally through the mouth. Of course, the air cannot actually follow this path. When inhaling, it goes straight down into the lungs as always. But by breathing with this circular feeling, the diaphragm draws air more deeply into the lungs, so breathing is more efficient. This type of breathing is called *fukushiki kokyū* (abdominal breathing). Another term frequently used for the pattern of three slow breaths before a technique is *kiyomeri kokyū* (purification breaths), since their purpose is to cleanse both the mind and body of toxins.

As the third breath is drawn in, the initial movement of the *waza* is begun. If possible, the third breath should be held throughout the *waza*. However, in longer *waza* this is not always possible, especially for beginners. The objective in those cases is to breathe in such a way that the opponent cannot detect your breathing and exploit it. This involves breathing soundlessly, and letting the breath fill the *tanden*, so there will not be any noticeable swelling of the chest cavity or rising of the shoulders to alert an enemy to the pattern of your breathing.

Although breath control is crucial for maximizing balance, power, and stamina while fighting, the most important aspect of breath control is mental, rather than physical. Physically, the act of breathing brings fresh, oxygen-rich air into the body as we inhale, and expels impure, carbon dioxide-laden air as we exhale. Thus, breathing serves to purify our bodies in the physical sense, so our goal in *iaijutsu* is to use our breathing to purify our minds at the same time.

As a beginner this is done by consciously "drinking in" positive thoughts and emotions while inhaling, and releasing negative thoughts and emotions while exhaling. Negative thoughts and emotions, such as fear, worry, doubt, selfishness, jealousy, and hatred, are self-destructive and burdensome. Science has shown that excesses of these emotions are actually toxic to the body, leading to ulcers, higher incidence of cancer, impairment of the immune system, and susceptibility to disease. So it is quite beneficial—even necessary—to regularly cleanse the body and mind of these influences. But our minds cannot contain a vacuum. There is always something filling our thoughts. To truly drive out the destructive influences, we must replace them with positive thoughts. So, while we fill our lungs with fresh air, at the same time we fill our minds with refreshing feelings like confidence, faith, compassion, love, respect, and courage.

After a time of consciously practicing this mental cleansing, called *jaki o dasu* (expelling evil), it will become a habit. Once it has become habitual in *iaijutsu* practice, it will become part of our normal lifestyle, so that we are constantly refreshing and cleansing our mind and body as we go about our daily lives.

# KAMAE

## Structure

There are no "stances" in *iaijutsu*!

Despite this fact, proper stances are vital to correct technique. *Kamae* means "structure," and the position of our feet, legs, and hips, which we typically call "stance" in English, is the base for sound body structure. It is another of *iaijutsu's* infinite paradoxes that great emphasis is placed on correct stance, or *kamae*, while at the same time it is also stressed that *iaijutsu* stances are all natural and therefore *kamae* is essentially nonexistent. Historically, *iaijutsu* has not given names to stances, the way some other forms of *budō* have done. Nevertheless, to facilitate description of proper structure, we will use a few terms to denote common body positions.

Although the *seiza* and *tatehiza* positions are not considered stances as such, we have included descriptions of them here as *kamae*, since they are the beginning positions for some thirty-five of the *waza* you will practice in Eishin-Ryū, and having the correct structure in these positions is essential to successful performance of those *waza*.

## 7L: SEIZA

*Seiza* (see fig. 7L.6) is the formal kneeling-seated position used during audiences with those of high rank, in tea ceremony, and in other similarly ritualistic or formal occasions like negotiations.

To sit in *seiza* from a standing posture, first make sure that your left thumb is hooked over your *tsuba* to prevent your sword from unsheathing, then bend at the waist and knees and use your right hand to tuck the inside leg of your *hakama* behind your left knee first (fig. 7L2), then your right knee (fig. 7L.3). Do not do this with a loud slap of your hand, which is considered rude, but simply tuck the fabric into the creases of your knees as they bend. This ensures that your *hakama* will not entangle your feet as you later attempt to rise. Continue squatting and place your left knee on the floor first (fig. 7L.4), then your right knee (fig. 7L.5). Flatten your feet against the floor with your big toes just touching, then sit down onto your heels (fig. 7L.6).

Figures 7L.1–6. Assuming *seiza* posture

Many students find *seiza* uncomfortable at first, but with a few weeks' training, most find their knees and ankles adapting quite readily to it. For older *iaidōka* or those with injuries or infirmities that prevent them sitting in *seiza*, most *sensei* will permit them to stand instead, sometimes designating a special area for such students so as not to interfere with or distract from the performance of others.

# 7M: TATEHIZA

Unlike *seiza*, *tatehiza* did not originate as a formal sitting position, but was the posture taken by samurai while relaxing. When first experiencing the discomfort of *tatehiza*, many find it difficult to imagine it as a way of resting. It is likely, however, that *tatehiza* was one of the few comfortable positions a samurai could assume while dressed in *yoroi*, the pleated bamboo battle armor, which may account for its common usage. *Tatehiza* is often considerably uncomfortable initially, especially for students who have not first become accustomed to *seiza*. It is also less familiar to many students, so it is presented in both front (figs. 7M.1–10) and side (figs. 7M.11–20) views.

To sit in *tatehiza* from a standing position, again make sure your thumb is controlling your *tsuba*, then bend at the knees and waist and use your right hand to tuck your *hakama* behind your left knee (figs. 7M.3 and 7M.14). Even though *tatehiza* is not a formal sitting position, it is still considered rude to noisily slap your *hakama* into place. Lower yourself onto your left knee (figs. 7M.4 and 7M.15), then move your right foot to the front (figs. 7M.6–7 and 7M.16–17). Now position your left foot beneath you on its side, so that the inner ankle bone is centered under your body (figs. 7M.8 and 7M.19) and tuck the right leg of your *hakama* behind your right knee. Next, draw your right foot back even with your left knee and sit down onto your left foot so that your behind is centered on your ankle-bone (figs. 7M.9 and 7M.19). Finally, straighten your back and rest your right wrist comfortably atop your right knee (figs. 7M.10 and 7M.20). You are now in the position commonly used by samurai to relax when off duty.

*Shisei* must also be erect while seated in *tatehiza*, as shown in figure 7M.10. For most Westerners, there is a tendency to lean forward to alleviate some of the weight from the left ankle to ease the discomfort of *tatehiza*, so be sure to keep the line from your buttocks to your head as straight as possible. At first you may also feel as if your balance is precarious in *tatehiza* and be tempted to tense your upper body to remain erect, so you must make a conscious effort to keep your shoulders and upper body relaxed.

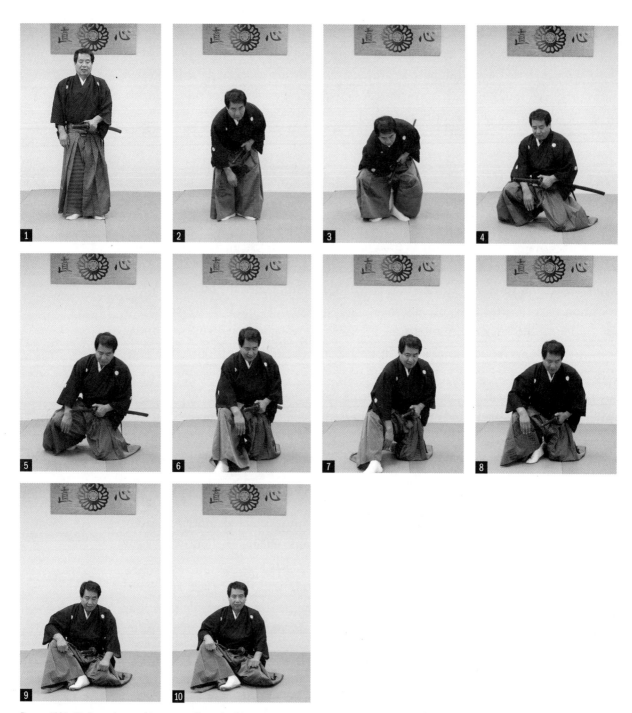

Figures 7M.1–10. Assuming *tatehiza* posture (front view)

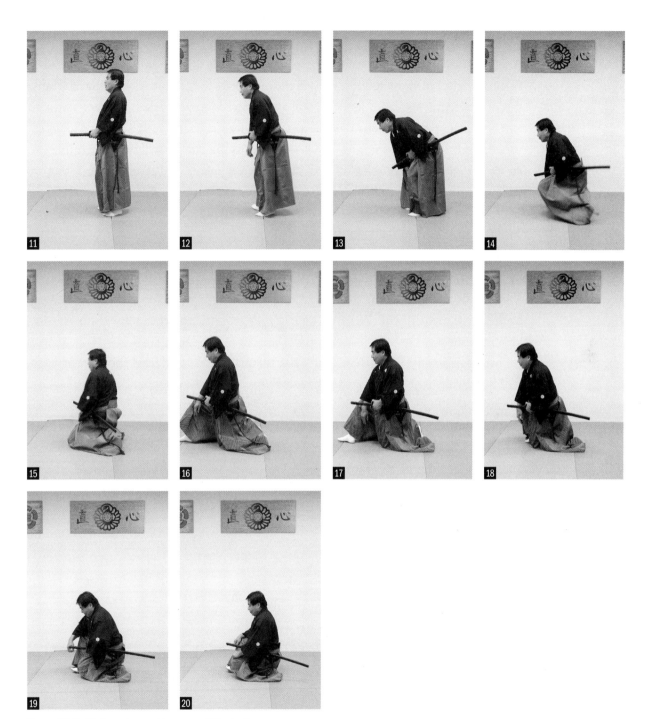

Figures 7M.11–20. Assuming *tatehiza* posture (side view)

# 7N: STANDING POSTURES

Another reason we can say that *iaijutsu* has no stances is that the standing postures used in *iaijutsu* are all identical to those used in the related art of *kenjutsu*, so we utilize the same descriptive terms for them. It should be remembered, however, that different styles do occasionally use different terms for these stances or postures, as we will attempt to note.

Probably the most basic and universal stance is the one we will typically call *seigan no kamae*. Some styles refer to it as *chūdan no kamae* ("mid-level stance"), but we will more often use the term *seigan no kamae* for this posture, since *"seigan"* (straight at the eyes) accurately describes pointing the *kissaki* directly at the opponent's eyes. Another term occasionally used is *hito no kamae* (person stance).

In *seigan no kamae*, the feet are kept shoulder width apart, separated back-to-front by the distance of a medium stride, with the front knee bent so the shin is vertical. The heel of the back foot is slightly raised (or only lightly touching the floor) and the back knee is slightly bent. When using *seigan no kamae*, the right foot is almost always kept in front (see figs. 7N.1–2).

In *seigan no kamae*, the hands grip the *tsuka* at the natural level about navel high, with the blade angled upward so the *kissaki* points at the opponent's eyes (or where the opponent's eyes would be, if he were standing at neutral distance). The right hand should push slightly forward and the left hand should pull slightly rearward, as if you are trying to stretch the *tsuka* about a quarter inch. This opposing tension stabilizes and energizes the blade. Your left hip, left hand, *tsuba*, and *kissaki* should form a straight line pointing toward the spot between your opponent's eyes so that your left hip is effectively reinforcing the sword.

Figure 7N.1. *Seigan no kamae* (front view)  Figure 7N.2. *Seigan no kamae* (side view)

It is imperative to adhere to all other elements of *kihon*—*tsuka no nigiri kata*, *chakugan*, and so on—as part of this and all other *kamae*. *Kamae* is complete structure, not merely stance or posture. *Seigan no kamae* is a neutral stance that can be used with equal effectiveness for either attack or defense. Of the various defensive postures, *seigan* is the safest, since from it can be initiated a defense against any kind of attack and the protruding sword serves as a barrier against an opponent moving too close.

*Jōdan no kamae* (high-level stance) is an attacking stance. It is sometimes called *ten no kamae* (heaven stance), because the sword is pointing skyward. It is also referred to as *hi no kamae* (fire stance), because your fighting spirit must be so strong and evident that it nearly "burns" the opponent, oppressing his spirit and resolve. Without such strong spirit behind it, *jōdan no kamae* is merely a weak and dangerously exposed posture.

The foot position for *jōdan no kamae* is a little taller than that for *seigan*, and the *left* foot is usually kept forward. The position of the feet is more akin to the *hanmi dachi* of *aikidō* or *kendō*, with the rear foot pointed outward (60 to 75 degrees, to facilitate driving forward from the ball of the foot), both knees comfortably flexed, and the feet spread about the distance of a normal walking step. In *iaijutsu*, we usually refer to this posture as *shizentai* (natural stance).

The sword is held directly overhead, with the *kissaki* angled upward at a 45- to 60-degree angle. The *tsukagashira* should be a bit forward of the forehead and the *tsuba* roughly centered above the skull. The elbows should be spread to a comfortable width, just wide enough to allow unobstructed forward vision. In samurai movies, you may see the elbows pulled quite wide, but this is done for cinematic effect only, and should not be practiced in the *dōjō*. It is vital that the upper body remain almost square to the opponent to avoid exposing the left underarm and elbow to attack. Figures 7N.3–4 show *jōdan no kamae*.

Figure 7N.3. *Jōdan no kamae* (front view)   Figure 7N.4. *Jōdan no kamae* (side view)

*Gedan no kamae* (low-level stance) is considered a defensive stance, and for this reason it is sometimes called *shubi no kamae* (defense stance) or *chi no kamae* (earth stance) because the sword is pointed toward the ground (fig. 7N.5). However, *gedan* is far from the neutral, guarded posture that is *seigan*. Instead, by deliberately exposing the head and upper body, *gedan* is actually an invitation to attack, especially when the opponent is standing in *jōdan*. If a *kiriageru* (upward cut) is initiated from *gedan*, it is impossible for an opponent in *jōdan* to block it in time. Yet if the opponent responds to this threat with an attack, it can be readily blocked or counterattacked from *gedan*.

The overall posture of *gedan no kamae* is the same *shizentai* as that for *jōdan*, except that the sword is pointed downward with the cutting edge turned slightly toward the opponent, and the stance is usually right foot forward.

Figure 7N.5. *Gedan no kamae* (front view)

Figure 7N.6. *Gedan no kamae* (side view)

Figure 7N.7. *Gedan no kamae* (reverse angle side view)

Another common stance using *shizentai* is *hassō no kamae* (eight-phase stance), sometimes called *kanshi no kamae* (watching stance), which is essentially a neutral stance, although it bears the appearance of an attacking posture. *Hassō* is a versatile posture, from which you can easily shift to *jōdan* or *seigan*, as well as directly attack or defend (see figs. 7N.8–9). For this reason, *hassō no kamae* is one of the most frequently used stances in Eishin-Ryū, especially in *kumitachi* (simulated combat exercises). Another name sometimes applied to *hassō* is *in no kamae*, *in* being the Japanese word for the better-known Chinese concept of yin—the passive, yielding component of yin and yang—although in some styles *in no kamae* is different from *hassō*.

*Hassō no kamae* again uses the same *shizentai* as that for *jōdan* and *gedan*, except that the sword is held high at the side of the body and pointed upward. The natural gripping position of the hands should cause the blade to be angled back about 45 degrees. The elbows should be held naturally, almost relaxed, as if the sword was suspended in air and your arms were hanging from it. The *tsuba* should be about the level of your jaw, about four to six inches from your right cheek. If held at the correct angle, when you sight down the tsuka and it points directly at your opponent's big toe, you are precisely in *kirima* (cutting range), as described later in this chapter.

Figure 7N.8. *Hassō no kamae* (front view)  Figure 7N.9. *Hassō no kamae* (side view)

*Waki no kamae* (figs. 7N.10–11) or *wakigamae* is also sometimes called *kanshi no kamae*, because it is also a neutral or "watching" stance. The name is sometimes shortened to *wakigamae*. Occasionally, it is referred to as *yō no kamae*, the *yō* being the *yang* to *hassō*'s *yin*, since it is more overtly aggressive in nature and appearance. In *waki no kamae*, the feet are spread wider than the stances previously described—a long stride or nearly twice shoulder width apart—with the front knee bent severely to make the stance low and stable. The sword is held at the rear hip with the edge facing outward and the blade slanting down to the rear alongside *(waki)* the body. This is by no means a defensive posture, since the sword is not in a position to readily guard. Instead, the position of the sword is hidden from the opponent's view, making it harder for him to judge its reach. This uncertainty, if coupled with strong fighting spirit (see "Kihaku," later in this chapter) as in *jōdan no kamae*, puts tremendous pressure on the opponent.

Figure 7N.10. *Waki no kamae* (front view)   Figure 7N.11. *Waki no kamae* (side view)

*Chūdan no kasumi* (middle-level haze) is something of a hybrid, combing elements of both *gedan no kamae* and *seigan no kamae*. It utilizes the same wide stance as *waki no kamae* and the angular sword position of *gedan no kamae*, but keeps the *kissaki* pointed at the opponent's eyes, like *seigan no kamae*. It is a versatile stance, since both attack and defense can readily be initiated from it. It lends itself naturally to a thrusting attack, yet the hands can easily shift to *furikaburi* for a *kirioroshi* (downward) or *kesagiri* (diagonal) cut. The power and versatility of this stance make it extremely intimidating.

Figure 7N.12. *Chūdan no kasumi* (front view)

Figure 7N.13. *Chūdan no kasumi* (side view)

# MAAI
## Distance

As soon as you begin to draw your sword for the first time, you will become aware of the concept of distance. Obviously, controlling the distance between yourself and your opponent is of life-or-death importance in *iaijutsu*.

Generally, your starting position should be the distance from which you can correctly cut the opponent by taking one full step forward. This places you out of the adversary's reach unless he takes such a step. If you are too close, you are obviously in danger, and if you are too far away, your opponent will see and deflect your attack too easily. Due to differences in body size, arm length, and speed of motion, correct *maai* varies for everyone.

To determine this safe starting distance, you must work backward from the correct attacking distance; and to determine the correct attacking distance, you must first understand how to strike with the sword. The cutting area of the blade is not the middle, as many novices suppose, and it is certainly not the portion closest to the *tsuba*. The slicing area, called the *monouchi*, is the one-third of the blade (approximately ten inches) closest to the *kissaki* (fig. 70.1), as explained in chapter 4.

If you remember that the cutting ability of the blade comes from *enshin ryoku* (centripetal force) rather than muscle strength, this is easier to understand. The closer to the *kissaki*, the faster the blade is moving at the time of impact, so the more cutting power it has. Since the blade must slice—not strike—the target, enough blade must be employed to cut deeply. The balance of speed and slicing depth predicates the ideal location of the *monouchi* as the one-third of the blade nearest the *kissaki*. In actuality, the *monouchi* is not the entire last one-third of the blade, since the three or four inches nearest the *kissaki* are susceptible to breaking, but the area indicated in figure 70.1, which does not include those last few inches.

Thus, *kirima*—the correct distance from which to effectively cut—is the distance at which, when swung naturally and correctly, the *monouchi* will strike the target immediately after the arms reach their full extension. The correct starting distance— sometimes called *mazakai* (safe distance)—is determined by taking one large or lunging step backward from *kirima*.

monouchi

Figure 70.1. *Monouchi*

Obviously, both the *mazakai* and *kirima* will vary individually, depending on your height and the reach of your arms while swinging the sword, the distance you cover in one stride, and the speed at which you can close that distance. It is therefore something you will learn and determine through practice and develop a feel for as your experience grows.

The final and perhaps most important distance involved in *iaijutsu* is that by which the opponent's blade should miss you during an attempted attack. This distance determines how far you move when evading an adversary's cut. It is important to dodge an opponent's cut so that it misses by just the slightest margin. If you move too far out of an opponent's reach, you will also have moved out of counterattacking range, so it is crucial to practice this aspect of *maai* diligently, and several Eishin-Ryū *kumitachi* (sparring exercises) provide opportunities for this.

The Japanese say: "*Issun no maai o mikiru*," which means to ascertain a distance of one inch. This entails observing the opponent's attack to determine how close his attacking momentum will carry him and how far his sword will reach toward his intended target. If you can cause your opponent to miss by just one inch, then you are well within counterattacking range immediately afterward.

To attain skill in judging the opponent's striking distance demands countless hours of training in the *dōjō*. By trial and error—often painful error—you will eventually be able to instinctively retreat just a hair's breadth beyond an attacker's reach, and in a single fluid motion step in for a counterattack that is both too quick for your adversary to block and too close for him to avoid. The highest ideal of this *maai* is sometimes called *kami no hitoe*—the thickness of a single sheet of paper—in which the opponent's sword would cut your garment but not quite graze your skin. If you reach this level of skill, you have truly mastered *maai*.

# HAPPŌ GIRI
## Eight Direction Cutting

By combining the *kihon* thus far described—*tsuka no nigirikata*, *nukitsuke*, *furikaburi*, *kirioroshi*, *chiburi*, *nōtō*, *shisei*, *chakugan*, *kokyū*, *kamae*, and *maai*—you can begin training in the fundamentals of *iaijutsu*. A helpful exercise that combines these elements is Happō Giri, the eight-direction cuts.

Begin standing with good posture (fig. 7P.1) with your *katana* in *taitō*, having already performed the essential *sahō* and *reihō*. Shift into *iaigoshi* while performing *koiguchi no kirikata* (fig. 7P.2), then step forward with your right foot and perform *nukitsuke* (first cut) as shown in figures 7P.3–4. Remaining in place, raise the sword to *furikaburi* (fig. 7P.5) and perform the second cut, *kirioroshi* (fig. 7P.6). Without moving your feet, shift the sword to *gyaku* (left side) *waki no kamae* and execute *kiriage*, an upward left-to-right diagonal cut, as depicted in figures 7P.7–8, then reverse the sword and perform *kesa-giri*, a downward right-to-left diagonal cut (figs. 7P.9–10). Now draw your right foot backward to about twice shoulder width in a stable stance while preparing the sword for a horizontal cut (fig. 7P.11), then perform the fifth cut: a left-to-right lateral *suihei-giri* (sometimes called *yoko ichimonji*) parallel to the floor (fig. 7P.12).

Figures 7P.1–11. Happō Giri exercise

Figures 7P.12–24. Happō Giri exercise

Next, step forward with the left foot while lowering the sword to *waki no kamae* (fig. 7P.13), then execute *gyaku-kiriage*, an upward right-to-left diagonal cut (fig. 7P.14), reverse the sword (fig. 7P.15) and perform *gyaku kesa-giri* (fig. 7P.16), a downward left-to-right diagonal cut. Draw the left foot back to about twice shoulder width in a stable stance while preparing for the eighth and final cut (fig. 7P.17), then perform a right-to-left horizontal *suihei-giri* (fig. 7P.18). Step forward with the right foot into *seigan no kamae* (fig. 7P.19), reverse the grip of your right hand on the *tsuka* (fig. 7P.20) and perform *gyakute nōtō* (figs. 7P.21–23). Finally, draw your left foot even with your right foot and lower your hands to your sides.

When performed in this fashion, you should finish in *seigan no kamae* with your feet in the exact positions they were in at the completion of *nukitsuke*. This allows you to not only confirm that you are taking equal-length steps when moving from one *kamae* to another, but also to repeatedly perform Happō Giri in a small or crowded space. After practicing Happō Giri a sufficient number of times, be sure to perform *sahō* and *reihō* before leaving the training area.

# KIHAKU
## Intensity

It is axiomatic that *iaijutsu* techniques executed with insufficient power and focus will be ineffective. However, as we have previously mentioned, power involves far more than simply applying muscle strength. In fact, muscle strength will often thwart the *iaijutsu* student who is attempting a powerful cutting technique. From the physical point of view, *te no uchi*, the subtleties of technique, will provide far more cutting power than sheer muscle strength.

But power is more than simply good technique as well. The driving force behind a truly powerful technique is predominantly mental. It comes from developing a single-minded focus and intensity the Japanese call *kihaku*.

*Kihaku* is a combination of several mental factors, including self-confidence, determination, belief in the cause for which we are fighting (*shinnen*), and all-out commitment. It stems from an unremitting resolve not to lose or fail. As we explained in detail in chapter 2, you are more likely to achieve a victory if you are determined not to lose rather than trying to win. Thus, the best way for a *budōka* to win is simply not to lose.

If we focus on winning, we place an expectation on ourselves that can induce unnecessary tension. The desire to win also tends to make us the aggressor, and this aggressiveness can easily lead to mistakes in our efforts to win. Conversely, if our sole objective is not to lose, we can unleash an indomitable spirit that is unencumbered by anxiety, heroic expectations, and the pressure to succeed. Instead, our mind and body are free to react naturally and instinctively to our opponent—guided by our training—and with this kind of *kihaku*, we are more likely to prevail.

These factors, in fact, all work together. If we have trained arduously, we can have justifiable faith in our physical ability. Based on this self-confidence, we can make the determination not to lose the battle we are facing. And knowing that we are fighting out of sincere and right motives for a just cause, we can make an all-out commitment to the battle without the slightest hesitation or reservation. This unrestrained fighting spirit—*kihaku*—then becomes the driving force behind the physical techniques.

*Kihaku* manifests itself in the dignity with which we conduct ourselves, knowing our cause to be just, the intensity with which we move (*kibi-kibi to shita dosa*), and the sincerity of heart (*kokoro no koma*) that is evident in our respect and poise. These are the qualities that set apart the advanced *iaijutsu* practitioner from the beginning student.

# ZANSHIN
## Warrior Spirit

*Zanshin* is a term that appears to be unique to the Japanese language; there is certainly no adequate translation of it in English. Taken literally, it means "remaining spirit," "leftover spirit," or "excess spirit," but it is usually explained as "leaving your spirit focused on the opponent." None of these terms does *zanshin* justice, however. Unfortunately, there is no easy way to define or explain *zanshin*. It is simply a state of mind that must be experienced to be understood. And once understood, it defies accurate description.

"Warrior spirit" may be the easiest way for Westerners to conceptualize *zanshin*. It is a complex state of mind that encompasses indomitable will—the will not to lose that we explained earlier—a projection of fighting spirit that should be almost palpable to the opponent, mental and physical readiness to respond to attack, and an intense state of alertness, all of which are tempered with a complete lack of fear, worry, excitement, or tension. *Zanshin* is almost a paradox in itself, since it combines the fiercest possible fighting spirit with the calm peace of mind of *heijōshin*.

When practicing *iaijutsu* technique, *zanshin* should arise as you begin inhaling your *kokyū* cleansing breaths. This would correspond to the moment a threat is perceived. This intense state of mind then continues throughout *nukitsuke*, *kirioroshi*, *chiburi*, and even *nōtō*. In fact, by its very nature, *nōtō* is one of the most crucial times in which to retain *zanshin*. It is natural for almost anyone to maintain fighting spirit while drawing the sword, blocking a strike, or cutting. But one of the most vulnerable moments for the samurai is when the battle appears to be over and the sword is being resheathed. The best time for a wounded opponent to make a dying effort to defeat you is at the midpoint of *nōtō*—the point at which the *kissaki* is just entering the *koiguchi*. From this point, you cannot draw with any power or effect, but you do not have time to complete *nōtō* and draw again. That is the reason for the slight pause at this moment during Shoden *nōtō*. It serves as a visible expression and reminder of the need for *zanshin*. Thus, *chiburi* and *nōtō* are the times when your *zanshin* should be most evident.

When the *tsuba* first contacts the left hand, there should still be a very strong sense of your *zanshin*, since your sword is still not completely in the *saya*. As a practical matter, you would not fully close the *tsuba* against the *saya*, wedging the *habaki* tightly into the *koiguchi*, where it will be difficult to redraw, until you were certain your opponent was finished. Your *zanshin* should continue, just as evident as at the height of battle, until your right hand is removed from the *tsuka-gashira* at the end of the *waza*.

It is probably because so much attention is paid to *zanshin* after the opponent has been defeated that many people have the misconception that the "remaining spirit" of *zanshin* refers only to the martial spirit that is remaining *after* the fight. Although *zanshin* is most noticeable during *chiburi* and *nōtō*—that is, "after the fight"—it must be present from the moment the technique begins.

Just as there is no simple way to describe this state, there is no simple way to learn *zanshin*. It is a state of mind that can only be developed by dedicated training. It may have been easier for the samurai of old to practice *zanshin*, because there was the very real and imminent possibility that his training would be put to the test with his life at stake. For the modern *iaidōka*, however, it takes a bit of imagination to develop *zanshin*.

Visualization helps many people practice and develop their fighting spirit. By imagining that you are actually facing an opponent while performing *iaijutsu* techniques, you can more readily enter a mental state of alert concentration. By pretending that your life is at stake, you can imitate the fierce resolve and willpower necessary to win the imaginary battle. And if you finish each *waza* anticipating that your defeated foe might spring up for one final attack, or that another enemy might be lurking nearby just waiting for a lapse in your concentration to attack, you can more easily practice that state of calm yet wary preparedness that is *zanshin*. Also, it is a mistake to limit the focus of *zanshin* to the most recently defeated opponent. A correctly executed *kirioroshi* will have assured that your last opponent poses no further threat, and your *waza* is not truly complete unless it contained a properly performed *kirioroshi*. So, instead of fixing your gaze where your last opponent would now lie during *chiburi* and *nōtō*, it is preferable to return your gaze to *enzan no metsuke* as you perform *chiburi* and *nōtō*, while maintaining intense *zanshin*. If, in fact, another adversary is lurking nearby at this point, the intensity of your *zanshin* alone should wither his spirit and prevent his attack.

*Zanshin* would hardly qualify as an aspect of *iaijutsu* if it did not have a somewhat paradoxical nature—fortunately, *zanshin* readily meets this criterion. As already mentioned, *zanshin* literally means "remaining spirit," and is often associated with the warrior spirit remaining after combat, yet it is to be present at all times, before, during, and after the battle. On the other hand, the Japanese have a saying, *Meijin ni zanshin nashi* (The supreme master has no *zanshin*). This suggests that at the highest levels of training, you no longer exhibit *zanshin*.

What this really means is that the highly advanced master has so much *zanshin* active every moment of his or her life—even during sleep—that to the untrained eye it appears that *zanshin* is absent. Instead, however, what is absent is not *zanshin*, but the lack of *zanshin*, so that in such a master there is no noticeable difference between being at rest or at the peak of mortal combat.

A final word about *zanshin* is that it underlies every other aspect of *iaijutsu*. It is the driving force behind all of the physical techniques. Its courage is manifest in the erect posture of *shisei*. It is the nearly palpable resolve-crushing spirit evident in *kamae*. It shines from the eyes to challenge the opponent in *chakugan*. It energizes every breath in *kokyū*. It emboldens the samurai to maintain correct, opponent-pressuring *maai*. And it provides the ferocious single-minded focus of *kihaku*.

# SEME

## Pressure

Closely related to *zanshin* is the principle of *seme*. *Seme* is usually translated as "pressure," but an equally appropriate term might also be "intimidation." It is a term used frequently throughout this book, especially when explaining techniques and movement. The general concept of *seme* is to always and relentlessly maintain pressure against your opponent(s) to suppress their ability to attack, to oppress their spirit, to force mistakes, and basically to dominate them. *Seme* is accomplished by a combination of technique, strategy, and samurai spirit.

Technique is used to create a credible threat to the opponent's safety. Examples of this are *seigan no kamae*, in which the *kissaki* remains pointed at the opponent's eyes as a visible threat, or keeping the *kissaki* fixed on the opponent's *seichūsen* at the completion of *yoko-chiburi*. The presence of the *kissaki* serves as a visible barrier to the opponent's ability to approach within *kirima* (cutting range) and is thus an element of *seme*.

Similarly, strategy can be a form of *seme*. For instance, by moving diagonally instead of linearly, we may be able to limit an opponent's options for attack or defense, while at the same time presenting fewer possible target areas on ourselves and exposing potential target areas on the opponent.

As explained in chapter 2, if our *bushi damashii* (samurai spirit) and determination are strong enough, an opponent may be so intimidated by it that he or she will hesitate to act, or make a mistake at a crucial moment that allows us to prevail.

By combining these three aspects of *seme*, it becomes one of our most potent weapons. As you progress in your training, you will find that *seme* is involved in practically every facet of *iaijutsu* and is the key to prevailing in battle.

# BUNKAI AND ŌYŌ
## Analysis and Application

The Japanese terms *bunkai* and *ōyō* are not typically used in *iaijutsu*. They are more commonly used in *karate-dō*, but they are applicable to all forms of *budō*, and so deserve mention here. *Bunkai* (divide and study) is the process of examining something—in this case the techniques of *iaijutsu*—by breaking it into its component parts and studying each individual part carefully to determine how and why it is effective, as well as what errors might cause it to fail and what alternatives might work better. *Ōyō* means "method of use" or "practical application."

To perform *iaijutsu waza* without consideration for their *ōyō* (practical application or use) would reduce the art to nothing more than a set of graceful movements. In order to correctly perform any *iaijutsu waza*, you must not only understand its *ōyō*, but you must also visualize yourself in the situation implied by its *ōyō* and fulfilling that purpose by your performance. For example, if the technique involves severing an opponent's leg, then your *kamae* and the angle and direction of your cut must reflect that purpose precisely. This is why, in the chapters that follow containing descriptions of the *waza* of Eishin-Ryū, we explain the *ōyō* of each *waza*.

*Bunkai* is the process by which you study each element of a technique to align your performance with its purpose (*ōyō*). In the example mentioned, in order to sever an opponent's leg, you must consider how *te no uchi* (use of the hands) will affect the angle, speed, and power of the cut to be sufficient for that purpose, what *kamae* (stance and posture) will best accomplish the intended cut, and so forth.

*Iaijutsu* is not merely following a prescribed pattern by rote, but carefully studying each movement with the goal of constantly improving your performance of it (*bunkai*) in order to achieve its intended purpose (*ōyō*). So, while you may rarely hear the terms *ōyō* and *bunkai* mentioned in the *dōjō*, they are essential practices that should be integral to your training.

# MACHIGAI
## Mistakes

In *iaijutsu*, a confrontation ends in the blink of an eye, and one of the combatants lies dead on the ground. The samurai could not afford to make a mistake. Mistakes, very simply, meant death.

On the other hand, the only way to learn an art as difficult and complex as *iaijutsu* is to make mistakes. So in one respect, you must train with an intensity of *kihaku*, as if there is no room for mistakes—as if they would be fatal—while in another respect, you must accept the fact that mistakes are a normal part of the learning process.

It is important, therefore, not to dwell on your mistakes, whether they are simply training errors in the *dōjō* or mistakes that have a serious impact in your life. If you allow errors in your past to affect your future attempts, at the very least you will find yourself losing confidence and going into a slump. At the worst, you can become so paralyzed by the fear of failure that you will no longer even try. Furthermore, your mind will inevitably try to achieve whatever you visualize. So if you keep visualizing yourself making that same old mistake over and over, you are effectively programming your subconscious to repeat it.

Instead, pay attention to your mistakes without dwelling on them. Try to determine what caused the error and how it can be corrected or avoided in the future, then *visualize yourself acting correctly*. In this way, rather than being a setback or hindrance, each mistake becomes an investment in your future success. Remember, too, that it is far better to have tried and failed—and learned from the experience—than never to have tried, never to have learned, and never to have truly lived.

# Chapter 8

# Ōmori-Ryū Seiza Waza

## Shoden Waza

初
伝
正
座

Originally, Hayashizaki-Ryū, and subsequently Eishin-Ryū, *iaijutsu* consisted only of techniques performed from the *tatehiza* (crouching) and *tachiwaza* (standing) positions. However, with the establishment of the Tokugawa Shōgunate in 1603, the status of the samurai class was further elevated, making it essential that techniques be devised to address situations that might arise during occasions of great formality or courtly ritual.

A seventeenth-century expert *(tatsujin)* in Shinkage-Ryū Kenjutsu, Ōmori Rokurōzaemon, combined five *kenjutsu kumitachi* (formal partner exercises) and *battōjutsu* (sword drawing techniques) with the social rituals of Ogasawara-Ryū Seiza Reihō (the etiquette of tea ceremonies) to create a series of formal Seiza *waza*, which begin in this traditional Japanese kneeling-seated position. The ninth-generation headmaster of Eishin-Ryū, Hayashi Rokudayū, also studied *kenjutsu* under Ōmori Rokurōzaemon and incorporated these Seiza *waza* into Eishin-Ryū Iaijutsu. In recognition of their origin, these *waza* are known as the Shoden Ōmori-Ryū Seiza *waza*.

We often explain the term *shoden* as "initial level." The Japanese word *den*, however, carries a much deeper and more interesting meaning than simply "level" or "stage." It is a complex concept with no single-word equivalent in English that does it justice. In essence, *den* is the process of personally passing knowledge and information from one generation to the next in parental fashion. Even "heritage," "transmission," or "legacy," at least in their current usage, fail to impart the richness of nuance that we find in *den*.

The Ōmori-Ryū Seiza *waza* are normally the first *waza* taught to beginning *iaijutsu* students, probably because so many of them are merely variations and practical applications of *iaijutsu* fundamentals.

Prior to the succession of seventeenth headmaster, Ōe Masamichi, all but one of the Shoden *waza* bore names different from those by which they are presently known in Eishin-Ryū, as shown below:

| Present Name | Previous Name |
|---|---|
| 1. Mae | Shohattō (First Draw) |
| 2. Migi | Satō (Left Sword) |
| 3. Hidari | Utō (Right Sword) |
| 4. Ushiro | Atari-tō (Striking Sword) |
| 5. Yaegaki | Inyō Shintai (Yin-Yang Mind and Body) |
| 6. Ukenagashi | Ryūtō (Flowing Sword) |
| 7. Kaishaku | Juntō (Assisting Sword) |
| 8. Tsukekomi | Gyakutō (Reverse Sword) |
| 9. Tsukikage | Shinchūtō (True-Motives Sword) |
| 10. Oikaze | Korantō (Running Tiger Sword) |
| 11. Nukiuchi | Nukiuchi (Sudden Attack) |

A notable feature of the Shoden *waza* is the use of the Ōmori-Ryū, or "Wet Umbrella," *chiburi*. Reread the detailed description of this *chiburi* in chapter 7, and practice it several times until you can perform it smoothly and without major noticeable flaws before practicing the *waza* in this chapter.

Another characteristic of this group of *waza* is the Shoden *nōtō*, also described in detail in chapter 7. This style of *nōtō* features broad, gracefully unhurried sweeping motions of the sword.

Review all of the fundamentals in chapter 7 in order to be able to readily follow the descriptions of *waza* in this chapter, since they are presented in much less detail here.

## 8A: MAE

The first *waza*, Mae (Front) or Seiza Mae, contains all the major elements of *kihon* in their most basic form, as described in chapter 7: *nukitsuke, furikaburi, kirioroshi, chiburi,* and *nōtō*. The simplicity of this *waza* is deceptive: while it is the easiest *waza* to learn and perform, it takes true mastery to perform it with the necessary power and precision.

Mae begins facing straight ahead in *seiza* posture (fig. 8A.1) while taking the three preparatory *kiyomeri kokyū* breaths. You are facing a single opponent, who is also seated directly in front of you. As you begin inhaling the third time, you sense his intention to attack …

Figures 8A.1–12. Ōmori-Ryū Seiza *waza:* Mae

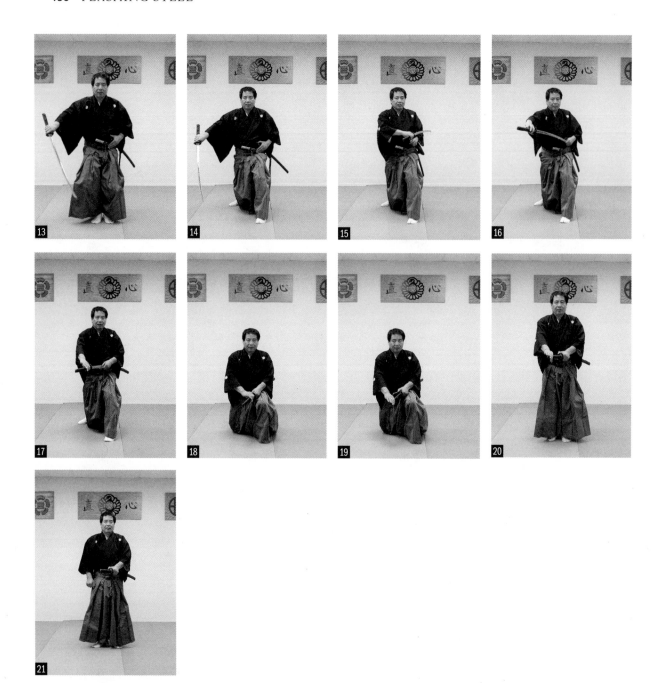

Figures 8A.13–21. Ōmori-Ryū Seiza *waza:* Mae

Perform *koiguchi no kirikata* and begin *nukitsuke* as you rise on your knees (fig. 8A.2). It is essential in all Seiza *waza* that you rise onto the balls of your feet as you begin to rise from *seiza* (fig. 8A.3). If your toes remain flat on the floor, you will be unable to push forward with your rear foot. Step forward with your right foot, still kneeling on your left knee, and complete *nukitsuke* at your shoulder level (opponent's eye level in *seiza*), as shown in figure 8A.5. Perform *furikaburi* while remaining on one knee (figs. 8A.6–7).

To increase the power and reach of *kirioroshi*, shuffle forward during the cut by pushing with the left foot while stepping farther forward with the right foot, then allowing the left foot to slide forward so that it resumes the same spacing as before (fig. 8A.9). This shuffle should draw you forward some six to twelve inches during *kirioroshi*. Follow *kirioroshi* with Ōmori-Ryū (Wet Umbrella) *chiburi*, rising to your feet by pushing up with both feet and drawing your left foot forward, even with the right, as depicted in figures 8A.10–13.

It is not necessary to reach full standing posture at the exact moment the sword completes *chiburi*. Usually, the sword finishes *chiburi* just a moment before you fully rise. Also remember to remain in *iaigoshi* when rising. While maintaining *zanshin*, slide your right foot slowly back (fig. 8A.14), then perform Shoden *nōtō* while gradually lowering onto your left knee (figs. 8A.15–18). In all Seiza *waza*, time this movement so that your right knee touches the floor at the exact moment the *tsuba* touches your left hand at the *koiguchi*. Hook your left thumb over the *tsuba*, then slide your right hand to the *tsuka-gashira* (fig. 8A.19), and rise to a standing position (fig. 8A.20). Still maintaining *zanshin*, take two steps back to reach your original starting position, as shown in figure 8A.21. At this point, now standing fully erect, remove your right hand from the *tsuka-gashira* and return it to your right side while your left hand releases the *saya* and *tsuba* and returns to your left side.

# 8B: MIGI

The second *waza*, Migi ("Right") is nearly identical to Mae, except that it begins turned 90 degrees to the right, and therefore includes a 90-degree turn to the left during *nukitsuke*. As a result, *nukitsuke* ends with the left foot forward and the foot positions are the mirror image of those in Mae. Earlier this *waza* was called Satō (Left Sword) because of this initial pivot, but the name was subsequently changed to Migi because it was less confusing to students to name it for its starting orientation.

Begin by turning 90 degrees to your right as you assume the initial *seiza* posture (fig. 8B.1), then take the three preparatory breaths. As you begin your third breath, you sense the intention of the person seated on your left to attack …

Figures 8B.1–20. Ōmori-Ryū Seiza *waza:* Migi

Perform *nukitsuke*, pivoting 90 degrees to your left as you rise and step forward with your left foot. Follow with *furikaburi* and *kirioroshi*, just as in Mae, but with your foot positions reversed. *Chiburi* and *nōtō* will also be the mirror image of Mae, after which rise to a standing position with *iaigoshi* and, maintaining *zanshin*, step back to your starting position.

# 8C: HIDARI

The third *waza*, Hidari (Left) is the mirror image of Migi, and the movements are nearly identical to Mae, except that it begins turned 90 degrees to the left (as shown in fig. 8C.1).

Figures 8C.1–20. Ōmori-Ryū Seiza *waza:* Hidari

Therefore, it begins with a 90-degree turn to the right during *nukitsuke*. Earlier this *waza* was called Utō (Right Sword) because of this initial pivot, but the name was subsequently changed to Hidari, again because it was less confusing to students to name it for the starting direction.

Begin by turning 90 degrees to your left as you take the initial *seiza* posture and begin *kiyomeri kokyū* cleansing breaths. As you inhale the third time, you sense the intention of the person on your right to attack.

Perform *nukitsuke*, pivoting 90 degrees to your right as you rise, and stepping forward with your right foot. From this point, the *waza* is performed exactly the same as Mae, with *furikaburi, kirioroshi,* Ōmori-Ryū *chiburi,* and Shoden *nōtō* while lowering onto your left knee. After securing the *tsuba* with your left thumb, slide your right hand to *the tsuka-gashira,* rise, and step back to your original starting position.

## 8D: USHIRO

Ushiro (Rear) is the fourth in the initial series of *waza*, completing the four possible directions of attack, so it begins facing rearward from your original orientation (fig. 8D.1).

Take the three cleansing breaths while in this rear-facing *seiza* posture. As you take in your third cleansing breath, you sense the intention of someone seated directly behind you to attack.

Pivot 180 degrees to your left as you perform *nukitsuke,* finishing left foot forward. For beginners it is acceptable to swing both feet 30 to 45 degrees to the right to initiate this turn, then pivot on the ball of the left foot and the right knee, but advanced students should do so without making this a separate step in the sequence (as shown in figure 8D.2). From there, exactly as in Migi, perform *furikaburi, kirioroshi,* and *chiburi,* followed by Shoden *nōtō* while lowering onto your left knee. Rise to a standing position, then take two steps back to your original starting point and place your hands at your sides.

Figures 8D.1–5. Ōmori-Ryū Seiza *waza:* Ushiro

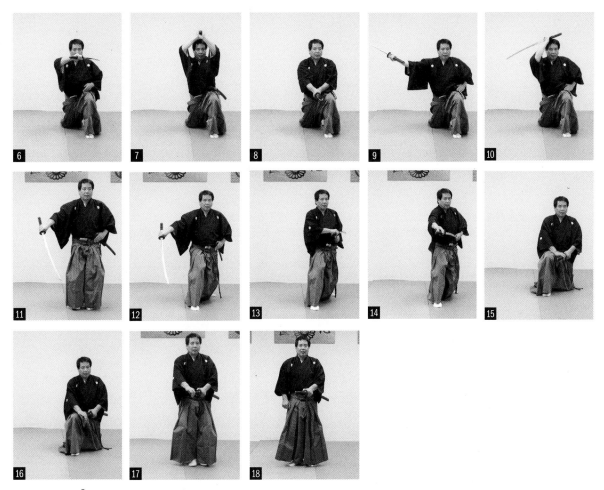

Figures 8D.6–18. Ōmori-Ryū Seiza *waza:* Ushiro

# 8E AND 8F: YAEGAKI

The fifth *waza*, Yaegaki (Barriers within Barriers), displays an increased level of complexity over the first four Shoden *waza*. In addition, there are two similar but distinct versions of Yaegaki, Omote and Ura.

The nuances of Omote and Ura are difficult to translate into simple terms. As a general rule, Omote and Ura denote opposite sides of the same object, such as the head and tail of a coin, or the two sides of a sheet of paper or a door. This meaning carries with it the notion of one side being readily visible, and the other side being hidden from view. So, while we use the simple translation of "front" and "back" for Omote and Ura, the terms also connote "apparent" and "hidden," "facing" and "reversed," or any number of similar meanings, as well as the implication of an inseparable connection between the two sides.

## 8E: YAEGAKI OMOTE

Yaegaki Omote (Front) begins facing straight ahead in *seiza* position (fig. 8E.1) exactly as in Mae. As you inhale the third cleansing breath, you sense the intent of the person in front of you to attack.

Rising to one knee, exactly as in Mae, perform *nukitsuke*, ending with your right foot forward. Rise to a three-fourths standing position during *furikaburi* (fig. 8E.6), stepping forward with your left foot, then dropping back to one knee while performing *kirioroshi*, as depicted in figures 8E.7–8.

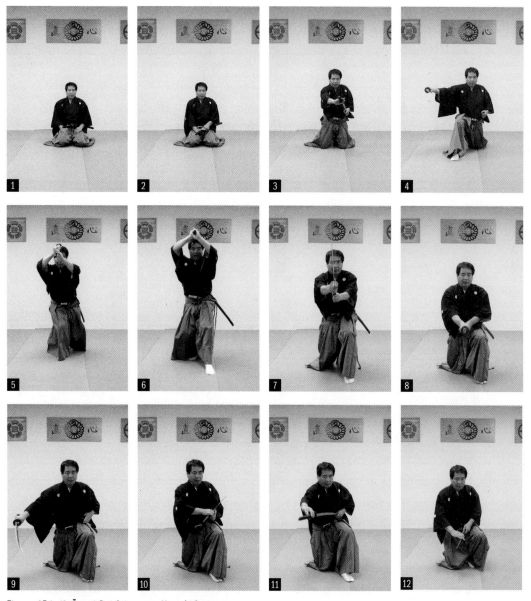

Figures 8E.1–12. Ōmori-Ryū Seiza *waza:* Yaegaki Omote

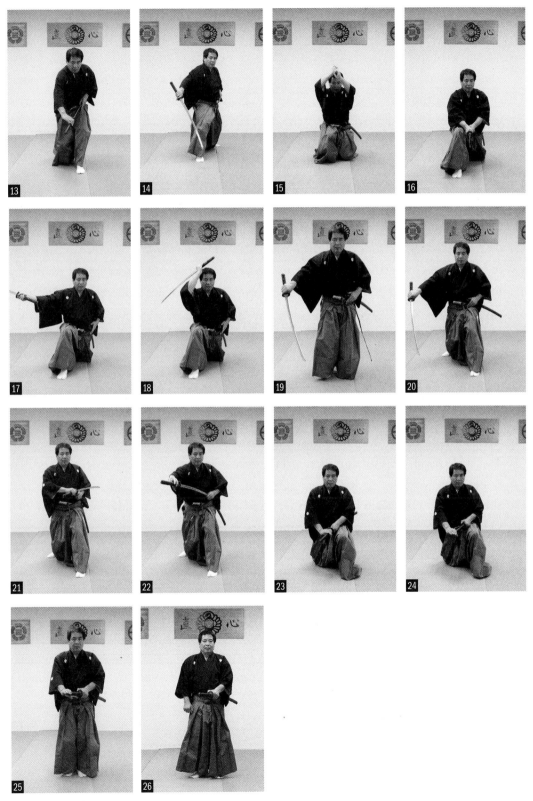

Figures 8E.13–26. Ōmori-Ryū Seiza *waza:* Yaegaki Omote

Perform Eishin-Ryū *(yoko) chiburi* (fig. 8E.9). While performing Shoden *nōtō*, slide your left foot backward at the same pace the sword is entering the *saya*, until about two-thirds of the blade is sheathed, as depicted in figure 8E.12. Begin to rise while drawing the sword at a slight downward angle, as shown in figure 8E.13, and finish using the back of the blade *(mine)* to guard in front of your right leg, as shown in figure 8E.14. Drop to one knee with your right foot forward (fig. 8E.15) during *furikaburi*. With the same lunging shuffle as in Mae, perform *kirioroshi* (fig. 8E.16). This time, follow with Ōmori-Ryū *chiburi*, rise, slide your right foot back, and finish with Shoden *nōtō*. At the completion of the *waza*, rise to your feet (remaining in *iaigoshi*), then step three steps back to your starting place and return your hands to your sides.

The basic *ōyō* (practical application) of Yaegaki Omote is a defense against a single attacker directly in front of you. As with Mae, *nukitsuke* and *kirioroshi* are used first to blind, then to finish, this opponent. However, the opponent was able to evade the brunt of your first *kirioroshi* and "plays possum" until you are vulnerable during *nōtō*, then makes a surprise attempt to sever your right leg. You use the second *nukitsuke* to block this slash to the leg, and a second *kirioroshi* to be certain he will not make another such attempt.

## 8F: YAEGAKI URA

Yaegaki Ura ("Back") begins facing straight ahead in seiza position (fig. 8F.1) just as in Yaegaki Omote. This *waza* is identical in every respect to Yaegaki Omote, except that rather than blocking an attempted cut to the leg on the second *nukitsuke*, as shown above in figure 8E.14, in Ura, *nukitsuke* cuts horizontally at shoulder level (fig. 8F.14).

From this point, Yaegaki Ura continues in exactly the same manner as Yaegaki Omote, by dropping to one knee during *furikaburi*, shuffling forward *kirioroshi*, then Ōmori-Ryū *chiburi*, rising to *iaigoshi* standing height, sliding your right foot back, and finishing with Shoden *nōtō*. At the completion of the *waza*, rise to your feet (again remaining in *iaigoshi*), then step three steps back to your initial position.

The *ōyō* for Yaegaki Ura is essentially the same as that of Omote, except that rather than the first attacker lying in wait for a second attack, a second attacker appears from concealment behind *(ura)* the first. Thus, the second *nukitsuke* and *kirioroshi* are identical to the first set.

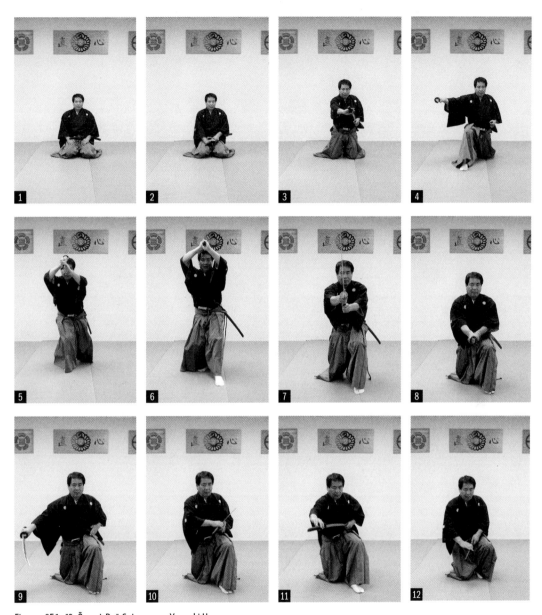

Figures 8F.1–12. Ōmori-Ryū Seiza *waza:* Yaegaki Ura

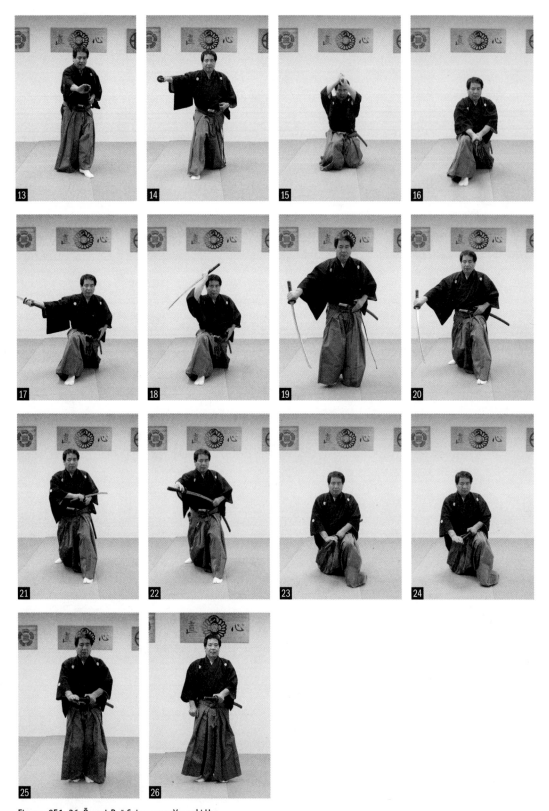

Figures 8F.1–26. Ōmori-Ryū Seiza *waza:* Yaegaki Ura

# 8G: UKENAGASHI

Since Yaegaki Omote and Ura are considered variations of the same technique, Ukenagashi (Flowing Block) is considered to be the sixth *waza* of the Shoden series.

Figures 8G.1–20. Ōmori-Ryū Seiza *waza*: Ukenagashi

Ukenagashi begins in *seiza*, facing 45 degrees to the front-right, as shown in figure 8G.1. In this *waza*, your opponent is to your left with his sword already drawn and about to attack.

As you inhale the final cleansing breath, look 45 degrees to your left and perform *koiguchi no kirikata*. Begin to rise, stepping forward with your left foot as you draw about one-third to one-half of the sword (fig. 8G.2). This makes you appear vulnerable and precipitates the opponent's strike. Rise to a standing position (with *iaigoshi*) as you complete *nukitsuke*, drawing the sword overhead, with the *kissaki* angled downward to your left, as shown in figure 8G.3, which will cause the opponent's strike to slide down the slope of your sword to your left. In a continuously flowing movement, twist your body 90 degrees to your left without yet moving your feet, and perform a one-handed *furikaburi* (fig. 8G.4), then lift your left foot (fig. 8G.5) and lunge toward the attacker with *kirioroshi* (moving your left foot first, then your right foot), bringing your feet together while maintaining *iaigoshi* (fig. 8G.6–7). With *zanshin*, step back with your left foot into a wide stance, with both knees bent for stability, and perform "drip" *chiburi*. Conclude with *gyakute nōtō*, so that you finish facing front, rise in *iaigoshi* while maintaining *zanshin*, and step back to the starting position.

*Ukenagashi* means "flowing parry," which is the hallmark technique of this *waza*. In application, the force of the opponent's *kirioroshi* striking your obliquely angled blade as you rise actually impels your counteract. In addition, the opponent is momentarily off-balanced when his attack fails to meet resistance, and these two factors assure your victory.

## 8H: KAISHAKU

The seventh Shoden *waza* is Kaishaku (Suicide Assistant). This *waza* contains proper technique and etiquette for assisting a fellow samurai in committing suicide by *seppuku*. It is easiest to understand and practice if described and illustrated in its proper context.

Kaishaku begins facing straight ahead in *seiza* with the customary three cleansing breaths. Step forward with your right foot while beginning *nukitsuke*, drawing the blade slowly and quietly, so as not to disturb the concentration of the person committing *seppuku*. As you finish *nukitsuke*, rise and step back with your right foot into a stable stance with both knees flexed (the same stance used for *waki no kamae*) and the sword held level overhead, then slowly lower the sword behind your head until the *kissaki* is at eye level. As shown in figure 8H.5, the *kissaki* should be at the edge of your left eye's peripheral vision. This is the equivalent of *furikaburi*. Pause in this position.

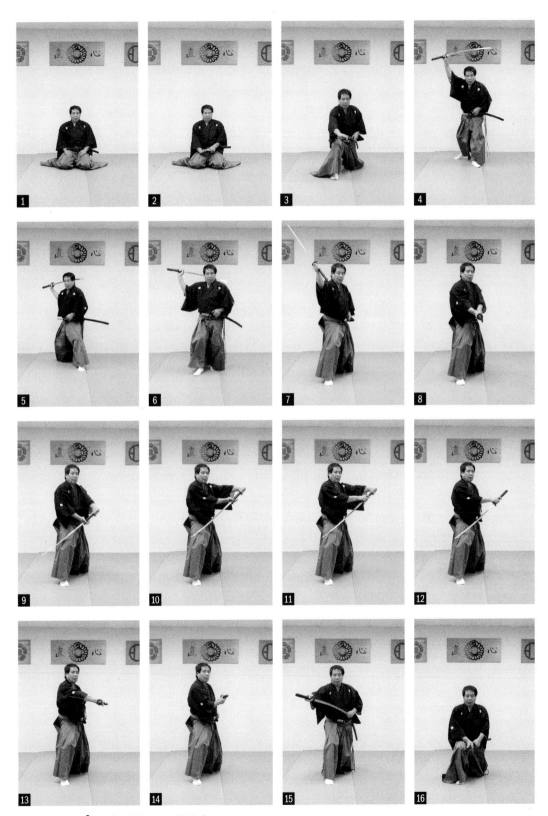

Figures 8H.1–16. Ōmori-Ryū Seiza *waza:* Kaishaku

In actual use, you would wait until the samurai you are assisting has finished the horizontal cut across his abdomen. By twisting his dagger upward toward his sternum, the samurai would signal completion of his suicide efforts. At this point, you step forward with your right foot, swinging the sword one-handed in a diagonal arc angled 45 degrees to your lower-left (fig. 8H.7), using your left hand to stop the *tsuka* and halt the travel of the blade precisely (fig. 8H.8). In actual practice, stopping the blade in this manner would prevent it from completely severing the samurai's neck, so his head would not roll or bounce away disgracefully. *Chiburi* and *nōtō* are identical to those in Ukenagashi. While maintaining *zanshin*, rise to a standing position and step back to your starting point, standing fully erect with your hands at your sides.

In ancient times, serving as *kaishakunin* to a samurai performing *seppuku* was one of the most solemn duties of a samurai. It demanded the utmost of the *kaishakunin* in every respect: skillful swordsmanship, dignified demeanor, control of emotions, concentration, adherence to formal etiquette, respect, compassion, and extreme sensitivity to the behavioral cues of the samurai committing *seppuku*. The slightest lapse in any aspect of the *kaishakunin's* duties could turn the honorable act of *seppuku* into a ghastly and humiliating spectacle. For this reason, Kaishaku was diligently practiced by samurai of sufficiently high standing that they might be called upon to serve as *kaishakunin*, and it was practiced with profound intensity and decorum.

If we wish to develop respect, compassion, *heijōshin*, and true samurai spirit, we must practice Kaishaku the same way today, treating it with the solemnity and respect we would accord to any sacred ritual. We should always perform Kaishaku as if we were really preserving the dignity and honor of a fellow samurai who is committing *seppuku*, and never take its practice lightly. Accordingly, Kaishaku is a technique that should never be performed at a public demonstration.

## 8I: TSUKEKOMI

The eighth Shoden *waza* is Tsukekomi (Seize Opportunity), which begins in *seiza* position facing straight ahead. At the inhalation of your third cleansing breath, begin *nukitsuke*, stepping forward with your right foot and leaning slightly forward to deliberately expose your head to attack, as shown in figure 8I.3, while drawing one-third to one-half of the blade. Rise quickly to full height (in *iaigoshi*), completing *nukitsuke* with the sword angled like an *ukenagashi*-type block (fig. 8I.4) that rises into *furikaburi* as part of a continuous motion (fig. 8I.5). Lunge forward, leading with your right foot into *iaigoshi* with your feet together, and execute *kiritsuke* (fig. 8I.6). *Kiritsuke* is a straight downward cut like *kirioroshi* that stops at the opponent's jaw level with the blade angled upward at about 45 degrees, cutting only the head.

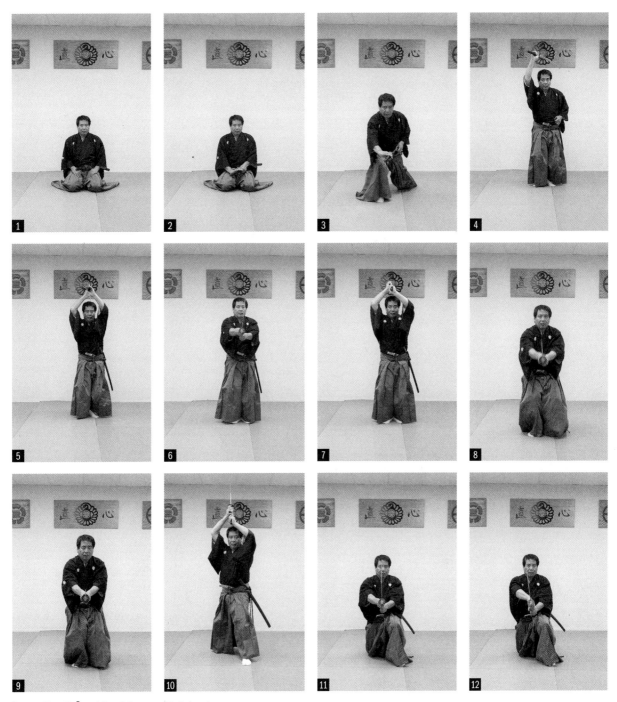

Figures 81.1–12. Ōmori-Ryū Seiza *waza:* Tsukekomi

Raise the sword overhead in a second *furikaburi*, then shuffle-step forward again with a complete *kirioroshi* (fig. 81.8), also with feet together in *iaigoshi* standing posture. Step back with the right foot into *shizentai*—natural upright stance—holding the sword in *jōdan no kamae,* as shown in figure 81.10. After a brief pause, lower onto the right knee, bringing the sword down in front of yourself, using the blade to protect your face and torso, as depicted in figure 81.11. Holding this posture, first invert your grip on the *tsuka* with your right hand (fig. 81.12), then cup your left hand beneath the *tsuba*, as shown in figure 81.13.

Figures 81.13–23. Ōmori-Ryū Seiza *waza:* Tsukekomi

Swiveling the sword on its *tsuba* in your left hand, use your right hand to turn it edge upward, pointing down and to your left at about a 45-degree angle (fig. 8I.14), then draw the *tsuka* toward your right shoulder, letting the *mine* slide across the base of the fingers in your left hand, as shown in figure 8I.15. This motion, which mimics wiping the blade on a cloth or the hem of your *hakama*, serves as *chiburi*. Use your left hand to guide the *kissaki* to your left side and the *mine* into the crook of your arm, and perform *gyakute* (reversed-hand) *nōtō* in the same manner as following a "drip" *chiburi*. Rise and return to the starting position.

Here again is a *waza* whose *ōyō* is subtle and somewhat complex. As with Ukenagashi, your opponent's sword is already drawn and ready to attack. Your apparent vulnerability as you begin *nukitsuke* (fig. 8I.3) lures the attacker into striking prematurely. In this case, you rise holding your sword in an Ukenagashi-type blocking position as a precaution, but your rearward movement should completely evade the opponent's cut. With the opponent's attack thwarted, you then have the opportunity for counterattack. In this case, either your first *kiritsuke* is not fully effective, requiring the follow-up *kirioroshi*, or—as in the case of Yaegaki Ura—a second attacker was lurking behind the first.

# 8J: TSUKIKAGE

Tsukikage (Moon Shadow), the ninth *waza* in the Shoden series, begins in *seiza* facing 45 degrees to the left (fig. 8J.1). As you begin your third *kiyomeri kokyū* breath, look to your right as you grasp the *tsuka* in preparation for *nukitsuke*. Rise to a semi-standing position (in *iaigoshi*) during *nukitsuke*, cutting upward with the blade angled upward at about a 45-degree angle as shown in figure 8J.4 to the underside of the opponent's arms as he attempts *kirioroshi*.

Maintaining *iaigoshi* and holding the sword in this upward-angled position— with the feeling that you are keeping your head protected by the blade—step forward with your left foot (fig. 8J.6). As you step forward next with your right foot, perform *furikaburi* then *kirioroshi* in a continuous motion so that the blade completes the downward cut as your right foot lands (figs. 8J.7–8). Ōmori-Ryū *chiburi* is performed from a *standing* position in Tsukikage.

Step back with your right foot and also do Shoden *nōtō* in a standing position. Do not lower onto one knee during *nōtō* in Tsukikage. Step back to your starting point after completing *nōtō*.

Tsukikage is another situation in which the attacker is already bearing down on you, sword drawn. As he strikes at your unguarded head, you use *nukitsuke* to slash his forearms as they swing his sword down at you (fig. 8J.4). After driving forward to off-balance him and push his arms back, you finish the attacker with *kirioroshi*.

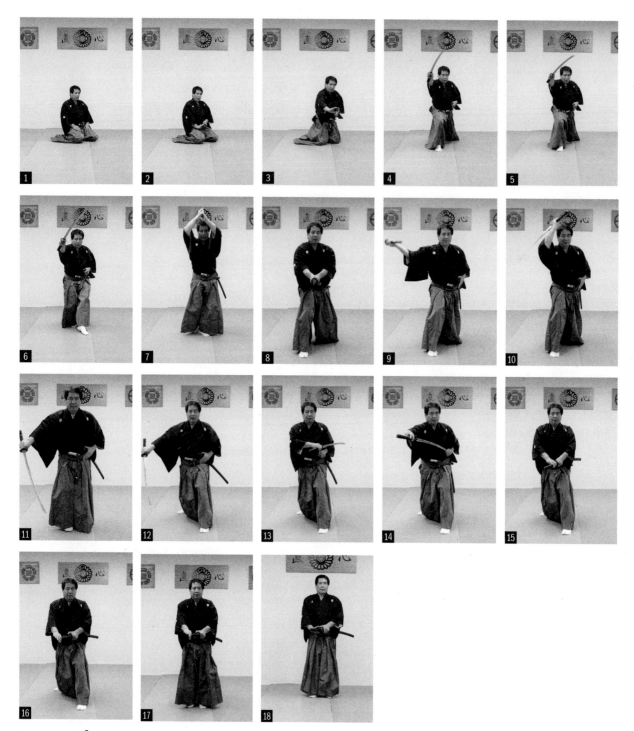

Figures 8J.1–18. Ōmori-Ryū Seiza *waza:* Tsukikage

# 8K: OIKAZE

Oikaze (Chase the Wind), the tenth Shoden *waza,* is the only one that begins from a standing position. It is also the first *waza* students learn that employs *chidori-ashi* footwork. A *chidori* (literally "thousand birds") is a plover, a seabird commonly seen at Japanese shorelines and beaches. The *chidori* is known for its peculiar running style, in which it takes extremely small, rapid steps. *Chidori-ashi* is a running method that imitates this pattern. By taking many small, fast steps on the balls of the feet, it not only helps the runner accelerate faster from a standstill, but allows the runner to change direction quickly, so it is used when chasing an adversary who is likely to zig and zag unexpectedly to evade pursuit. Its use can also be symbolic of having run much farther than the distance actually covered using *chidori-ashi.*

As you inhale the third cleansing breath, rise onto your tiptoes as you grasp the *tsuka* in preparation for *nukitsuke,* then crouch slightly forward into *iaigoshi* as you perform *koiguchi no kirikata.* Run forward in *chidori-ashi* (figs. 8K.3–6) as you begin *nukitsuke,* taking two or three normal-size steps (figs. 8K.7–9) as you complete the level draw after covering a distance of about ten to fifteen feet (fig. 8K.10) with your right foot leading. Step forward with the left foot during *furikaburi,* then another step with the right foot during *kirioroshi,* as shown in figure 8K.12. Ōmori-Ryū *chiburi* is again performed from a *standing* position in Oikaze, followed by a standing Shoden *nōtō,* then return to your starting point.

The situation in Oikaze may seem troubling at first, because it is obvious that you are chasing someone and cutting them down from behind. However, Oikaze involves a condition known in Japanese as *jōiuchi* (orders from above), in which you have been instructed to either capture or execute an enemy or criminal who flees at the sight of you. You are carrying out your duty as an official of the sovereign government. You are acting lawfully, morally, and have no choice in the matter. In this situation, *nukitsuke* would either be used to hamstring the opponent as he runs, or blind him as he turns to fight. *Kirioroshi* of course follows to finish him with dignity.

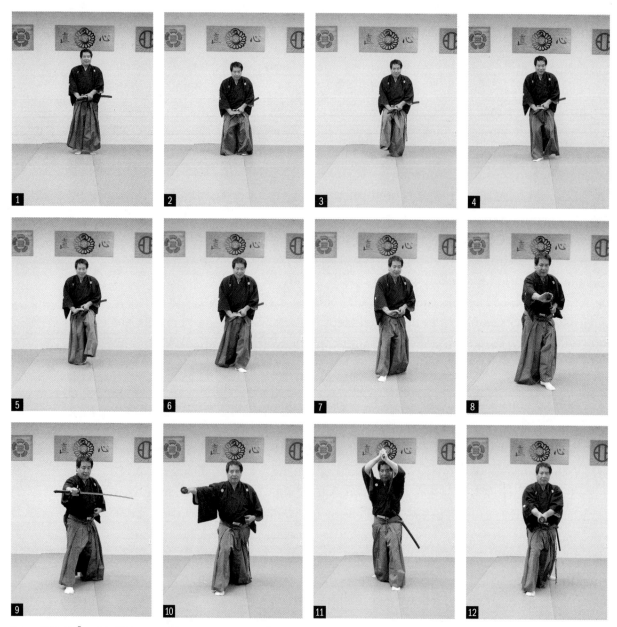

Figures 8K.1–12. Ōmori-Ryū Seiza *waza:* Oikaze

Figures 8K.13–21. Ōmori-Ryū Seiza *waza:* Oikaze

Figures 8L.1–14. Ōmori-Ryū Seiza *waza:* Nukiuchi

## 8L: NUKIUCHI

Last in the Shoden series, Nukiuchi (Sudden Attack) begins facing straight ahead in *seiza* posture. On your third cleansing breath, grasp the *tsuka* and perform *koiguchi no kirikata*, then draw the sword straight up so that *nukitsuke* becomes *furikaburi* in a single motion as you rise up tall on your knees and get set on the balls of your feet (fig. 8L.4).

During *kirioroshi*, spread your knees wide for balance and stability while remaining on the balls of your feet. Do not allow your sword to strike the floor during *kirioroshi* (fig. 8L.7). As you perform a *yoko* (Eishin-Ryū) *chiburi* (fig. 8L.8), draw your knees back into the proper width for *seiza*, which will raise your hips and allow Shoden *nōtō* without your *kojiri* striking the floor. Remain on the balls of your feet during *nōtō* and gradually settle back onto your heels just as the *tsuba* meets your left hand (fig. 8L.11). After you slide your right hand to the *tsuka-gashira*, flatten your feet against the floor, and lower yourself into *seiza* position.

The *ōyō* for Nukiuchi involves another instance of *jōiuchi*. In this *waza*, it is readily apparent that you are slaying someone who is bowing to you, which might seem an underhanded thing for a samurai to do. In this situation, however, rather than fleeing as did the adversary in Oikaze—either being ignorant of, or accepting his fate—the enemy bows to you, giving you the opportunity to end his life with merciful speed.

# Chapter 9

# Chūden Tatehiza Waza

中伝立膝

## Chūden Waza

The techniques that made up Hayashizaki-Ryū during its formative years were predominantly those we now refer to as the Okuden *waza*, including both the Okuden Suwariwaza performed from *tatehiza* (crouching) and most of the Okuden Tachiwaza (standing) techniques.

However, with the adaptation of Hayashizaki-Ryū techniques to the slightly shorter *katana* by the seventh-generation headmaster, Hasegawa Eishin, additional techniques were added to the style. The Chūden Tatehiza *waza*—or at least most of them—were among those added by Hasegawa Eishin when the style took on his name. Unlike the Shoden *waza*, the Chūden *waza* were not renamed by the seventeenth headmaster, Ōe Masamichi.

In chapter 8 we explained the meaning of *den*, as in Shoden and Chūden. Just as we usually refer to Shoden as "initial level" or "beginning level" techniques, we describe Chūden *waza* as "middle level" or "intermediate level" techniques.

One characteristic of Chūden *waza* is that all but one (Makkō) begin in *tatehiza* posture. *Tatehiza* (Standing Knee) is a posture that most Westerners find particularly uncomfortable, but which the samurai of feudal Japan frequently used when relaxing while wearing *yoroi*, the wide-woven bamboo armor common to that age. A samurai in *yoroi* could not comfortably sit in *seiza* or cross-legged in *agura*, which probably accounts for the use of *tatehiza* in nearly half the techniques of Eishin-Ryū.

To assume the *tatehiza* position, squat as though preparing to sit in *seiza* and use your right hand to sweep your *hakama* free of your left leg as you lower onto your left knee. Tuck your left foot beneath you and sit on it with the ankle bone centered between your buttocks. The right foot remains flat on the floor, with the knee elevated. A more thorough explanation with illustrations is provided in chapter 7 under the heading "Tatehiza." At the beginning of a *waza*, your hands should be resting in loosely clenched fists atop your right knee and left thigh while you perform your preparatory *kiyomeri kokyū* breathing.

Because *tatehiza* was a position used for resting, most of the techniques in the Chūden series are noticeably more defensive in nature than those found in Shoden or Okuden *waza*, since they involve responses to a surprise attack. This is apparent in the fact that many of the techniques begin by moving away from the direction of attack, rather than toward the attacker, as is more common in the Shoden *waza*.

Two other characteristics of this series of *waza* are that Eishin-Ryū *chiburi*—the "flicking" type—is used exclusively, and Chūden *nōtō* is also exclusively employed.

Remember from chapter 7 that Chūden *nōtō* differs from Shoden *nōtō* in that when the *mine* is placed along the left forearm, only one-half to two-thirds of the blade is aligned on the arm, rather than the entire blade. From this point, the blade is drawn forward more quickly than in Shoden *nōtō*. Once the *kissaki* drops into the *koiguchi*, however, the blade is sheathed at about the same steady pace as in Shoden *nōtō*.

Although the Chūden *waza* are now sometimes taught earlier in a student's training, traditionally they were taught about the time the student entered the Ha stage of Shu ▪ Ha ▪ Ri (see chapter 5), while during the Shu phase, the student trained predominantly in the Shoden *waza* (chapter 8) and Tachiuchi no Kurai (chapter 15).

## 9A: YOKOGUMO

The first Chūden *waza*, Yokogumo (Cloud Bank), is essentially a *tatehiza* equivalent of Mae in the Shoden *waza*. Yokogumo begins facing straight ahead in *tatehiza* posture (fig. 9A.1) while taking the *kiyomeri kokyū*. As you inhale the third time, raise your hands to the *tsuka* and perform *koiguchi no kirikata*. As with the Seiza *waza*, in Chūden *waza* it is essential that you simultaneously set the ball of your left foot on the floor (fig. 9A.3) as you perform *nukitsuke*, so that you can push forward with your rear foot. Finish *nukitsuke* by stepping forward with your right foot as shown in figure 9A.7.

Note: As a more advanced variation of this *waza*, you may step backward with the left foot during *nukitsuke*. Yokogumo is usually practiced with the forward step described here, since it is easier to perform in this fashion, but the backward step is more consistent with the nature of a defense against a surprise attack and should be mastered by intermediate to advanced students.

Perform *furikaburi* while scooting your left knee forward for a better purchase (fig. 9A.8), then shuffle forward to increase the power of *kirioroshi*, while remaining in a kneeling position as shown in figure 9A.9. Follow with Eishin-Ryū *(yoko) chiburi*. Note that in Chūden *waza*, you remain in the kneeling posture during *chiburi*, rather than rising to your feet as in the Shoden *waza*. *Nōtō* is also performed a bit differently in *tatehiza* posture.

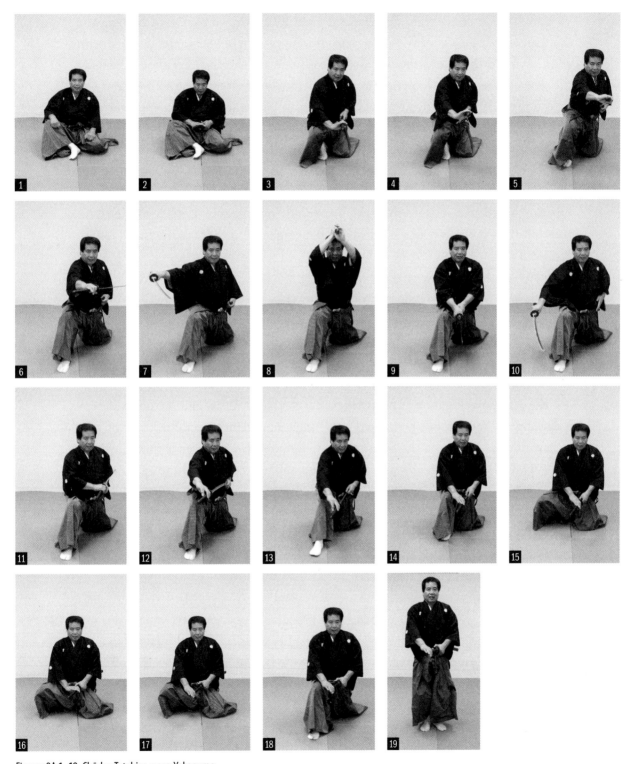

Figures 9A.1–19. Chūden Tatehiza *waza:* Yokogumo

While the sword is being sheathed, the right foot is drawn backward at about the same speed that the sword is entering the *saya*. As your right heel comes into line with your left knee, the sword should be about 80 percent sheathed. Without changing the speed of the moving foot, slide it in a small clockwise circular motion—about one foot in diameter—so that the *tsuba* contacts your left hand at the same instant your right heel comes to rest beside your left heel in a squatting position (fig. 9A.16).

Notice from the illustration that your body will have turned slightly to the right as your right foot made this circular motion. Try to minimize this twisting action of the torso, so you remain facing as directly as possible to the front, even though your hips are turned somewhat to the right. You should now be squatting on your heels as your left thumb hooks over the *tsuba*, and your right hand slides to the *tsuka-gashira* (fig. 9A.17).

Step forward with your right foot, reaching much the same position as at the end of *nukitsuke* (fig. 9A.18), and rise to a standing position (in *iaigoshi*), sliding your left foot forward to meet your right. Take two or three steps back to reach your original starting position. At this point, now standing fully erect, remove your right hand from the *tsuka-gashira* and return it to your right side while your left hand releases the *saya* and *tsuba* and returns to your left side to complete the *waza*.

The *ōyō* for Yokogumo is nearly identical to that of Mae, and it, too, is deceptively simple. You are being attacked by a single opponent directly in front of you. A key difference between the Shoden and Chūden *waza*, however, is that in *chūden* the opponents are assumed to be more skillful and aggressive than the opponents in Shoden *waza*, which is why you must initially retreat from attacks in several Chūden *waza*. By sensing his intention to attack before he acts, you are able to draw more quickly, slashing his eyes to blind him, thus gaining the time to prepare for and execute *kirioroshi*.

# 9B: TORA NO ISSOKU

The second Chūden *waza*, Tora no Issoku (One Leg of a Tiger), begins facing straight ahead in *tatehiza* posture (see fig. 9B.1). As you take your third cleansing breath, begin *nukitsuke*, rising and drawing the *tsuka* at a slightly downward angle, stepping back with your left foot and blocking in front of your right leg (with the blade edge forward) as shown in figure 9B.5. During *furikaburi*, drop to one knee with your right foot leading, then shuffle forward while performing *kirioroshi*. Tora no Issoku ends identically to Yokogumo, with Eishin-Ryū *chiburi* and Chūden *tatehiza nōtō*, then rising and returning to your starting point.

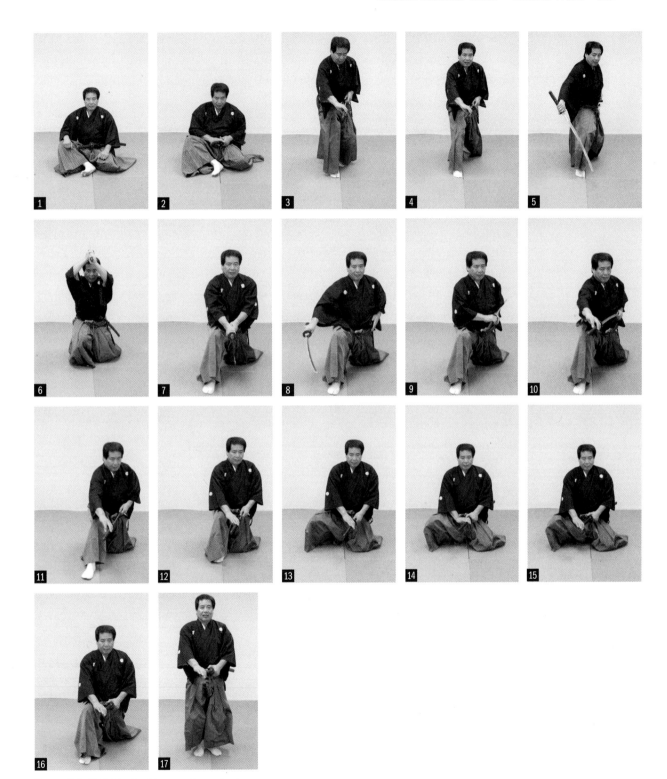

Figures 9B.1–17. Chūden Tatehiza *waza:* Tora no Issoku

The application for Tora no Issoku is only slightly different than that for Yokogumo. Your attacker is directly in front of you. In this case, you have not beaten him to the draw, however. Instead, you must use *nukitsuke* to block his *nukitsuke* attack to your leading leg, then follow with *kirioroshi*.

## 9C: INAZUMA

The third *waza*, Inazuma (Lightning), begins facing straight ahead in *tatehiza* posture.

As you inhale the third breath, begin *nukitsuke.* As you rise and step back with your left foot, use *nukitsuke* to cut upward into the underside of the opponent's arms in a fashion similar to the *nukitsuke* of the Shoden *waza*, Tsukikage (fig. 9C.4). Drive your sword forward (fig. 9C.5) as you drop to one knee, right foot leading, during *furikaburi* (fig. 9C.6), then shuffle forward while performing *kirioroshi* (fig. 9C.7). Inazuma also ends identically to Yokogumo, with Eishin-Ryū *chiburi*, and Chūden *tatehiza nōtō.* Rise to standing position and step back to your starting point.

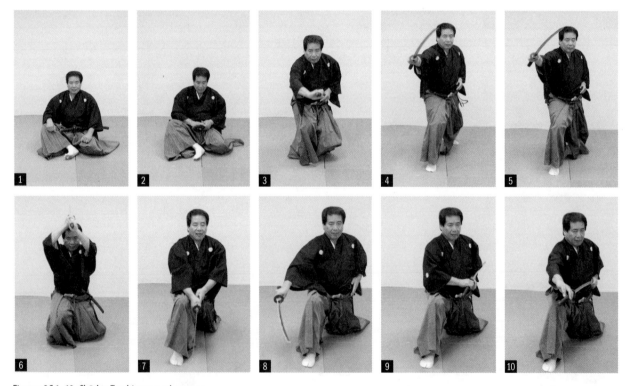

Figures 9C.1–10. Chūden Tatehiza *waza:* Inazuma

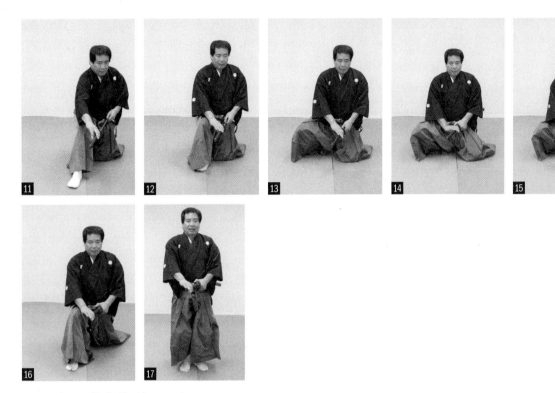

Figures 9C.11–17. Chūden Tatehiza *waza:* Inazuma

In Inazuma, your opponent is again attacking from your front. This time, however, his sword was already drawn and he is attacking with *kirioroshi.* Your upward *nukitsuke* slashes his arms just as they reach full extension during *kirioroshi,* then you force his arms back and finish him with a *kirioroshi* of your own.

# 9D: UKIGUMO

Ukigumo (Floating Clouds) is the fourth in this Chūden series of *waza,* and begins in *tatehiza* posture facing 90 degrees to the left of your normal orientation.

Note: In order to provide the best perspective, the photographs are shown at a 45-degree angle to the left, rather than at 90 degrees, with the exception of figure 9D.1, which is face-on. When performing Ukigumo, remember to begin facing 90 degrees to the left, so that you finish facing directly forward, not 45 degrees to the right, as shown in the photographs.

On the third breath of *kokyū,* grasp the *tsuka* with your left hand and rise, stepping to your left as you twist the *tsuka* a half-circle counterclockwise, ending back at your left hip as shown in figure 9D.2. Your right hand should still be resting at your right thigh. While stepping across with your left foot in front of your right, grasp the *tsuka* with your right hand and circle it clockwise, beginning *nukitsuke* as the *tsuka* rises past the six o'clock position (figs. 9D.4–5). As you complete *nukitsuke*, turn your body slightly to the left, aligning your shoulders with the blade and lowering your center of gravity by bending both knees slightly and twisting your left ankle so your weight rests on the outer edge of the foot (fig. 9D.6).

Without allowing the blade to move, turn your body one quarter turn to the right (see fig. 9D.7) and place the palm of your left hand against the *mine*. Step back with your right foot and drop to one knee, turning your body another 45 degrees while pushing the blade downward to your right until it is pointing almost straight out from your right knee, as shown in figure 9D.8. Use your left hand to gently "flip" the blade upward during *furikaburi* (fig. 9D.9), then perform *kirioroshi* at a slight angle down and to the left, ending with your right hand just to the left of your left knee, as shown in figure 9D.10. With your left foot still forward, perform Eishin-Ryū *chiburi*, and Chūden *tatehiza nōtō*. Rise to standing position and step back to your starting point, then place your hands at your side.

Figures 9D.1–10. Chūden Tatehiza *waza*: Ukigumo

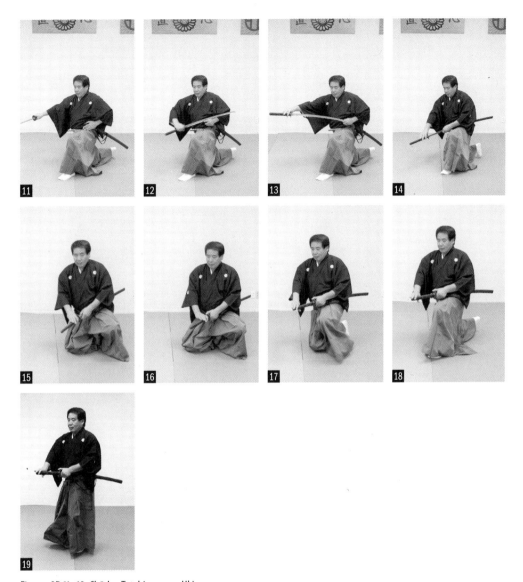

Figures 9D.11–19. Chūden Tatehiza *waza:* Ukigumo

Ukigumo anticipates that you are seated in the midst of a group of people when one or more attack you. The circular movements that give Ukigumo its name (Floating Clouds) are used to avoid striking other people seated around you as you avoid an opponent's attempt to grab your *tsuka* to prevent you from drawing. Without these movements, it is likely that your sword would bump against or entangle with the bystanders, hindering your ability to draw and defend yourself.

## 9E: YAMAOROSHI

The fifth Chūden *waza*, Yamaoroshi (Mountain Wind), begins facing 90 degrees to the left in *tatehiza*. As you inhale the third cleansing breath, look to your right (at about a 45-degree angle) as you grasp the *tsuka* with both hands, then step at a 45-degree angle to your right as you rise to one knee, twisting the *tsuka* in a clockwise circle and striking with the *tsukagashira*.

Figures 9E.1–12. Chūden Tatehiza *waza:* Yamaoroshi

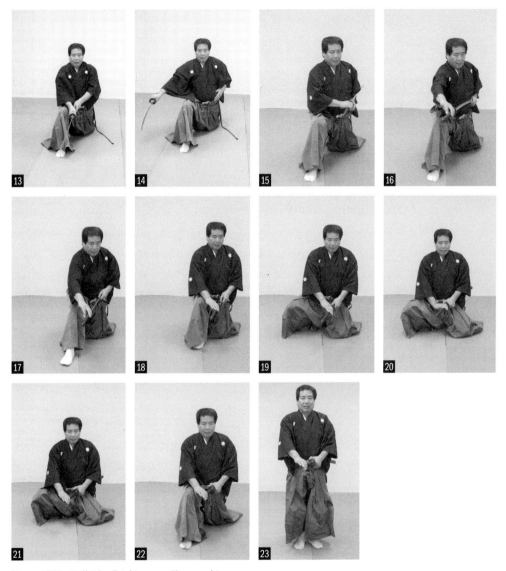

Figures 9E.13–23. Chūden Tatehiza *waza:* Yamaoroshi

This action avoids an opponent's attempt to grab your *tsuka* and strikes the opponent in the face. *Nukitsuke* is performed by drawing all but the last few inches of the blade, then using a powerful snap of your right wrist with a simultaneous leftward twist of your hips as your left foot slides forward almost to your right foot to perform *saya-banari,* finishing with the blade angled upward at about 45 degrees, as depicted in figures 9E.5–7.

Without allowing the sword to move from the finish of *nukitsuke*, place the palm of your hand on the *mine* at about midway along the blade, turn your body 90 degrees to the right, extend your right leg, then push the blade horizontally to the right while shifting your body weight toward your right leg, as depicted in figures 9E.8–10. Use your left hand to gently "flip" the blade upward during *furikaburi*, while sliding your body and left foot to the right so that you scoot beneath the overhead blade, then perform *kirioroshi* straight downward with a small step forward with your right foot (fig. 9E.13). From this position, perform Eishin-Ryū *chiburi* and Chūden *tatehiza nōtō*, then rise to standing position and step back to your starting point.

The *ōyō* for Yamaoroshi is another defense against an attempt to grab your *tsuka*. This time, rather than being seated directly to your right, as in Ukigumo, your opponent is seated diagonally in front and to the right of you. As he reaches for your *tsuka*, you twist the *tsuka* away from—or out of—his grasp, then strike his face with the *tsuka-gashira* (fig. 9E.4), stunning him just long enough for you to counterattack with *nukitsuke* (fig. 9E.7), slash the blade free (fig. 9E.10), and finish him with *kirioroshi* (fig. 9E.13). This swirling, slashing counterattack brings to mind the harsh icy winds that blow down the slope of a mountain, hence the name Yamaoroshi.

# 9F: IWANAMI

Iwanami (Waves Breaking against the Rocks) is the sixth *waza* of the Chūden series. It begins in *tatehiza*, facing 90 degrees to the right (fig. 9F.1). As you inhale the final cleansing breath, look 90 degrees to your left with your peripheral vision, and begin to rise, stepping back with your left foot as you draw about three-fourths of the sword at a slight downward angle (fig. 9F.3). Place the fingertips of your left hand against the *mine* to guide the last few inches of the blade from the *saya* (fig. 9F.4), then pivot 90 degrees to your left while using both hands to turn the blade over as you rise to a standing position (with *iaigoshi*), as shown in figure 9F.5. Stutter-step with your right foot to confuse your opponent's timing, then step forward with your right foot while dropping to one knee and thrusting the blade forward with an upward rolling motion, using your left hand to steady and guide the blade, as depicted in figure 9F.7. Leaving your left hand in position against the *mine*, twist the blade 90 degrees to your right, step sideways with your right foot, and shuffle to your right while pushing the blade horizontally to slash it free of your opponent (figs. 9F.8–9). As in Ukigumo and Yamaoroshi, use the fingers of your left hand to "flip" the blade overhead during *furikaburi*, while simultaneously sliding your body beneath the upraised sword. Then, with a slight forward step of the right foot, perform *kirioroshi* straight down to finish your attacker before performing Eishin-Ryū *chiburi* and Chūden *tatehiza nōtō*. Rise to standing position and step back to your starting point.

Iwanami involves an attack initiated from your left side. You draw and prepare to thrust (fig. 9F.5), then use the stutter-step to throw the opponent's timing off as you perform a reinforced thrust that enters beneath the opponent's sternum and is driven upward into the chest. The upward curling motion of this thrust is reminiscent of a wave crashing against a rocky shoreline, giving the *waza* its name.

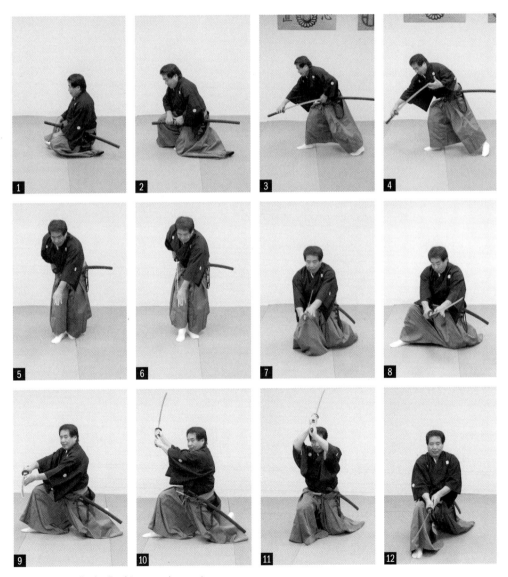

Figures 9F.1–12. Chūden Tatehiza *waza:* Iwanami

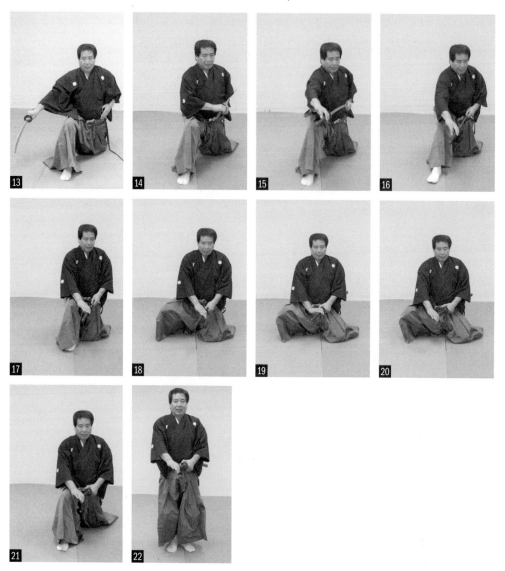

Figures 9F.13–22. Chūden Tatehiza *waza:* Iwanami

## 9G: UROKOGAESHI

The seventh Chūden *waza* is Urokogaeshi (Sudden Turn). This *waza* is the Chūden equivalent of Migi in the Shoden *waza*, so it begins facing 90 degrees to the right in *tatehiza* posture.

As you take your third cleansing breath, look 90 degrees to your left, then perform a level *nukitsuke*, stepping rearward with your left foot in a sharp left turn (fig. 9G.2–6). Drop to one knee, with your right foot forward during *furikaburi*, followed by *kirioroshi*, Eishin-Ryū *chiburi*, and Chūden *tatehiza nōtō*. Rise to standing position and step back to your starting point.

The attack in Urokogaeshi is coming from your left side, and the *ōyō* is essentially the same as in Migi: sensing an adversary's intention to attack, you turn suddenly and slash across the opponent's eyes with *nukitsuke*, then finish with *kirioroshi*. Our translation of the name Urokogaeshi as "Sudden Turn," while descriptive of its technique, fails to capture the full imagery of the original Japanese. *Uroko* means "fish scales," and Urokogaeshi describes the way a fish twists itself nearly in half, its scales flashing in the water, as it turns from peril. This is the character you should seek in Urokogaeshi: a quick, twisting turn and the bright flash of *nukitsuke* at the onslaught of danger.

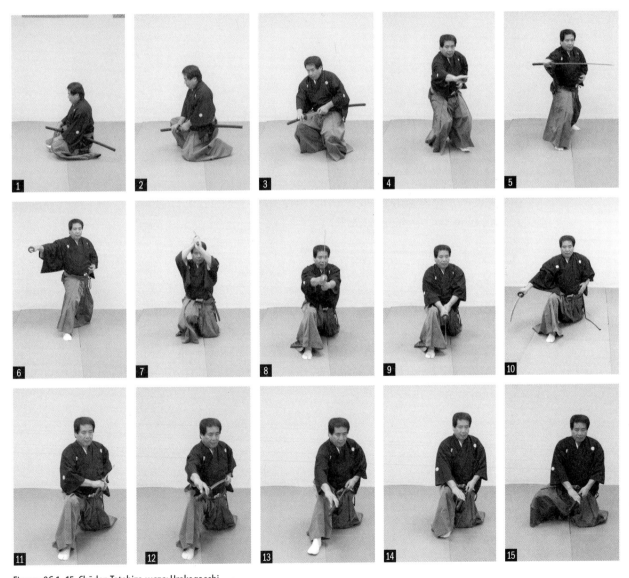

Figures 9G.1–15. Chūden Tatehiza *waza:* Urokogaeshi

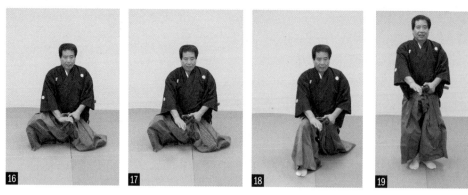

Figures 9G.16–19. Chūden Tatehiza *waza:* Urokogaeshi

## 9H: NAMIGAESHI

The eighth Chūden *waza* is Namigaeshi (Returning Wave), the *tatehiza* equivalent of Ushiro in the Shoden *waza*. Thus, Namigaeshi begins facing to the rear. At the inhalation of your third cleansing breath, perform *nukitsuke*, pivoting 180 degrees to your left and rise with a level, standing draw (figs. 9H.2–8). Drop to one knee, right foot forward, during *furikaburi*, then perform *kirioroshi*, Eishin-Ryū *chiburi*, and Chūden *tatehiza nōtō*. Rise to standing position and step back to your starting point.

Namigaeshi is basically the Chūden equivalent of Seiza Ushiro, so its *ōyō* is essentially the same. As you sense an attack from the rear, you peek over your left shoulder, turn during *nukitsuke*, and slash your opponent's eyes, then finish him with *kirioroshi*. With its power derived from turning sharply in the opposite direction of the movement of the sword during *nukitsuke*, *namigaeshi* is reminiscent of the manner in which one wave is drawn from the shoreline by the undertow created by the wave following it.

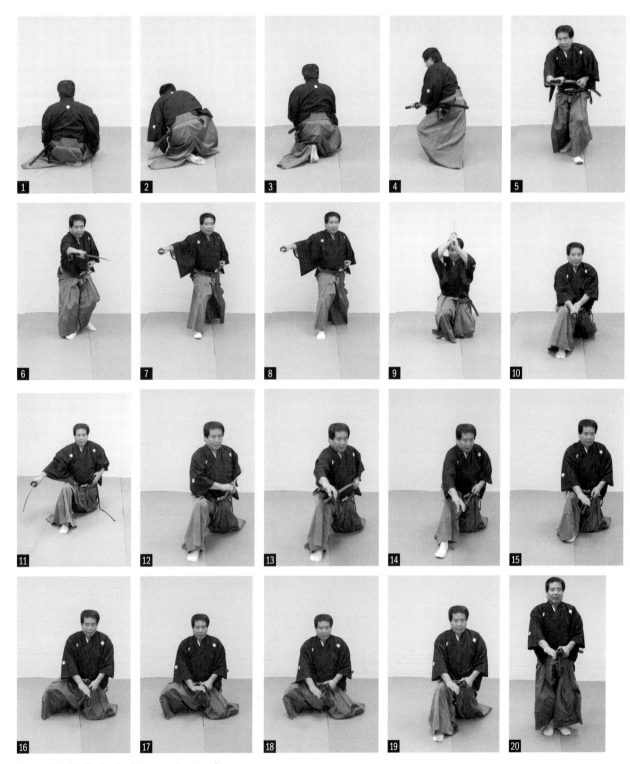

Figures 9H.1–20. Chūden Tatehiza *waza:* Namigaeshi

## 91: TAKIOTOSHI

Takiotoshi (Cascading Waterfall), the ninth *waza* in the Chūden series, begins in *tatehiza* facing to the rear. This *waza* is a defense against an attacker who grabs the end of your *saya* (the *kojiri*) and raises it so you will be unable to draw in defense against another attacker in front of you.

As you take your final cleansing breath, glance over your left shoulder as you grasp the *tsuka* while stepping back with your left foot (fig. 91.2) and performing *koiguchi no kirikata*. Rise to a standing position (in *iaigoshi*) with a shuffle to the rear while thrusting sharply downward on the *tsuka* to break the opponent's grip, as shown in figure 91.3.

Figures 91.1–8. Chūden Tatehiza *waza:* Takiotoshi

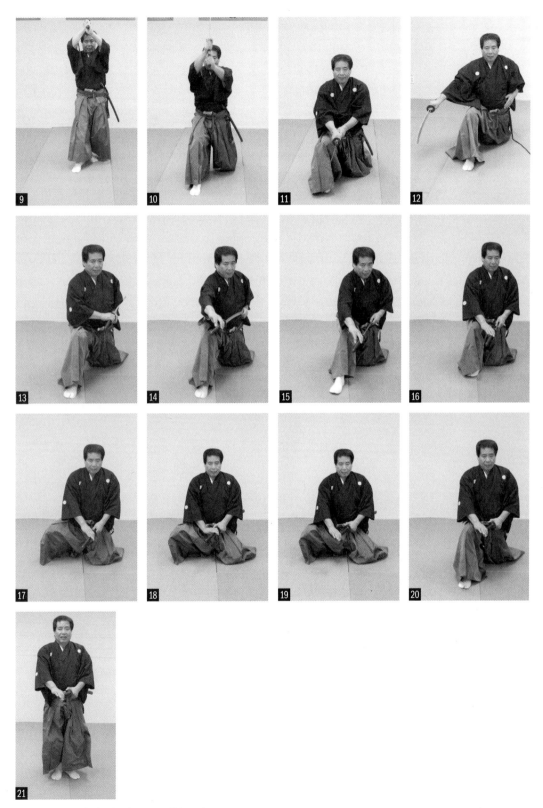

Figures 9I.9–21. Chūden Tatehiza *waza:* Takiotoshi

Still looking over your shoulder at your opponent, draw your left foot slightly ahead of your right foot, while twisting the *tsuka* in a clockwise direction to wrench the *kojiri* completely free of the rear attacker's grasp (fig. 9I.4) and take a step forward with your right foot while performing *nukitsuke* (fig. 9I.5). As the sword is nearly drawn, pivot 180 degrees left on the balls of both feet, so that the twist of your hips pulls the last couple of inches of blade from the *saya*. Keep the blade close by your right hip, held flat with the edge turned away from your body, as depicted in figure 9I.6. With a left-right shuffle-step forward, execute a one-handed thrust to the opponent's solar plexus, as shown in figure 9I.7. Withdraw the *kissaki* from the opponent by pulling your right hand slightly back while twisting the blade a quarter turn counterclockwise, so the *mine* is upward (fig. 9I.8), then perform *furikaburi* while beginning to step forward with the right foot (fig. 9I.9), so that the sword is directly overhead, poised for *kirioroshi* just as the right foot passes the left foot. Complete the step forward by dropping to one knee during *kirioroshi*, as depicted in figure 9I.11. Complete the *waza* with Eishin-Ryū *chiburi* and Chūden *nōtō*. Rise to standing position and step back to your starting point.

Figures 9J.1–10. Chūden Tatehiza *waza:* Takiotoshi (side view)

Presented above in side view is the sequence from figures 9I.3–11. This affords a clearer view of the movement of the sword to escape the attacker's grasp and the thrust and *kirioroshi* that finish him.

The name Takiotoshi comes from the swirling, dancing movements of the sword as you evade the grasp of your attackers, turn, thrust, and slash downward—motions reminiscent of the bounding path of a small waterfall cascading down a rocky mountainside.

## 9K: MAKKŌ

Last in the Chūden series, Makkō (Face to Face) is nearly identical to Nukiuchi in the Shoden *waza*. Like Nukiuchi, Makkō begins facing straight ahead in *seiza* posture (fig. 9K.1). On your third cleansing breath, draw the sword straight up so that *nukitsuke* and *furikaburi* occur in a single motion as you rise up tall on your knees and get set on the balls of your feet (see fig. 9K.5) for *kirioroshi*. Conclude with Eishin-Ryū *chiburi* (drawing your knees back to the proper separation for *seiza*) and Chūden *nōtō*, remaining on the balls of your feet during *nōtō* while you gradually settle back onto your heels just as the *tsuba* meets your left hand. After you slide your right hand to the *tsuka-gashira*, rise up slightly, flatten your feet against the floor, and lower yourself into *seiza* position.

The key distinctions between Makkō and Nukiuchi are: (1) in Makkō, *nukitsuke*, *furikaburi*, and *kirioroshi* are performed almost as a single action, as well as more quickly than in Nukiuchi; and (2) Chūden *nōtō* is employed in Makkō.

*Ōyō* for Makkō is identical to that of Nukiuchi: a case of *jōiuchi* (orders from above) to execute the enemy facing you. As the opponent bows, you swiftly draw and cut in a sudden and continuous motion. The increased speed, power, and accuracy with which you perform Makkō should not be something you deliberately train yourself to achieve, but simply the result of several years of consistent repetition of Nukiuchi, resulting in swifter and smoother execution of the technique.

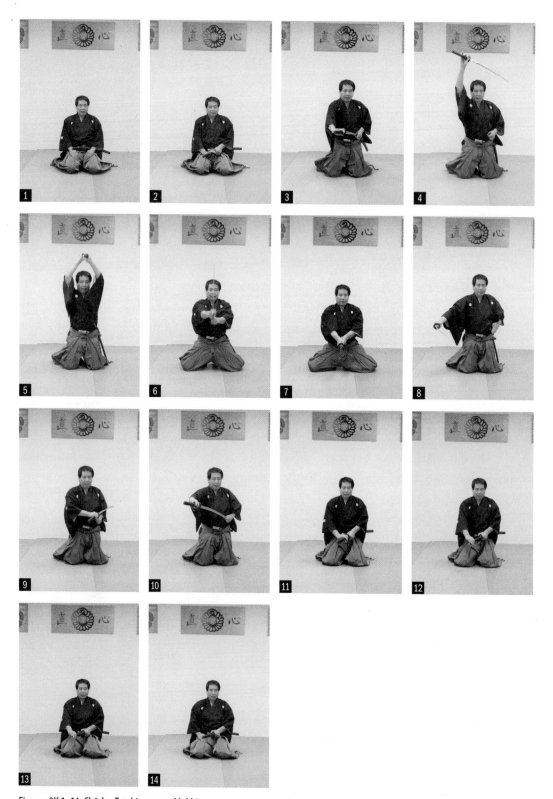

Figures 9K.1–14. Chūden Tatehiza *waza:* Makkō

Chapter 10

# Chūden Hayanuki
**Rapid Practice Exercise**

中伝速抜

The Chūden Tatehiza *waza* presented in chapter 9 are, in many respects, the foundation of Eishin-Ryū in an almost literal sense. They are the techniques that were first created by our style's namesake, Hasegawa Eishin, and they were specifically developed for the *daitō*—the "modern" samurai sword that remained in common use from the late sixteenth century until the end of the samurai era.

Therefore, developing skill in, and comprehensive knowledge of the Chūden *waza* is essential to becoming proficient in the Eishin-Ryū style. Typically, beginners are taught the Shoden (Ōmori-Ryū) *waza* along with the Shoden Battō-Hō presented in chapter 13. The Chūden Tatehiza *waza* are usually taught to intermediate students. The fact that the Shoden and Chūden *waza* are taught earlier in a student's training does not mean that they are of lesser significance or value than the Okuden *waza* that are taught to more advanced students. The descriptions of *shoden* (beginning lore), *chūden* (intermediate lore), and *okuden* (deep lore) should not be interpreted as meaning that the *techniques* are beginner, intermediate, or advanced, but only that the *student* being taught these techniques has a beginner, intermediate, or deep-level understanding of *iaijutsu* at the time these *waza* are introduced.

Thus, when first learning the Shoden *waza*, the student will gain only a superficial knowledge of their performance and application. When initially learning the Chūden *waza*, the student will gain a deeper level of understanding of those techniques from the outset of that training. And when learning the Okuden *waza*, the student will derive significantly more profound knowledge from them than he or she gained during earlier instruction.

For this reason, it is vital that intermediate students—those typically holding *shodan*, *nidan*, and *sandan* ranks—practice the Chūden *waza* as the bedrock of their training. To facilitate daily practice of the Chūden *waza* the seventeenth headmaster

203

of Eishin-Ryū, Ōe Masamichi, created an exercise called Hayanuki. The name Haya-nuki means "fast draw" or "quick draw," but that does not mean that the sword is drawn more quickly in the Hayanuki exercise. Instead it means that the exercise permits practice of the nine Tatehiza *waza* of the Chūden series in less time than it normally takes to perform those nine *waza* individually.

For example, the first Chūden *waza*, Yokogumo, takes about fifty seconds to complete from its beginning in a standing position to its completion after resuming a standing position. The first twenty seconds are spent lowering into the *tatehiza* posture and taking the three cleansing breaths. The core of the *waza*—*nukitsuke, furik-aburi, kirioroshi, yoko chiburi,* and the first half of Chūden *nōtō*—together take only about fifteen seconds to complete. An additional fifteen seconds is spent completing *nōtō*, rising to a standing position and stepping back to the starting point of the *waza*.

In the Hayanuki exercise, the practitioner lowers into *tatehiza* only once at the beginning of the exercise, performs *kiyomeri kokyū* (purifying breaths) only once, then performs nine *waza* in succession, completing *nōtō* with *zanshin* only after the final *waza*, then rising and returning to the starting point only once. This eliminates thirty-five to forty-five seconds from each of eight *waza*. The Seiza *waza* Makkō is not included in the Hayanuki exercise, so the total time needed to practice the Chūden *waza* is reduced from eight or nine minutes to no more than two minutes. This is the purpose for which Hayanuki was intended—to quickly practice drawing, not to practice drawing quickly.

When performing Hayanuki it is therefore essential to perform all of the movements at the same speed as when performing each *waza* individually. The objective is not to hurry the movements, but simply to eliminate the repetitive lowering into and rising from the *tatehiza* posture. Rushing the movements is probably the single most common—and detrimental—mistake people make when performing Hayanuki.

From a standing position facing straight ahead, lower into *tatehiza* as described in chapter 9, with your left foot beneath you and its ankle bone centered between your buttocks. The right foot remains flat on the floor, with the knee elevated and angled slightly outward, as shown in figure 10A.1. Your hands should be resting in closed (but not clenched) fists atop your right knee and left thigh. Begin with *kiyo-meri kokyū*, taking three preparatory cleansing breaths. Ideally, the remainder of the Hayanuki exercise should be completed in three to six additional breaths.

As you inhale the third time, raise your hands to the *tsuka* and perform *koiguchi no kirikata*. Set the ball of your left foot on the floor (fig. 10A.3) to push forward with your rear foot as you perform *nukitsuke*, finishing with your right foot forward, as shown in figure 10A.7.

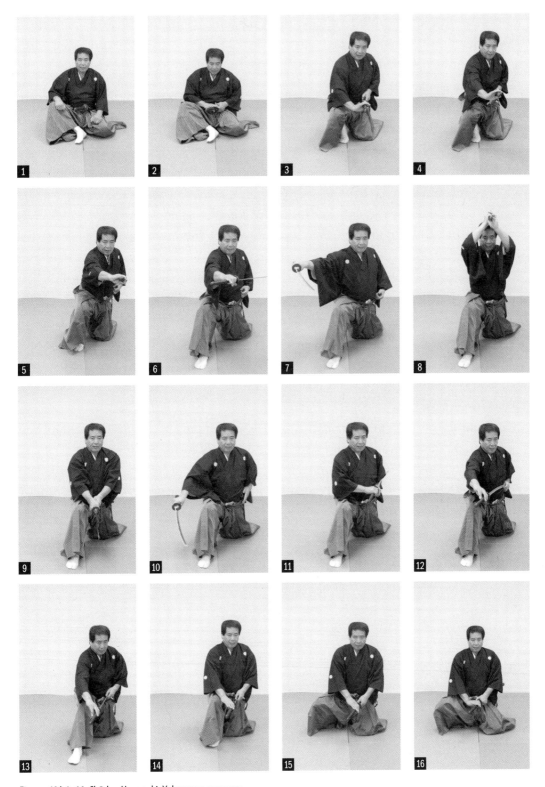

Figures 10A.1–16. Chūden Hayanuki: Yokogumo sequence

Note: In the Hayanuki exercise, the Yokogumo sequence is usually performed with the forward step described here, rather than the rearward step preferred when Yokogumo is performed as a stand-alone *waza*, so that the exercise finishes in the same place it started.

Perform *furikaburi* while scooting your left knee forward for a better purchase (fig. 10A.8), then shuffle forward to increase the power of *kirioroshi*, while remaining in a kneeling position as shown in figure 10A.9. Then perform Eishin-Ryū (*yoko*) *chiburi*.

Begin Chūden *nōtō*, drawing the right foot rearward at about the same pace that the sword is entering the *saya*, but instead of completing *nōtō* as you draw your heels together (fig. 10A.16), immediately begin the next (Tora no Issoku) sequence of the exercise.

From the position shown in figure 10A.16, rise while stepping back with the left foot and drawing your sword into a sweeping block in front of your right leg (with the blade edge forward) as shown in figure 10B.3, exactly as performed in the Chūden *waza* Tora no Issoku. During *furikaburi*, drop to your left knee with your right foot leading, then shuffle forward while performing *kirioroshi*. Perform Eishin-Ryū *chiburi* and begin Chūden *tatehiza nōtō*, again beginning the next sequence when your right heels draw together.

From the position in figure 10B.12, rise while stepping back with the left foot and perform *nukitsuke* as an upward lateral cut just above head height (fig. 10C.2). Press forward (fig. 10C.3), then drop to your left knee, right foot leading, during *furikaburi* and shuffle forward while performing *kirioroshi*. Again perform Eishin-Ryū *chiburi*, then begin Chūden *tatehiza nōtō*. When your heels have drawn together, begin the next Hayanuki sequence.

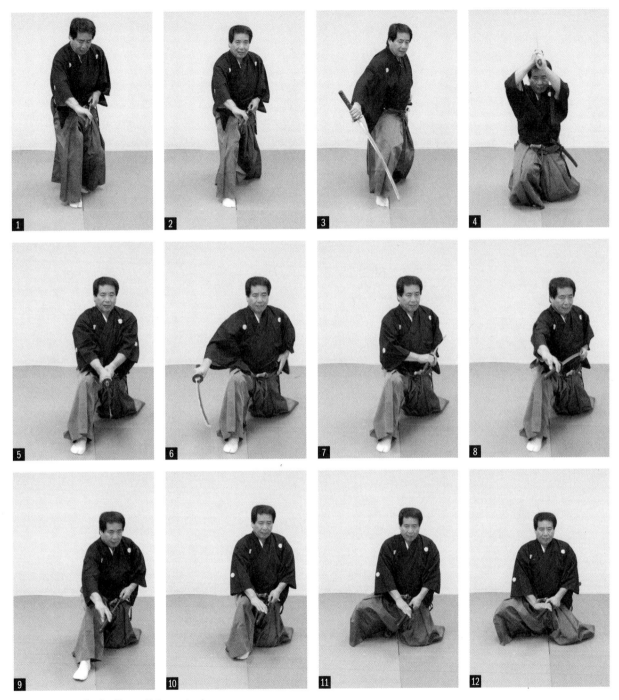

Figures 10B.1–12. Chūden Hayanuki: Tora no Issoku sequence

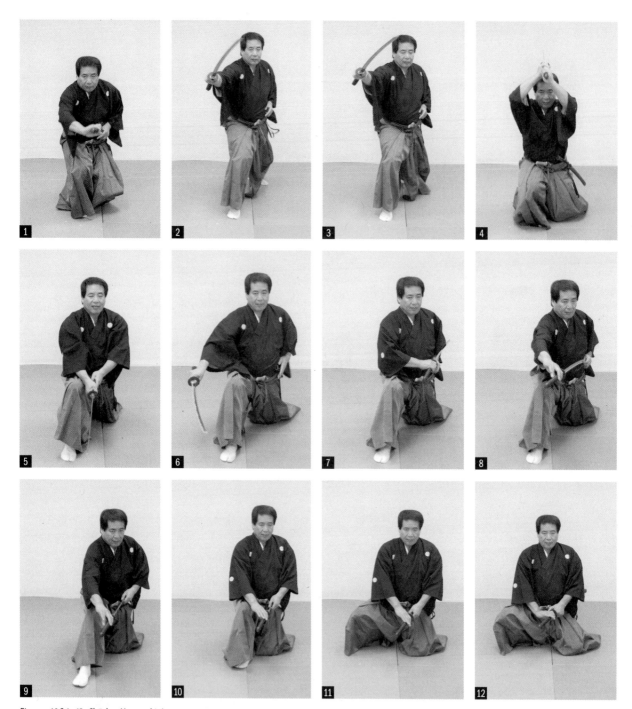

Figures 10C.1–12. Chūden Hayanuki: Inazuma sequence

Note: The photographs depict the Ukigumo sequence at a 45-degree angle, rather than the angle at which it is performed in the Hayanuki exercise. In these photographs, the sequence starts facing 45 degrees to the left, but in the exercise, the Ukigumo sequence begins facing straight ahead. Similarly, the photographs show the sequence concluding facing 45 degrees to the right, but in practice it should end facing 90 degrees to the right.

From the position shown in figure 10C.12, quickly complete *nōtō*, securing the *tsuba* with your left thumb, then rise and step to your left with your left foot while swinging the *tsuka* in a half-circle counterclockwise, ending back at your left hip as shown in figure 10D.1. Your right hand should be resting at your right thigh at this point. While stepping across with your left foot in front of your right, grasp the *tsuka* with your right hand and circle it clockwise, beginning *nukitsuke* as the *tsuka* rises past the six o'clock position (figs. 10D.2–4). As you complete *nukitsuke*, turn your body slightly to the left, aligning your shoulders with the blade and lowering your center of gravity by bending both knees slightly and twisting your left ankle so your weight rests on the outer edge of the foot (fig. 10D.5).

Without allowing the blade to move, turn your body one quarter turn to the right (see fig. 10D.6) and place the palm of your left hand against the *mine* as you step back with your right foot and drop to one knee. Turning your body another quarter turn, push the blade downward to your right until it is pointing almost straight out from your right knee, as shown in figure 10D.7. Use your left hand to gently flip the blade upward during *furikaburi* (fig. 10D.8), then perform *kirioroshi* at a 45-degree angle down and to the left, ending at the position outside the left knee shown in figure 10D.9. At this point, you should be facing 90 degrees to the right of the direction you were facing as you began this sequence. With your left foot still forward, perform Eishin-Ryū *chiburi*, and perform partial *nōtō* as before, except that your *left* foot draws back as the sword is sheathed, rather than your right foot.

Note: The photographs that follow depict the Yamaoroshi sequence from its normal perspective, beginning at a 90-degree angle to the left of your original starting position of the Hayanuki exercise. Instead, in Hayanuki, you will be facing the opposite direction (90 degrees to the right of your starting position) at the beginning of the Yamaoroshi sequence, and finish facing to the rear, rather than the front.

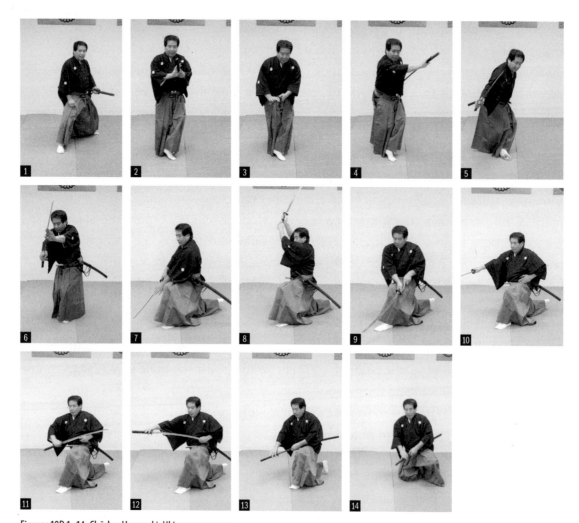

Figures 10D.1–14. Chūden Hayanuki: Ukigumo sequence

To initiate the next (Yamaoroshi) sequence, look to your right at about a 45-degree angle and step in that direction with your right foot while twisting the *tsuka* in a clockwise circle and striking with the *tsukagashira*. As in the Chūden *waza* Yamaoroshi, *nukitsuke* is performed by drawing all but the last few inches of the blade, then using a powerful snap of your right wrist with a simultaneous leftward twist of your hips as your left foot slides forward almost to your right foot, finishing with the blade angled upward at about 45 degrees, as depicted in figure 10E.7.

Without allowing the sword to move from the finish of *nukitsuke*, place the palm of your hand on the *mine* at about midway along the blade, turn your body 45 degrees to the right, extend your right leg, then push the blade horizontally to the right while shifting your body weight onto your right leg, as depicted in figures 10E.8–10. Use your left hand to gently flip the blade upward into *furikaburi*, while sliding your body and left foot to the right so that you scoot beneath the overhead blade, then perform *kirioroshi* straight downward with a small step forward with your right foot (fig. 10E.13). At this point, you should be facing directly to the rear of the position in which you began the Hayanuki exercise. Now perform Eishin-Ryū *chiburi* and partial Chūden *tatehiza nōtō* in the normal fashion.

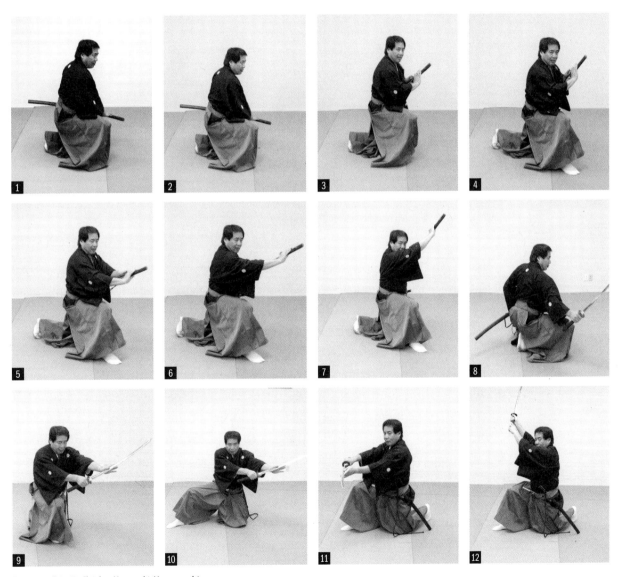

Figures 10E.1–12. Chūden Hayanuki: Yamaoroshi sequence

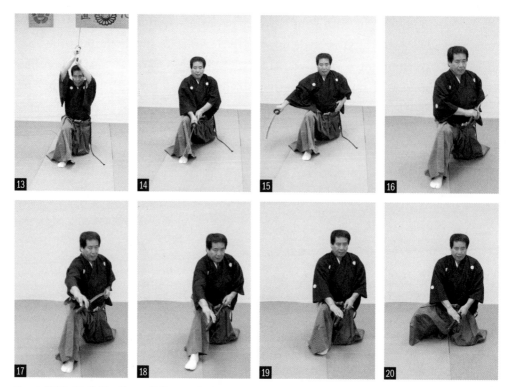

Figures 10E.13–20. Chūden Hayanuki: Yamaoroshi sequence

Note: The photographs that follow depict the Iwanami sequence from its normal perspective, beginning at a 90-degree angle to the right of your original starting position of the Hayanuki exercise. Instead, in Hayanuki, you will be facing to the rear (180 degrees from your starting position) at the beginning of the Iwanami sequence, and finish facing 90 degrees to the right, rather than to the front.

Begin the Iwanami sequence by rising and stepping back with your left foot as you draw about three-fourths of the sword (fig. 10F.1). Place the fingertips of your left hand against the *mine* to guide the last few inches of the blade from the *saya*, then pivot 90 degrees to your left while using both hands to turn the blade over as you rise to a standing position (feet together, with *iaigoshi*), as shown in figure 10F.2. Stutter-step with your right foot, then step forward with your right foot while dropping to one knee and thrusting the blade forward and upward so that the *kissaki* follows a crescent-shaped path, using your left hand to steady and guide the blade, as depicted in figure 10F.6. Leaving your left hand in position against the *mine*, twist the blade 90 degrees to your right, step sideways with your right foot and shuffle to your right while pushing the blade horizontally to tear it free of your opponent (figs. 10F.7–8).

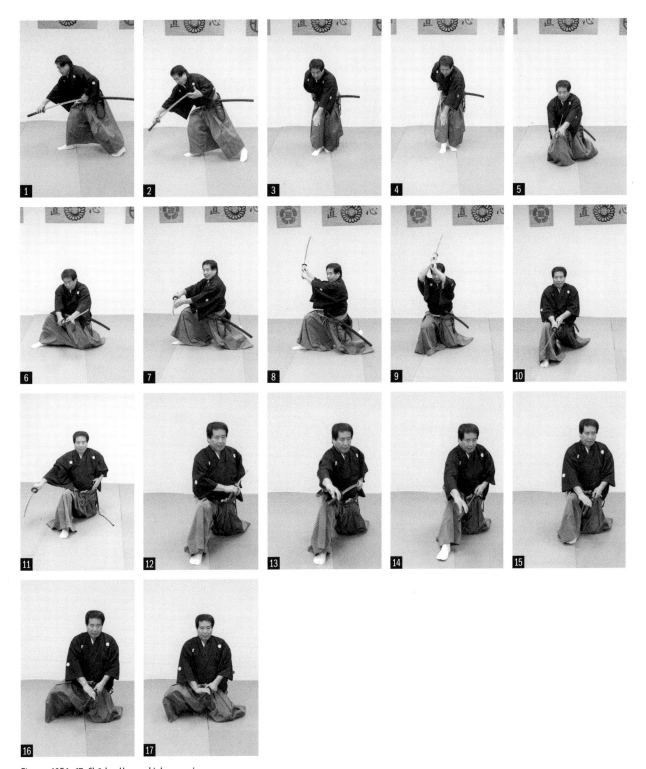

Figures 10F.1–17. Chūden Hayanuki: Iwanami sequence

As in Yamaoroshi, use the fingers of your left hand to "flip" the blade overhead into *furikaburi*, while simultaneously sliding your body beneath the upraised sword. Then, with a slight forward step of the right foot, perform *kirioroshi* straight down to finish your attacker before performing Eishin-Ryū *chiburi* and the usual partial Chūden *tatehiza nōtō*. At the completion of this sequence you will be facing 90 degrees to the right of your original orientation (90 degrees to the left from the beginning of the Iwanami sequence).

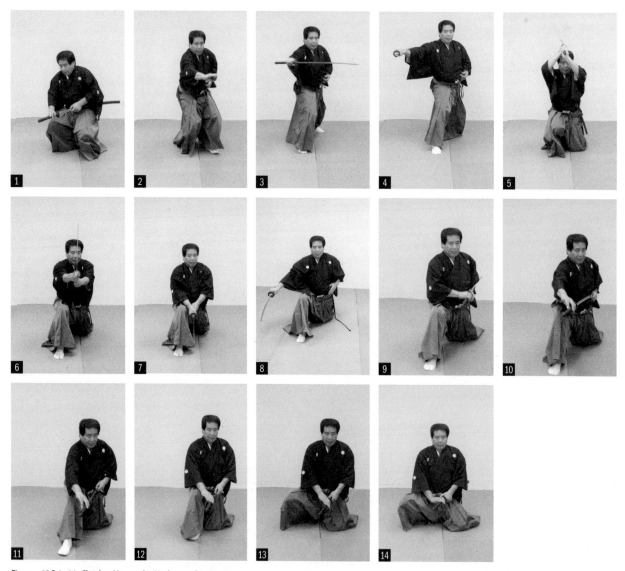

Figures 10G.1–14. Chūden Hayanuki: Urokogaeshi sequence

The Urokogaeshi sequence starts from its customary position in Hayanuki. Look 90 degrees to your left, then rise, pivoting 90 degrees to your left and stepping rearward with your left foot while performing a level *nukitsuke* (fig. 10G.1–3). Drop onto your left knee, with your right foot forward during *furikaburi*, followed by *kirioroshi*, Eishin-Ryū *chiburi*, and partial Chūden *tatehiza nōtō*. At the conclusion of this sequence, you are once again facing in the direction in which you started the Hayanuki exercise.

Note: The Namigaeshi sequence is depicted in the photographs below 180 degrees from the direction it is performed in Hayanuki. When performed by itself, Namigaeshi begins facing rearward, but as part of the Hayanuki exercise, it begins facing forward.

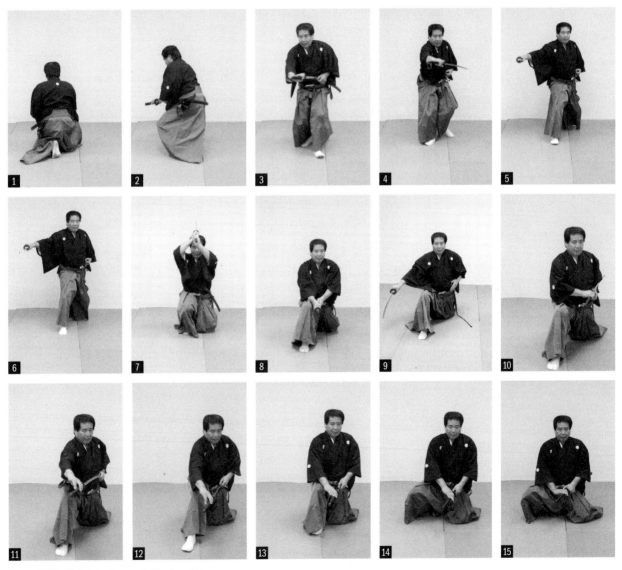

Figures 10H.1–15. Chūden Hayanuki: Namigaeshi sequence

Rise and turn 180 degrees to your left while performing *nukitsuke* as a level, standing cut to the rear (figs. 10H.2–6). Lower onto your left knee, right foot forward, during *furikaburi*, then perform *kirioroshi*, Eishin-Ryū *chiburi*, and partial Chūden *tatehiza nōtō*. When finished with this sequence, you will again be facing to the rear of your original orientation.

The Hayanuki exercise ends with the Takiotoshi sequence, which is depicted in the photographs that follow exactly as it is performed in Hayanuki, facing to the rear at the outset and finishing facing to the front.

Glance over your left shoulder, set your left foot (fig. 10I.1), then step forcefully back and rise to a standing position (in *iaigoshi*) while thrusting sharply downward on the *tsuka* to drive the *kojiri* upward with enough power to break the opponent's grip, as shown in figure 10I.2.

Still looking over your shoulder at your opponent, draw your left foot slightly ahead of your right foot, while twisting the *tsuka* in a clockwise direction up to your right shoulder (to wrench the *kojiri* free of the attacker's grasp). Step forward with your right foot while performing *nukitsuke*. As the sword is nearly drawn, pivot 180 degrees left on the balls of both feet, so that the twist of your hips pulls the last couple of inches of blade from the *saya*. Keep the blade close by your right hip, held flat with the edge turned away from your body, as depicted in figure 10I.5. With a left-right shuffle-step forward, execute a one-handed thrust to the opponent's solar plexus, as shown in figure 10I.6. Withdraw the *kissaki* from the opponent by pulling your right hand slightly back while twisting the blade a quarter-turn counterclockwise, so the *mine* is upward (fig. 10I.8), then perform *furikaburi* while beginning to step forward with the right foot, so that the sword is directly overhead, poised for *kirioroshi* just as the right foot passes the left foot. Complete the step forward by dropping to one knee during *kirioroshi* as depicted in figure 10I.10. You will once again be facing in the direction in which you began the Hayanuki exercise. Complete your performance with Eishin-Ryū (*yoko*) *chiburi* and full Chūden *nōtō* with *zanshin*, then rise to a standing position.

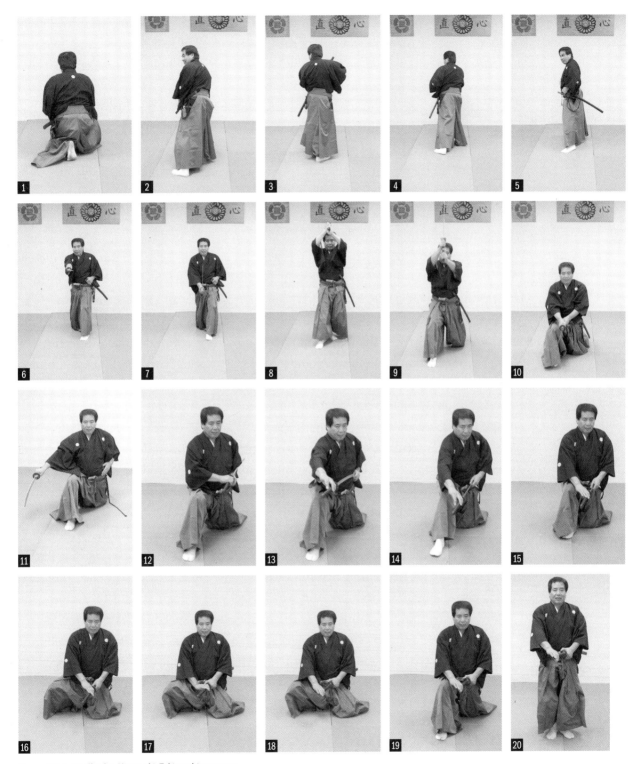

Figures 10I.1–20. Chūden Hayanuki: Takiotoshi sequence

This completes the Chūden Hayanuki. Remember that the purpose of this exercise is to practice correct execution of the Chūden *waza* in a more expeditious manner, so the movements should not be rushed. Nevertheless, it should only take about two minutes to complete the entire exercise.

It is also important to understand that Hayanuki is not a substitute for regular training in the full Chūden *waza*. In fact, Shimabukuro Hanshi was always reluctant to teach students the Hayanuki, because he did not want them to substitute practicing Hayanuki for practicing the full-length individual Chūden *waza*. Hayanuki were intended to be practiced only when training time did not permit practice of each complete Chūden *waza*. It was undoubtedly for this reason that he decided to omit Hayanuki from previous editions of *Flashing Steel*.

There is also a danger in treating Hayanuki as if it is a type of *kata*. It is merely a training exercise. Performed as a sequence, the individual *waza* lose much of their practicality, which is why Hayanuki is considered merely an *exercise*, not a *waza*. The Chūden *waza* represent situations in which a samurai is attacked while resting in the *tatehiza* posture. After the first such attack, no samurai would remain in *tatehiza* or a kneeling position while undergoing additional attacks. This is why each Chūden *waza* stands alone.

Although stringing the Chūden *waza* together into the Hayanuki may look impressive to people unfamiliar with the art of *iaijutsu*, there is a long-standing tradition that Hayanuki not be performed in public demonstrations of any kind. It is a personal training exercise that one might think of as equivalent to calisthenics or running on a treadmill. We therefore urge you to perform only complete individual *waza* during any public performances or demonstrations.

Despite the several risks inherent to performing Hayanuki for the wrong purposes, a disciplined *iaidōka* can derive significant benefit from proper training in this exercise. It can prove useful in helping a student more quickly learn the entire Chūden *waza* curriculum. Furthermore, the self-control and focus required to perform the entire series without succumbing to the temptation to speed up its movements will greatly improve a student's performance of all *iaijutsu waza*. For this reason alone, if done mindful of these cautions, practicing Hayanuki can be extremely beneficial for the intermediate *iaidōka*.

## ALTERNATIVE TRAINING METHODS

Once a student becomes familiar with the pattern and execution of the Hayanuki, he or she can practice the Katate Hayanuki variation. Katate Hayanuki means "one-handed fast draw." Its only difference from the standard Hayanuki pattern is that all cuts—*nukitsuke*, *hiki-daoshi tsuki*, and *kirioroshi*—as well as *furikaburi* are performed with the right hand only. In this way, Karate Hayanuki not only helped develop greater wrist, arm, shoulder, chest, and back strength to support the sword arm, but also considerably improves the student's *te no uchi* and control of the sword.

The Hayanuki can also be performed from a standing position. Of course, it is preferable that the exercise be initiated from the *tatehiza* posture whenever possible. However, there are many circumstances in which *tatehiza* is not a viable option for some *iaidōka*. Students recovering from injuries or surgery, for example, may find it painful or even harmful to sit in *tatehiza* or to perform the Hayanuki sequence kneeling. The ground or floor may be of a material, such as gravel or uneven tile, not conducive to or suitable for kneeling. In situations of this kind, students wishing to practice Hayanuki should perform them from a standing position in order to benefit from the training under circumstances that would otherwise prevent it.

One final caution: avoid the temptation to embellish the Hayanuki. There are now videos posted on the internet depicting people performing hybrid versions of the Hayanuki that add elements derived from other portions of the *iaijutsu* curriculum. These hybrids appear to have been created to improve the "showmanship" of the Hayanuki, which is antithetical to its intended training purpose. The *iaijutsu* curriculum and training regimen we now follow in the twenty-first century are the product of over four hundred years of thoughtful development by masters of the art with decades of both training and experience in teaching, including several who had applied this training in actual combat. It is the epitome of arrogance for anyone lacking equivalent knowledge, training, and experience to attempt to "improve" the curriculum and training methods such *sensei* have developed.

Chapter 11

# Okuden Tachiwaza

## Standing Okuden Waza

The Okuden (Deep-Level) Tachiwaza (standing techniques)—or at least most of them—were part of Hayashizaki-Ryū during its formative years. With the adaptation of Hayashizaki-Ryu techniques to the slightly shorter *katana* by seventh-generation grandmaster Hasegawa Eishin, most or all of the *tachiwaza* had to be modified in some respect to accommodate the newer sword design.

Following the progression from Shoden (initial level) to Chūden (middle level), we have now reached Okuden, or deep-level techniques. It was once customary to begin training in the Okuden *waza* late in the Ha period of Shu ▪ Ha ▪ Ri, so that mastery of the Okuden techniques occurred during Ri, when the student was already considered a master of swordsmanship. In more recent times, it is not unusual for students to begin learning Okuden *waza* shortly after becoming *yudansha*, the equivalent of a black belt.

As we find in translating many Japanese words, *oku* holds some interesting nuances, and "deep" really does not convey its full flavor. *Oku* actually describes the "innermost," that which lies at the very core or heart of a matter. So, in a real as well as literal sense, the Okuden *waza* are truly the *core* curriculum of Musō Jikiden Eishin-Ryū Iaijutsu.

One characteristic of the Okuden Tachiwaza is that all except the three Itomagoi *waza* are performed from a standing or walking posture. As a result, most of the responses to attack are bolder, since you have greater mobility and power while standing. A standing samurai is also less susceptible to a surprise attack than when sitting in *seiza* or relaxing in *tatehiza*.

Most Tachiwaza employ a standard pattern of footwork that begins standing erect, with your feet together as if "at attention" while taking your three cleansing breaths. As you finish inhaling the third breath, hold that breath and step forward with your *right* foot. As you step with your left foot, both hands rise simultaneously to grasp the *tsuka* and perform *koiguchi no kirikata*. Then, as you take your third step (right foot again), you perform *nukitsuke*.

The stance used during Okuden *kirioroshi* is also different from that used in the Shoden and Chūden *waza*. Rather than finishing with your hips squarely forward in a stance similar to the *zenkutsu dachi* (front stance) used in *karate-dō*, with the back leg straight and heel slightly off the ground, Okuden Tachiwaza use what we sometimes call a "power stance" or "cutting stance." Unique to the Okuden *waza*, this power stance is a modified version of the "front stance" used in the Shoden and Chūden *waza*. The front leg is bent and bears about 60 percent of your weight, but your hips and shoulders are turned about 30 degrees from directly forward. Your rear leg is bent slightly, with the foot pointing directly sideways and flat on the floor. This stance, illustrated in figure 11A.1, permits greater use of the hips and generates considerably more cutting power and stability than the stance used in Shoden and Chūden *waza*. Like all other stances in Eishin-Ryū, there is no prescribed name for this stance, but we typically refer to it as *okuden kamae* (deep-level structure), *okuden kiridachi* (deep-level cutting stance), or in English as "power stance."

Figure 11A.1. Okuden Tachiwaza power stance

Two other characteristics of this series of *waza* are that the "flicking" type Eishin-Ryū *chiburi* is used almost exclusively, as well as Okuden *nōtō*, which was described in detail in chapter 7.

## 11B: YUKIZURE

The first Okuden *waza*, Yukizure (Escorted), is a defensive technique used when walking in the custody of two opponents, one at either shoulder. In such a situation, you are likely being taken to be executed or interrogated, so you are under obligation to your lord to escape if at all possible. As you finish inhaling the third *kiyomeri kokyū* cleansing breath, take your first step forward with your right foot. Your second step (left foot) is made with a distinct movement toward your left side that knocks one opponent off balance as you raise your hands to the *tsuka*. With the left hand gripping the *saya* at the same moment your right hand grasps the *tsuka*, perform *koiguchi no kirikata*. As you take your third step, turn 45 degrees to your right as you perform *nukitsuke*, drawing the sword in a downward-slashing arc with the power stance described previously, ending with the *kissaki* pointing upward at about a 45-degree angle, as shown in figure 11B.9. Perform *furikaburi* while turning 90 degrees to your left as you step forward with your right foot, and perform *kirioroshi*, also in the power stance (fig. 11B.12). Follow this with Eishin-Ryū *chiburi* and Okuden *nōtō* while remaining in the power stance, exhibiting *zanshin*. After your right hand slides to the *tsuka-gashira*, maintain *iaigoshi* while sliding your left foot up to meet your right foot, then pivot 45 degrees to your right and step back to your original starting position. At this point, now standing fully erect, remove your right hand from the *tsuka-gashira* and return it to your right side while your left hand releases the *saya* and *tsuba* and returns to your left side.

The *ōyō* and techniques of Yukizure are more abrupt and bold than those of the Shoden and Chūden *waza*. In Yukizure, you are being escorted by two samurai, possibly because you previously had no opportunity to escape or were invited to accompany them under false pretenses. When you realize their treachery or sense their intention to kill or capture you, you seize the opportunity to counterattack by lurching against the one on your left. While he is off balance, you draw and kill the foe on your right before he can react, then finish the first adversary before he can recover his balance. It is typical of Okuden *waza* that they present both technique and strategy and are thus "deeper" (*oku*) than Shoden or Chūden *waza*.

Figures 11B.1–8. Okuden Tachiwaza: Yukizure

Figures 11B.9–18. Okuden Tachiwaza: Yukizure

## 11C: TSUREDACHI

The second Okuden *waza*, Tsuredachi (Companions), involves a situation similar to that in Yukizure. In this case, however, your opponents are escorting you at an angle instead of side-by-side; the one to your left is a half-step behind you, and the one to your right is a half-step ahead. As you take your second step (left foot) of the *waza*, raise your hands to the *tsuka*, with the left hand gripping the *saya* at the same moment your right hand grasps the *tsuka*. Then, as you take your third step, perform *koiguchi no kirikata* while turning 45 degrees to your right and thrusting forward with both hands, as if performing *tsuka-ate* (a strike with the *tsuka-gashira*). Next pull the *saya* back, performing *nukitsuke*, and take a half step to your rear while turning your left shoulder aside and making a one-hand chest-level thrust to the rear.

As illustrated in figure 11C.9, this thrust should be horizontal, with the blade turned sideways—edge away from you—and with the underside of your right forearm reinforcing the *tsuka*. Raise the sword in *furikaburi* and take a shuffle-step forward as you execute *kirioroshi* at a 45-degree angle to your right front, as depicted in figure 11C.11. Once again, note that the *tsuki* (thrust) and *kirioroshi* are performed in *okuden kamae* (power stance) in this *waza*.

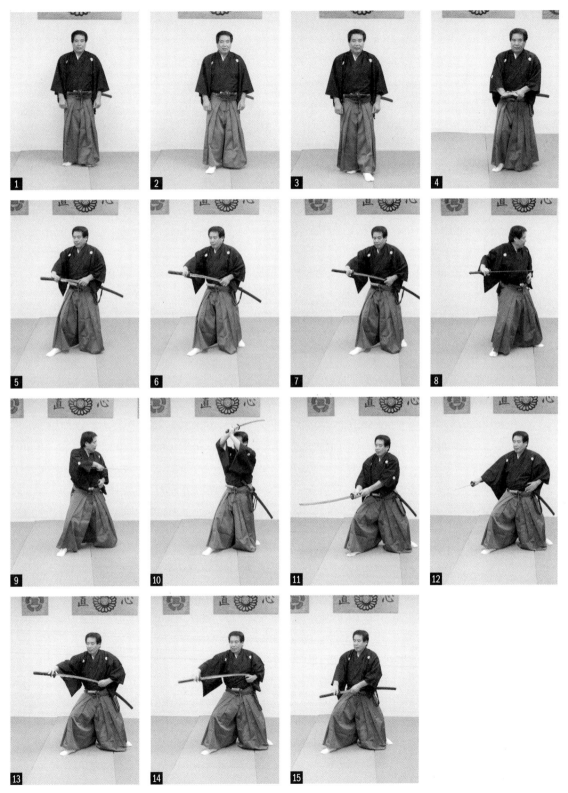

Figures 11C.1–15. Okuden Tachiwaza: Tsuredachi

Complete the *waza* with Eishin-Ryū *chiburi* and Okuden *nōtō*. After your right hand slides to the *tsuka-gashira*, maintain *iaigoshi* while sliding your left foot up to meet your right foot, then pivot 45 degrees to your left and, maintaining *zanshin*, step back to your original starting position.

*Ōyō* for Tsuredachi is only slightly different than that for Yukizure. You are again dealing with two opponents, only they are escorting you at an angle, rather than at your sides. This time, your action begins as you take your third step of the *waza* (with your right foot). You lunge toward the opponent to your right-front, knocking him temporarily off balance. Then, by merely pulling back the *saya*, you perform *nukitsuke*. The shuffle-step toward your left-rear not only ensures that you are within striking distance for the thrust that dispatches the opponent behind you, but also blocks him from making a normal *nukitsuke* and distances you from the enemy to your front. Before the opponent at your front can recover, you lunge ahead and finish him with *kirioroshi*.

# 11D: SŌMAKURI

The third *waza*, Sōmakuri (All Around), is the most complex of the Tachiwaza, earning its name with a total of five cutting strokes that attack nearly every major target on the body. As you take your second step (left foot), position your hands for *koiguchi no kirikata*. On your third step, perform *koiguchi no kirikata* and draw about half the blade, then step abruptly back with the right foot, completing *nukitsuke* overhead as an *uke-nagashi*-type block that continues into *furikaburi* (fig. 11D.2). Next, take a shuffle-step forward—right foot, then left foot—performing *yokomen-giri* (side-of-the-head cut) to your opponent's left temple (see fig. 11D.7). With another shuffle-step forward, perform *furikaburi* (fig. 11D.8) and make an angular cut to the right side of the opponent's neck, as shown in figure 11D.9. Your next step forward lands in the power stance with an angular cut—slanting about 45 degrees down to your left—at rib level on your opponent's left side (fig. 11D.11). Without moving your feet, and chiefly using a twist of your wrists, flip the sword back, next to your left side at waist level, then take another shuffle-step forward—lunging with the right foot, then letting your left foot "drag" forward—as you perform a *yoko ichimonji* (level horizontal) cut from left to right. Allow your follow-through from *yoko ichimonji* to carry the blade around and up into *furikaburi* in a single fluid motion, drawing your left foot forward to meet your right foot, then take another step forward with your right foot as you finish with *kirioroshi* (fig. 11D.17) in *okuden kamae*. Complete the *waza* with Eishin-Ryū *chiburi* and Okuden *nōtō*, then draw your left foot up to meet your right foot, and step back to your original starting position.

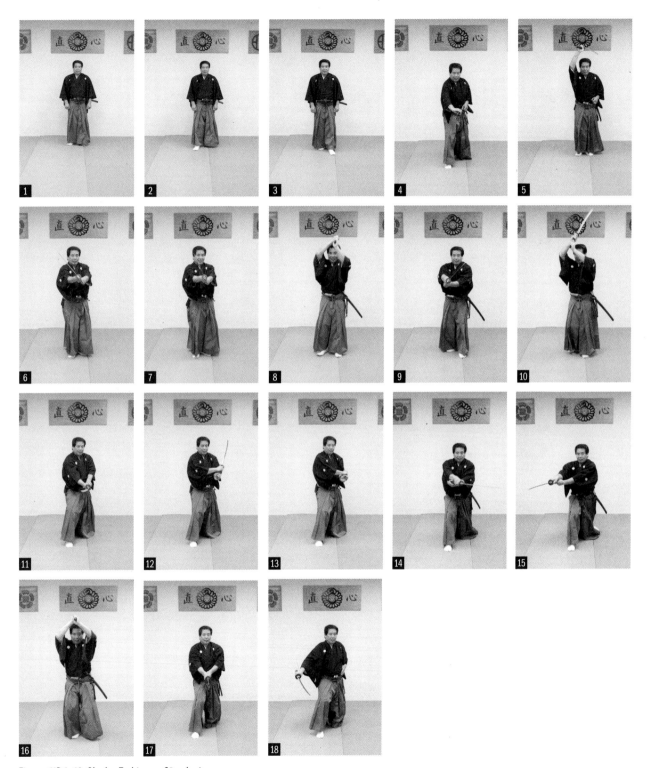

Figures 11D.1–18. Okuden Tachiwaza: Sōmakuri

The sequence of cuts (figs. 11D.4–17, above) are shown below in side view to provide further detail of the footwork and angles of attack.

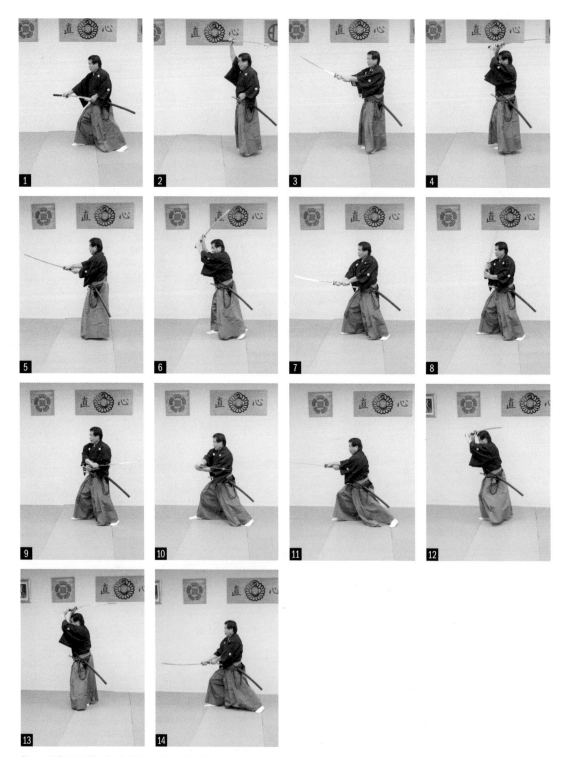

Figures 11E.1–14. Okuden Tachiwaza: Sōmakuri (side view)

*Ōyō* for Sōmakuri includes several possible interpretations. The most basic application is against a single attacker who is back-pedaling to escape your counterattacks after his first unsuccessful attack. Because of his deft evasive movements, your first four counterattacks do not finish him. At the other extreme, you are defending against up to five opponents who rush at you single-file. This is not as unlikely as it may at first seem, since a single-file onslaught has the strategic advantage of making it difficult for you to determine the number and relative positions of your attackers, as well as the timing and nature of their attacks. Bearing this in mind, more experienced students should perform Somakuri with the feeling that there could be an endless number of opponents rushing toward them, and they could continue slashing through them in a similar manner indefinitely.

# 11F: SŌDOME

Sōdome (Stop Everything) is the fourth in the Okuden series of *waza*, and contains techniques that are extremely awkward and difficult to master.

As you finish your third cleansing breath, take your first step forward with your right foot. Raise your hands to the *tsuka* as you take your second step (left foot), gripping the *saya* with your left hand at the same moment your right hand grasps the *tsuka*. Then, as you take your third step, perform *koiguchi no kirikata* followed by *nukitsuke* as a downward angular cut in the power stance, as shown in figure 11F.6.

Note that the blade is angled upward at about a 45-degree angle. The power for this strike is derived from the reverse rotation of your hips, snapping them to your left during *saya-banari*—opposite from the direction of the travel of the sword.

After a slight pause, step forward with your left foot—just slightly ahead of your right foot—as you perform *nōtō*, twisting your hips forward once again, as depicted in figure 11F.10. When you have nearly completed *nōtō*, with only a couple of inches of blade unsheathed, step forward with your right foot again and perform *nukitsuke* exactly as before (fig. 11F.12). Again step forward with your left foot as you perform *nōtō*, then perform a third *nukitsuke*, exactly as before (fig. 11F.18). Now shift to a "front stance" as you do one-handed Eishin-Ryū *chiburi*, followed by Okuden *nōtō*. Once your right hand has reached the *tsuka-gashira*, maintain *iaigoshi* while sliding your left foot up to meet your right foot, then step back to your original starting position.

To present the footwork and timing of the multiple *nukitsuke* and *nōtō* combinations in Sōdome more clearly, the sequence of movements shown in figures 11F.3–18 below are also depicted in side view following the forward-facing series.

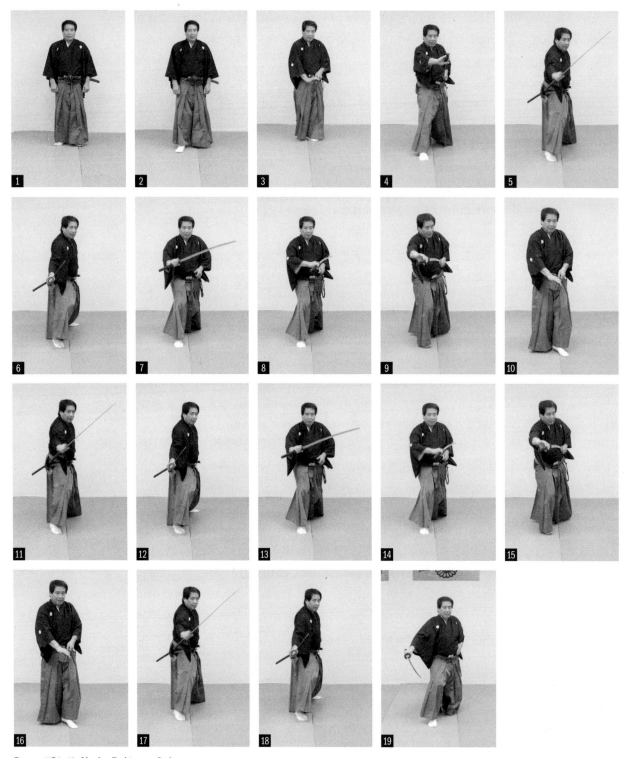

Figures 11F.1–19. Okuden Tachiwaza: Sōdome

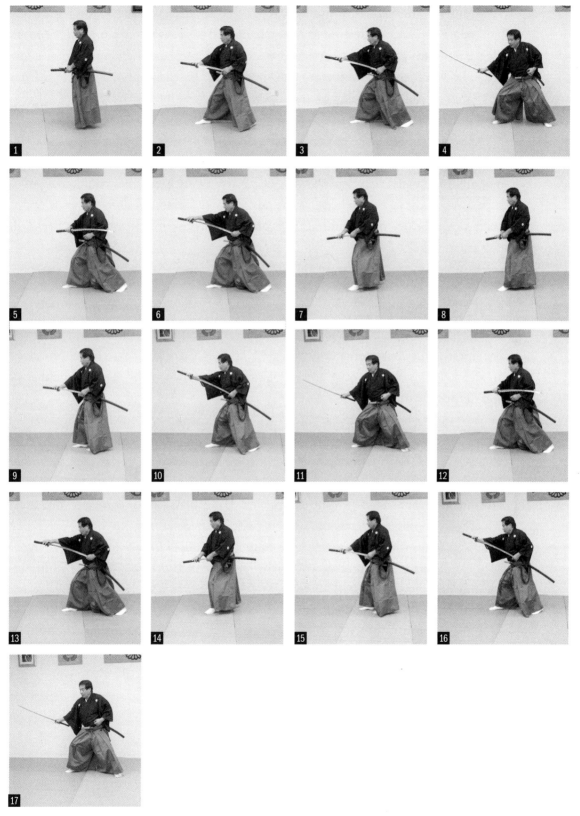

Figures 11G.1–18. Okuden Tachiwaza: Sōdome (side view)

Sōdome is another *waza* with several possible variations of its *ōyō*. It is most commonly interpreted as a defense against an ambush while walking along an *azemichi*, the narrow path that separates one rice paddy from another, often bordered by a low hedge in which enemies could conceal themselves. As each opponent springs from concealment, you use the downward-slicing *nukitsuke* before he has a chance to complete his attack.

An equally appropriate use of Sōdome is against a series of opponents rushing up at you as you descend a flight of temple, castle, or garden steps—or down a narrow mountainside path with dense undergrowth from which enemies could emerge. In such cases as these, you would use the advantage of being uphill to cut your opponents down before they could achieve proper purchase for their feet as they rush upward to attack.

## 11H: SHINOBU

The fifth Okuden *waza*, Shinobu (Stealthy), is quite unique in nature, and its apparent simplicity is characteristically deceptive. In this *waza*, you sense the approach of an attacker stalking you on a dark, moonless, or overcast night in which neither of you can see the other …

As you finish inhaling your third cleansing breath, take your first step forward with your right foot and perform *koiguchi no kirikata*. Begin *nukitsuke* as you take your second step (left foot) at about a 45-degree angle to your left (fig. 11H.4). *Nukitsuke* should be slow and very quiet. Complete *nukitsuke* while taking your third step, crossing your right foot in front of your left. Bend both knees, lowering your body while maintaining erect posture as you twist 90 degrees to your right. Extending your arm almost fully, lightly tap the floor twice with the *kissaki*, as depicted in figure 11H.8. Still facing 45 degrees to your right, step forward with your left foot while performing *furikaburi*, then step 90 degrees to the right with your right foot and execute *kirioroshi* (fig. 11H.12) in *okuden kamae*. Finish with Eishin-Ryū *chiburi* and Okuden *nōtō*, then then step back to your original starting position.

The *ōyō* for Shinobu reflects the uniqueness of this *waza*. Knowing that both you and your opponent are stalking each other by sound, you step silently to your left as you draw your sword, then reach far to your right—where your opponent expects to find you—and make a slight noise by tapping the *kissaki* on the ground. Thinking it to be a misstep, your enemy will attack in the direction of the sound, and—guided by the *tachikaze* (whoosh) of his sword—you defeat him with *kirioroshi*.

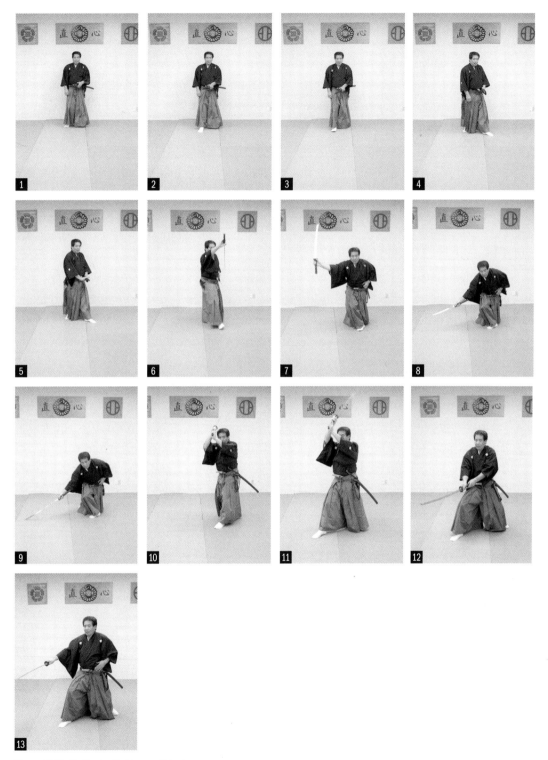

Figures 11H.1–13. Okuden Tachiwaza: Shinobu

Shinobu is an excellent example of the ways that *bunkai* and *ōyō* must determine how you perform a *waza*. Without an understanding of its *ōyō*, Shinobu would make no sense. But knowing its purpose allows you to analyze *(bunkai)* each aspect of the *waza* in order to perform it correctly. Your footsteps must be absolutely silent, so as not to betray your position. You must also draw your sword with complete silence. Tapping the floor with the *kissaki* must be done in a manner that sounds like a samurai's *waraji* (straw sandal) tapping or scraping loose gravel, twigs, or leaves. If it sounds like a sword tapping the ground, your opponent will recognize your subterfuge and move to counter it.

## 11: YUKICHIGAI

Yukichigai (Passing By) is the sixth *waza* of the Okuden series, and deals with another common type of ambush. In this instance, your attackers are walking toward you, one behind the other, and passing on both sides of you—with the one on your left in the lead. Just as the first opponent passes, he turns to attack from your rear quarter, while his accomplice simultaneously attacks from your front-right.

As you finish inhaling the third time, take your first step forward with your right foot. As you take your second step (left foot), raise your hands to the *tsuka*, with the left hand gripping the *saya* at the same moment your right hand grasps the *tsuka*. Then, as you take your third step, perform *koiguchi no kirikata* while turning 45 degrees to your right and thrusting forward with both hands, performing *tsuka-ate* (striking with the butt of the handle) at face height (fig. 11I.4).

Next, pull the *saya* back, performing *nukitsuke* as you pivot—without changing the position of your feet—180 degrees to your left, completing *nukitsuke* as an *ukenagashi*-type overhead block, as depicted in figure 11I.6.

In a continuous motion—still without moving your feet—raise your left hand to the *tsuka* during *furikaburi*, then cut downward with *kirioroshi*, as shown in figure 11I.8.

Raise the sword into *furikaburi* as you pivot—still without moving your feet—180 degrees to your right and finish with another *kirioroshi* (fig. 11I.10).

Complete the *waza* with Eishin-Ryū *(yoko) chiburi*, followed by Okuden *nōtō*. After moving your right hand to the *tsuka-gashira*, maintain *iaigoshi* while sliding your left foot up to meet your right foot, then step back to your original starting position. At this point, now standing fully erect, remove your right hand from the *tsuka-gashira* and return it to your right side while your left hand releases the *saya* and *tsuba* and returns to your left side.

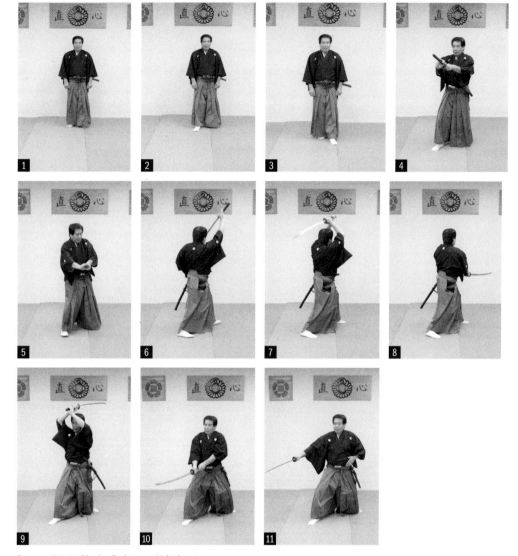

Figures 111.1–11. Okuden Tachiwaza: Yukichigai

The *ōyō* for Yukichigai involves elements of timing and speed, as well as economy of motion. With two enemies attacking simultaneously, there is no time to lose and no room for error. In the fraction of a second it takes for the attacker to your rear to turn in preparation for his strike, you must drive your *tsuka-gashira* into the face of the assailant to your front. By pivoting as you draw, your sword is protecting your body from the attacker behind you even before your draw is complete. Your *ukenagashi* and *kirioroshi* must follow only a split second apart, so you will be able to pivot and finish the attacker to your front before he can recover from the blow to his face and resume his assault.

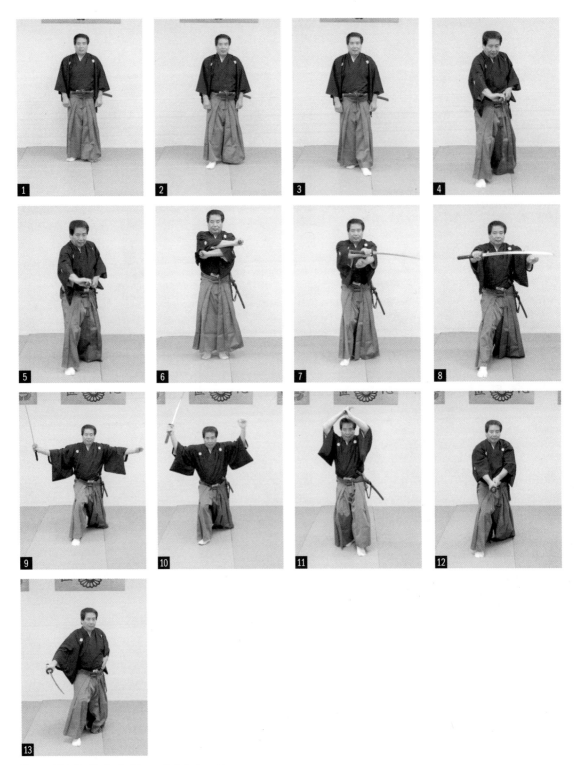

Figures 11J.1–13. Okuden Tachiwaza: Sode Surigaeshi

# 11J: SODE SURIGAESHI

The seventh in this series is Sode Surigaeshi (Brushing Sleeves), which, like many of the Okuden *waza*, has quite a unique character. You are faced by a single attacker who is lurking amid a crowd of innocent bystanders, using them as human shields as he prepares to attack you. You must avoid injuring these bystanders while pushing through the crowd to confront and defeat this attacker.

As you finish inhaling your third cleansing breath, take your first step forward with your right foot. As you take your second step (left foot), raise your hands to the *tsuka* in preparation for *nukitsuke*. Then, as you take your third step, perform *koiguchi no kirikata* and draw most of the sword (fig. 11J.5). As you complete *nukitsuke*, step back with your right foot, rising on tiptoe and crossing your arms in front of you, so that the sword is pointing straight back behind you, edge upward, as illustrated in figure 11J.6. Lower your hips and take a long stride forward with your right foot, spreading your arms to the sides, as shown in figures 11J.7–9. Slide your left foot up to meet your right foot as you raise the sword to *furikaburi*, then step forward with your right foot to perform *kirioroshi* in *okuden kamae*. Without changing your stance, perform Eishin-Ryū *chiburi* and Okuden *nōtō*, then step back to your original starting position.

Further detail of the relationship between the footwork and movement of the sword can be seen in the side view below.

Figures 11K.1–9. Okuden Tachiwaza: Sode Surigaeshi (side view)

The situation in Sode Surigaeshi is as interesting as the technique used to over-come it. To avoid cutting the bystanders, you draw your sword and fold your arms across your chest, so your sword is pointed away from them. You must lower your hips as you lunge forward through the crowd in order to gain the leverage needed to push them aside. By keeping your sword edge-up as you swing your arms to the sides, you avoid accidentally slashing any of the bystanders as you push your way clear of them. Then, once free of the crowd, you can continue the motion into *furikaburi* and dispose of your attacker with *kirioroshi.* By not waiting for your opponent to burst through the crowd at you, you have seized the initiative and are able to catch him unprepared. Obviously, this *waza* takes its name from the act of pushing aside the innocent bystanders—with your sleeves brushing theirs as you clear a path to your opponent.

## 11L: MONIRI

The eighth Okuden *waza* is Moniri (Gate Entry), which portrays an effective defense against another ambush attempt. In Moniri, your enemies are lying in wait at a narrow entry gate—the kind that are still quite common in Japan. Passing through such a gate is a vulnerable moment for a samurai, since its sides hamper a normal drawing motion and its low top beam prevents *kirioroshi.* Two ambushers are wait-ing on the far side of the gate, while a third stalks you from behind. This presents a challenging situation, because if you turn to deal with the attacker to your rear, the two in front will rush through the gate behind you. But, if you attempt to pass through the gate, all three will converge on you while you are confined within its framework.

At the completion of your three cleansing breaths, take your first step forward with your right foot. As you take your second step (left foot), raise your hands to the *tsuka* and perform *koiguchi no kirikata.* On your third step, draw most of the sword and complete *nukitsuke* on your fourth step (left foot) by pulling the sword back to your right side, parallel to the floor and edge away from you next to your hip (fig. 11L.6). Step forward with your right foot and perform a one-handed thrust (fig. 11L.7), supporting the *tsuka* against the underside of your forearm with the blade horizontal. Pivot 180 degrees to your left as you grasp the *tsuka* with both hands and perform *furikaburi,* then step forward with your right foot. Normally, you would use the momentum of your stride to add power to *kirioroshi.* In this case, however, make sure you have taken a complete step while still in *furikaburi, then* perform *kirioroshi.* This delay ensures that your swing will not be blocked by the top beam of the gate. Again, pivot 180 degrees to your left during the second *furikaburi,* and step forward—once more delaying *kirioroshi* until you have completed the step forward with your right foot, clearing the gate. Now perform Eishin-Ryū *chiburi* and Okuden *nōtō,* then step back to your original starting position.

Figures 11L.1–12. Okuden Tachiwaza: Moniri

It may be easier to visualize the essential timing of the footwork with *kirioroshi* in the side view presentation below.

There are many subtle aspects of the *ōyō* for Moniri that warrant explanation. The unusual *nukitsuke*, for instance, is used to prepare for a straight thrust. The sword must be fully drawn and ready on the fourth step (left foot in front). When you step forward with the right foot and thrust, you are stepping through the gate, thus using it for your protection as you thrust your sword into one of the two ambushers on the far side of the gate. Then you turn while still protected by the gate as you perform *furikaburi*, but you must step completely clear of the gate before using *kirioroshi* on the attacker who was behind you.

Figures 11M.1–9. Okuden Tachiwaza: Moniri (side view)

If you try to use your body's momentum for a more powerful cut, you risk striking the top of the gate on the upswing. With your blade wedged deep in the wood and your hands overhead exposing your entire torso, you will almost certainly lose the battle. Similarly, as you pivot and step back through the gate to perform *kirioroshi* on the last assailant, you must complete your step first, then swing the sword. When done at full speed, this subtle difference in timing is difficult to see. Yet correctly performing this Moniri makes all the difference in the world—a life-or-death difference in application—so it must be given close attention in your practice. Moniri is another excellent example of the need to integrate *bunkai* and *ōyō* into your routine *iaijutsu* training.

# 11N: KABEZOE

Kabezoe (Against the Wall), the ninth *waza* in the Okuden group, contains an unusual-looking defense designed for a situation that was quite common in major cities in feudal Japan—and even today in the older sections of large Japanese cities. By Western standards, Japanese streets and alleys seem narrow. Four centuries ago, before automobiles or even bicycles, this was even more the case. It was not unusual for a samurai to find himself walking down a narrow alley that was little more than the width of his own shoulders. Kabezoe provides a means of defense if attacked in this situation.

At the completion of your cleansing breaths, step forward with your right foot, then as you take your second step (left foot), perform *koiguchi no kirikata*. On your third step, draw your right foot even with your left foot and rise onto tiptoe as you draw almost straight upward, allowing your elbows to spread no wider than the width of your shoulders, as shown in figure 11N.3. Allow the *kissaki* to swing around just past your shoulder and behind you as you raise your left hand to the *tsuka* for *furikaburi*, as illustrated in figure 11N.4. While still on tiptoe, perform *kirioroshi*, allowing the *kissaki* to swing down to about knee level, rather than stopping its travel level with your navel as you normally would (fig. 11N.7). Remaining on tiptoe, perform an abbreviated *chiburi* with a snap and twist of your right wrist (fig. 11N.8).

Then a modified Okuden *nōtō*, keeping your left elbow snug against your side and raising the *tsuka* to face level during the rapid portion of *nōtō*, as depicted in figure 11N.12.

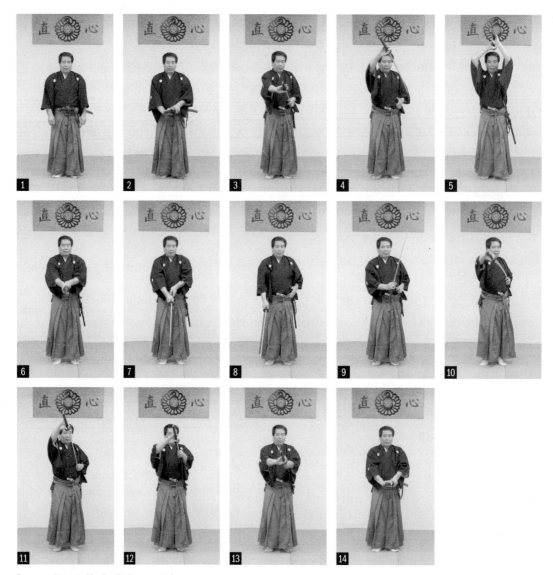

Figures 11N.1–14. Okuden Tachiwaza: Kabezoe

While completing the slow portion of *nōtō*, lower yourself to a flat-footed stance (in *iaigoshi*) as you lower both hands to a normal finishing position. After moving your right hand to the *tsuka-gashira*, step back to your original starting position. Once you are standing fully erect, remove your right hand from the *tsuka-gashira* and return it to your right side while your left hand releases the *saya* and *tsuba* and returns to your left side.

In the side view below, some aspects of the movement of the sword within narrow confines during *nukitsuke*, *furikaburi*, and *kirioroshi* can be better seen.

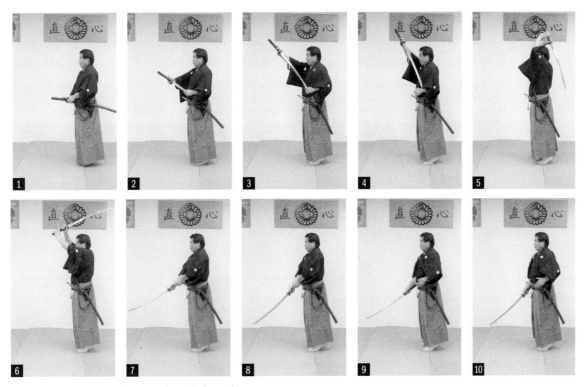

Figures 110.1–10. Okuden Tachiwaza: Kabezoe (side view)

The narrow alleyways that Kabezoe anticipates were another favorite trap, since the cramped space prevents a normal *nukitsuke*. The unusual, compressed *nukitsuke* and *kirioroshi* of Kabezoe allow you to draw and defeat your opponent in these narrow confines. Likewise, the *chiburi* and *nōtō* peculiar to this *waza* permitted resheathing of the sword in such limited space.

## 11P: UKENAGASHI

Last of the Okuden Tachiwaza, Ukenagashi (Flowing Block) follows the basic principle of its Shoden namesake—the continuous-motion draw, block, and counterattack—but performed while standing or walking, rather than seated.

As you finish inhaling your third cleansing breath, take your first step forward with your right foot. On your second step, your left foot crosses in front of your right, so you are turned about 45 degrees to the right as you perform *koiguchi no kirikata* and draw about one-third to one-half of the sword (fig. 11P.3).

Your right foot now steps a little farther to the right and to the rear of your left—in a triangular pattern much like that used in the Shoden version of Ukenagashi—as you twist your upper body 45 degrees to your left and complete *nukitsuke* as a rising *ukenagashi* (see fig. 11P.6). Twist your upper body another 45 degrees to your left as the sword swivels into *furikaburi*, grasp the *tsuka* with your left hand, and shuffle-step (left foot, then right foot) forward with *kirioroshi*. As shown in figure 11P.10, *kirioroshi* is completed with the feet together in *iaigoshi*. Remain facing 45 degrees to the left of your original direction, step back with your left foot into a power stance as you perform Eishin-Ryū *chiburi* and Okuden *nōtō*, slide your left foot up to meet your right foot, pivot 45 degrees to your right, then step back to your original starting position.

Figures 11P.1–12. Okuden Tachiwaza: Ukenagashi

The application for this variation of Ukenagashi is identical to that for the Shoden version, except that it occurs in a standing position. Your opponent is directly in front of you, with his sword drawn and ready as you approach. As you come within his striking range, you step to your right and begin to draw, apparently exposing yourself to attack. As your opponent strikes at what he perceives as your vulnerability, you draw, block, and counterattack in a single motion.

The sidestepping and twisting motion employed in the blocking phase of Ukenagashi is called *tenshin* (body-shift) and is used to throw the opponent off balance by suddenly removing the resistance he expects to meet with his powerful *kirioroshi*. This is the reason you must turn and step to your left during *kirioroshi*, since your opponent's momentum will carry him stumbling forward to about this point after failing to meet the anticipated resistance of your block.

## ITOMAGOI

The aptly named Itomagoi (Farewell Visit) *waza* are three slightly different variations of a single theme. They are conceptually the same as the Shoden *waza* Nukiuchi, or the Chūden *waza* Makkō, differing only in nuances of their execution.

One difference common to all three Itomagoi *waza* is that the continuous-motion nukitsuke-furikaburi-kirioroshi is performed even more quickly than in Makkō. Another shared difference, of course, is that the Itomagoi *waza* employ Okuden *nōtō*.

Although they are normally included as "Tachiwaza" in the Eishin-Ryū curriculum, the Itomagoi *waza* are all performed in *seiza* position, just as their Shoden and Chūden counterparts. They are differentiated from each other simply by being numbered *ichi* (one), *ni* (two), and *san* (three).

## 11Q: ITOMAGOI ICHI

Begin in *seiza* posture (fig. 11Q.1) by taking the customary three cleansing breaths.

As you finish inhaling the third time, begin to bow by leaning slightly forward and moving your hands toward the floor. Just as your fingertips graze the floor, immediately grasp the *tsuka*, perform *koiguchi no kirikata*, and draw the sword straight up so that *nukitsuke* and *furikaburi* occur in a single motion as you rise up tall on your knees and get set on the balls of your feet (fig. 11Q.3–7). As in Nukiuchi and Makkō, do not allow your sword to strike the floor during *kirioroshi*. Use Eishin-Ryū *chiburi* (simultaneously retracting your knees to normal *seiza* width) and Okuden *nōtō*. Remain on the balls of your feet during *nōtō* and gradually settle back onto your heels just as the *tsuba* meets your left hand. After you slide your right hand to the *tsuka-gashira*, rise up slightly, flatten your feet against the floor, and lower yourself into *seiza* position.

Ōyō for Itomagoi Ichi is identical to that of Nukiuchi or Makkō. You are on a *jōiuchi* mission to capture or execute the enemy seated in front of you in formal *seiza* posture. In this more subtle (*oku*) situation, your foe suspects that you may be under such orders, so he waits for you to bow. As you begin to bow, he follows, giving you the split-second opportunity to draw and strike in a sudden and continuous motion.

Figures 11Q.1–15. Okuden Tachiwaza: Itomagoi Ichi

# 11R: ITOMAGOI NI

Itomagoi Ni is identical to Itomagoi Ichi except the extent to which you begin to bow. From *seiza* posture (fig. 11R.1), begin by taking the customary three cleansing breaths.

As you finish inhaling the third time, begin to bow by leaning slightly forward and placing your hands on the floor, just as you would for a normal *zarei*. The moment your hands are in position to bow (fig. 11R.6), immediately grasp the *tsuka* and perform *koiguchi no kirikata*, rise, and draw the sword straight up so that *nukitsuke* and *furikaburi* occur in a single motion, exactly as in Itomagoi Ichi, followed immediately with *kirioroshi*. The waza ends with Eishin-Ryū *chiburi*, Okuden *nōtō*, and your return to seiza posture exactly as in Itomagoi Ichi. Since the rest of the waza is presented in figures 11Q.3–15, above, shown below is only the portion of Itomagoi Ni that is different—the initiation of the bow.

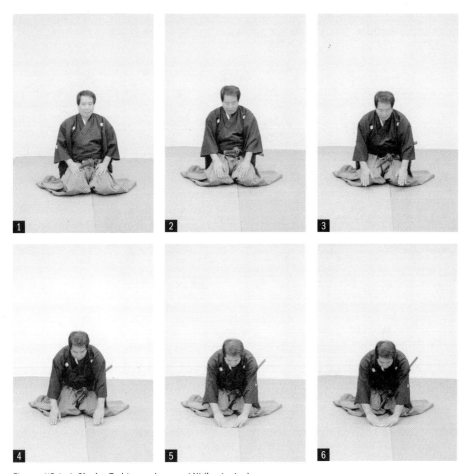

Figures 11R.1–6. Okuden Tachiwaza: Itomagoi Ni (beginning)

*Ōyō* for Itomagoi Ni is identical to that of Itomagoi Ichi, except that your enemy is even more suspicious of you than his counterpart in Itomagoi Ichi. In this case, he hesitates until your hands touch the floor in preparation to bow (fig. 11R.6), so that you are beginning to bend forward in your bow before he returns your bow. Once again, you have a split-second opportunity to draw and strike in order to carry out your orders.

## 11S: ITOMAGOI SAN

Itomagoi San takes the situation a degree further than Itomagoi Ichi and Ni, so the only difference is the extent of your initial bow. From *seiza* posture (fig. 11S.1), take the customary three cleansing breaths. As you finish inhaling the third time, you bow fully in *zarei* (fig. 11S.3). Pause for a moment, then complete the *waza* exactly as in Itomagoi Ichi and Itomagoi Ni (figs. 11Q.3–15). Conclude with Eishin-Ryū *chiburi*, Okuden *nōtō*, and return to *seiza*. Once again, only the extent of the bow is depicted below, since the remainder of the *waza* is identical to the other Itomagoi *waza*.

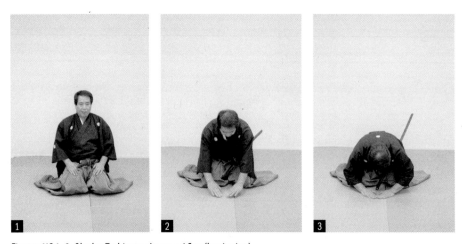

Figures 11S.1–3. Okuden Tachiwaza: Itomagoi San (beginning)

*Ōyō* for Itomagoi San is identical to that of Itomagoi Ichi and Ni, except that in this case your enemy is completely distrustful of you. He therefore waits until you have performed a full bow before he follows suit. But honor and etiquette require that he return your bow, giving you a split-second chance to fulfill your *jōiuchi* mission by rising suddenly while the opponent is bowing forward and executing him before he can react.

# CONCLUSION

As with the Ōmori-Ryū Seiza *waza,* many of the Okuden Tachiwaza had different names prior to changes made by Ōe Masamichi (the seventeenth headmaster of Eishin-Ryū):

| Present Name | Previous Name |
|---|---|
| 1. Yukizure | Yukizure (Escorted) |
| 2. Tsuredachi | Tsuredachi (Companions) |
| 3. Sōmakuri | Gohōgiri (Five-Way Cut) |
| 4. Sōdome | Hanashiuchi (Severing Strikes) |
| 5. Shinobu | Yoru no Tachi (Night Sword) |
| 6. Yukichigai | Yukichigai (Passing By) |
| 7. Sode Surigaeshi | Ken no Koto (Brushing Sword) |
| 8. Moniri | Kakuresute (Ambushed) |
| 9. Kabezoe | Hito Naka (In the Middle) |
| 10. Ukenagashi | Yurumi Nuki (Relaxed Draw) |
| 11. Itomagoi | Itomagoi (Farewell Visit) |

# Chapter 12

# Okuden Suwariwaza

## Seated Okuden Waza

The Okuden Suwariwaza (crouching techniques), like the Okuden Tachiwaza, were part of Hayashizaki-Ryū during its formative years. They too were modified by Hasegawa Eishin to adapt their techniques to the modern shorter sword (*daitō*) design.

All of the Okuden (Deep-Level) Suwariwaza begin in *tatehiza* (standing knee) posture. If you have practiced the Chūden *waza* for several months or longer before moving on to the Okuden series, you may by now find *tatehiza* less uncomfortable than before. For a detailed description of the *tatehiza* position, refer to the explanatory material in chapters 7 and 9.

Like all other Okuden techniques, the Suwariwaza exclusively employ Eishin-Ryū *chiburi* (the "flicking" type) and Okuden *nōtō*, as described in chapter 7. Since Okuden *waza* should not be attempted until the Chūden *waza* have been practiced extensively, and these elements are now thoroughly familiar to the reader, *nōtō* and *chiburi* have been presented for review only for the first Suwariwaza, Kasumi, and then omitted from the photographic sequences for the remainder of this chapter.

## 12A: KASUMI

The first Okuden Suwariwaza, Kasumi (Haze), begins facing straight ahead in *tatehiza* posture (see fig. 12A.1) while taking the three preparatory *kiyomeri kokyū* breaths.

As you finish inhaling the third time, raise your hands to the *tsuka*, with the left hand gripping the *saya* just before your right hand grasps the *tsuka*, and perform *koiguchi no kirikata* and *nukitsuke*. In this instance, rather than finishing *nukitsuke* with the *kissaki* pointing back toward your opponent's position, allow the blade's momentum to carry it well to your right, as shown in figure 12A.5. Turn the sword and sweep it back to your left side at knee level, scooting your left knee forward for additional reach, in a movement called *kirikaeshi* (returning cut), as illustrated in figures 12A.6–8. Perform *furikaburi*, then step forward with the right foot for *kirioroshi*. Conclude with Eishin-Ryū *chiburi* and Okuden *nōtō*.

In Okuden Suwariwaza, your right foot slides rearward during *nōtō*, in much the same manner as in the Chūden *waza*, with one exception: you begin sliding your right foot back *after* you have finished the rapid stage of Okuden *nōtō*. Thereafter, the retracting foot keeps pace with the slow and steady insertion of the *katana* into its *saya*. As your right heel comes into line with your left knee, the sword should be about 80 percent sheathed and, without changing the speed of the moving foot or the remaining *nōtō*, it traces a small clockwise circle and comes to rest beside your left heel just as the *tsuba* contacts your left hand, as shown in figure 12A.14.

From this position, step forward with your right foot, then rise to a standing position (in *iaigoshi*), sliding your left foot forward to meet your right. Take two or three steps back to reach your original starting position. At this point, now standing fully erect, remove your right hand from the *tsuka-gashira* and return it to your right side while your left hand releases the *saya* and *tsuba* and returns to your left side.

The *ōyō* of Kasumi is identical to Yokogumo in the Chūden *waza*. However, as an Okuden *waza*, it takes the situation to a deeper level. You are being attacked by an opponent who is directly in front of you. Anticipating his action, you are able to draw more quickly than him, but he recoils, avoiding your attempted slash at his eyes, so you immediately shift to *kirikaeshi*, cutting his leg to immobilize him while you prepare for and execute *kirioroshi*. Kasumi, translated here as "Haze," possibly gets its name from the blur of motion in which *nukitsuke* flows into *kirikaeshi*, and then into *furikaburi* and *kirioroshi* in a continuous sequence.

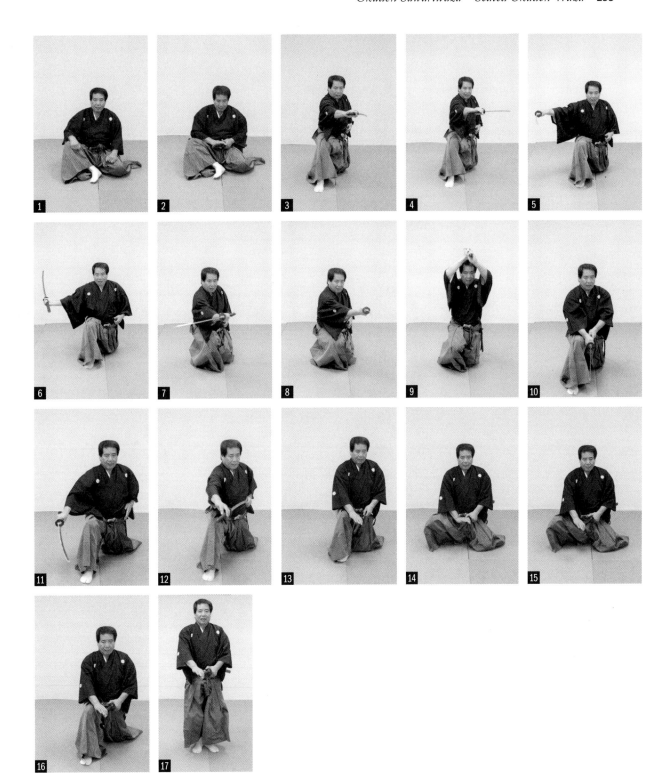

Figures 12A.1–17. Okuden Suwariwaza: Kasumi

## 12B: SUNEGAKOI

The second Okuden *waza*, Sunegakoi (Shin Protection) begins facing straight ahead in *tatehiza* posture while you take your three preparatory breaths. At the top of the third breath, begin *nukitsuke*, drawing the *tsuka* at a slight downward angle. Complete *nukitsuke* by rising as you draw—stepping back with your left foot—and blocking in front of your right leg (with the blade edge forward) as shown in figure 12B.5.

Drop to one knee, right foot leading, during *furikaburi*, then shuffle forward while performing *kirioroshi*, finishing with Eishin-Ryū *chiburi* and Okuden *nōtō*. Rise to standing position and step back to your starting point.

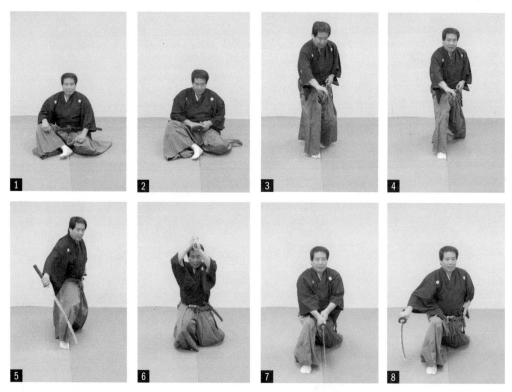

Figures 12B.1–8. Okuden Suwariwaza: Sunegakoi

*Ōyō* for Sunegakoi is identical to its Chūden counterpart, Tora no Issoku. In fact, the only visible differences between the two are that Sunegakoi is performed more quickly than Tora no Issoku, and uses Okuden *nōtō*. In both instances, your attacker is directly in front of you, and you have not beaten him to the draw. Instead, you must use *nukitsuke* to block his *nukitsuke* attack directed at your leading leg, then counter-attack with *kirioroshi*.

## 12C: SHIHŌGIRI

In the third Suwariwaza, Shihōgiri (Four-Way Cut), you begin by facing straight ahead in *tatehiza* posture while performing *kiyomeri kokyū*. At the top of the third breath, begin *koiguchi no kirikata*, then step at a 45-degree angle to your right-front as you begin *nukitsuke* (fig. 12C.3), and finish *nukitsuke* by turning your hips left to perform a level thrust at a 45-degree angle to your left-rear, as shown in figure 12C.5.

Figures 12C.1–11. Okuden Suwariwaza: Shihōgiri

Turn your upper body back toward the right-front during *furikaburi*, then shuffle forward while performing *kirioroshi* at 45 degrees to your right-front (fig. 12C.7). Turn 90 degrees to your left while raising the sword in *furikaburi*, and step forward (right foot front) with *kirioroshi* at 45 degrees to your left-front (fig. 12C.9). Perform *furikaburi* again while turning 45 degrees to your right, and step forward (right foot front) with *kirioroshi* in the direction you were originally facing (fig. 12C.11). Complete Shihōgiri with Eishin-Ryū *chiburi* and Okuden *nōtō*, rise to standing position, and step back to your starting point.

Interestingly, *ōyō* for Shihōgiri is usually explained differently than the way in which the *waza* is performed, and this difference deserves detailed examination. In Shihōgiri, you are surrounded by attackers on four sides: right-front, left-front, left-rear, and right-rear, whom you must dispatch in order of the imminence of their threat. Their plan of attack is to have the opponent to your right-front grab your *tsuka* to prevent you from defending yourself, while the enemies to your rear attack, followed by the remaining attacker at your front-left. Thus, although it is not usually practiced as a strike, the first movement—rising to begin *nukitsuke*—is considered to *imply* a *tsuka-ate* (handle-strike).

The next most dangerous foe is the one to your left-rear, so you make a lethal thrust past your left shoulder, which would be performed essentially as practiced in this *waza*. The opponent at your right-rear is next in degree of threat, and is this opponent who is understood to receive the first *kirioroshi* in the *waza*, even though it is practiced to the front-right, instead of the right-rear.

Next comes the opponent to your left-front, who has now had time to turn and begin his attack. You must quickly turn and deal him a *kirioroshi*, roughly to the position practiced in the *waza*.

Lastly, having recovered from the agonizing blow to the face from your *tsuka*, the opponent to your right-front receives the final *kirioroshi*, which is delivered to the front-center in the *waza*.

## 12D: TOZUME

Tozume (Boxed In by Doors) is the fourth in this series of *waza*, and begins in *tate-hiza* posture facing straight ahead.

After the third breath of *kokyū*, perform *koiguchi no kirikata* and rise, stepping firmly to your right as you complete *nukitsuke* with a downward cut that ends with the blade angled upward at about 45 degrees, as illustrated in figure 12D.3. During *furikaburi*, turn 90 degrees to your left and step strongly forward with your right foot with *kirioroshi* (fig. 12D.5). Finish with Eishin-Ryū *chiburi* and Okuden *nōtō*, rise, and step back to your starting point.

The *ōyō* for Tozume is somewhat subtle. Your two opponents are at angles to your right-front and left-front, but are crouching behind a pair of *byōbu* (folding decorative screens) or *fusuma* (interior sliding doors). The powerful forward step taken on *nukitsuke* and *kirioroshi* is designed to knock down each of these barriers, both hampering your enemy's attack and exposing him to counterattack.

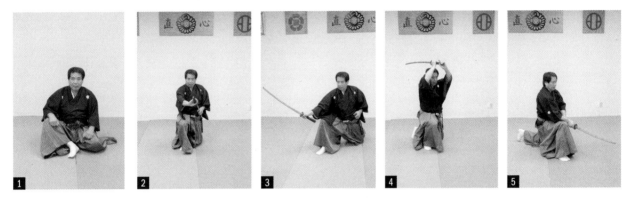

Figures 12D.1–5. Okuden Suwariwaza: Tozume

# 12E: TOWAKI

The fifth Okuden *waza*, Towaki (Beside the Door), involves a situation very similar to that dealt with in Tozume. Once again, you begin facing straight ahead in *tatehiza* during *kiyomeri kokyū*. As you inhale the third cleansing breath, look to your right (at about a 45-degree angle) as you grasp the *tsuka* with both hands, then step at a 45-degree angle to your right as you rise to one knee and draw the blade forward, then thrust back past your left shoulder at a 45-degree angle to your left-rear (fig. 12E.4). Immediately turn to your right-front as you raise your sword in *furikaburi*, then step forward with your right foot and execute *kirioroshi*. Conclude with Eishin-Ryū *chiburi* and Okuden *nōtō*, rise, turn 45 degrees to your left while maintaining *iaigoshi*, then step back to your starting point.

The *ōyō* for Towaki is similar to that of Tozume, because your opponents are hiding behind lightweight barriers, waiting for the ideal moment—or perhaps a signal—to attack. In this case, however, one is concealed behind you and one to your front at opposite corners, giving them the greatest advantage in a simultaneous attack. As you sense their presence and intent, you draw and stab to the rear, thrusting through one *byōbu* or *fusuma*, then step forward, knocking the second screen down onto the other attacker as you defend with *kirioroshi*.

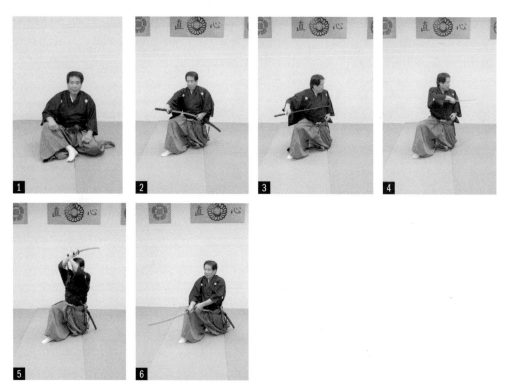

Figures 12E.1–6. Okuden Suwariwaza: Towaki

## 12F: TANASHITA

Tanashita (Beneath a Shelf) is the sixth *waza* of the Okuden series. It begins in *tate-hiza*, facing forward. However, to more clearly portray this *waza*, it is shown below in side view. To perform this *waza* with the proper feeling, body position, and technique, it is important to understand its *ōyō*. Tanashita takes its name literally, since you are crouching beneath a shelf, such as those common in Japanese gardens, or perhaps a raised porch of the type that customarily surrounded a Japanese home or teahouse in feudal times.

As you take your third cleansing breath, raise your hands to the *tsuka* for *koiguchi no kirikata*. As you begin to draw your sword, take a long, crouching step forward with your right foot, sliding it along the floor. As shown in figure 12F.3, be sure to keep your head low, as if hunkered beneath a low overhang. When the *kissaki* clears the *koiguchi*, remain crouched low and draw your left foot forward until your left knee is beside your right heel as you raise the sword over your back in a modified *furikaburi* (see fig. 12F.5). Push with your left foot as you take another long step forward with your right foot, straightening your back only as your weight comes to bear on your front leg and you perform *kirioroshi* (fig. 12F.7). As your momentum carries you onto your front leg, allow your rear leg to slide forward into the normal kneeling posture shown.

Your movements should have the feeling and appearance of emerging from beneath the shelf or porch and stepping far enough clear of its overhang to make a full, unobstructed swing during *kirioroshi*. To achieve this requires that you visualize yourself in this situation during practice.

Complete the *waza* with Eishin-Ryū *chiburi* and Okuden *nōtō*, rise to a standing position, and step back to your starting point.

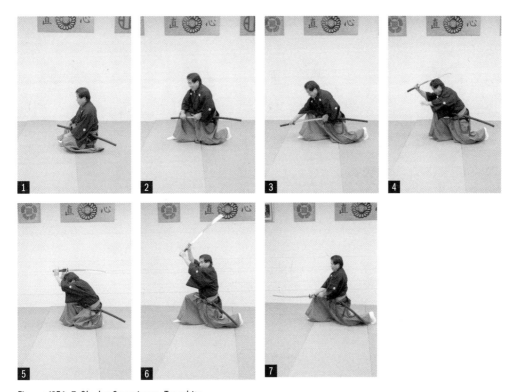

Figures 12F.1–7. Okuden Suwariwaza: Tanashita

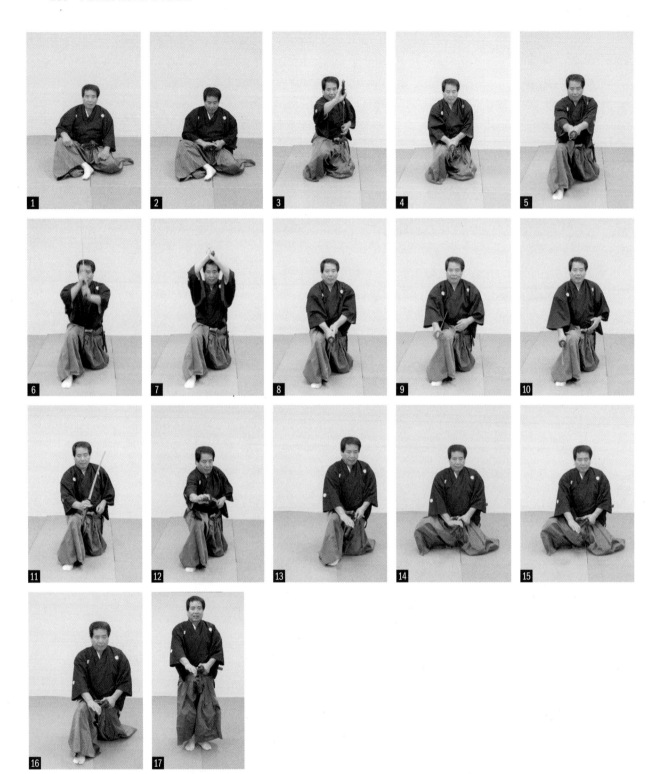

Figures 12G.1–17. Okuden Suwariwaza: Ryōzume

# 12G: RYŌZUME

The seventh Okuden *waza* is Ryōzume (Boxed In on Both Sides). The situation in this *waza* is the equivalent of that found in the Tachiwaza called Kabezoe. You are seated in *tatehiza*, sandwiched between two barriers, such as in a narrow hallway, and confronted by an opponent directly ahead of you.

As you finish your third cleansing breath, raise your hands to the *tsuka* for *koiguchi no kirikata*, then draw the sword at an upward angle of about 45 degrees as you rise to one foot. When the *kissaki* leaves the *koiguchi*, pull the *tsuka* back toward your navel and grasp it with your left hand, as shown in figure 12G.4. With a shuffle-step forward, perform a two-handed thrust to the opponent's midsection. Pull back on the *tsuka* again to withdraw the blade from the adversary, then raise the sword in *furikaburi*, take another shuffle-step forward, and finish with *kirioroshi*.

Due to the tight confines for which this technique was designed, *chiburi* has been modified for Ryōzume. By bending your wrist upward, raise the *kissaki* a few inches while raising the *tsuka* enough to swing it from the inside to the outside of your right leg—keeping the *tsuba* even with your knee—and snap your wrist down, so the *kissaki* again drops slightly below level, finishing as shown in figure 12G.10.

*Nōtō* in Ryōzume is also adapted to cramped quarters by keeping both elbows close to the body, flipping the *kissaki* back toward the left shoulder (fig. 12G.11) to initiate *nōtō*, and raising the right hand to about face height during the rapid portion of *nōtō* (fig. 12G.12), rather than keeping it level. Bearing in mind your high degree of vulnerability during *nōtō*, raising the *tsuka* in this fashion allows you to keep your right hand closer to the center of your body and away from the obstruction on your right. After the accelerated portion of *nōtō*, it is completed in the usual fashion; then rise to standing position, and step back to your starting point.

In Ryōzume, you are boxed in by walls or obstacles on both sides, making a normal *nukitsuke* impossible. So, when your opponent begins his attack, you instead draw and thrust straight forward, inflicting an abdominal wound that delays your opponent's attack until you can finish with *kirioroshi*.

# 12H: TORABASHIRI

The final Okuden Suwariwaza is Torabashiri (Running Tiger), a *tatehiza* technique with similarities to the Shoden *waza* called Oikaze. In Torabashiri, your opponent begins a surprise attack, but when he realizes that you can successfully defend yourself, retreats as you rise to your defense. Thus, as you complete your three cleansing breaths, grasp the *tsuka* for *koiguchi no kirikata*, rising on the balls of your feet as shown in figure 12H.2. In a manner similar to Oikaze, take a number of *chidori-ashi* (tiny, rapid stutter-steps) forward, ending with a normal step with your left foot, then a normal step with your right foot as you complete *nukitsuke* in a standing position (fig. 12H.6).

Crouch down as you raise your *katana* in *furikaburi* (fig. 12H.7), then take a shuffle-step forward as you perform *kirioroshi* (fig. 12H.8).

After Eishin-Ryū *chiburi*, begin Okuden *nōtō*, starting to slide your right foot back. Just before you would normally circle it beneath you (fig. 12H.12), a second (concealed) attacker begins an assault. Draw both feet slightly together to gain the best possible footing, then take a number of *chidori-ashi* steps backward as you begin *nukitsuke* again. Your last step back is a full step with your left foot as you complete *nukitsuke* (figs. 12H.15–16). Crouch down as you again raise your *katana* in *furikaburi* (fig. 12H.17), then take a shuffle-step forward as you perform the final *kirioroshi*. Once again, perform Eishin-Ryū *chiburi* and Okuden *nōtō*, this time completing *nōtō* by sliding your right foot back and circling it beneath yourself as you resheath the sword. Rise to standing position and step back to your starting point.

Figures 12H.1–10. Okuden Suwariwaza: Torabashiri

Figures 12H.11–18. Okuden Suwariwaza: Torabashiri

# CONCLUSION

Again, many of the Suwariwaza also had different names prior to changes made by Ōe Masamichi, the seventeenth *sōshihan* of Eishin-Ryū:

| Present Name | Previous Name |
| --- | --- |
| 1. Kasumi | Mukōbarai (Sweep Opponent) |
| 2. Sunegakoi | Tsukadome (Stop Attack) |
| 3. Shihōgiri | Shisumi (Four Corners) |
| 4. Tozume | Misumi (Three Corners) |
| 5. Towaki | Mukōzume (Boxed In by Opponents) |
| 6. Tanashita | Tanashita (Beneath a Shelf) |
| 7. Ryōzume | Ryōzume (Boxed In on Both Sides) |
| 8. Torabashiri | Torabashiri (Running Tiger) |

Chapter 13

# *Battō-Hō*

## Military Waza

The Battō-Hō are a relatively recent addition to the Eishin-Ryū curriculum. The Okuden *waza* were derived from the original *waza* of Hayashizaki-Ryū that were created in the late sixteenth century. The Chūden Tatehiza *waza* were added by the seventh headmaster and namesake of our style, Hasegawa Eishin, in the late sixteenth or early seventeenth century. The Shoden (Ōmori-Ryū) *waza* were developed during the time of ninth headmaster Hayashi Rokudayū in the early to mid-seventeenth century. The Bangai no Bu were created by seventeenth headmaster Ōe Masamichi in the early twentieth century and are therefore not considered *koryū waza*.

Created in 1939 by Kōno Hyakuren of the Shimomura-Ha lineage (see chapter 1), the Battō-Hō are, at just over eighty years, the newest techniques in the Eishin-Ryū curriculum. The Battō-Hō were created in order to train Japanese naval officers in the fundamentals of *iaijutsu* during the Second Sino-Japanese War. Developed under the auspices of the Dai Nippon Butoku-Kai, where Kōno was serving as an instructor at its Budō Senmon Gakkō, these techniques were initially called the Dai Nippon Battō-Hō. In the aftermath of World War II they came to be more commonly called Eishin-Ryū Battō-Hō.

Since the Eishin-Ryū Battō-Hō were created as a separate set of techniques for the specific purpose of training military officers in *iaijutsu* in much the same way the Seitei Iai Kata (see chapter 18) were created specifically to train *kendōka*, they were not considered part of the core curriculum of Eishin-Ryū, and therefore not included in the earlier editions of *Flashing Steel*.

In recent years, however, the Battō-Hō have been practiced by increasing numbers of *iaidōka* worldwide, not only among practitioners of Eishin-Ryū, but among *iaidōka* from many styles. It wasn't until after the publication of the second edition of *Flashing Steel* in 2008 that, due to his failing health, Miura Takeyuki Sōshihan named Shimabukuro Hanshi as his eventual successor. As he considered the burden of this responsibility, Shimabukuro Hanshi looked to the example of Masaoka Katsutane, who merged the teachings of Shimomura-Ha and Tanimura-Ha to create what is now recognized as the Masaoka-Ha lineage, and decided to incorporate the Eishin-Ryū Battō-Hō into the core curriculum of Masaoka-Ha.

This decision was not made lightly, nor simply to expand the curriculum of the Masaoka-Ha tradition in order to broaden its appeal. It was instead made after a lengthy and in-depth analysis of the purpose and methods of the Battō-Hō, from which Shimabukuro Hanshi concluded that the Battō-Hō present a training scenario different from the rest of the Eishin-Ryū curriculum and would expand the knowledge and skill of practitioners of Masaoka-Ha.

Soon after deciding to incorporate the Battō-Hō into his future teachings, Shimabukuro Hanshi set about diligently promulgating them to his students around the world. In 2008 he released a set of three DVDs through *Black Belt Magazine*, in which he demonstrated the Battō-Hō, and in 2011 he coauthored with current *sōshihan* Carl Long Hanshi the book *Samurai Swordsmanship: The Battō, Kenjutsu, and Tameshigiri of Eishin-Ryū*, in which the Battō-Hō are described and depicted in thorough detail. Since full details on the performance of the Battō-Hō are already available in those formats, this chapter presents only a general overview of the Battō-Hō and their underlying principles.

The Eishin-Ryū Battō-Hō are divided into two distinct sets of techniques: the Shoden no Bu (Beginning Level Group) and the Okuden no Bu (Deep-Level Group), as listed below:

| *Waza* Name | Meaning of the Name |
|---|---|
| SHODEN NO BU | |
| Juntō Sono Ichi | Standard Sword No. 1 |
| Juntō Sono Ni | Standard Sword No. 2 |
| Tsuigekitō | Pursuing Attack |
| Shatō | Angled Sword |
| Shihōtō Sono Ichi | Four-Direction Sword No. 1 |
| Shihōtō Sono Ni | Four-Direction Sword No. 2 |
| Zantotsutō | Behead and Thrust |

| *Waza* Name | Meaning of the Name |
|---|---|
| OKUDEN NO BU | |
| Zenteki Gyakutō Sono Ichi | Front Enemy Reversed Sword No. 1 |
| Zenteki Gyakutō Sono Ni | Front Enemy Reversed Sword No. 2 |
| Tatekitō | Many Enemies Sword |
| Koteki Gyakutō | Rear Enemy Reversed Sword |
| Koteki Nukiuchi | Rear Enemy Sudden Attack |

Note: As a result of his research into the Battō-Hō, Shimabukuro Hanshi created the technique we now call Zenteki Gyakutō Sono Ichi to match the footwork pattern of Juntō Sono Ichi and fully integrate the principles and methods of both Shimomura-Ha and Tanimura-Ha into the Battō-Hō. The technique named Zenteki Gyakutō Sono Ni above was originally called simply Zenteki Gyakutō. Not all branches of Eishin-Ryū practice both the Sono Ichi and Sono Ni variations.

Battō-Hō means "sword-drawing methods." *Battō-jutsu*, or "art of sword-drawing," was one of the earliest terms for the art we more often call *iaidō* or *iaijutsu* today. Nevertheless, there is a subtle but crucial difference between the way the Battō-Hō are performed and the way most other *waza* in the Eishin-Ryū curriculum are performed. This difference stems from the fact that the Battō-Hō were created to train military officers in methods of sword combat. While the Shoden *waza*, Chūden *waza*, Okuden Suwariwaza, and roughly half the Okuden Tachiwaza address self-defense situations in which the *iaidōka* is attacked unexpectedly, the Battō-Hō are designed to employ *iaijutsu* techniques under battlefield conditions. When attending a formal function (the setting of most Shoden *waza*) or relaxing in camp (the setting of the Chūden *waza*), the *iaidōka* is aware of the possibility of a surprise attack but is engaged in some other activity until the moment the attacker makes his or her intentions known. The same is true of the Okuden Suwariwaza scenarios and several of the Okuden Tachiwaza.

In the Battō-Hō, however, the *iaidōka* is already on the battlefield and ready to engage in combat with a clearly identified enemy or enemies even before performance of the technique begins, and this fact alters the mindset and actions of the *iaidōka*, which is central to the nature of the Battō-Hō techniques themselves. Thus, a notable characteristic of the Battō-Hō is the more aggressive posture, footwork, and *seme* (intimidating pressure) evident at the beginning of each Battō-Hō technique. Also, consistent with a battlefield scenario, all of the Battō-Hō are *tachiwaza*—techniques performed in a standing position.

# SHODEN BATTŌ-HŌ

The Shoden Battō-Hō all begin in the same fashion: three *kiyomeri kokyū* (purifying breaths) followed by taking three steps forward. Those three steps all follow the same basic pattern: while stepping forward with the right foot, the left hand rises and grasps the *saya* with the thumb on the *tsuba*; as the left foot begins moving forward, the left hand performs *koiguchi no kirikata*, feeding the *tsuka* into the right hand as it grasps the *tsuka* and begins *nukitsuke*; then, as the right foot lands in the third step forward, *nukitsuke* is completed. In the Shoden Battō-Hō the Shimomura-Ha method of *nukitsuke* is used, as well as Shimomura-Ha *furikaburi*, both of which are explained in detail in chapter 7.

Several Okuden Tachiwaza, such as Yukizure, Tsuredachi, and Yukichigai, begin by taking two or three steps forward walking in a normal manner. In each of those scenarios, however, you are trying not to give away your intent to take defensive measures, so to disguise your intentions, you walk in a normal manner, as if taking a casual stroll, until the moment you initiate your action. Conversely, in the Shoden Battō-Hō, you are on a battleground and already engaged in combat. Your opponent is fully aware of your intentions, so there is no reason to mask them.

Thus, in the Shoden Battō-Hō, you begin standing in normal upright posture (see fig. 13A.1). Your first step is initiated by lowering into *iaigoshi* by flexing your hips, knees, and ankles as you begin moving your right foot forward, and in your subsequent steps, you remain in this athletic and aggressive posture with your hips, knees, and ankles poised to spring suddenly and powerfully forward. Your mental focus and intensity should reflect this readiness to drive ferociously at your opponent, like a pouncing tiger, yet you must maintain an erect posture and not hunch or lean forward as you move to engage your adversary. Figure 13A.2 shows the completion of the first forward step, with the left hand positioned at the *tsuba* to perform *koiguchi no kirikata*. As you begin to step forward with your right foot, raise your right hand to the *tsuka* slightly forward of the point at which you will grip it and use *koiguchi no kirikata* to push the *tsuka* into the right hand. This is what we mean by "feeding" the *tsuka* into the right hand. Without pause, the right hand continues to push the *tsuk-agashira* toward the opponent's *me no ma* (space between the eyes), beginning *nukitsuke* as the left foot is stepping forward (fig. 13A.3), then *saya-banari* and completion of *nukitsuke* as the right foot steps forward (fig. 13A.4). This coordinated timing of *nukitsuke* and *ashi-sabaki* (footwork) is critical to keeping you out of range of your opponent to preclude any effective countermeasures and concealing the type of *nukitsuke* cut (in this example, *suihei-giri*) employed until it is too late for the opponent to anticipate and defend against it.

Since this beginning is common to all seven of the Shoden Battō-Hō, it will not be explained in detail in the descriptions that follow, but abbreviated simply as, "Take three steps forward ..."

Similarly, all seven of the Shoden Battō-Hō end in the same manner. After *chiburi*, perform Shoden *nōtō* in the manner described in chapter 7. Once the *habaki* is seated in the *saya*, hook your left thumb over the *tsuba* at about the one o'clock position, then slide your right hand along the *tsuka* to the *tsukagashira*. Pause for a moment in this position, maintaining *zanshin* (awareness of your surroundings) to be sure you are not subject to further attack, then lower your right hand, closing it into a loose fist in front of your right thigh and about even with the *tsuba*. Return to the starting point of the *waza* by taking a small step back with your left foot, followed by a slightly longer rearward step with your right foot, then three more steps of normal length. In the descriptions that follow, this sequence will be abbreviated as "Perform Shoden *nōtō* and return to your starting position" to avoid unnecessary repetition of these details.

# 13A: JUNTŌ SONO ICHI

Take three steps forward, completing *nukitsuke* as a *suihei-giri* (horizontal cut) with the right foot forward (fig. 13A.4). Maintaining *seme* (see chapter 7), begin stepping forward with the left foot, performing *furikaburi* in mid-stride, then *kirioroshi* as your left foot reaches its final position (fig. 13A.6). *Ō-chiburi* (see chapter 7), drawing your right foot even with your left foot as you complete *chiburi*. Then perform Shoden *nōtō* and return to your starting position.

Figures 13A.1–5. Shoden Battō-Hō: Juntō Sono Ichi

Figures 13A.6–13. Shoden Battō-Hō: Juntō Sono Ichi

## 13B: JUNTŌ SONO NI

Take three steps forward, completing *nukitsuke* as a *suihei-giri* (horizontal cut) with the right foot forward (fig. 13B.4). Maintaining *seme*, draw your left foot even with your right while performing *furikaburi*, then step forward with your right foot and *kirioroshi* (fig. 13B.6). The timing of footwork and sword handling should be essentially the same as in Juntō Sono Ichi, the only difference being which foot is forward upon *kirioroshi* and the distance traveled between the completion of *nukitsuke* and *kirioroshi*. Without moving your feet, *yoko-chiburi* (see chapter 7), then perform Shoden *nōtō* and return to your starting position.

Juntō Sono Ichi and Juntō Sono Ni address an identical combative situation, but offer two different solutions to the timing and distance between yourself and your opponent after *nukitsuke*. Juntō Sono Ichi (left foot forward) allows a slightly quicker *kirioroshi*, but covers a shorter distance than does Juntō Sono Ni (right foot forward), depending on what your opponent does after being cut by your *nukitsuke*. They are essentially the same *waza*, with the choice of right or left foot leading being dependent on the opponent's aggressiveness and actions, and would be made on the spot.

Figures 13B.1–11. Shoden Battō-Hō: Juntō Sono Ni

# 13C: TSUIGEKITŌ

Take three steps forward, completing *nukitsuke* as a *gyaku-kesagiri* (left-to-right downward diagonal cut) with the right foot forward (fig. 13C.4). Maintaining *seme*, draw your left foot even with your right while performing *furikaburi*, then lunge forward, leading with your right foot and drawing both feet together with *kiritsuke* (fig. 13C.7), then lunge forward again in the same manner with *furikaburi* and *kirioroshi* (fig. 13C.9). Step back with the right foot into *jōdan no kamae*. Pause to determine that no further threats exist, then step back with your left foot into *seigan no kamae*. Maintaining *zanshin*, *yoko-chiburi*, and Shoden *nōtō*, return to your starting position.

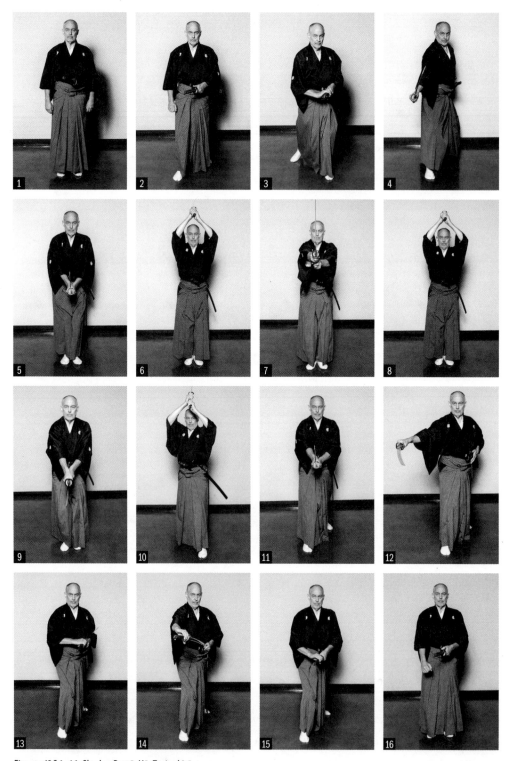

FLASHING STEEL

Figures 13C.1–16. Shoden Battō-Hō: Tsuigekitō

Tsuigekitō means "pursuing-attack sword," so this *waza* emphasizes the aggressive pursuit of an opponent rapidly retreating after your initial *gyaku-kesagiri*. The underlying concept is constant *seme* (pressure) and pursuit, but without rushing. Haste produces sloppiness and vulnerability, whereas unrelenting pressure and unhurried but constant advancement keeps your opponent off balance, retreating, and prone to mistakes.

## 13D: SHATŌ

Take three steps forward, completing *nukitsuke* as a *jōdan-suihei-giri* (high-level left-to-right horizontal cut) with the right foot forward (fig. 13D.4). This first cut is to the underside of the opponent's arms, which are in *jōdan no kamae*. Step forward with the left foot while performing Tanimura-ha *furikaburi* (see chapter 7) and *gyaku-kesagiri* (fig. 13D.6). Step forward and slightly to your right with your right foot while performing *furikaburi*, then *kesagiri*, allowing the momentum of your cut to turn your body and swing your left leg 45 degrees to your left, as shown in figure 13D.8. Raise the sword to *seigan no kamae*, *yoko-chiburi*, and Shoden *nōtō*. Draw your left foot even with your right, then pivot 45 degrees to your right and step back to your starting position.

Figures 13D.1–9. Shoden Battō-Hō: Shatō

Figures 13D.10–16. Shoden Battō-Hō: Shatō

Shatō (Angle Sword) is usually interpreted as an encounter with two opponents who are lined up directly in front of you. The high-level cut of *nukitsuke* severs the muscles and tendons in the nearest opponent's raised arms, before finishing him with *gyaku-kesagiri*. As the first opponent falls, the second immediately attacks with either a *tsuki* or *kiriroshi* over the first attacker's falling body, which you sidestep with the slight movement to your right during *furikaburi*, then counterattack with *kesagiri*, turning farther away from the second opponent's line of attack as you cut.

## 13E: SHIHŌTŌ SONO ICHI

Take three steps forward, turning 45 degrees sharply to your right and beginning *nukitsuke* on the third step, as shown in figure 13E.3. Perform *saya-banari* by turning your hips to the left (fig. 13E.4) and shuffle-step to your left-rear with *chūdan soetezuki* (mid-level thrust with the *tsuka* braced against the underside of your right wrist), as shown in figure 13E.5. Shuffle-step to your front-right with *furikaburi* and *kiriroshi* (fig. 13E.6). Turn the edge of your blade 90 degrees to your left, then with your right foot, step 90 degrees to your left-front with *furikaburi* and *kiriroshi* (fig. 13E.7). Step 45 degrees to your right-front with *furikaburi* and *kirioroshi* (fig. 13E.8). *Yoko-chiburi*, Shoden *nōtō*, and return to your starting position.

Figures 13E.1–13. Shoden Battō-Hō: Shihōtō Sono Ichi

Shihōtō Sono Ichi (Four-Direction Sword Number One) includes subtleties of strategy and execution that are not readily apparent merely by viewing photographs or watching a video of its performance. It is therefore vital to perform this *waza* with those elements in mind.

In both of the Shihōtō scenarios, you deal with four attackers: three in front of you and one directly behind you, as shown in figure 13E.14.

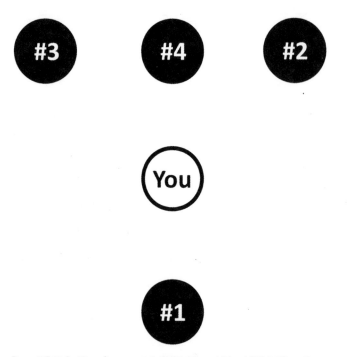

Figure 13E.14. Position of opponents in Shihōtō Sono Ichi and Shihōtō Sono Ni

This attack configuration is intended to make you stop to face the three opponents in front of you, so that the opponent behind you (#1 in fig. 13E.14) can readily cut you down from your unprotected blind side. To counter this strategy, you continue moving forward as if intent on attacking opponent 4, directly in front of you, then in mid-stride, just as opponent 1 begins to attack with *kirioroshi*, you suddenly lunge to your right-front while drawing your sword. This momentarily freezes opponent 2 and at the same time causes opponent 1 to miss. Instead of completing *nukitsuke* with a cut to opponent 2, you turn 45 degrees left (keeping the other two opponents in view), and thrust your sword into the chest of opponent 1 before he can recover from his failed attempt to cut you. In this position, your sword is across your body, serving as protection against an attack from either opponent 3 or opponent 4, so *furikaburi* must be performed with a readiness to use it as a parry against either of those attackers as you turn and perform *kirioroshi* to attacker 2 at your right-front. At this point, you appear vulnerable to an attack from your left, particularly from opponent 4, who is nearest to you, which is why you turn the edge of your blade toward him and begin *furikaburi* as if you intend to cut opponent 4 with *suihei-giri* or *gyaku-kiriage*. This feint keeps opponent 4 at bay (and you out of reach of his sword) while appearing to give opponent 3 an opportunity to attack from your left side, so you step past opponent 4 and perform *kirioroshi* to opponent 3 while he is moving toward you in preparation for attack. At this point, opponent 4 will attempt to attack you, so *furikaburi* should be performed with readiness to use it as an *ukenagashi* deflection as you raise the sword overhead for the final *kirioroshi*.

In addition to performing Shihōtō Sono Ichi with this strategy foremost in mind, you should feel prepared at any moment to defend and counterattack against any of the remaining opponents. This is an *ura* (obscured) meaning of Shihōtō—that you could apply the strategic principles of the *waza* to counterattack the four opponents in any order, depending on their actions or reactions during the encounter, not only the sequence described here.

# 13F: SHIHŌTŌ SONO NI

Take three steps forward, turning 45 degrees sharply to your right and beginning *nukitsuke* on the third step, as shown in figure 13F.4. Perform *saya-banari* by turning your hips to the left and shuffle-step to your left-rear with *chūdan soetezuki* (mid-level thrust with the *tsuka* braced against the underside of your right wrist), as shown in figure 13F.5. Shuffle-step to your front-right with *furikaburi* and *kirioroshi* (fig. 13F.6). Turn the edge of your blade 90 degrees to your left, then with your right foot step 90 degrees to your left-front with *furikaburi* and *kirioroshi* (fig. 13F.7). Step 45 degrees to your right-front with *furikaburi* and *kirioroshi* (fig. 13F.8). *Yoko-chiburi*, Shoden *nōtō*, and return to your starting position.

Figures 13F.1–5. Shoden Battō-Hō: Shihōtō Sono Ni

Figures 13F.6–13. Shoden Battō-Hō: Shihōtō Sono Ni

Shihōtō Sono Ni (Four-Direction Sword Number Two) differs from Shihōtō Sono Ichi in only one seemingly minor way: the counterattack to opponent 3 is performed with the left foot leading (see fig. 13F.7), rather than the right foot. However, this is more than merely a difference in footwork. It reveals a significant difference in the timing and spacing (*maai*) of the attackers. As illustrated in figure 13F.14, stepping toward opponent 3 with the right foot (Shihōtō Sono Ichi) moves you eighteen to twenty-four inches closer than does stepping with the left foot (Shihōtō Sono Ni). Also, simply pivoting on the right foot and stepping toward opponent 4 with the left foot is a quicker movement, which means *kirioroshi* occurs sooner. Thus, Shihōtō Sono Ni addresses a situation in which opponent 3 is either closer or attacks more aggressively than in Shihōtō Sono Ichi. For similar reasons, the footwork in Shihōtō Sono Ni moves you farther toward opponent 4, since your lead (left) foot becomes the rear foot for this cut, while in Shihōtō Sono Ichi your rear (left) foot remains in place while you pivot to cut opponent 4. It is therefore vital to perform this *waza* with those differences in timing and distance in mind.

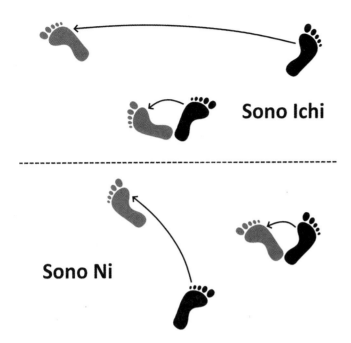

Figures 13F.14. Footwork patterns of Shihōtō Sono Ichi and Sono Ni

# 13G: ZANTOTSUTŌ

Take three steps forward. On the third step complete *nukitsuke* as a *gyaku-kesagiri* (downward left-to-right) cut. Maintaining *iaigoshi*, draw your left foot even with your right foot while pulling the *tsukagashira* toward your navel, as shown in figure 13G.5. Step forward deeply with your right foot, thrusting fully to *jōdan* with your arms as your right foot completes its stride, thus initiating the *tsuki* with your hips and completing it with your arms for maximum penetration and power. Again draw your left foot even with your right foot while pulling the *tsukagashira* toward your navel, then *furikaburi* and *kirioroshi* as you step forward with your right foot. *Yoko-chiburi* and Shoden *nōtō*, then return to your starting position.

Zantotsutō means "beheading thrusting sword," which describes the nature of this *waza*. The *gyaku-kesagiri* performed as *nukitsuke* cuts the opponent from the side of the neck to the center of the chest, partially decapitating him. This is followed with a lunging thrust to the throat, then *kirioroshi* to end his suffering. Avoid the temptation to rush through Zantotsutō. Its movements flow together so well that a smooth, steady pace provides all the speed necessary for its execution.

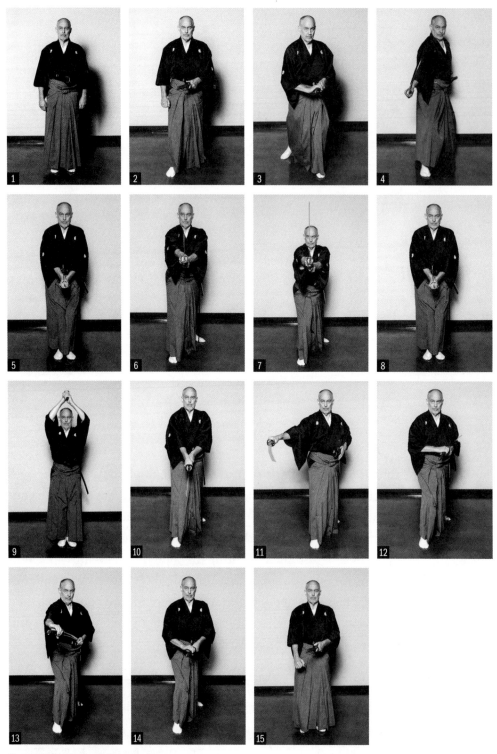

Figures 13G.1–15. Shoden Battō-Hō: Zantotsutō

# OKUDEN BATTŌ-HŌ

The next five *waza* of this series are the Okuden Battō-Hō, which are performed with some characteristic differences from the Shoden Battō-Hō described above. Being Okuden *waza*, they are less obviously confrontational in appearance, which serves to disguise your intentions. Thus, you begin stepping forward with your hands moving naturally at your sides, rather than the left hand grasping the *saya* on the first step and right hand rising to the *tsuka* on the second step as in the Shoden Battō-Hō. Instead, both hands rise to the sword simultaneously, and not until you begin *nukitsuke*. From the moment you begin *nukitsuke* until the completion of your final cut in each *waza*, your sword should be in continual motion without noticeable pauses between *nukitsuke*, *furikaburi*, and each cut. This requires extreme focus and concentration, plus a high level of sword handling skill, to maintain *hasuji* (correct alignment of the blade). Otherwise your cuts will bind in the opponent's body and not be complete.

Another key characteristic of the Okuden Battō-Hō is that *suihei-giri* (horizontal) *nukitsuke* is never used. Most subsequent cuts are diagonal, rather than vertical *kirioroshi*. Only the *waza* Tatekitō employs vertical *kirioroshi*. All cuts in Okuden Battō-Hō are made in the *okuden kamae* power stance, *yoko-chiburi* is used exclusively, and all *nōtō* are performed as Okuden *nōtō* (see chapter 7). The final difference is that upon completion of *nōtō*, the right hand remains in contact with the *tsuka-gashira* until you have returned to the starting position of the *waza*.

# 13H: ZENTEKI GYAKUTŌ SONO ICHI

After *kiyomeri kokyū*, step forward with your right foot, then left foot. As you begin your third step forward (right foot), raise both hands to the *tsuka*, perform *koiguchi no kirikata* and *nukitsuke* as *kiriage* (upward left-to-right diagonal cut). While stepping forward with the left foot, perform Tanimura-Ha *furikaburi* and *gyaku-kesagiri* (downward left-to-right diagonal cut) in power stance. Raise the sword to *seigan no kamae*, *yoko-chiburi*, Okuden *nōtō*, and return to your starting position.

Zenteki Gyakutō Sono Ichi means "Front Enemy Reversed Sword Number One," and it deals with an opponent directly in front of you. A vital subtlety to this *waza* to keep in mind when training is that, as an Okuden *waza*, the initial *kiriage* must cut the opponent's right arm and torso at the same time. This means that energy must be transmitted from the right hand to both the *monouchi* and *kissaki* simultaneously. This requires a high degree of proficiency in *te no uchi* (inside the hands) and years of training to achieve.

Figures 13H.1–14. Okuden Battō-Hō: Zenteki Gyakutō Sono Ichi

# 131: ZENTEKI GYAKUTŌ SONO NI

After *kiyomeri kokyū*, step forward with your right foot, then left foot. As you begin your third step forward (right foot), raise both hands to the *tsuka*, perform *koiguchi no kirikata* and *nukitsuke* as *kiriage* (upward left-to-right diagonal cut). Draw the left foot even with your right foot during Tanimura-Ha *furikaburi* and step forward with your right foot to execute *kesagiri* (downward right-to-left diagonal cut) in power stance. Raise the sword to *seigan no kamae*, *yoko-chiburi*, Okuden *nōtō*, and return to your starting position.

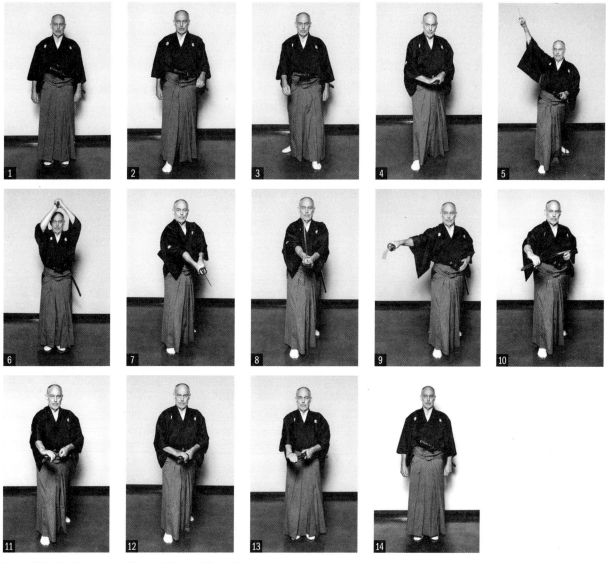

Figures 131.1–14. Okuden Battō-Hō: Zenteki Gyakutō Sono Ni

The primary distinction between Zenteki Gyakutō Sono Ni (Front Enemy Reversed Sword Number Two) and Zenteki Gyakutō Sono Ichi is whether the left foot or the right foot is forward during the final cut. As is the case with other pairs of *waza* differentiated by a change of the leading foot, the distinction is not trivial. It significantly alters the timing and distance factors of the *waza* in order to deal with a more aggressive opponent in Sono Ichi or one who retreats from the *kiriage* in Sono Ni. The timing of both Zenteki Gyakutō variations should be identical.

## 13J: TATEKITŌ

After *kiyomeri kokyū*, step forward with your right foot, then left foot. As you begin your third step forward (right foot), raise both hands to the sword, perform *koiguchi no kirikata* and step suddenly to your right-front with your right foot as you begin *nukitsuke*, as shown in figure 13J.5. Twist your hips to the left to perform *saya-banari* and shuffle to your left-rear with *soetezuki* (level thrust bracing the *tsuka* against the underside of your right wrist). Using the movement to protect the left side of your head, *furikaburi* and shuffle to your right-front with *kirioroshi*. Step 90 degrees to your left-front with your left foot and *kirioroshi*. *Yoko-chiburi*, Okuden *nōtō*, draw your right foot even with your left foot, pivot 45 degrees to your right, and return to your starting position.

Figures 13J.1–9. Okuden Battō-Hō: Tatekitō

Figures 13J.10–15. Okuden Battō-Hō: Tatekitō

Tatekitō means "Many Enemies Sword," yet only three opponents are represented in this *waza*. This is similar to Sōmakuri in the Okuden Tachiwaza (chapter 11), in which the five adversaries in the *waza* are used to represent any large number of enemies attacking you. Therefore, Tatekitō should be performed in anticipation that several more opponents would be charging toward you after the *kirioroshi* to your left-front, and you would continue the pattern of alternately counterattacking them.

## 13K: KOTEKI GYAKUTŌ

After *kiyomeri kokyū*, step forward with your right foot, then left foot. On your third step forward (right foot), raise both hands to the sword, perform *koiguchi no kirikata*, and pivot suddenly 180 degrees to your left, executing *nukitsuke* as a *kiriage* (fig. 13K.5). Immediately pivot 180 degrees to your right with *furikaburi* and *kesagiri*. Raise the sword to *seigan no kamae*, *yoko-chiburi*, Okuden *nōtō*, draw your left foot even with your right foot, and return to your starting position.

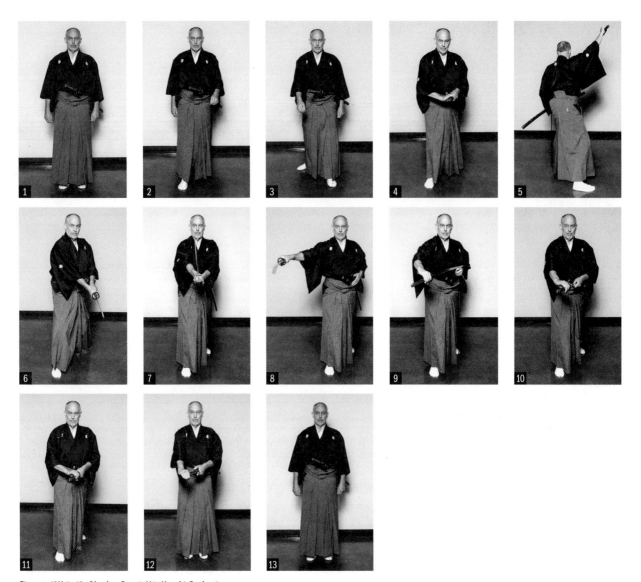

Figures 13K.1–13. Okuden Battō-Hō: Koteki Gyakutō

At first glance, Koteki Gyakutō (Rear Enemy Reversed Sword) may appear simple for a *waza* considered to be *okuden* (deep learning). It is not the pattern or footwork that is difficult to master, however, but the *te no uchi* (sword handling) required to perform a deep, fatal cut one-handed as *kiriage* and maintain *hasuji* (correct blade alignment), then immediately executing *kesagiri* as you turn swiftly in the opposite direction from the *kiriage* cut.

# 13L: KOTEKI NUKIUCHI

After *kiyomeri kokyū*, step forward with your right foot, left foot, and right foot. On your fourth step forward (left foot), raise both hands to the sword, perform *koiguchi no kirikata*, and pivot suddenly 180 degrees to your right, executing *nukitsuke* as a one-handed *gyaku-kesagiri* (fig. 13L.6). Immediately pivot 180 degrees to your left with *furikaburi* and *gyaku-kesagiri* (downward left-to-right diagonal cut). Raise the sword to *seigan no kamae*, *yoko-chiburi*, Okuden *nōtō*, draw your right foot even with your left foot, and return to your starting position.

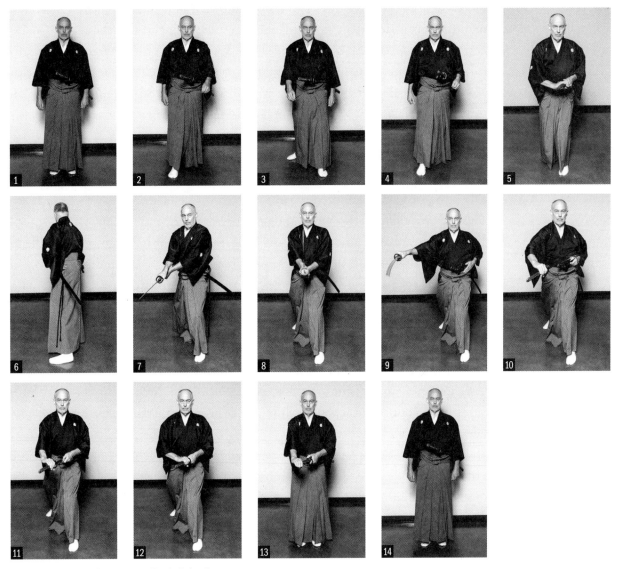

Figures 13L.1–14. Okuden Battō-Hō: Koteki Nukiuchi

Koteki Nukiuchi (Rear Enemy Sudden Attack) is another *waza* that may appear simple, but is supremely difficult to perform with correct *te no uchi* (sword handling) for a deep, fatal cut one-handed as *gyaku-kesagiri* and to maintain *hasuji* (correct blade alignment) while pivoting quickly in the opposite direction to perform the final *gyaku-kesagiri*.

## BATTŌ-HŌ TRAINING REGIMEN

It is now commonplace in Masaoka-Ha Eishin-Ryū to introduce the Shoden Battō-Hō early in a student's training. Juntō Sono Ichi and Juntō Sono Ni are often among the first *waza* taught to students once they can perform the basics (*nukitsuke, furikaburi, kirioroshi, chiburi,* and *nōtō*). Depending on how frequently a student trains and how rapidly he or she develops proficiency, another of the Shoden Battō-Hō is typically taught every month or two, so that a beginning student can expect to learn all seven of the Shoden Battō-Hō in the first nine to twelve months of training in *iaijutsu*.

There is a saying in *karate-dō* and other forms of *budō*: "*Manabu no tame ni, hyakkai. Jukuren no tame ni senkai. Satori no tame ni manga o okonau.*" This axiom is usually translated as, "A hundred repetitions to learn [a technique]. A thousand repetitions for proficiency. Ten thousand repetitions for mastery [complete understanding]." While this phrase is not commonly used in *iaijutsu*, it is certainly applicable to our training. For example, after performing Juntō Sono Ichi a hundred times, you should expect to make no major errors—wrong foot forward, wrong type of cut, wrong form of *chiburi*, loss of balance, and so on—but many of the finer details will still need considerable improvement. By the time you have performed Juntō Sono Ichi a thousand times, however, you should be proficient even in the finer points of the art and only occasionally making a noticeable mistake. Your *nukitsuke* should have consistently level *hasuji*, your *kirioroshi* should be a large circular arc that generates cutting power, your *chiburi* should exhibit *seme* (pressure on the opponent), and *nōtō* should be consistently smooth and level.

If you train three days per week and perform Juntō Sono Ichi five times every time you train, you can expect to complete a hundred repetitions of the *waza* and thereby learn (memorize) it in less than two months. A thousand repetitions will take fifteen to sixteen months, so you can be proficient in its performance in a year and a half with just regular attendance at the *dōjō*.

But you still have twelve more *years* of training ahead of you to reach the ten thousand repetitions necessary for in-depth understanding and mastery.

What this means regarding the Battō-Hō is that, if you have been training consistently and diligently, you will be just beginning to achieve proficiency in the fundamentals of *iaijutsu* and the first couple of Shoden Battō-Hō about the time you are introduced to the significantly more difficult Okuden Battō-Hō. Ordinarily, you would not yet be at a stage of your training at which you have begun learning the Chūden *waza* or *chūden* strategy and tactics, yet you will now be attempting to perform *okuden* techniques that employ *okuden* skills and tactics for the first time. This presents students with a significant challenge.

It is, however, a challenge with a purpose. From an instructional perspective, introducing more challenging techniques earlier in a student's training not only provides greater variety in order to hold the student's interest in the art, but it also affords the student more time to improve his or her skills and tends to assist in faster skill development.

Chapter 14

# *Bangai no Bu*

## Supplemental Waza

The word *bangai* means "extra," "additional," "supplemental," or "outside the scope," so the Bangai no Bu are a group *(bu)* of *waza* that are supplemental to the core Eishin-Ryū curriculum. The Bangai no Bu were created—or perhaps it would be more accurate to say *curated*—by Ōe Masamichi, the seventeenth headmaster of Eishin-Ryū in the early twentieth century. It is generally believed that they are a set of ancient *waza* that Ōe Sōshihan considered important for *iaidōka* to practice, but didn't fit well into the Shoden, Chūden, or Okuden categories.

Originally, there were only the three *waza* in the Bangai no Bu: namely Hayanami, Raiden, and Jinrai, all created or selected by Ōe Sōshihan. Sometime later a fourth *waza*, Akuma Barai (known in some branches of Eishin-Ryū as Shihōgiri or Shihō Barai), was added to the set, possibly by Ōe's student Yamamoto Harusuke. Other branches of Eishin-Ryū have added still more *waza* to their Bangai curricula, but we have chosen to include only the original three created by Ōe Sōshihan here.

Being so few in number, not having a clear place in the Eishin-Ryū curriculum, and in some ways being extraneous (another nuance of the word *bangai*), the Bangai no Bu tended to be neglected in most instruction in Eishin-Ryū, and thus were not included in the first two editions of *Flashing Steel*.

As with the Battō-Hō, when Shimabukuro Hanshi was designated as the successor to Miura Sōshihan, he decided to ensure that the Bangai no Bu would be preserved in the Masaoka-Ha lineage and began teaching these techniques to some of his higher-ranking students, and even included them occasionally in his public demonstrations beginning around 2010.

The Bangai no Bu are considered to be *okuden* (deep-level) *waza*, and are typically taught only to students of *yondan* (see chapter 21 for ranking standards) or higher rank, based upon their instructor's individual evaluation of their preparedness to learn and train in these *waza*.

A key characteristic of the Bangai *waza* are that they involve situations in which multiple opponents are converging on you simultaneously and therefore employ methods of preventing them from all striking at once. This distinguishes the Bangai from most other *waza* in the Eishin-Ryū curriculum, which in most cases involve either single attackers, or situations in which multiple opponents are precluded from attacking simultaneously, either by their positions or evasive actions.

The Bangai *waza* all begin in the same fashion: three *kiyomeri kokyū* (purifying breaths), then three steps forward. However, those three steps differ from the typical pattern of most other Okuden Tachiwaza, so this is an important distinction to make in the performance of the Bangai *waza*. Generally, in Okuden Tachiwaza, both hands rise to grasp the *tsuka* on the third step, disguising your intentions until the last moment before acting. But the Bangai *waza* combine the normal walking footwork of the Okuden Tachiwaza with the timing of the hand actions of the Shoden Battō-Hō in their opening movements.

Thus, while stepping forward with the right foot, the left hand rises and grasps the *saya* with the thumb on the *tsuba* as the left foot begins moving forward, the left hand performs *koiguchi no kirikata*, feeding the *tsuka* into the right hand as it grasps the *tsuka* and begins *nukitsuke*, then as the right foot lands in the third step forward, *nukitsuke* is completed as in the Shoden Battō-Hō. But, like the Okuden Tachiwaza, the walking posture remains upright and natural, rather than using the aggressive posture of the Battō-Hō.

Since this pattern is common to all of the Bangai *waza*, it will not be explained in detail in the descriptions that follow, but abbreviated simply as, "Take three steps forward …"

Similarly, all of the Bangai *waza* end in the same manner: with *yoko chiburi*, followed by Okuden *nōtō* (described in chapter 7). Once the *habaki* is seated in the *saya*, hook your left thumb over the *tsuba* at about the one o'clock position, then slide your right hand along the *tsuka* to the *tsukagashira*. Pause for a moment in this position, maintaining *zanshin* (awareness of your surroundings) to be sure you are not subject to further attack while drawing your rear foot even with your leading foot, then lower your right hand to a natural position beside your right thigh. The hand should remain open and relaxed, roughly in the shape of a parenthesis, with the thumb aligned with the index finger so that it does not protrude. This is another slight difference from both the Okuden Tachiwaza, in which the right hand remains on the *tsukagashira* until you have returned to the starting position, and the Shoden Battō-Hō, in which your right hand forms a loose fist and remains slightly forward of the right thigh while stepping backward. This seemingly insignificant difference reflects a different level of *zanshin* from those other *waza*: a state of mind in which you are aware that there are no other enemies in the vicinity, as opposed to uncertainty about the safety of your environment. Now return to the starting point of the *waza* by taking a small step back with your left foot, followed by a slightly longer rearward step with your right foot, then three more steps of normal length, allowing your right hand to swing naturally.

In the descriptions that follow, this sequence will be abbreviated as "Perform *yoko chiburi*, Okuden *nōtō*, and return to your starting position" to avoid unnecessary repetition of these details.

## 14A: HAYANAMI (FAST WAVES)

In Hayanami, you are confronted with four opponents: one directly behind you, one directly in front of you, one to your front-right, and one to your front-left. As the name Hayanami (Fast Waves) suggests, they are attacking you in quick succession. However, it is important to remember that Hayanami does not mean you are counterattacking them in a rush. A major point and purpose of this *waza* is to act calmly and unhurriedly in the face of a collective onslaught. Tactics and timing, not haste, are the means by which you defeat the four opponents.

Take three steps forward, turning suddenly 45 degrees to the right on the third step and completing *nukitsuke* as *gyaku kesa-giri* (left-to-right downward diagonal cut) with the right foot forward in the *okuden kamae* power stance used in most Okuden Tachiwaza (fig. 14A.5). The feeling should be that you were intending to attack the opponent directly in front of you, but at the last moment attacked to the front-right instead.

Begin turning left, maintaining *seme* (see chapter 7) toward your left-front by turning your sword edge in that direction, and step 90 degrees to your left-front with *kirioroshi* (fig. 14A.6). Note that this *kirioroshi* is not performed in the power stance because you face an immediate threat from another opponent to your right-front. Raise your sword into a horizontal block (fig. 14A.7) against an attack coming from 45 degrees to your front-right. The sword should be level and at head height, about six inches in front of your forehead, with the *kissaki* pointing to your right and your right elbow in line with your left shoulder, so that the center of the blade is protecting the center of your head.

While drawing your left foot forward, maintaining *iaigoshi*, lower the blade to chest level at your left side and perform a sweeping 270-degree *suihei-giri* (horizontal cut) while stepping across with your left foot and pivoting 225 degrees to your right, as depicted in figures 14A.8–10. This three-quarter circle cut either wounds or keeps at bay all four of your opponents as you turn to engage the one attacking from behind you.

Perform *furikaburi* and *kirioroshi* while stepping forward (toward the starting point of the *waza*) with your right foot into a power stance (fig. 14A.12). Pivot 180 degrees to your left with *furikaburi* (fig. 14A.13), then step forward with your right foot into a power stance with *kirioroshi* (fig. 14A.14).

Finish the *waza* with *yoko chiburi*, Okuden *nōtō*, and step back to the original starting position.

Figures 14A.1–10. Bangai no Bu: Hayanami

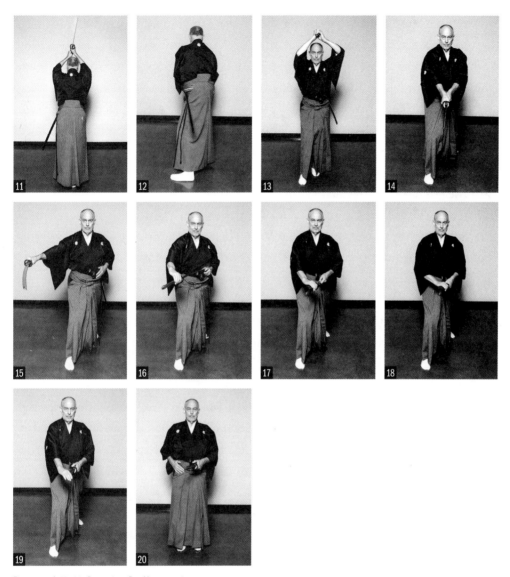

Figures 14A.11–20. Bangai no Bu: Hayanami

# 14B: RAIDEN (THUNDER AND LIGHTNING)

Raiden is another situation involving multiple attackers. It is similar to Takiotoshi in the Chūden *waza* (chapter 9), except that you are attacked while walking, rather than when seated in *tatehiza*. One of the opponents grabs your *kojiri* to prevent you from drawing your sword while the others are attacking you. The first movement of the *waza*—forcing the *tsuka* downward, then twisting it in a circle—frees your *saya* so that you can defend yourself.

Take three steps forward, grasping the *tsuka* with your right hand as your right foot completes the third step and thrusting it sharply downward (fig. 14B.4). Note that the arms are straight and the torso is leaning slightly forward so that the weight of the upper body—not just arm strength—is used to force the *tsuka* downward in order to raise the *kojiri* powerfully. Draw your left foot forward, even with your right foot, as you rotate the *tsuka* in a clockwise circular motion to the position in front of your right shoulder shown in figure 14B.5. At this point your hips should have turned about 45 degrees to your right, to add power from the legs, hips, and abdominal muscles to the strength of your arms in twisting the *kojiri* free of the opponent's grasp. Perform *koguchi no kirikata* and step forward with your right foot while continuing this circular motion and begin *nukituke*. When you have completed this forward step, all but about three inches of the blade should be drawn, as shown in figure 14B.6. It is vital that the movements from the position shown in figures 14B.4–6 be performed in one smooth, uninterrupted motion. There is no pause at the point shown in figure 14B.5. It is shown only to depict the degree of rotation that should be achieved by the time your left foot has come parallel to your right foot and the position at which you perform *koiguchi no kirikata* and begin stepping forward with your right foot.

Without letting the sword move, turn sharply 180 degrees to your left. The rearward rotation of your left hip will perform *saya-banari* (sword exiting the scabbard) automatically. At this point (fig. 14B.7) the *mine* (spine of the sword) should be almost touching your right side. Shift your left foot slightly to your left-front, then your right foot to your right for a well-balanced stance and perform *katate soetezuki* (one-handed reinforced thrust) with the blade level, edge facing to your right, and the *tsuka* pressed firmly against the underside of your right forearm for support. Pull the sword back with your right hand, turning it 90 degrees clockwise and keeping it aligned on your *seichūsen* (center line) with the *tsukagashira* at navel height in *seigan no kamae*, then bring your left hand (which was still holding the *saya*) to the *tsuka* as you step forward with your right foot and perform *furikaburi* and *kirioroshi* in the *okuden* power stance. As always, *furikaburi* should begin by pushing the *kissaki* forward as your body begins to move forward as if you are thrusting toward an opponent's throat. This detail is particularly important in all Okuden *waza*, since there should never be a moment of vulnerability or lapse in *seme* at this level.

After completing *kirioroshi*, raise the sword in a horizontal block against a *kirioroshi* coming from directly in front of you. The sword should be level at head height, about six inches in front of your forehead, with the *kissaki* pointing to your right and your right elbow in line with your left shoulder, so that the center of the blade is protecting the center of your head (fig. 14B.11).

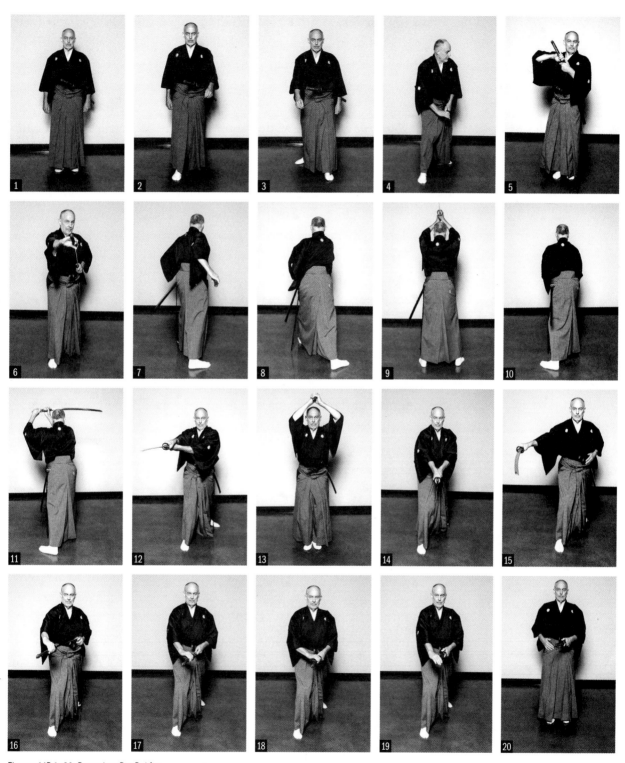

Figures 14B.1–20. Bangai no Bu: Raiden

While drawing your left foot forward, maintaining *iaigoshi*, lower the blade to chest level at your left side and perform a sweeping 180 degree *suihei-giri* (horizontal cut) while stepping across with your left foot and pivoting 180 degrees to your right, as depicted in figure 14B.12. This half-circle *suihei-giri* first cuts the torso of the attacker in front of you, then either wounds or forces back the opponent behind you.

Perform *furikaburi* and *kirioroshi* while stepping forward with your right foot into a power stance (fig. 14B.14). Finish the *waza* with *yoko chiburi*, Okuden *nōtō*, and step back to the original starting position.

The timing, distance, and footwork of Raiden are crucial, because they are the keys to the tactics of this *waza*. Once you have freed the *saya*, you lunge toward the opponent in front of you while beginning *nukitsuke*. This action forces the opponent to remain out of range of your sword as you turn suddenly and impale the attacker who grabbed your *saya*. Your forward step as you perform *furikaburi* and *kirioroshi* keep you out of range of the attacker behind you. And the half-step forward you take during the 180-degree *suihei-giri* assures that your cut is deep enough to be fatal while still maintaining a margin of safety from the opponent to your rear. Then you must draw your left foot forward during *furikaburi* in order to cut the final opponent with a single step forward.

You must therefore practice Raiden with these factors in mind, so that you train in the tactics and mindset of the *waza*, not just its movements. The purpose of training in Okuden *waza* is to develop *okuden* (deep-level) understanding and application of the strategy, tactics, and attitudes necessary to prevail against overwhelming odds, not merely to improve your sword handling technique.

# 14C: JINRAI (THUNDERCLAP)

In its outward appearance, Jinrai (Thunderclap) is a combination of Shihōtō Sono Ichi in the Battō-Hō and Sode Surigaeshi in the Okuden Tachiwaza. In this scenario, you are surrounded by a combination of attackers and innocent bystanders, like in a crowded street. One attacker is directly behind you and four in front—one at your right-front, one at your left-front, one directly ahead, and another lurking among the bystanders. Just as a thunderclap is unexpected and startling, your sudden, fierce counterattack in Jinrai is used to startle and temporarily immobilize and confuse your opponents.

Take three steps forward as if engaging the opponent directly in front of you, but veer sharply to your right-front on the third stride and perform *nukitsuke* to the point just before *saya-banari* (see fig. 14C.5), using the combination of deception and *seme* to prevent either of them attacking you and your movement to the right-front to evade the rear opponent's *kirioroshi*.

Perform *saya-banari* by turning your hips to the left and shuffle-step 45 degrees to your left-rear while executing *katate soetezuki* (one-handed reinforced thrust) at chest level (fig. 14C.6). Note that your body and head should be facing the opponent in the center, so that all of your opponents remain in your field of view at this time. Even though the sequence of movements in this *waza* is prearranged, you should feel ready to defend against or counterattack any of them at this point, rather than following the prescribed sequence by rote.

Grasp the *tsuka* with your left hand and perform *furikaburi*, guarding against attacks from your left as you raise the sword, then shuffle-step to your right-front with *kirioroshi* in the power stance as shown in figure 14C.7.

Turn the edge of the sword toward the center (now to your left-front) opponent as you begin turning your body in that direction as if your intention is to attack the nearest opponent with *gyaku kiri-age* (right-to-left upward diagonal cut). With your right foot, step 90 degrees to your left with *furikaburi* and *kirioroshi* in the power stance (fig. 14C.8).

Now turn the edge of the sword counterclockwise to again threaten the center (now to your right-front) opponent with a possible *kiri-age* (left to right upward diagonal cut) as you turn in that direction. Step 45 degrees with your right foot to your right-front while performing *furikaburi* and *kirioroshi* in the power stance (fig. 14C.9). During this *furikaburi* you should maintain a readiness to perform it as an Ukenagashi-type deflection, even though *furikaburi* is not done in this manner in the *waza*.

Draw your right foot back even with your left foot while crossing your arms at chest level, so that the *kissaki* points straight back from your left shoulder, edge upward (fig. 14C.10), then take a long stride forward with your right foot, sweeping both arms outward to push away the bystanders in front of you. Step forward with your left foot during *furikaburi* and step forward with your right foot for *kirioroshi* in the power stance (fig. 14C.13). Finish the *waza* with *yoko chiburi*, Okuden *nōtō*, and step back to the original starting position.

Although few in number, the Bangai *waza* have an important role in training at the *okuden* level, and we do not recommend practicing them until you have achieved proficiency in the Okuden Tachiwaza. This is not because we consider them more advanced than other Okuden *waza*, but it is due to their complexity and the potential to develop bad habits by training in them prematurely.

A key distinction of Okuden *waza* is that movements should flow more fluidly from one to the next at the *okuden* level, with the blade seldom coming to a stop at the completion of each cut. With a greater number of cuts in each Bangai *waza* than the typical Okuden Tachiwaza, this can lead to sloppy swordsmanship—which is precisely the opposite of what Okuden *waza* should be. It is supremely difficult to maintain proper *hasuji* (edge alignment) when quickly changing from one cutting angle to another in the Bangai *waza*. It takes far longer to unlearn bad habits and then relearn good habits than it takes to learn good habits in the first place, so we strongly recommend resisting the temptation to practice the Bangai no Bu *waza* before you have trained several years in the main Okuden *waza*.

Figures 14C.1–19. Bangai no Bu: Jinrai

Chapter 15

# *Tachiuchi no Kurai*

## Katachi

太刀打之位

It is probable that some form of *kumitachi* (practice fencing) has been part of the regimen of Eishin-Ryū from its earliest days, since partner training and contests using
*bokken* (wooden swords) in place of *shinken* ("live" swords) have been common practice in most styles of swordsmanship for many centuries.

However, the Tachiuchi no Kurai—prearranged *bokken* sparring involving two
partners—that we currently practice in Eishin-Ryū are of relatively recent development, having evolved through alteration, augmentation, and simplification of earlier
forms of *kumitachi* as they were passed from one generation to the next. In effect,
they are *koryū* (ancient) exercises that have been undergoing gradual modification
for centuries, taking their current form during the tenure of seventeenth *sōshihan*, Ōe
Masamichi. The formal name for this group of exercises, Tachiuchi no Kurai, means
"sword-striking circumstances," but for the sake of brevity they are often called *katachi*
(patterns).

Each of these ten *katachi* (patterned drills) was created to promote practice of a
key principle of Eishin-Ryū under controlled but reasonably realistic conditions.

Prior to practicing the Tachiuchi no Kurai, you should perform *sahō* and *reihō* just
as if you were preparing for any other aspect of *iaijutsu* training. Treat your *bokken*
just as you would treat an *iaitō* or *shinken*, by performing *tōrei* as you take up your
*bokken* and bowing to your partner.

In a formal setting, the highest level of sincerity and respect is shown by performing your preparation and etiquette in a *seiza* position, facing your partner. In the
description of each *katachi*, we are assuming that the partners have already performed
the appropriate *sahō* and *reihō*, so our narrative describes only the techniques in the
*katachi* itself.

In each *katachi*, one partner practices a key principle of *iaijutsu*, and the other partner provides the appropriate attack and defense to facilitate this training. The partner who practices the principle intrinsic to the *katachi* has historically been called Shitachi (Using Sword) and the partner assisting called Uchitachi (Striking Sword). Shimabukuro Hanshi preferred the more human terms, Shikata (Using Person or simply User) and Uchikata (Striking Person or Striker), since it is not the *swords* who are in training, but the *people*. These terms have since become the preference of many of Shimabukuro Hanshi's students and are used extensively in the following description, but either set of terms is acceptable and should be considered interchangeable.

Even though Shikata is the one practicing the key technique of each Katachi, it is equally important to develop aptitude in the role of Uchikata, both for development of your swordsmanship skills and the refinement of such character traits as humility, cooperation, and self-sacrifice.

Following the climactic technique of each *katachi*, the training partners shift into a position called *ai-seigan* (mutual *seigan no kamae*). This position is a key element of every *katachi*, and since it is not a feature of any Eishin-Ryū *waza*, a few thoughts about *ai-seigan* are warranted. *Ai-seigan* is more than just a formal way of ending each *katachi*. It is the last opportunity Shikata and Uchikata have to win or lose the battle represented by a *katachi*, making *ai-seigan* as essential an element of *kumitachi* as *nukitsuke* or *kirioroshi*, and is therefore explained in detail in our description of the first *katachi*, Deai.

Some other characteristics common to all ten Tachiuchi no Kurai are the *chiburi* and *nōtō*. Eishin-Ryū *chiburi* is performed at the completion of each *katachi*. This is followed by a simulated *nōtō*, using the left hand to simulate the *koiguchi*, and sliding the *bokken* through the opening of the hand as if sheathing it. It is not customary or necessary to slide the *bokken* through your belt to simulate it being in the *saya*.

Another characteristic not found in the *waza* of Eishin-Ryū is *kiai*—the loud shout that accompanies each striking motion in the *katachi*. This means that sometimes only Shikata or Uchikata will *kiai*, since only one of the two is using an attacking technique, while the other is receiving it. In several cases, however, such as the first attacks of Deai, Tsukekomi, Ukenagashi, Ukekomi, and others in which the partners are attacking simultaneously, both partners will *kiai*. Generally, when making a cut (*nukitsuke, kirioroshi, kesa-giri,* etc.) the *kiai* should be voiced as "*Ei!*" or "*Ya!*" and when performing a *tsuki* (thrust) it should be "*Hō!*" or "*Tō!*" in order to best match the movement of the diaphragm during *kiai* with the corresponding contraction of the abdominal muscles performing the technique.

# 15A: DEAI

The first *katachi*, Deai (First Meeting), is designed to employ the *iaijutsu* fundamentals *nukitsuke* and *kirioroshi* in simulated attack and defense with a training partner. For safety, however, Shikata applies *nukitsuke* toward Uchikata's leg, rather than an eye-level strike, and Uchikata blocks the *kirioroshi*.

Being the first *katachi* taught to most beginners and their first attempt to engage in *kumitachi*, Deai is often taught a little differently than it should be performed once a student has gained confidence and proficiency at mock combat with a living opponent. This allows students to train at a slower pace at first and gradually increase the speed and power of their performance as their skills improve. The description that follows explains the movements as they should be performed by beginning to intermediate students who are already familiar with the *katachi*.

Begin facing your partner at a distance of about eight paces. Both partners perform *kiyomeri kokyū*, just as if preparing to perform a *waza* (see fig. 15A.1), at the completion of which Uchikata (on the right) grasps his *tsuka* in preparation to draw and Shikata (on the left) immediately responds by doing the same (fig. 15A.2). Both partners simultaneously take several *chidori-ashi* steps toward each other (fig. 15A.3).

*Chidori-ashi* is a footwork pattern named for the *chidori*, a common seabird often found on Japanese beaches and shorelines. The *chidori*, whose name means "thousand birds," is renowned for its characteristic way of running in tiny, extremely fast and nimble steps, as if tiptoeing at high speed. This is an apt description of *chidori-ashi*, in which you run as quickly as possible on the balls of your feet in *iaigoshi*, taking steps that are only three or four inches long. This footwork allows you to quickly accelerate from a standstill, change direction unexpectedly, and represents having run a much longer distance than is actually traveled in a dozen or more *chidori-ashi* steps.

Having taken ten or more *chidori-ashi* steps, Shikata and Uchikata take three additional normal walking strides *(ayumi-ashi)* toward each other. On the third step, leading with the right foot, each performs *nukitsuke*. Shikata's *nukitsuke* is directed toward Uchikata's right knee, while Uchikata's *nukitsuke* attacks Shikata's right knee, resulting in the two cuts blocking each other (fig. 15A.5). By bending his knees, Shikata presses forward against Uchikata's sword, forcing Uchikata slightly back to protect his knee, then draws his left foot even with his right and performs *furikaburi*, while Uchikata draws his right foot back to his left while shifting to *seigan no kamae* (figs. 15A.6–7). Shikata continues forward with *kirioroshi* while Uchikata steps back with his left foot and blocks this strike with *jōdan uke* as shown in figure 15A.9. This *jōdan uke* should be made with the sword parallel to the floor just above eyebrow level and three to four inches in front of the face. Uchikata's right elbow should be directly in front of his right shoulder for maximum stability.

The manner in which Shikata and Uchikata separate from this position (fig. 15A.9) into *ai-seigan* (mutual *seigan no kamae*) is a crucial element of training to develop good swordsmanship. Neither partner can give the other an opportunity for attack as they move apart, and both should feel ready to instantly exploit such an opening if it is offered. Uchikata initiates this by pressing his sword toward Shikata while swinging his *kissaki* toward Shikata's *seichūsen* (center line) and sliding Shikata's blade slightly off line to Uchikata's left side. Shikata responds to this threat by shuffling (*yori-ashi*) backward and lowering his sword to *seigan-no-kamae* to hold the *seichūsen*. Uchikata also moves back with *yori-ashi* until they are in *ai-seigan* (fig. 15A.10).

This apparently minor movement and its subtleties is as crucial to correct performance of Deai as the *nukitsuke*, *kirioroshi*, or *jōdan uke*. There is no point in becoming skillful in the major aspects of *iaijutsu* only to be killed for providing the opponent with an easy opportunity to attack you while disengaging from an encounter. Maintaining constant awareness of your and your opponent's vulnerabilities to attack is the foundation for developing *zanshin* (situational awareness), making it one of the most practical aspects of *kumitachi* training.

As its name implies, *ai-seigan* is a position in which Shikata and Uchikata face each other in *seigan no kamae*, as depicted in figure 15A.10, with the tips of their swords crossed. Practically every detail of this position is vital to the survival of both participants as they disengage from combat. Of utmost importance is *kamae* (structure), so it may be beneficial to reread the description of *seigan no kamae* in chapter 7. Without sound structure, your opponent will easily be able to deflect your sword and kill you in *ai-seigan*, so be aware of *te no uchi* and the alignment of your feet, hips, and blade in this position. How and where the tips of the swords cross is also crucial. Only one to three inches of the blades should cross each other. Being any closer to your opponent in *ai-seigan* places you in imminent danger of attack. Ideally, the two blades should cross just behind the *yokote*. The blades should cross on the *omote* side, meaning the side on your left to keep your opponent's blade at the maximum distance from your exposed hand. Crossing on the *ura* side puts your right hand six or more inches closer to your opponent's blade.

The key factor in *ai-seigan* is the contact between the two blades. By exerting slight pressure against your opponent's blade, you can feel whether or not your opponent has solid kamae and *te no uchi*. With practice you can also feel slight movements or changes in pressure that signal your opponent's intentions, and you should be ready to respond to those signals with appropriate attacking or defending measures.

Figures 15A.1–8. Tachiuchi no Kurai: Deai

Figures 15A.9–16. Tachiuchi no Kurai: Deai

Figures 15A.17–22. Tachiuchi no Kurai: Deai

From *ai-seigan*, each *katachi* concludes in the same manner: while maintaining ai-seigan, both participants first move to the center point between their respective starting positions, then separate while maintaining *zanshin* and step back in *seigan no kamae* to their original starting positions, ending right foot forward, about eight paces apart. Normally, this requires three full steps backward by each partner. Once back at their original starting positions (fig. 15A.12), each partner levels his sword and pushes his hips slightly forward, then performs *Eishin-Ryū chiburi*.

Both perform *nōtō* (customarily Uchikata begins *nōtō* slightly before Shikata, but Shikata completes *nōtō* prior to Uchikata), drawing their rear foot forward in *iaigoshi* as their swords are "sheathed" into their left hands, slide their right hands down to the *tsuka-gashira*, then rise to a full standing position.

As mentioned earlier, Deai is often taught a bit differently than it should be performed once students are familiar with its pattern of movements. Many instructors begin by having the students omit the *chidori-ashi* at the beginning and just take three slow, deliberate steps toward each other to perform *nukitsuke*. This allows students to focus on timing and distance control. Once students have developed the timing to perform *nukitsuke* safely and with proper *maai* (distance control), then the *chidori-ashi* are added and the stepping pattern performed at a faster pace.

Similarly, to ensure student safety, some instructors add a pause following the *nukitsuke* (fig. 15A.5) to give Uchikata a moment to prepare to move backward, and another pause when Shikata is in *furikaburi* (fig. 15A.7) to allow Uchikata to prepare for *jōdan uke*. Another safety practice some follow is having *nukitsuke* and *kirioroshi* performed at half-speed until students demonstrate familiarity with the pattern of Deai.

Another common safety practice is for Shikata to announce the name of the *katachi* about to be practiced—in this case, "Deai"—and for Uchikata to repeat the name prior to initiating the attack. This ensures that both partners will be practicing the same drill.

Once students develop familiarity with Deai, it should be performed with full speed and cutting power. In addition, intermediate and advanced students (*yūdansha*) should continue running, rather than walking, after the *chidori-ashi*, which is how Deai would occur on the battlefield.

## 15B: TSUKEKOMI

The second *katachi*, Tsukekomi (Take Advantage), provides practice of the principle of quickly seizing the initiative and advantage as an opponent attempts to sustain momentum following an initially unsuccessful attack.

Both partners perform *kiyomeri kokyū*, just as if preparing to perform a *waza* (see fig. 15B.1), at the completion of which Uchitachi (on the right) and Shitachi (on the left) engage in a manner identical to the opening sequence of Deai, performing *chidori-ashi* followed by three *ayumi-ashi* strides forward and executing simultaneous *nukitsuke* as cuts toward each other's right knee (fig. 15B.4). At this point, however, the roles are reversed. Uchikata begins to press forward, threatening Shikata's knee, but Shikata quickly steps forward and slightly to his left with his left foot and seizes Uchikata's right hand (figs. 15B.5–6), gripping it with the thumb at the base of Uchikata's little finger and the index and middle fingers between Uchitachi's index finger and thumb to ensure control of the wrist.

Figures 15B.1–8. Tachiuchi no Kurai: Tsukekomi

Figures 15B.9–1. Tachiuchi no Kurai: Tsukekomi

Figures 15B.17–22. Tachiuchi no Kurai: Tsukekomi

At this point, Shikata's left foot should be just outside Uchikata's right foot, allowing Shikata to sweep Uchikata's foot or buckle Uchikata's knee if necessary, and Uchikata's right hand should be pinned against Shikata's left thigh. Shikata finishes with a thrust between the ribs (fig. 15B.7) that would, if extended fully, penetrate the lungs and pericardium.

To separate from this position with *zanshin*, Shikata must push Uchikata's hand aside with the first step back to ensure that Uchikata cannot counterattack (fig. 15B.8). Once they have reached *ai-seigan* (fig. 15B.10), both partners return to their starting positions, perform *chiburi* and *nōtō* as previously described, and rise to a standing position.

An important detail of Tsukekomi is the means by which Shikata controls and captures Uchikata's right hand after the two perform *nukitsuke*. If Shikata simply attempts to seize Uchikata's wrist, Uchikata may be able to avoid being grabbed by moving his hand. Uchikata's elbow, however, cannot move as quickly or as far, so Shikata must make first contact with Uchikata's right arm at the elbow as shown in figure 15B.23 below, thereby preventing Uchikata from swinging his sword in Shikata's direction. Then Shikata slides his left hand down Uchikata's arm to the wrist (fig. 15B.24), seizing it and taking full control of Uchikata's sword arm.

Another key factor in Tsukekomi is yielding to the pressure Uchikata exerts on Shikata's sword after the mutual *nukitsuke*. This sudden release of pressure is what breaks Uchikata's balance (*kuzushi*), shifting *Uchikata's* weight onto his front leg, and allows Shikata to seize the initiative—and Uchikata's wrist. It is therefore imperative when practicing Tsukekomi that Uchikata apply this pressure and Shikata wait until feeling that pressure before acting.

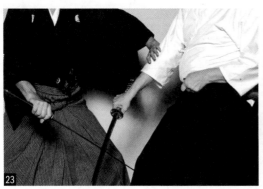

Figures 15B.23–24. Detail of capture of Uchikata's wrist

# 15C: UKENAGASHI

The main principle practiced in Ukenagashi (Flowing Block) is that found in several Eishin-Ryū *waza*: allowing the opponent's attack to glance off an angled parry, then counter-striking in a continuous flowing motion before the attacker can recover his balance.

The partners begin, facing each other about eight paces apart, with *kiyomeri kokyū*, then—initiated by Uchikata and instantly followed by Shikata—both partners draw their *bokken*, stepping forward with their right feet into *seigan no kamae* (figs. 15C.2–4). As Uchikata next takes a step forward with his left foot, Shikata takes a step back with his right foot to maintain their separation, both assuming *hassō no kamae*. From this point (fig. 15C.5), both partners step forward three paces. As soon as they are within attacking distance, Uchikata steps forward with his right foot in a *yokomen-giri* aimed at Shikata's left temple, and Shikata steps left foot backward with an identical strike. Thus, they clash in the middle, still just out of range, as shown in figure 15C.8. Shikata must ensure that his *yokomen-giri* cuts to Uchikata's *seichūsen*; otherwise he cannot seize the initiative at this point.

Here, Shikata begins to press forward with a thrust to Uchikata's face, which Uchikata steps back to evade, swinging his sword in a circular arc with a *yokomen-giri* directed at Shikata's right temple. Shikata meets this by stepping forward with a mirror-image *yokomen-giri* (fig. 15C.10), again cutting to Uchikata's *seichūsen*. Now on the *ura* (back) side of each other's blades, their *kote* (forearms) are both vulnerable, so Shikata sustains his initiative by attempting to cut Uchikata's exposed right *kote*, which Uchikata avoids by shuffling (*yori-ashi*) back and taking *jōdan no kamae* (fig. 15C.12).

Seeing that Shikata's *kissaki* is off his *seichūsen* following the attempted cut to *kote*, Uchikata steps forward with *kirioroshi*, but Shikata responds by shuffling left with *ukenagashi*, raising the *katana* to take Uchikata's *kirioroshi* as a glancing strike that propels Shikata's blade in a fierce arc that ends with *kirioroshi* to Uchikata's head (figs. 15C.14–18). The partners then move to *ai-seigan*, separate with *zanshin*, and return to their starting positions in the customary manner.

Figures 15C.1–4. Tachiuchi no Kurai: Ukenagashi

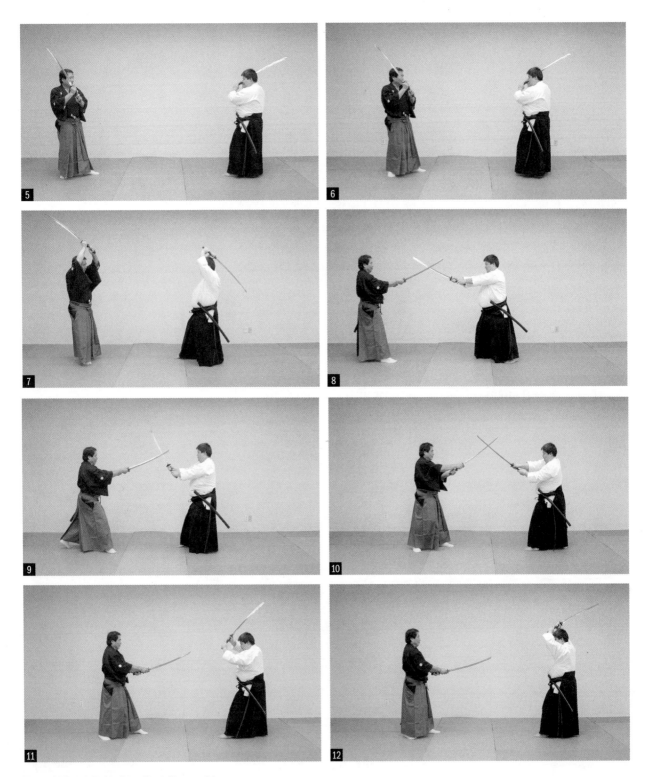

Figures 15C.5–12. Tachiuchi no Kurai: Ukenagashi

Figures 15C.13–20. Tachiuchi no Kurai: Ukenagashi

Figures 15C.21–28. Tachiuchi no Kurai: Ukenagashi

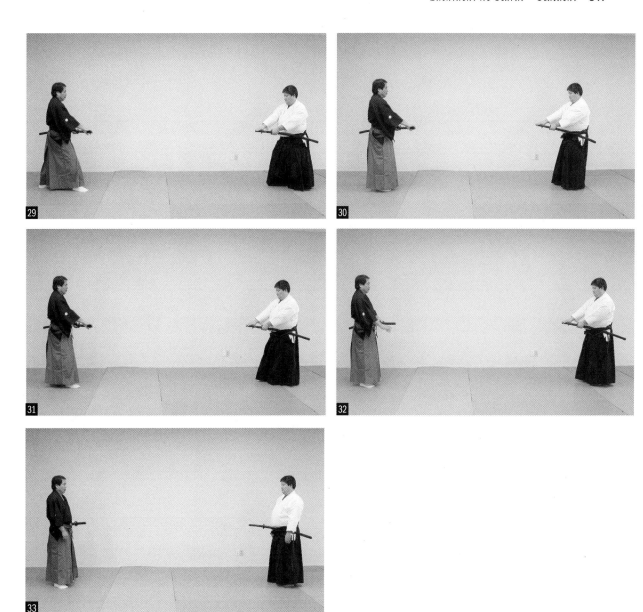

Figures 15C.29–32. Tachiuchi no Kurai: Ukenagashi

## 15D: UKEKOMI

Ukekomi (Receive and Move In) is the fourth *katachi*, which employs a different type of counterattack to a situation almost identical to Ukenagashi.

The partners again face each other about eight paces apart during *kiyomeri kokyū*. With Uchikata initiating, both training partners draw their *bokken*, stepping forward with their right feet into *seigan no kamae* (fig. 16D.4).

Figures 15D.1–8. Tachiuchi no Kurai: Ukekomi

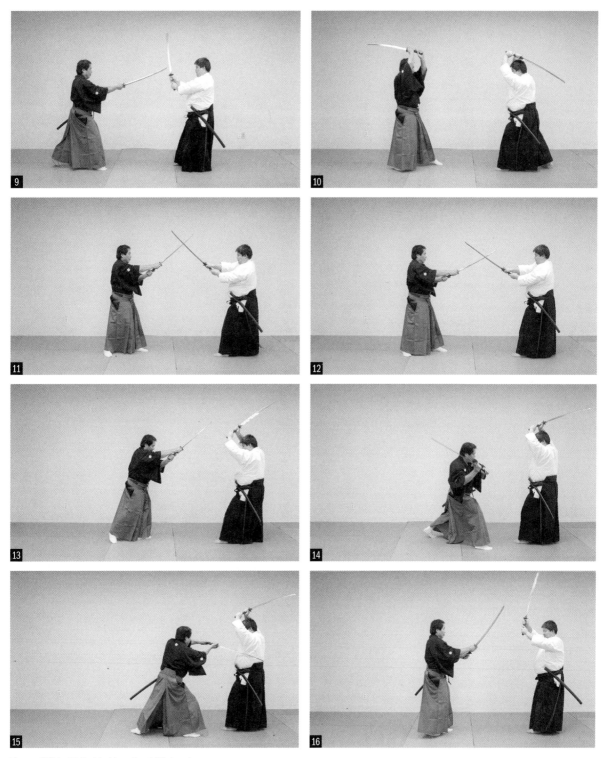

Figures 15D.9–16. Tachiuchi no Kurai: Ukekomi

Figures 15D.17–2. Tachiuchi no Kurai: Ukekomi

Figures 15D.25–30. Tachiuchi no Kurai: Ukekomi

As Uchikata next takes a step forward with his left foot, Shikata takes a step back with his right foot to maintain their separation, both assuming *hassō no kamae* (fig. 16D.5). Both partners step forward three paces. As soon as they are within attacking distance, Uchikata steps forward with his right foot in a *yokomen-giri* aimed at Shikata's left temple, and Shikata steps left foot backward with an identical strike. Thus, they again clash in the middle, still just out of range, as shown in figure 15D.8. Shikata must ensure that his *yokomen-giri* cuts to Uchikata's *seichūsen*; otherwise he cannot seize the initiative at this point.

Shikata begins to press forward with a thrust to Uchikata's face, which Uchikata steps back to evade, swinging his sword in a counterclockwise arch with a *yokomen-giri* strike aimed at Shikata's right temple. Shikata meets this by stepping forward with a mirror-image *yokomen-giri*. Shikata attempts to cut Uchikata's exposed right *kote*. This time, however, as Uchikata steps back into *jōdan no kamae*, Shikata immediately follows in, stepping slightly to the right and outside Uchikata's *seichūsen*, with *kiriage* (upward diagonal cut) to Uchitachi's left side (which in application would slice Uchikata from the left hip to right shoulder), as depicted in figures 15D.15. The partners then move to *ai-seigan*, separate with *zanshin*, and return to their starting positions in the customary manner.

## 15E: TSUKIKAGE

The fifth *katachi*, Tsukikage (Moon Shadow), primarily trains students to calculate the trajectory and distance of an opponent's strike and evade it, while remaining in range for an immediate counterattack. This provides essential training in sensing and reacting to an opponent's movement, speed, reach, and timing.

The training partners face each other at a distance of about eight paces apart. On their third cleansing breaths, with Uchikata initiating, both Shikata and Uchikata draw their *bokken* and step forward with their right feet into *seigan no kamae* (fig. 15E.4). Taking a step forward with the left foot, Uchikata assumes *hassō no kamae*, but Shitachi remains in *seigan*. After a brief pause, Shikata lowers his sword to *gedan no kamae*, creating an apparent vulnerability to attack. Both partners then walk forward three paces in *ayumi-ashi*. When they reach attacking range, Uchikata steps right foot forward and directs a *yokomen-giri* toward Shikata's left temple, Shikata raises his sword to receive the attack. Both then shuffle (*yori-ashi*) slightly forward, pushing their swords *tsuba* to *tsuba* (called *tsubazeria* in Japanese), as depicted in figure 15E.12.

In *tsubazeria*, both partners must be sensitive to each other's strength and match it exactly. In a real battle, this would be a crucial opportunity for victory. If one slacks off slightly, the other could easily push through with a thrust or short slice to the throat. Therefore, each partner must exactly match the other's intensity and force. The correct position for *tsubazeria* is shown in figure 15E.1.

Figure 15E.1. Tsubazeria

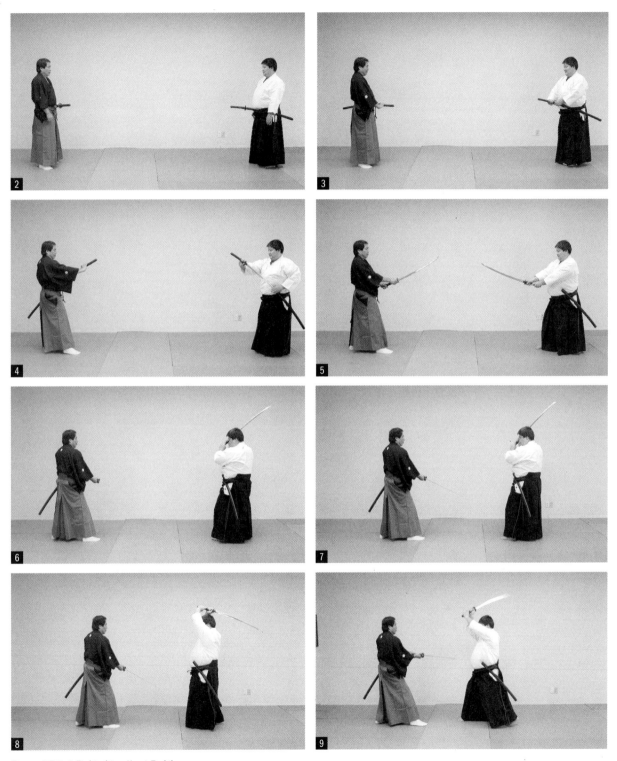

Figures 15E.2–9. Tachiuchi no Kurai: Tsukikage

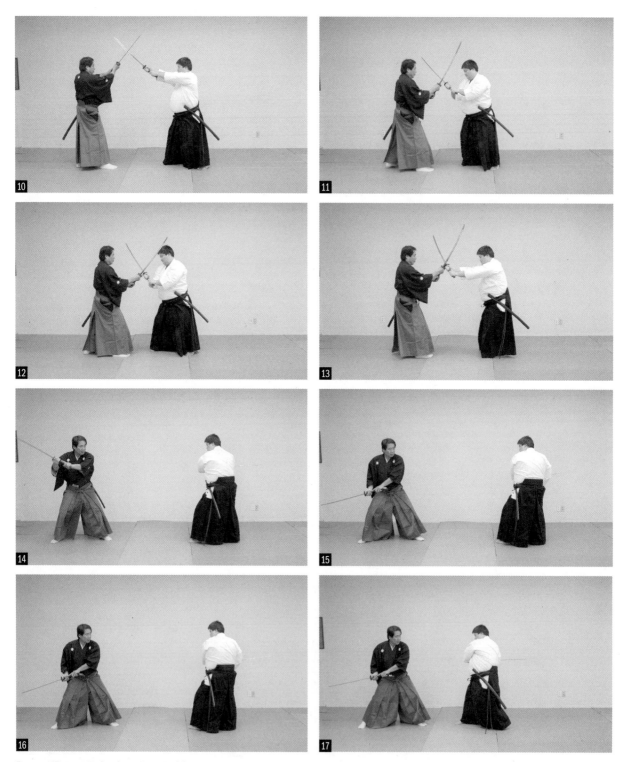

Figures 15E.10–17. Tachiuchi no Kurai: Tsukikage

Figures 15E.18–25. Tachiuchi no Kurai: Tsukikage

Figures 15E.26–33. Tachiuchi no Kurai: Tsukikage

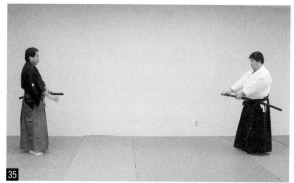
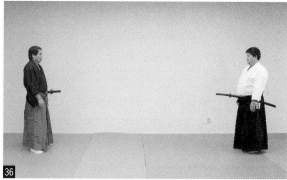

Figures 15E.34–36. Tachiuchi no Kurai: Tsukikage

When it becomes apparent that neither can gain an advantage or overpower the other, both partners simultaneously push away from each other, stepping back with their right feet into *waki no kamae*, as shown in figure 15E.15. Again, it is essential that both partners push simultaneously and with equal power. If either the timing or strength of the push is off, one partner will be toppled and the other will gain instant victory. From this position, Uchikata steps forward with a cut to Shikata's forward leg (figs. 15E.17–18).

Note: *Waki-no-kamae* offers the opponent three major targets: the leading knee, since it is the closest; the leading side or arm; and the leading shoulder. In ancient times it is probable that Uchikata would select whichever of these targets appeared most vulnerable, given their relative positions. For beginners, we now suggest that Uchikata cut for Shikata's left knee, because it is the easiest for Shikata to evade and therefore the safest option. Intermediate and advanced students should also practice with Uchikata cutting for the torso (ribs) or left shoulder to train for more realistic battlefield conditions.

With a sharp leftward twist of the hips, Shikata draws his left foot back to his right foot, pulling it out of reach of Uchikata's attempted cut (figs. 15E.18–19) and, the moment Uchikata's *bokken* passes, steps forward with the right foot to deliver *kirioroshi* (figs. 15E.20–21).

The critical element of this *katachi* is the timing of this evasion and counterattack by Shikata. If Shikata moves prematurely, Uchikata could adjust the attack to succeed, so Shikata cannot react until Uchikata is sufficiently committed to the attack that its path cannot be altered. This means the attack will barely miss the forward leg— applying the concept of *issun no maai* from chapter 7. Likewise, if the counterattack is not made the moment Uchitachi's attack misses, Uchitachi will be able to recover and evade or block it. As long as Uchikata cuts with full speed and power, Shikata can initiate his counterattack the moment his feet have drawn together without danger of running into Uchikata's *bokken*. But if Uchikata cuts slowly, hesitantly, or incompletely, Shikata may be struck by Uchikata's *bokken* during *kirioroshi*, so it is imperative that Uchikata commit fully to the technique and trust Shikata to perform correctly.

The name of this *katachi*, Tsukikage (Moon Shadow), refers to the way in which Uchikata is enticed to attack where Shikata's leg or side appears to be (its shadow), rather than where the target (moon) actually is while Uchikata's sword is passing through its shadow.

Following the decisive *kirioroshi*, both Shitachi and Uchitachi conclude the *katachi* by assuming *ai-seigan*, then returning to their respective starting points in the customary manner.


# 15F: SUIGETSUTŌ

Suigetsutō (Solar Plexus Thrust) is the sixth *katachi*, and is used to practice a deflection and continuous-motion counterattack against a thrust to the solar plexus.

It begins with the partners facing each other about eight paces apart during *kiyomeri kokyū*, then Uchitachi initiates both Shikata and Uchikata drawing their *bokken* while stepping forward with their right feet into *seigan no kamae* (fig. 15F.4). Uchikata next takes a step forward with his left foot, and Shitachi takes a right-foot step back to maintain their separation, both assuming *hassō no kamae*. Both walk forward in *ayumi-ashi*, making any necessary adjustment to the attacking distance as they approach, then Uchikata steps forward with a right-foot-forward *yokomen-giri* cut aimed at Shikata's left temple, which Shikata steps left-foot backward to meet with an identical strike, clashing in the middle, as shown in figure 15F.8. Having cut down to Uchikata's *seichusen*, Shitachi begins to press forward with a thrust to Uchitachi's face, which Uchitachi steps back to evade, swinging his sword in a circular arc with a *yokomen-giri* aimed at Shikata's right temple.

Figures 15F.1–8. Tachiuchi no Kurai: Suigetsutō

Figures 15F.9–16. Tachiuchi no Kurai: Suigetsutō

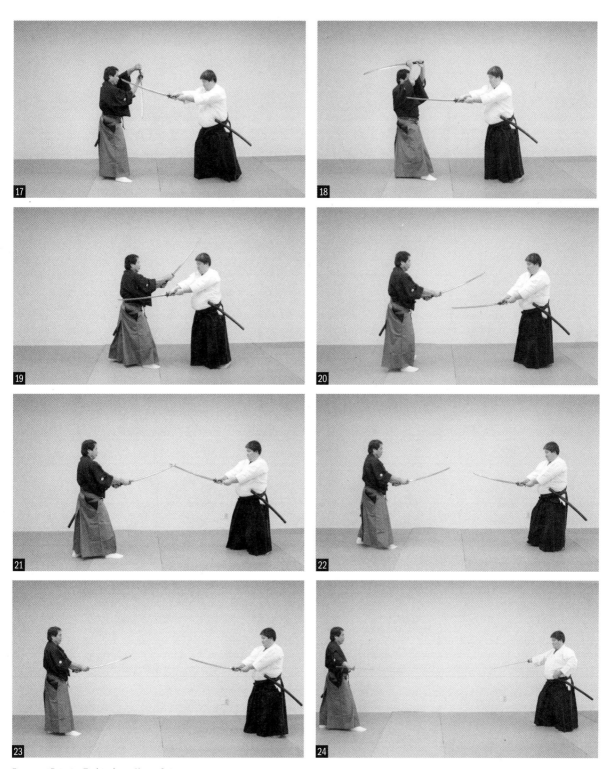

Figures 15F.17–24. Tachiuchi no Kurai: Suigetsutō

Figures 15F.25–32. Tachiuchi no Kurai: Suigetsutō

Shitachi meets this by stepping left foot forward with a mirror-image *yokomen-giri*. This time, however, Shikata continues to drive forward, clockwise with another *yokomen-giri* aimed at Uchikata's left temple, which is met by Uchikata in mirror-image. To prevent Shikata from continuing to press his attacks, Uchikata shuffles (*yori-ashi*) back while maintaining *seigan no kamae* and trying to control the *seichūsen*.

The moment Uchikata's retreating foot touches the floor, he drives fiercely forward with a thrust to Shikata's solar plexus (fig. 15F.16). Shitachi raises his hands slightly so that Uchitachi's thrust is deflected to his right while he shuffles slightly to his left, completing *furikaburi* and *kirioroshi* in a circular, fluid motion (fig. 15F.17–19). The partners then shift to *ai-seigan*, separate with *zanshin*, and return to their starting positions in the customary manner.

# 15G: ZETSUMYŌKEN

The seventh *katachi* is Zetsumyōken (Unbeatable Sword), which is used to practice a *tsuka-ate* (handle-strike) technique.

The partners face each other about eight paces apart during *kiyomeri kokyū*, then with Uchikata initiating both partners draw their *bokken*, stepping forward with their right feet into *seigan no kamae*. Taking a step forward with the left foot, Uchikata assumes *hassō no kamae*, while Shikata steps backward with the right foot into *hassō no kamae*. Both partners walk forward while in *hassō no kamae* to close within attacking distance, then Uchikata attacks with *yokomen-giri* toward Shikata's temple, and Shikata steps back, countering the attack with a mirror-image cut toward Uchikata's temple (fig. 15G.8). Both have attempted to cut to the *seichu*, but neither has done so, leaving them equally disadvantaged. So both then drive forward with *yori-ashi*, pushing their swords *tsuka* to *tsuka* (called *tsukazeria*), as depicted in figure 15G.10.

Note that this position is slightly different from *tsubazeria*, which was performed in Tsukikage. The balance of opposing forces is maintained in the handles, with the contact point being the gap between Shitachi's and Uchitachi's hands, rather than just above the *tsuba*. This causes the swords to be nearly vertical and the partners more closely positioned. The correct position for *tsukazeria* is illustrated in figure 15G.1. The partners remain in this position struggling for dominance for a few seconds, with neither gaining an advantage.

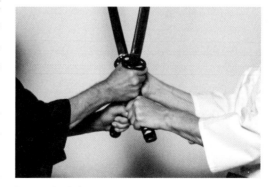

Figure 15G.1. Tsukazeria

Figures 15G.2–9. Tachiuchi no Kurai: Zetsumyōken

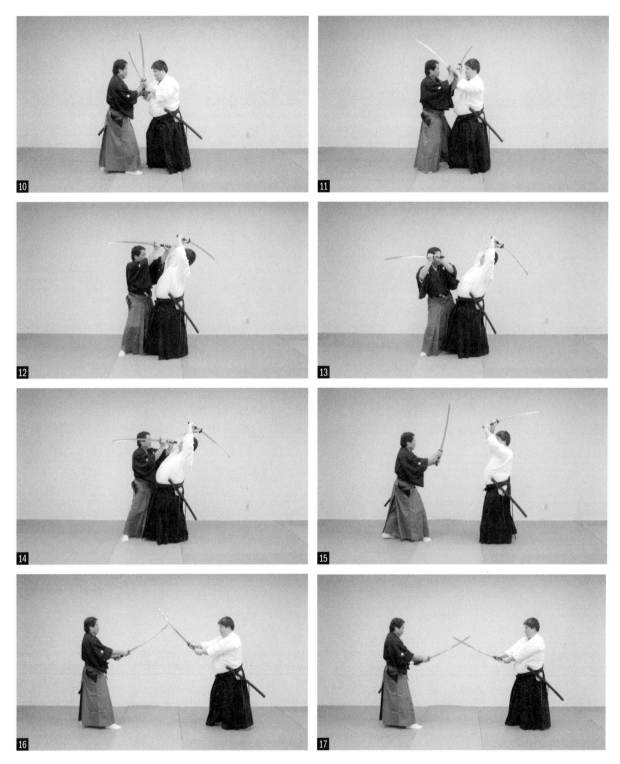

Figures 15G.10–17. Tachiuchi no Kurai: Zetsumyōken

Figures 15G.18–25. Tachiuchi no Kurai: Zetsumyōken

Figures 15G.26–29. Tachiuchi no Kurai: Zetsumyōken

Using the *tsuka* as a fulcrum, Shikata lowers his stance while stepping left foot forward. This sudden reduction in counter-pressure causes Uchikata's sword to lurch forward while Shikata pivots his *tsukagashira* sharply upward, lifting Uchikata's hands with it (figs. 15G.11–12). Shikata immediately follows with a *tsuka-ate* strike to Uchikata's face with the *tsukagashira* (figs. 15G.13–14).

The matched force of Uchitachi in *tsukazeria* against Shitachi provides the vulnerability that makes this technique work. The moment Shikatai's sword pivots, the sudden release of Uchikata's own pushing force causes his sword to ride up over Shikata's. This, coupled with the leverage Shikata gains, creates the break in Uchikata's balance and the opening to the face, which allows Shikata to make the strike. The *katachi* ends at this point, since the stunned Uchikata could be easily finished by any technique of Shikata's choosing. After moving to *ai-seigan*, both Shikata and Uchikata step back to their respective starting points in the usual manner.

## 15H: DOKUMYŌKEN

Eighth in the Tachiuchi no Kurai is Dokumyōken (Miraculous Sword), which incorporates one of the most difficult techniques found in the *katachi*.

On their third cleansing breaths, both Shikata and Uchikata draw their bokken, stepping forward with their right feet into *seigan no kamae*. With Uchikata stepping forward and Shikata stepping back to maintain their separation, both partners raise their swords to *hassō no kamae* and approach each other with *ayumi-ashi*. Once in attacking range, Uchikata attacks with *yokomen-giri* to Shikata's left temple while Shikata steps back with a mirror-image counterattack, so that both meet in the middle (fig. 15H.7). This time, Uchikata has cut to Shikata's *seichūsen*, so Uchikata then steps forward and attacks with *yokomen-giri* to Shikata's right temple (fig. 15H.11), so Shikata steps back and meets this with a mirror-image counterattack, again stymieing Uchikata's attack. But, Uchikata has again controlled the *seichūsen*, so Uchikata steps forward with *kirioroshi*, forcing Shikata to step back once again.

Shikata must do something to seize the initiative from Uchikata, so he steps back and blocks overhead (*jōdan uke*) using his left hand to reinforce the *mine* against the strength of Uchitachi's cut (fig. 15H.15). With a powerful twist of the hips, Shikata sweeps Uchikata's blade aside to the right (figs. 15H.16–18), then steps forward with a reinforced thrust to Uchikata's exposed right side (fig. 15H.19–20), using the left hand along the mine to guide the *kissaki* to its target.

Shikata now steps forward, forcing Uchikata to step back, as both take *ai-seigan*, then both return to their starting points in the usual fashion.

The success of Dokumyōken depends entirely on Shikata sweeping Uchikata's sword rearward with the movements depicted in figures 15H.18–20. If Shikata merely forces Uchikata's sword to the side, Uchikata can easily counter with *kiri-kaeshi* (returning cut) to Shikata's right side. So, the sweeping movement must begin with Shikata's sword level and pushing Uchikata's sword upward and straight back for the first several inches of travel. Then, as Uchikata's hands rise above head level, Shikata can begin turning his blade clockwise for the duration of the sweeping motion, which will fling Uchikata's *kissaki* toward his left heel.

Figures 15H.1–8. Tachiuchi no Kurai: Dokumyōken

Figures 15H.9–16. Tachiuchi no Kurai: Dokumyōken

Figures 15H.17–24. Tachiuchi no Kurai: Dokumyōken

Figures 15H.25–32. Tachiuchi no Kurai: Dokumyōken

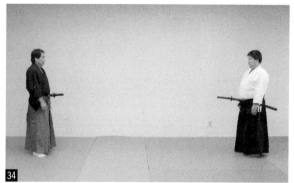

Figures 15H.33–34. Tachiuchi no Kurai: Dokumyōken

# 15I: SHINMYŌKEN

Shinmyōken (Clear Mind Sword) is the ninth *katachi*, and also presents a high degree of difficulty in terms of Shikata's timing to parry Uchikata's attack.

After *kiyomeri kokyū*, Uchikata draws, stepping forward with the right foot into *seigan no kamae*. Taking a step forward with the left foot, Uchikata raises the sword to *jōdan no kamae* and walks toward Shikata to close within attacking distance. Shikata does not draw or take a defensive posture as Uchikata approaches. Once in attacking range, Uchikata steps forward with the right foot and attacks with *kirioroshi* toward Shikata's *shōmen* (center of the head). Now Shikata draws, using *nukitsuke* to block the *kirioroshi* and, in a continuous, fluid motion deflects Uchikata's strike to the right side, grasping the *tsuka* with the left hand and continuing around in a circular motion to finish with a cut to Uchikata's neck, as shown in figures 15I.8–15.

Both Shikata and Uchikata assume *ai-seigan*, then step back to their respective starting points in the usual manner.

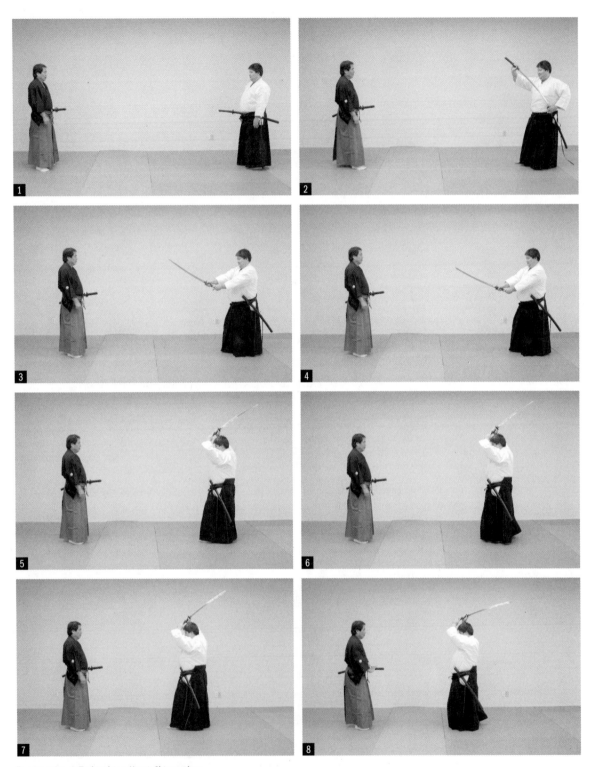

Figures 15I.1–8. Tachiuchi no Kurai: Shinmyōken

Figures 15I.9–16. Tachiuchi no Kurai: Shinmyōken

Figures 15I.17–24. Tachiuchi no Kurai: Shinmyōken

Figures 15I.25–29. Tachiuchi no Kurai: Shinmyōken

The key aspect of Shinmyōken is the sweeping deflection illustrated in figures 15I.8–15. Additional detail of this portion of the *katachi* is shown and explained below. The initial contact with Uchikata's sword must be made with the flat of the blade near the *shinogi* (bevel); not the edge. The right wrist then begins turning clockwise, rolling the sword over as it begins sweeping to the right, so that its *mine* pushes Uchikata's *mine* downward. Notice that the left hand is added after initial contact has been made (fig. 15J.2), then both wrists are twisted clockwise as Uchikata's sword is swept down and aside, adding power and momentum to the technique (figs. 15J.3–6). This not only protects Shikata's sword from damage, but ensures that Uchikata cannot counter the technique.

Figures 15J.1–6. Detail of Tachiuchi no Kurai: Shinmyōken

A temptation when performing this *katachi* is to begin the parry-and-counterattack motion before the block has been fully effective. If Uchikata is performing the *kiri-oroshi* with realistic follow-through, this timing error can result in a painful knot on Shikata's head.

## 15 K: UCHIKOMI

Uchikomi (Clash Together) is the final technique of the Tachiuchi no Kurai, and it appears to be deceptively simple.

On their third *kiyomeri kokyū* breaths, both Shikata and Uchikata draw their *bokken*, stepping forward with their right feet into *seigan no kamae*. Both then raise their swords to *hassō no kamae*, with Uchikata taking a step forward as he does so, and Shikata taking a step back to maintain their separation. Both partners then approach each other in *ayumi-ashi*. Once in cutting range, Uchikata steps forward with a *yokomen-giri* cut to Shikata's temple and Shikata steps forward to meet the attack with a mirror-image cut to Uchikata's temple. Both *yori-ashi* forward to *tsubazeria* (*tsuba-to-tsuba* standoff). As with Tsukikage, it is essential that both partners be sensitive to each other's pressure to maintain equilibrium and not provide an opportunity for the other to attack. In fact, this is the essence and purpose of Uchikomi, which ends in a draw. So this sensitivity and matching force are even more pronounced. Once it is clear that neither can gain the advantage, both partners gradually slacken the force of their pushing. In a real battle, each would be sensitive to the other's possible treachery, so they must draw back from one another at exactly the same pace, feeling their partner's intentions as registered by the exertion against the crossed swords as a quintessential expression of *zanshin*.

As the mutual force gradually abates, Uchikata and Shikata simultaneously and slowly step apart until they reach *ai-seigan*. From there, they return to their respective starting points in *seigan no kamae*, then perform *chiburi* and *nōtō* to conclude in the customary manner.

The greatest impediment to performing Uchikomi well is that Shikata and Uchikata both know it is supposed to end in a draw, so they don't struggle realistically for dominance. Instead, they go through the motions without any intention of winning the encounter. This would not be the case in real combat. Uchikata and Shikata would both be fighting for their lives and seeking an opportunity to kill the other. That doesn't mean they would be shoving ferociously at each other, however. Bear in mind the lesson learned from Zetsumyōken: if one opponent applies too much force, the other can gain advantage by suddenly yielding to that force and moving tangentially. Therefore, every action in Uchikomi must be strategic—seeking an advantage, while at the same time not providing the opponent an opportunity to turn the tables.

When you can perform Uchikomi as if you are in real combat, yet still reach a draw with your training partner, you have clearly reached the *okuden* level in your training.

At the conclusion of Tachiuchi no Kurai practice, you should perform *sahō* and *reihō* just as you did at the beginning, but in reverse order. To demonstrate the utmost mutual respect, the partners would sit in *seiza* posture, perform *tōrei* to their swords and *zarei* to each other, treating their *bokken* just as they would treat an *iaitō* or *shinken*. In less formal settings, it is sufficient simply to perform a standing bow to each other, followed by a standing *tōrei*, and *hairei* prior to leaving the *dōjō*.

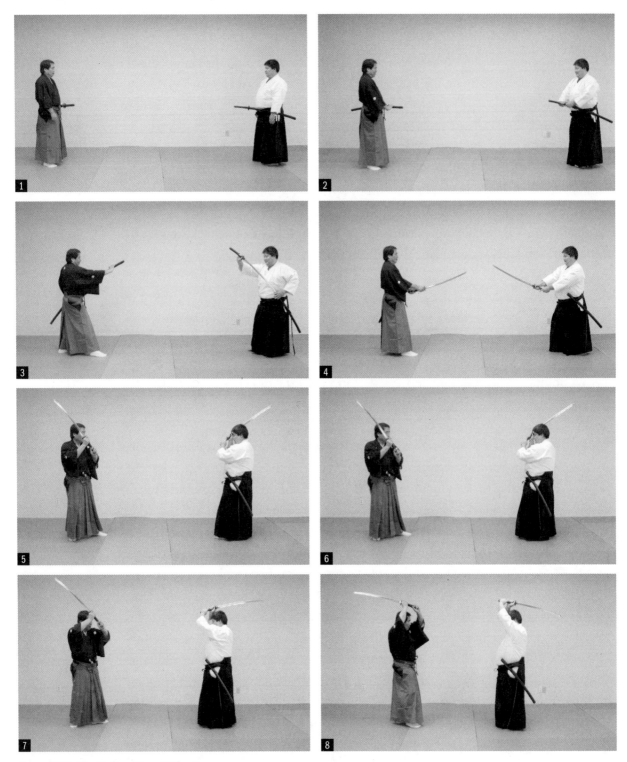

Figures 15K.1–8. Tachiuchi no Kurai: Uchikomi

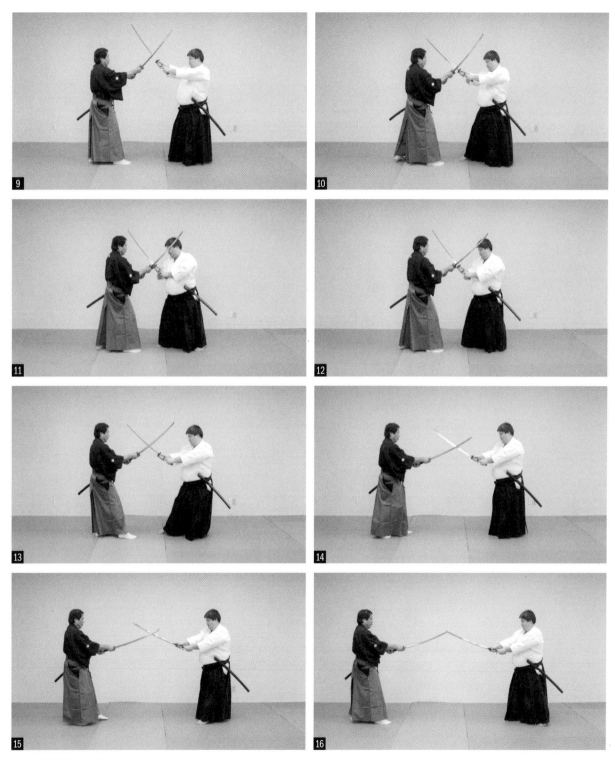

Figures 15K.9–16. Tachiuchi no Kurai: Uchikomi

Figures 15K.17–24. Tachiuchi no Kurai: Uchikomi

Figures 15K.25–28. Tachiuchi no Kurai: Uchikomi

# CONCLUSION

Every *katachi* in the Tachiuchi no Kurai series affords the opportunity to practice at least one major principle of *iaijutsu* under conditions simulating actual combat. Deai, for example, provides practice of the fundamentals of Eishin-Ryū: *nukitsuke, furikaburi,* and *kirioroshi*. Since Deai is performed with a partner, requiring that you adjust to another person's size, strength, speed, and movement, it also provides training in *maai* (distance control).

Deai, Tsukekomi, and Ukekomi all deal with seizing or reversing the initiative to gain a winning advantage over the opponent, and apply the principle of *seme* (pressure) to exert a measure of control over the opponent's actions. In Ukenagashi, Ukekomi, Suigetsutō, and Dokumyōken, a recurring principle is control of the opponent's *seichūsen* (center line) in order to maintain pressure *(seme)* and sustain your initiative. *Katachi* like Tsukikage and Suigetsutō apply the concept of *kage* (shadow), meaning not to be where you appear to be, or as vulnerable as you appear to be.

Bearing in mind our admonition in chapter 5, "*riron o shiru*" (understand the principles), what other *iaijutsu* principles did you notice being applied in the Tachiuchi no Kurai?

This should be a question in your mind every time you train in the Tachiuchi no Kurai, or any other aspect of *iaijutsu*. "What principles apply to this *waza* or this *katachi*?" "What should I be learning or improving as I do this?" And after your training session is complete, "What did I learn from that?" and "How did my *iaijutsu* improve from this?"

In chapter 5 we also stated, "*kaisū o kasaneru*" (develop through repetition). Repetition is always beneficial, but repetition with specific questions and objectives in mind will develop your skills even more quickly and fully. The most common and damaging mistake beginners—and even many experienced *iaidōka*—make is performing *kumitachi* by rote, rather than engaging in a mock life-or-death battle each time.

The primary purpose of *kumitachi* is to provide the *iaidōka* with a training experience that is as close to real combat as is safely possible. In this way, *kumitachi* not only reinforces such core principles of *iaijutsu* as *maai* (distance control), but it also trains the mind and spirit for the rigors and realities of combat. A battle between samurai is decided by a combination of strategy, reflexes, and sword-handling skills, and it all occurs in a split-second.

Even if the participants are applying proper stances, distance, and timing, *kumitachi* is of little benefit if the participants are merely clacking their *bokken* together in a prescribed sequence of movements. To derive the full and true benefit of *kumitachi*, each participant must attack and defend as if their life depended on it, earnestly trying to win the encounter even if their prescribed role (Uchikata) is to lose. The focus of *kumitachi* should be less about technique than about reading the opponent, sensing his or her intentions, and moving instinctively, but strategically, in response to the opponent.

Ideally, then, at least half of your training time and effort should be devoted to perfecting your performance of *kumitachi*.

Chapter 16

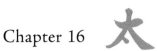

# *Tachiuchi no Kata*

## Katachi Variations

According to Masaoka Katsutane, the Tachiuchi no Kata were created by his *sensei* Ōe Masamichi, which places their origin in the late Meiji or early Taishō era—probably around 1900. Most of them are similar to Tachiuchi no Kurai, so it is likely they were derived from or created as variations of the *katachi* described in chapter 15. Although they were created in the modern era, they bear the characteristics of the *koryū* (ancient) Tachiuchi no Kurai.

The Tachiuchi no Kata were not included in previous editions of *Flashing Steel* primarily because they have rarely been practiced in the postwar era and are not customarily taught as part of the core curriculum of Eishin-Ryū, even in the Masaoka-Ha line. We have elected to include them in this edition of the book, primarily to preserve them for future reference, but also to provide *iaidōka* with some useful variations of the Tachiuchi no Kurai that involve differences in application, distance, and timing, and that in many cases are more challenging to perform.

Prior to practicing the Tachiuchi no Kata, you should perform *sahō* and *reihō* just as if you were preparing for any other aspect of *iaijutsu* training. Treat your *bokken* just as you would treat an *iaitō* or *shinken*, by performing *tōrei* as you take it up, and bow to your training partner.

As with the Tachiuchi no Kurai, the highest level of sincerity and respect is exhibited by performing your preparation and etiquette in a *seiza* position, facing your partner. In the description of each *kata*, we are assuming that the partners have already performed these rituals of proper etiquette, so our narrative describes only the techniques in the *kata* itself.

Just as in the Tachiuchi no Kurai, the partner who practices the principle intrinsic to the *kata* is called Shikata (User) and the partner assisting is called Uchikata (Striker), although the commonly used terms Shitachi and Uchitachi are equally

355

acceptable. Even though Shikata is the one practicing the key technique of each *kata*, it is equally important to develop proficiency in the role of Uchikata, both for development of your swordsmanship skills and the refinement of such character traits as humility, cooperation, and self-sacrifice.

Some characteristics common to all seven Tachiuchi no Kata are the *chiburi* and *nōtō*. Eishin-Ryū *chiburi* is performed at the completion of each *katachi*. This is followed by a simulated Shoden *nōtō*, using the left hand to simulate the *koiguchi*, and sliding the *bokken* through the opening of the hand as if sheathing it. It is not customary or necessary to slide the *bokken* through your belt to simulate it being in the *saya*, but neither is it prohibited, if you prefer to do so.

Another characteristic shared with the Tachiuchi no Kurai is *kiai*—the loud shout that accompanies each striking or thrusting motion in the *kata*. This means that sometimes only Shikata or Uchikata will *kiai* when only one of the two is using an attacking technique. Generally, when making a cut (*nukitsuke, kirioroshi, kesa-giri,* and so on) the *kiai* should be voiced as "*Ei!*" or "*Ya!*" and when performing a *tsuki* (thrust) it should be "*Hō!*" or "*Tō!*" in order to best match the movement of the diaphragm during *kiai* with the corresponding contraction of the abdominal muscles performing the technique.

## 16A: DEAI

The first *katachi*, Deai (Collision), is designed to employ the *iaijutsu* fundamentals *nukitsuke* and *kirioroshi* in simulated attack and defense with a training partner. It is nearly identical to its Tachiuchi no Kurai counterpart, except that it is performed with a higher degree of aggressiveness.

Begin facing your partner at a distance of about eight paces. Both partners perform *kiyomeri kokyū*, just as if preparing to perform a *waza* (see fig. 16A.1). Uchikata (on the right) initiates the action by grasping the *tsuka* and rising onto the balls of his feet, followed instantly by Shikata (on the left). Both partners take several *chidori-ashi* steps, then continue running—not walking, as in the Tachiuchi no Kurai—in normal strides toward each other. As they reach cutting distance, both take a final step forward with the right foot and perform *nukitsuke* (fig. 16A.4) as cuts toward each other's right knee. Without hesitation, Shikata drives forward, forcing Uchikata's sword rearward, causing Uchikata to withdraw his right leg. Drawing his left foot even with his right, Shikata performs *furikaburi* (fig. 16A.5) and lunges forward with his right foot, executing *kirioroshi*—all in a continuous motion. Uchikata steps back with his left foot and blocks this cut with *jōdan uke*, as shown in figure 16A.6.

This is a more aggressive performance of Deai than in the Tachiuchi no Kurai, demanding a higher level of skill of both participants. *Seme* (mental and physical pressure against the opponent) is the core principle underlying its successful execution. In essence, Shikata maintains such intense *seme* that Uchikata has no opportunity to seize the initiative and is forced to retreat.

The *kata* concludes in the same manner as in the Tachiuchi no Kurai version: both participants separate while maintaining *zanshin* and step back to their original starting positions, ending right foot forward, about eight paces apart. Once back at their original starting positions, each partner levels his sword and pushes his hips slightly forward, then performs Eishin-Ryū *chiburi*.

Both perform *nōtō* (with Uchikata beginning *nōtō* slightly before Shikata), drawing their rear foot forward in *iaigoshi* as their swords are "sheathed" into their left hands, slide their right hands down to the *tsukagashira*, then rise to a full standing position.

Figures 16A.1–4. Tachiuchi no Kata: Deai

Figures 16A.5–11. Tachiuchi no Kata: Deai

# 16B: KOBUSHI DORI

The second *katachi*, Kobushi Dori (Fist Capture), is nearly identical to Tsukekomi in the Tachiuchi no Kurai, and provides practice of the same principle of seizing (or reversing) the opponent's initiative.

Both partners perform *kiyomeri kokyū*, just as if preparing to perform a *waza* (see fig. 16B.1). Uchikata (on the right) initiates the action by grasping the *tsuka* and rising onto the balls of his feet, followed instantly by Shikata (on the left). Both partners take several *chidori-ashi* steps, then continue running in normal strides toward each other. As they reach cutting distance, both take a final step forward with the right foot and perform *nukitsuke* (fig. 16B.4) as cuts toward each other's right knee. As Uchikata presses forward, attempting to force Shikata back, Shikata quickly steps forward with his left foot and seizes Uchikata's right hand (fig. 16B.5), gripping it with the thumb at the base of Uchikata's little finger and the index and middle fingers between Uchikata's index finger and thumb to ensure control of the wrist. Shikata then turns his hips to the right while bearing his weight down on Uchikata's right arm, freeing his sword from beneath Uchikata's, then turns his hips sharply to the left, impaling Uchikata with a *tsuki* through the lungs and pericardium (fig. 16B.6).

Figures 16B.1–4. Tachiuchi no Kata: Tsukekomi

Figures 16B.5–11. Tachiuchi no Kata: Tsukekomi

To separate from this position with *zanshin*, Shikata keeps his *kissaki* pressed against Uchikata's *suigetsu* (solar plexus) while releasing Uchikata's right hand and stepping back with his right foot. After pausing momentarily in *ai-seigan* (fig. 16B.7), both partners return to their starting positions, perform *chiburi* and *nōtō* as previously described, and rise to a standing position.

## 16C: ZETSUMYŌKEN

Zetsumyōken (Miraculous Sword) is the third *kata*, which employs principles similar to those in Ukekomi in the Tachiuchi no Kurai.

The partners face each other about eight paces apart during *kiyomeri kokyū*, then with Uchikata initiating the movements, both Shikata and Uchikata draw their *bokken* and step forward with their right feet into *seigan no kamae* (fig. 16C.2). As Uchikata next takes a step forward with his left foot, Shikata takes a step back to maintain their separation, both assuming *hassō no kamae* (fig. 16C.3). After a brief pause, both partners dash forward using *chidori-ashi* for about ten paces (fig. 16C.4), followed by a couple of normal running strides. As they near *kirima* (cutting distance), both perform *furikaburi* and step right foot forward with *yokomen-giri* toward each other's left temple, nullifying each other's cut (fig. 16C.5).

An important distinction between Zetsumyōken in the Tachiuchi no Kata and Ukekomi in the Tachiuchi no Kurai is that in Zetsumyōken, both partners step *forward* while executing this first *yokomen-giri*, whereas in Ukekomi, Uchikata steps rearward to receive the cut. This is a significant increase in Uchikata's aggressiveness, and it alters the *maai* (distance control) factors considerably.

Having cut to Uchikata's *seichūsen*, Shikata begins to press forward with a thrust to Uchikata's face, which Uchikata steps back to evade and counters with a *yokomen-giri* aimed at Shikata's right temple. Shikata meets this by stepping forward with a mirror-image *yokomen-giri* (fig. 16C.6), again cutting to Uchikata's *seichūsen*. Shikata again presses forward with a thrust to Uchikata's face, and Uchikata steps back into *jōdan no kamae* with the intention of using *kirioroshi* to preempt Shikata's next *yokomen-giri*. In response, Shikata steps to his right, outside the line of Uchikata's intended *kirioroshi*, while performing either *yokomen-giri* to Uchikata's left temple (fig. 16C.7) or *dōbarai-giri* (torso cut) to Uchikata's left side (fig. 16C.8), depending upon which presents as the better target given Uchikata's distance, timing, and exposure. The partners then separate with *zanshin* to *ai-seigan* (fig. 16C.9), pause, and return to their starting positions in the customary manner.

Figures 16C.1–12. Tachiuchi no Kata: Zetsumyōken

# 16D: DOKUMYŌKEN

Dokumyōken (Mysterious Sword) is the fourth *kata* and is used to practice a deflection and continuous-motion counterattack against a thrust to the solar plexus in a manner similar to Suigetsutō in the Tachiuchi no Kurai.

The partners begin facing each other about eight paces apart during *kiyomeri kokyū*, then with Uchikata initiating the movements, both Shikata and Uchikata draw their *bokken* and step forward with their right feet into *seigan no kamae* (fig. 16D.2). As Uchikata next takes a step forward with his left foot, Shikata takes a step back to maintain their separation, both assuming *hassō no kamae* (fig. 16D.3). After a brief pause, both partners dash forward using *chidori-ashi* for about ten paces (fig. 16D.4), followed by a couple of normal running strides. As they near *kirima* (cutting distance), both perform *furikaburi* and step right foot forward with *yokomen-giri* toward each other's left temple, nullifying each other's cut (fig. 16D.5).

Once again, this is a more aggressive attack than those used in similar Tachiuchi no Kurai, with both partners *running* forward while executing this first *yokomen-giri*, unlike the Tachiuchi no Kurai, in which Uchikata steps rearward to receive the cut, and it alters the *maai* (distance control) factors considerably.

Having cut to Uchikata's *seichūsen*, Shikata begins to press forward with a thrust to Uchikata's face, which Uchikata steps back to evade and counters with a *yokomen-giri* aimed at Shikata's right temple. Shikata meets this by stepping forward with a mirror-image *yokomen-giri* (fig. 16C.6), again cutting to Uchikata's *seichūsen*. Shikata again presses forward with a thrust to Uchikata's face, which Uchikata steps back to evade and counters with a *yokomen-giri* aimed at Shikata's left temple. Shikata meets this by stepping forward with a mirror-image *yokomen-giri* (fig. 16D.7).

To prevent Shikata from continuing to drive forward, Uchikata now steps back and lowers his sword into *seigan no kamae* in an attempt to gain control of the *seichūsen*. Shikata also lowers his sword, resulting in *ai-seigan* (fig. 16D.8). Having apparently gained control of the *seichūsen*, Uchikata immediately lunges forward with a *tsuki* (thrust) to Shikata's *suigetsu* (solar plexus), which Shikata counters by stepping to his left and raising his hands to the *ura* (back) side of Uchikata's sword (fig. 16D.9), then continuing in a circular path into *kirioroshi* to Uchikata's *shōmen* (fig. 16D.10).

The partners then separate with *zanshin* to *ai-seigan* (fig. 16D.11), pause briefly, and return to their starting positions in the customary manner.

Figures 16D.1–8. Tachiuchi no Kata: Dokumyōken

Figures 16D.9–15. Tachiuchi no Kata: Dokumyōken

# 16E: TSUBA DOME

The fifth *kata*, Tsuba Dome (Tsuba Block), is reminiscent of Tsukikage in the Tachi-uchi no Kurai, and provides another situation in which calculating the speed, extension, and timing of an opponent's cut in order to dodge it is the core principle.

The training partners face each other at a distance of about eight paces apart. On their third cleansing breaths, with Uchikata initiating, both partners draw their *bokken*, stepping forward with their right feet into *seigan no kamae* (fig. 16E.2). After a momentary pause, Shikata lowers his *kissaki* to *gedan no kamae* (fig. 16E.3), creating an apparent opening to attack.

Both partners then dash forward using *chidori-ashi* for about ten paces (fig. 16E.4), followed by a couple of normal running strides. As they near *kirima* (cutting distance) both perform *furikaburi* (fig. 16E.5) and step right foot forward with *yokomen-giri* toward each other's left temple, nullifying each other's cut (fig. 16E.6), their momentum driving then forward into *tsubazeria* (fig. 16E.7).

This is again a more aggressive attack than those used in similar Tachiuchi no Kurai, with both partners *running* forward while executing this first *yokomen-giri*, and it alters the *maai* (distance control) substantially. In addition, advanced *iaidōka* can employ *kirioroshi* in place of the *yokomen-giri* shown in figure 16E.6 to further increase the aggressiveness and realism of this *kata*. Since this greatly increases the risk of accidental contact, it is recommended that only highly skilled *iaidōka* attempt this variation.

In *tsubazeria*, both partners must be sensitive to each other's strength and match it exactly. After realizing that neither can gain an advantage, both partners simultaneously push away from each other, stepping back with their right feet into *waki no kamae*, as shown in figure 16E.8. Seeing Shikata's left side apparently exposed to attack, Uchikata steps forward with *kirioroshi* to Shikata's *shōmen* (center of the head).

Note: This *kirioroshi* is a considerably more dangerous attack—even with *bokken*—than the cut to the leg utilized in Tsukikage in the Tachiuchi no Kurai. Shikata must exercise precise timing to avoid being struck in the left arm or head by Uchikata while training, so it is recommended that readers not attempt to practice this *kata* until they have developed proficiency in the *katachi* Tsukikage.

With a sharp twist of the hips, Shikata draws his feet together, pulling the forward leg back to his right foot while raising his arms laterally into *furikaburi* (fig. 16E.9) as Uchikata's attempted *kirioroshi* passes. If Shikata raises his arms before withdrawing from the path of Uchikata's sword, he will be struck in the left arm. In a continuous motion, Shikata steps right foot forward with *kirioroshi* to Uchikata's *shōmen* (center of the head), as shown in figure 16E.10.

Figures 16E.1–8. Tachiuchi no Kata: Tsuba Dome

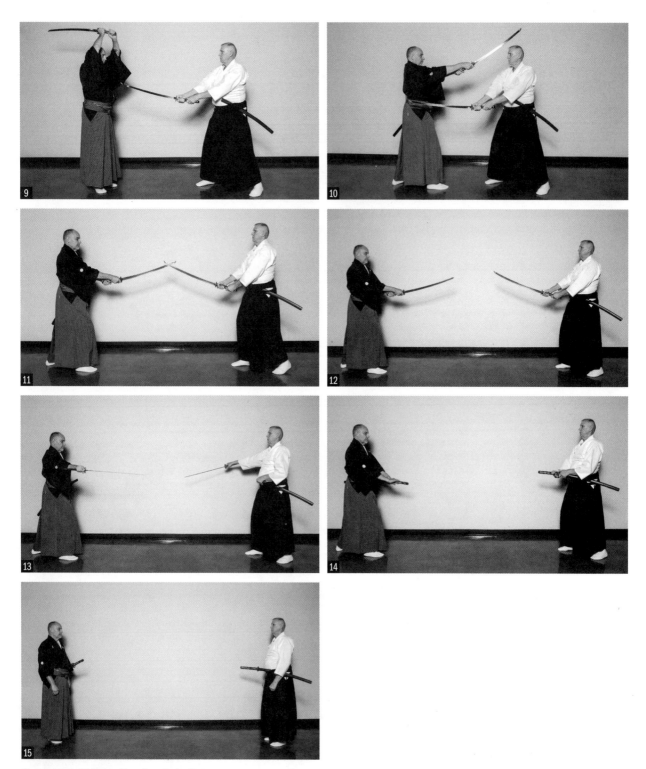

Figures 16E.9–15. Tachiuchi no Kata: Tsuba Dome

The critical element of this *katachi* is the timing of this evasion and counterattack by Shikata. If Shikata moves prematurely, Uchikata could adjust the attack to succeed, so Shikata cannot react until Uchikata is sufficiently committed to the attack that its path cannot be altered. This means the attack will nearly graze Shikata's torso as it passes, applying the concept of *issun no maai*. Likewise, if the counterattack is not made the moment Uchikata's attack misses, Uchikata will be able to recover and block it.

Following the decisive *kirioroshi*, both Shikata and Uchikata conclude the *katachi* by stepping back into *ai-seigan*, then returning to their respective starting points in the customary manner.

## 16F: UKENAGASHI

The principle practiced in Ukenagashi (Flowing Block) is that found in the Tachiuchi no Kurai of the same name, but in a slightly different manner and under far more challenging conditions.

The partners begin facing each other about eight paces apart during *kiyomeri kokyū*, then Uchikata (on the right) initiates the action by grasping the *tsuka* and rising onto the balls of his feet, followed instantly by Shikata (on the left). Both partners take several *chidori-ashi* steps (fig. 16F.3), then continue running in normal strides toward each other. As they reach cutting distance, Uchikata draws his sword directly overhead into *furikaburi* (fig. 16F.4) then steps forward with his right foot to execute *kirioroshi* to Shikata's *shōmen*. Shikata draws his sword directly overhead while stepping slightly to his right off the line of Uchikata's *kirioroshi*, allowing the natural angle of the blade to deflect Uchikata's cut (fig. 16F.5) and the impact of Uchikata's cut to propel Shikata's sword in a circular trajectory ending in *kirioroshi* to Uchikata's *shōmen* (fig. 16F.6).

The partners then separate with *zanshin* to *ai-seigan* (fig. 16F.7), then return to their starting positions in the customary manner.

It should be apparent that the timing and distance control involved in this variation of Ukenagashi is extremely challenging when performed running toward each other. The slightest error in timing could result in a serious injury to Shikata, so it is recommended that readers not attempt this *kata* until they are highly proficient in the performance of the Tachiuchi no Kurai version of Ukenagashi.

Figures 16F.1–8. Tachiuchi no Kata: Ukenagashi

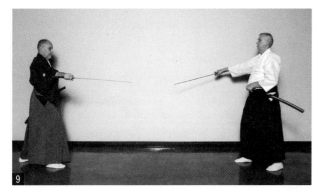

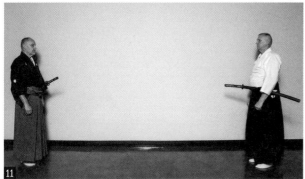

Figures 16F.9–11. Tachiuchi no Kata: Ukenagashi

# 16G: MAPPŌ

The final *kata* in the Tachiuchi no Kata series, Mappō (True Method), is different from any of the Tachiuchi no Kurai.

The training partners face each other at a distance of about eight paces apart. On their third cleansing breaths, with Uchikata initiating, both partners draw their *bokken*, stepping forward with their right feet into *seigan no kamae* (fig. 16G.2). After a momentary pause, Uchikata steps forward into *hassō no kamae* while Shikata remains in *seigan* (fig. 16G.3).

Both partners then dash forward using *chidori-ashi* for about ten paces (fig. 16G.4), followed by a couple of normal running strides. As they near *kirima* (cutting distance), both perform *furikaburi* (fig. 16G.5). Shikata accelerates forward, right foot leading, and executes *kirioroshi* before Uchikata can change the pace of his attack. Uchikata therefore twists his sword to his left into *jōdan uke* to receive the cut (fig. 16G.6).

Figures 16G.1–11. Tachiuchi no Kata: Mappō

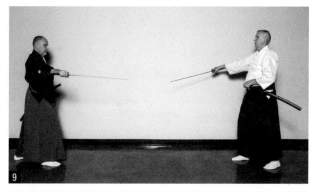

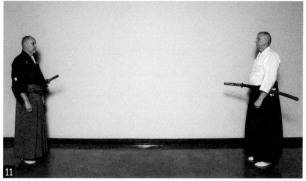

Figures 16G.1–11. Tachiuchi no Kata: Mappō

The principle underlying this *kata* is *maai* (distance control). As the two partners run toward each other, they must both adjust the timing of their steps to the other's in order to achieve proper *kirima* (cutting distance) for their intended attacks. In this case, Shikata accelerates suddenly and performs *kirioroshi* a half-step before Uchikata had timed his own attack, thus preempting it. To perform Mappō successfully requires extreme precision and sensitivity to Uchikata's timing.

The partners separate with *zanshin* to *ai-seigan* (fig. 16F.7), then return to their starting positions in the customary manner.

At the conclusion of Tachiuchi no Kurai practice, you should perform *sahō* and *reihō* just as you did at the beginning, but in reverse order. To demonstrate the utmost mutual respect, the partners would sit in *seiza* posture, perform *tōrei* to their swords and *zarei* to each other, treating their *bokken* just as they would treat an *iaitō* or *shinken*.

In less formal settings, it is sufficient to simply perform a standing bow to each other, followed by a standing *tōrei*, and *hairei* prior to leaving the *dōjō*.

# CONCLUSION

The Tachiuchi no Kata are clearly more difficult to perform than their Tachiuchi no Kurai counterparts. This, and the injuries resulting from that increased difficulty, may be the reasons that the Tachiuchi no Kata are seldom practiced in modern Eishin-Ryū.

On the other hand, they challenge experienced *iaidōka* with some interesting variations to the techniques found in the Tachiuchi no Kurai, and demonstrate that there is more than one correct or practical way of defending against a given attack. They offer students an opportunity to train against a more aggressive opponent in more intensely combative scenarios in order to improve their skills.

Although we have presented them chiefly for the sake of preserving them as part of the Masaoka-Ha heritage and history, we recognize that they may also serve to enhance your training after developing proficiency in the performance of the Tachiuchi no Kurai. If used in that way, in view of the danger they present to inexperienced *iaidōka*, we recommend that they be practiced after gaining proficiency in the Tsumeai no Kurai as well.

Chapter 17

# Tsumeai no Kurai

## Close Quarters Kumitachi

The exact origins of the Tsumeai no Kurai are no longer known, but either they, or a similar set of *kumitachi* performed from the *tatehiza* posture, have undoubtedly been an integral part of the training system Eishin-Ryū since the time of Hasegawa Eishin or perhaps earlier, since *waza* initiated from the *tatehiza* position have been an integral part of the *ryū* from the outset.

Like the Tachiuchi no Kurai, each of the Tsumeai no Kurai promotes the practice of a key principle of Eishin-Ryū under controlled but reasonably realistic conditions. The term *tsumeai no kurai* can be translated a couple different ways. *Tsumeai* and *tsumeawase* are both written with the same *kanji* and are commonly taken to mean "assorted" or "assortment." However, individually, *tsume* means "to pack," "cram," "box in," or "checkmate," and *ai* means "to join," "connect," "combine," or "be opposite," so the term could also be taken to mean "in close proximity," "closely opposing," or "close range." The latter seems particularly apropos, since most of the situations (*kurai*) in the Tsumeai no Kurai take place at close range, and therefore require slightly different tactics and a higher degree of skill than the Tachiuchi no Kurai. Typically, the Tsumeai no Kurai are rarely taught to students who are below *nidan* rank, and often not taught until *sandan* or above.

Prior to practicing the Tsumeai no Kurai, you should perform *sahō* and *reihō* just as if you were preparing for any other aspect of *iaijutsu* training. Treat your *bokken* just as you would treat an *iaitō* or *shinken*, by performing *tōrei* as you take up your *bokken*. Be sure to observe the appropriate formalities in bowing to your partner. These aspects of training are just as important as performing the *katachi*.

In a formal setting, the highest level of sincerity and respect is shown by performing your preparation and etiquette in a *seiza* position, facing your partner. In the description of each *katachi*, we are assuming that the partners have already performed these rituals of proper etiquette, so our narrative covers only the techniques in the *katachi* itself.

In each *katachi*, one partner practices a key principle of *iaijutsu*, and the other partner provides the appropriate attack and defense to facilitate this training. As with the Tachiuchi no Kurai, the partner who practices the principle intrinsic to the *katachi* is called Shikata (User) and the partner assisting is called Uchikata (Striker). Even though Shikata is the one practicing the key technique of each *katachi*, it is equally important to develop aptitude in the role of Uchikata, both for development of your swordsmanship skills and the refinement of such character traits as humility, cooperation, and self-sacrifice.

Some characteristics common to all ten Tsumeai no Kurai are the *chiburi* and *nōtō*. Eishin-Ryū *chiburi* (meaning *yoko-chiburi*) is performed at the completion of each *katachi*. This is followed by a simulated Chūden *nōtō* (see chapter 7 for details). If you don't have a *saya* for your *bokken*, use your left hand to simulate the *koiguchi*, and slide the *bokken* through the opening of the hand as if sheathing it. It is permissible, though not required, to slide the *bokken* through your *obi* to simulate it being in the *saya*.

Another characteristic not found in the *waza* of Eishin-Ryū is *kiai*—the loud shout that accompanies each cutting or thrusting motion in the *katachi*. This means that sometimes only Shikata or Uchikata will *kiai*, since only one of the two is performing an attacking technique, while the other is blocking. In several cases, however, such as the first attacks of Hassō, Kobushi Dori, Yaegaki, Urokogaeshi, and others in which the partners are attacking simultaneously, they will both *kiai* simultaneously. As a general rule, cuts should be accompanied by a *kiai* of "*Ei!*" or "*Ya!*" and thrusts by "*Hō!*" or "*Tō!*"

# 17A: HASSŌ

The first *katachi*, Hassō (Fast Departure), is designed to employ the *iaijutsu* fundamentals *nukitsuke* and *kirioroshi* in simulated attack and defense with a training partner in a manner similar to Deai in the Tachiuchi no Kurai. Instead of beginning with the participants standing eight paces apart, however, Hassō begins with them seated in close proximity in *tatehiza*.

Begin facing your partner at a distance of about three paces. This is roughly the distance from which you could touch fingertips if both of you extended your arms fully forward. From there, both Shikata and Uchikata sit in *tatehiza* in the manner described in chapter 7.

Both partners perform *kiyomeri kokyū*, just as if preparing to perform a *waza* (see fig. 17A.1), at the completion of which Uchikata (at right) begins *koiguchi no kirikata*, followed quickly by Shikata (at left). Both rise simultaneously as they begin *nukitsuke* (fig. 17A.2), with Uchikata stepping right foot forward at *saya-banari* and Shikata stepping left foot back, both cutting toward each other's upper shin (fig. 17A.3). Shikata draws his left foot even with his right and performs *furikaburi*, then lunges quickly right foot forward into a kneeling position with *kirioroshi*, while Uchikata steps back with his left foot and kneels with *jōdan uke* (overhead block), as shown in figure 17A.4.

Uchikata slowly lowers his sword, and Shikata's sword follows it down until it reaches *seigan* (*kissaki* pointing between Uchikata's eyes). Uchikata then moves his sword underneath Shikata's to the *omote* side until they are in *ai-seigan* (fig. 17A.5). Uchikata performs *yoko-chiburi*, with Shikata immediately following (fig. 17A.6). Uchikata initiates Chūden *nōtō* and Shikata follows, finishing slightly before Uchikata (figs. 17A.7–8). Both partners extend their right legs (fig. 17A.9) and rise to a standing position (fig. 17A.10), keeping their right hands on the *tsukagashira*. Then both draw their right feet back and lower their right hands (fig. 17A.11).

When performing Tsumeai no Kurai, it is more important than ever to treat the situation as if it was real combat with *shinken*. This is important, not only to train your mind under the most realistic conditions possible, but also for safety. Two key factors in the performance of Tsumeai no Kurai are *seme* (pressuring the opponent) and *sen* (seizing the initiative). Often, to seize the initiative and to prevent the opponent from counterattacking, Shikata must move so quickly and decisively that Uchikata has no opportunity to defend or counter the technique Shikata uses. A lapse in concentration under those conditions can easily lead to a serious injury.

Hassō exemplifies the use of *sen* (initiative) to preclude an effective defense. Note that Uchikata is the initiator of the first attack and Shikata is on the defensive at the outset, beginning to draw his sword after Uchikata and being forced to step back to avoid and block the first cut. To seize the initiative, Shikata must immediately turn the tables and drive Uchikata back. So, a key factor in Hassō is for Shikata to drive forward immediately after stopping Uchikata's initial attack. If done, correctly, this sudden reversal—the "fast departure" for which Hassō is named—prevents Uchikata from pressing his attack and forces him back and down into a kneeling position in which all he can do is capitulate.

Figures 17A.1–8. Tsumeai no Kurai: Hassō

Figures 17A.9–11. Tsumeai no Kurai: Hassō

## 17B: KOBUSHI DORI

The second *katachi*, Kobushi Dori (Fist Capture), provides another method for quickly seizing the initiative from an opponent who has initiated an unsuccessful attack.

Begin facing your partner at a distance of about three paces, then both of you sit in *tatehiza* and perform *kiyomeri kokyū* (see fig. 17B.1), at the completion of which Uchikata (at right) performs *koiguchi no kirikata* in preparation for an attack, and Shikata (at left) responds a moment later by beginning *nukitsuke*, as shown in figure 17B.2. The initial cut is identical to that performed in Hassō (fig. 17B.3).

Before Uchikata can react, Shikata quickly steps forward with his left foot and seizes Uchikata's right hand (fig. 17B.4), gripping it as shown close up in figure 17B.5, with the thumb at the base of Uchikata's little finger and the index and middle fingers between Uchikata's index finger and thumb to ensure complete control of the wrist. Shikata drops onto his right knee, pulling Uchikata down onto his left knee, and thrusts the *kissaki* into Uchikata's ribs (fig. 17B.6) at an angle that would, if extended fully, penetrate the lungs and pericardium. Note that in this position Uchikata's sword is trapped between the downward pressure of Shikata's left hand, the upward pressure of Shikata's sword, and Shikata's left hip, with Shikata's *tsuba* preventing Uchikata from cutting.

Figures 17B.1–8. Tsumeai no Kurai: Kobushi Dori

Figures 17B.9–13. Tsumeai no Kurai: Kobushi Dori

To separate from this position with *zanshin*, Shikata pushes Uchikata's sword hand toward Uchikata's left side while maintaining pressure against Uchikata's ribs with the *kissaki* and steps back with the left foot. This forces Uchikata to slide backward to escape the pressure of Shikata's *kissaki*, then return his sword to *ai-seigan*, as shown in figure 17B.7.

Uchikata performs *yoko-chiburi*, with Shikata immediately following (fig. 17B.8). Uchikata initiates Chūden *nōtō* and Shikata follows, finishing slightly before Uchikata (figs. 17B.9–10). Both partners extend their right legs (fig. 17B.11) and rise to a standing position (fig. 17B.12, keeping their right hands on the *tsukagashira*. Then both draw their right feet back and lower their right hands (fig. 17B.13).

Unlike Hassō, in which quickly and forcefully seizing the initiative is the key to gaining the advantage over Uchikata, in Kobushi Dori, Shikata essentially sidesteps Uchikata's attack. If Uchikata presses the attack by continuing his forward momentum, it actually works to Shikata's advantage in Kobushi Dori by unbalancing Uchikata. The principle practiced in Kobushi Dori (Fist Capture) is similar to Tsukekomi in the Tachiuchi no Kurai.

## 17C: NAMIGAESHI

The principle practiced in Namigaeshi (Returning Wave) is yet another variation of the principle found in Tsukekomi in the Tachiuchi no Kurai. In Namigaeshi, however, it is a counter to Uchikata's attempt to perform *kobushi dori*.

Begin as before, facing your partner at a distance of about three paces, then both of you sit in *tatehiza* and perform *kiyomeri kokyū* (see fig. 17C.1), at the completion of which Uchikata (right) performs *koiguchi no kirikata* in preparation for an attack, and Shikata (left) responds a moment later by beginning *nukitsuke*, as shown in figure 17C.2. The initial cut to the upper shin is again identical to that performed in Hassō (fig. 17C.3). This time, however, Uchikata steps forward with his left foot and attempts to grab Shikata's right hand, but Shikata retracts his hand while simultaneously seizing Uchikata's hand (fig. 17C.4). The manner in which Shikata grips Uchikata's hand is crucial to this technique. Shikata's middle, ring, and pinky finger grasp the base of Uchikata's thumb and Shikata's thumb lodges just below and between the knuckles of Uchikata's ring and pinky fingers, as shown in figure 17C.5, providing the leverage needed for the technique that follows shortly. As soon as this grip is secure, Shikata drops onto his right knee, using his weight to pull Uchikata forward and don, as well as pinning Uchikata's sword against the floor or ground, as depicted in figure 17C.6. Shikata releases his own sword and uses his right hand to reinforce his grip on Uchikata's hand (figs. 17C.7–8) while twisting Uchikata's wrist counterclockwise (from Shikata's perspective) and pivoting 90 degrees to his left to throw Uchikata to the ground or floor to Shikata's left side (figs. 17C.9–10) in a movement commonly called *kotegaeshi* in grappling arts like *jūdō*, *jūjutsu*, and *aikidō*.

Note: We recommend that when initially learning Namigaeshi, Uchikata also release his or her sword when Shikata forces it to the floor in order to avoid being struck with it during the *kotegaeshi* throw. In actual combat, Shikata would, in fact, attempt to strike Uchikata in the head with his or her own sword in order to off-balance Uchikata further. Later, when both partners are familiar with Namigaeshi, Uchikata should retain his or her sword, and the throw be performed in this manner, with Uchikata rolling to his or her right side to avoid being struck.

Having thrown Uchikata, Shikata then slides up against Uchikata, using his right knee in the small of Uchikata's back to keep Uchikata's body turned away, and presses Uchikata's right elbow against Shikata's left lower thigh, pinning it (and representing its dislocation), then punches Uchikata in the temple or base of the jaw, as shown in figure 17C.10. This strike is shown at the reverse angle in figure 17C.11 to better display the use of the right knee to immobilize Uchikata and the left knee to distend or dislocate Uchikata's right elbow. In actual combat, this punch would be replaced with a thrust of a *tantō* (dagger) or *wakizashi* (short sword), if Shikata was wearing one.

After striking, Shikata releases Uchikata. Both rise (fig. 17C.12) and warily move into position to retrieve their swords (fig. 17C.12). They simultaneously kneel, watching each other for signs of aggression, and pick up their swords (fig. 17C.14) and assume *ai-seigan* (fig. 17C.15) before rising in *ai-seigan* and returning to their original starting position (fig. 17C.16). Maintaining *ai-seigan*, both kneel with their right feet leading (fig. 17C.17), perform *yoko-chiburi* (fig. 17C.18), and Chūden *nōtō* (figs. 17C.19–20), then rise and conclude the *katachi* in the customary manner.

Namigaeshi introduces an element of *jūjutsu* into the Eishin-Ryū curriculum. It is the only *jūjutsu* technique included at the *chūden* level, but it serves as a hint that there is more to *iaijutsu* than swordsmanship alone. More *jūjutsu* techniques are included in the *okuden* curriculum, once *iaidōka* have developed proficiency in the use of the sword. It also underscores the fact that many aspects of *iaijutsu* simply cannot be learned in any other way than by personal instruction from a thoroughly knowledgeable *sensei*. Explanation alone is insufficient; the angles, pressures, timing, and precise placement of the body for performance of techniques like *kotegaeshi* can only be learned by experiencing them, because it is the minutiae that determine the success or failure of the technique.

A clue to the methodology of Namigaeshi is in the name of the technique. Taken literally, *namigaeshi* means "returning wave," but consider the effect of a returning wave. When a returning wave meets an incoming wave, it produces an undertow or rip current, which is an apt description for the curling motion applied to Uchikata's wrist in the *kotegaeshi* technique.

Figures 17C.1–8. Tsumeai no Kurai: Namigaeshi

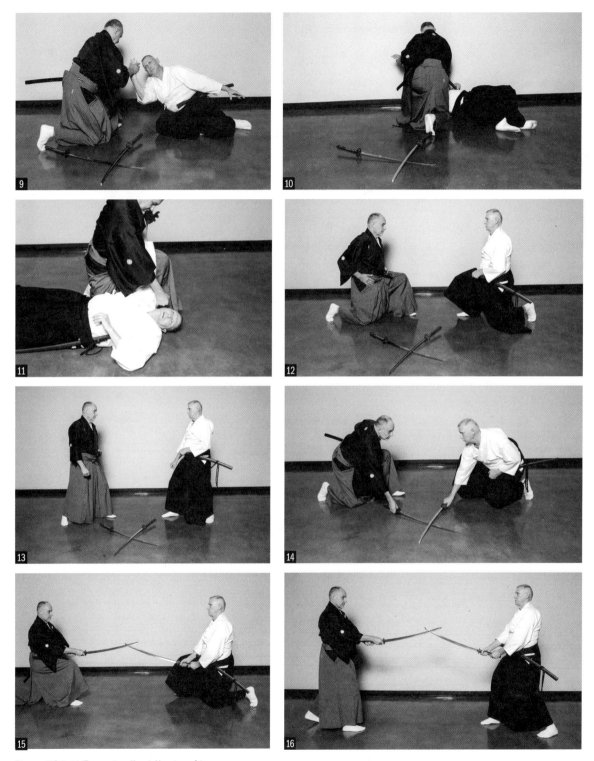

Figures 17C.9–16. Tsumeai no Kurai: Namigaeshi

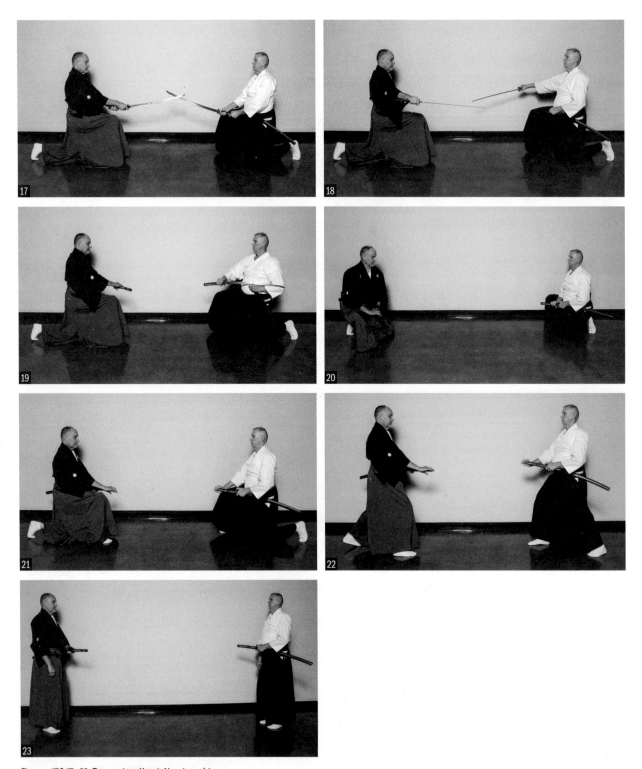

Figures 17C.17–23. Tsumeai no Kurai: Namigaeshi

# 17D: YAEGAKI

The fourth Tsumeai no Kurai is Yaegaki (Concentric Barriers), which provides a methodology for defending against a sustained series of highly aggressive attacks by Uchikata.

As with the previous *katachi* in this set, the training partners begin facing each other at a distance of about three paces, then both sit in *tatehiza* and perform *kiyomeri kokyū* (see fig. 17D.1). While inhaling his third breath, Uchikata (right) performs *koiguchi no kirikata* in preparation for an attack, and Shikata (left) responds a moment later by beginning *nukitsuke*, as shown in figure 17D.2. The initial cut to the upper shin is again identical to that performed in Hassō (fig. 17D.3).

Uchikata continues to drive forward, attacking quickly with *kirioroshi*, forcing Shikata to drop back into a kneeling position with a reinforced overhead block (fig. 17D.4), followed immediately by *Uchikata* stepping forward with a *yokomen-giri* to the right side of *Shikata's* head, which Shikata blocks by turning his sword vertical while stepping back again (fig. 17D.5). *Uchikata* immediately steps forward again, this time with a *yokomen-giri* to the left side of Shikata's head, which Shikata counters by stepping back and shifting his sword vertically to his left side, as depicted in figure 17D.6. Next, Uchikata lunges forward with another *kirioroshi*, which Shikata again receives with a reinforced overhead block (fig. 17D.7). As Uchitachi begins to raise his sword to *furikaburi* for another attack, Shikata seizes the initiative by rising with his sword beneath Uchikata's sword, forcing Uchikata to step back as he completes *furikaburi* and kneel in position to cut one of Shikata's exposed sides, which allows Shikata to step forward into a kneeling position with a *morote-zuki* (two-handed thrust) to Uchikata's throat, as shown in figure 17D.8.

The partners then rise and separate with *zanshin* to *ai-seigan* (fig. 17D.9), return to their starting positions, kneel in *ai-seigan*, and conclude the *katachi* with *chiburi* and *nōtō* in the usual manner.

Figures 17D.1–2. Tachiuchi no Kurai: Yaegaki

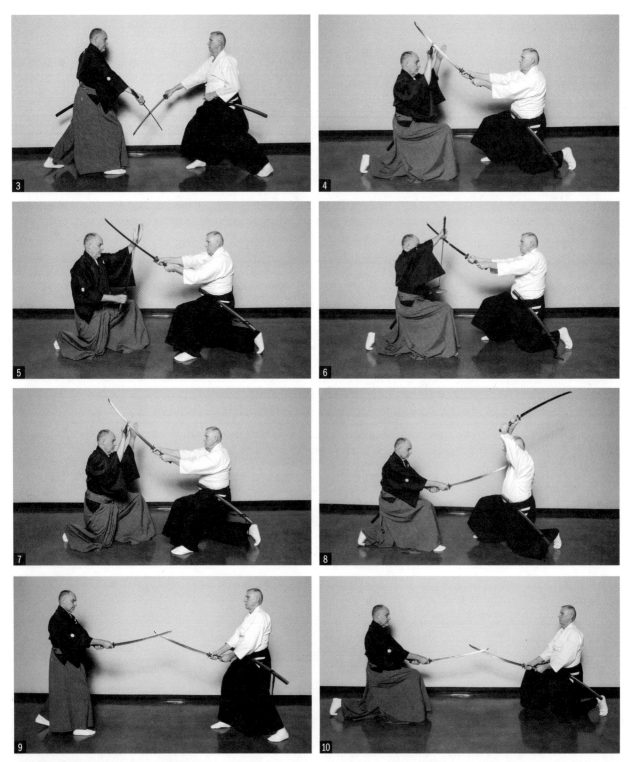

Figures 17D.3–10. Tachiuchi no Kurai: Yaegaki

Figures 17D.11–16. Tachiuchi no Kurai: Yaegaki

## 17-E: UROKO GAESHI

The fifth *katachi*, Uroko Gaeshi (Sudden Reversal), is a different response to the same situation as in Yaegaki, above, but involves Shikata seizing the initiative much sooner than in Yaegaki using the same technique found in Dokumyōken in the Tachiuchi no Kurai.

As before, the training partners begin facing each other at a distance of about three paces, then both sit in *tatehiza* and perform *kiyomeri kokyū* (see fig. 17E.1). While inhaling his third breath, Uchikata (right) performs *koiguchi no kirikata* in preparation for an attack, and Shikata (left) responds a moment later by beginning *nukitsuke*, as shown in figure 17E.2. The initial cut to the upper shin is once again identical to that performed in Hassō (fig. 17E.3). Uchikata immediately lunges right foot forward with *kirioroshi*, forcing Shikata to drop back into a kneeling position with a reinforced overhead block (fig. 17E.4). But before Uchikata can drive forward with a follow-up attack Shikata lunges left foot forward, forcing Uchikata's sword first upward—which necessitates Uchikata shuffling backward into a kneeling position—then sweeps Uchikata's sword to Shikata's right side while bringing Shikata's sword into position for a reinforced *tsuki* to Uchikata's throat, as shown in figure 17E.5.

Figures 17E.1–6. Tsumeai no Kurai: Uroko Gaeshi

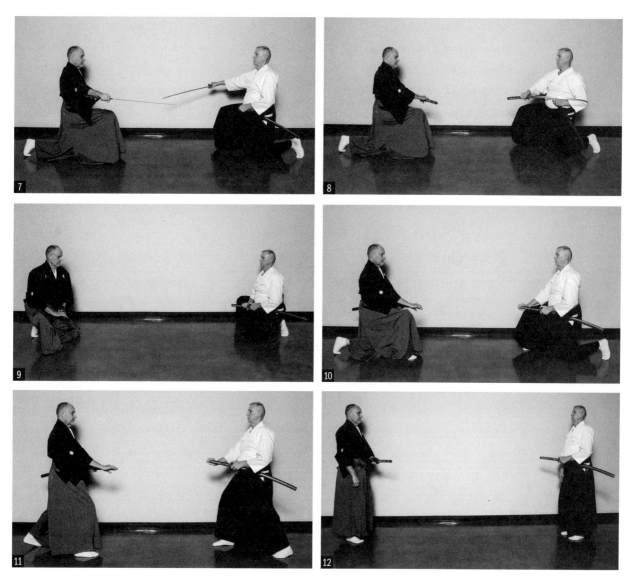

Figures 17E.7–12. Tsumeai no Kurai: Uroko Gaeshi

In actual combat, this reinforced sweeping motion of Shikata's sword would also inflict a shallow cut down the center of Uchikata's face, so in practice Uchikata should tilt his or her head slightly back to avoid being accidentally struck during this phase of the *katachi*.

The partners then separate with *zanshin* and return to their starting positions in the usual manner, as depicted in figures 17E.6–12.

The major emphasis when practicing Uroko Gaeshi is that Shikata must act the instant Uchikata's sword is blocked in figure 17E.4 in order to prevent Uchikata from sustaining his or her momentum. This sudden reversal of initiative is reflected in the name Uroko Gaeshi, which literally means "reversing fish scales" and alludes to the way the scales of a fish bend deeply when the fish turns sharply to elude a predator and flash in the sunlight. The need for this sudden reversal presents a risk of Shikata acting too soon, which can result in injury to one or both participants. To prevent this, it is essential that both partners maintain correct *kirima* (cutting distance) and sensitivity to each other's movements and intentions. This is another reason why the Tsumeai no Kurai should not be attempted by students ranking below *dan* level, because they will not yet have developed consistent *kirima* and sensitivity to a training partner's intentions.

## 17F: KURAI YURUMI

Kurai Yurumi (Relaxing) is the sixth Tsumeai no Kurai, and is a technique used to defend against an attacker charging at you while you are relaxing in the *tatehiza* posture. To non-Japanese people, *tatehiza* may neither look nor feel relaxing, but it was the preferred sitting position for samurai, especially those wearing *yoroi* (bamboo armor), making defense from *tatehiza* against a variety of surprise attacks an essential aspect of *iaijutsu* training.

In Kurai Yurumi, the training partners begin with Shikata seated in *tatehiza*, and Uchikata standing about eight paces away. Both perform *kiyomeri kokyū*, then Uchikata draws his *bokken*, stepping forward with his right foot into *seigan no kamae* (fig. 17F.2), then stepping forward with his left foot into *hassō no kamae* (fig. 17F.3). Uchikata then dashes forward and performs *kirioroshi* toward the seated Shikata, who draws his sword directly into *furikaburi* while rising (fig. 17F.4) and stepping back with his left foot, and drawing his right foot rearward, even with the left (fig. 17F.5) as Uchikata's sword passes, then steps right foot forward with *kirioshi*, finishing as shown in figure 17F.6.

The partners step back from this position into *ai-seigan* (fig. 17F.7), then maintain *seigan no kamae* while stepping back until they are about eight paces apart (fig. 17F.8), perform *yoko-chiburi* (fig. 17F.9), Chūden *nōtō* (figs. 17F.10–11), and lower their hands to their sides, as shown in figure 17F.12.

Kurai Yurumi applies the same principle found in the Shoden *waza* Tsukekomi, which is to evade the opponent's *kirioroshi* by stepping back just out of reach of Uchikata's *kissaki*, then stepping forward with a counter-cut before Uchikata has a chance to recover from his missed cut. It is a technique based primarily on distance control and perfect timing of these maneuvers. However, Shikata draws the sword at a slight angle to the left side—just outside the shoulder, as shown in figure 17F.5—so that it could be used as an *ukenagashi*-type deflection of Uchikata's cut, if necessary.

Figures 17F.1–8. Tsumeai no Kurai: Kurai Yurumi

Figures 17F.9–12. Tsumeai no Kurai: Kurai Yurumi

## 17G: TSUBAME GAESHI

The seventh *katachi* in the Tsumeai no Kurai set is Tsubame Gaeshi (Reversing Swallow), a name that alludes to the way in which swallows (*tsubame*) are able to instantly reverse direction (*gaeshi*) while in flight, and refers to the manner in which Shikata's sword suddenly reverses direction during its final cut (called *kiri-kaeshi*) in this *katachi*.

The partners face each other about eight paces apart during *kiyomeri kokyū*, then Uchikata draws his *bokken*, stepping forward with the right foot into *seigan no kamae* (fig. 17G.2). Taking a step forward with the left foot, Uchikata next assumes *hassō no kamae* (fig. 17G.3). After a brief pause, Uchikata dashes forward and performs *kirioshi*, which Shikata counters by stepping right foot forward and blocking with an upward *nukitsuke*, as depicted in figure 17G.4.

It is important to note the timing of this block, which stops Uchikata's *kirioroshi* near the top of its downward arc, before it reaches full speed and power, as well as exposing Uchikata's entire torso to counterattack. This forces Uchikata to retreat by stepping right foot back into *hassō no kamae*.

Figures 17G.1–8. Tsumeai no Kurai: Tsubame Gaeshi

Figures 17G.9–16. Tsumeai no Kurai: Tsubame Gaeshi

 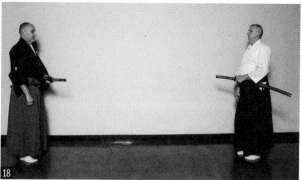

Figures 17G.17–18. Tsumeai no Kurai: Tsubame Gaeshi

Pressing his advantage, Shikata steps left foot forward into *hassō no kamae* (fig. 17G.5), then immediately steps right foot forward with a cut to Uchikata's left *yokomen*. To counter this, Uchikata steps left foot back, blocking the attack with a mirror-image strike toward Shikata's left temple, as shown in figure 17G.6). However, since Uchikata is retreating, he cannot cut as powerfully as Shikata, so Shikata's *kissaki* controls Uchikata's center line at this point. This allows Shikata to press forward, threatening Uchikata with the *kissaki* and forcing Uchikata to step back with his right foot while Shikata steps left foot forward with *yokomen-giri* to Uchikata's right temple. Once again, Uchikata counters this cut with a mirror-image cut to Shikata's right *yokomen* (fig. 17G.7), but he is still in the weaker position, so Shikata again threatens Uchikata with his *kissaki* and steps right foot forward with *kirioroshi*. Uchikata evades this *kirioroshi* by stepping back with his left foot (fig. 17G.8) and drawing his right foot rearward, even with his left foot, while raising his sword into *jōdan no kamae*. As his sword passes in front of Uchikata, Shikata draws his left foot even with his right foot, finishing the attempted cut, as shown in figure 17G.9.

In this position, Shikata appears to be exposed to counterattack, so Uchikata steps right foot forward with *kirioroshi*, but Shikata steps to his left-front while performing *kiriage* (upward diagonal cut) across Uchikata's torso (figs. 17G.10–11), then reverses the sword into *kiri-kaeshi* (returning cut) to Uchikata's exposed right *yokomen* (fig. 17G.12), shifting his right foot as necessary to achieve the correct *kirima* (cutting distance) based upon Uchikata's movements.

This final *kiri-kaeshi* is the "swallow's cut" for which Tsubame Gaeshi is named, and it should be performed as one smooth, continuous motion, rather than a separate *kiriage* and *kirikaeshi*.

The partners step back from this position into *ai-seigan* (fig. 17G.13), then maintain *ai-seigan* while stepping back until they are about eight paces apart (fig. 17G.14), perform *yoko-chiburi* (fig. 17G.15), Chūden *nōtō* (figs. 17G.16–17), and lower their hands to their sides, as shown in figure 17G.18.

# 17H: GANSEKI OTOSHI

Eighth in the Tsumeai no Kurai is Ganseki Otoshi (Impairing Vision), which incorporates the same principle found in Zetsumyōken in the Tachiuchi no Kurai, but with more difficult footwork and timing. *Ganseki* means "related to the eyes" and *otoshi* is "to drop," "fall," "lower," "reduce," or "decrease." The objective of Ganseki Otoshi is to impair the opponent's vision, and thereby incapacitate him or her.

This *katachi* begins with Shikata and Uchikata standing about eight paces apart (fig. 17H.1) during *kiyomeri kokyū*. As they inhale their third breaths, Uchikata begins *koguchi no kirikata*, followed immediately by Shikata, and both draw their *bokken*, stepping forward with their right feet into *seigan no kamae* (fig. 17H.2). With Uchikata initiating and Shikata immediately following, both partners raise their swords to *jōdan no kamae* (fig. 17H.3), with Uchikata stepping left foot forward and Shikata stepping right foot back to maintain their separation. With Shikata following Uchikata's lead by only a fraction of a second, both partners dash forward and execute *yokomen-giri* to the other's left temple, resulting in their swords intercepting each other just above head height (fig. 17H.4) and driving each other's cutoff line, and their combined momentum carries them forward into *tsubazeria* (fig. 17H.5).

You may recall that in Zetsumyōken in the Tachiuchi no Kurai, Shikata steps back to receive Uchikata's attack, thus keeping both partners out of range of each other's cuts as their swords clash. Ganseki Otoshi is a more aggressive variation in which the partners remain within reach of each other's cuts, requiring greater skill and timing for their safety during practice. It should also be noted that Ganseki Otoshi should ideally be performed with Shikata and Uchikata initially attacking with *kirioroshi*, but *yokomen-giri* as depicted here is recommended as a safer alternative unless both participants are highly skilled and experienced.

In *tsubazeria*, Shikata and Uchikata struggle to gain dominance. In this struggle, Shikata presses Uchikata's sword down, as if attempting to cut the side of Uchikata's neck, so Uchikata must push upward to avoid being cut. Feeling this upward pressure, Shikata then steps left foot forward while driving his left hand upward and pulling his right hand downward. The sudden loss of resistance against Uchikata's right hand propels Uchikata's hands upward, providing Shikata the leverage needed to swing his *tsuka* beneath Uchikata's right forearm and drive it upward, as shown in figure 17H.6. Shikata then executes a *tsuka-ate* strike between Uchikata's eyes with the *tsuka-gashira* (fig. 17H.7).

Figures 17H.1–8. Tsumeai no Kurai: Ganseki Otoshi

Figures 17H.9–13. Tsumeai no Kurai: Ganseki Otoshi

The partners step back from this position into *ai-seigan* (fig. 17H.8), then maintain *seigan no kamae* while stepping back until they are about eight paces apart (fig. 17H.9), perform *yoko-chiburi* (fig. 17H.10), Chūden *nōtō* (figs. 17H.11–12), and lower their hands to their sides, as shown in figure 17H.13.

# 171: SUIGETSUTŌ

The ninth Tsumeai no Kurai, Suigetsutō (Moon's Reflection Sword), is essentially the reverse of the principle practiced in the Tachiuchi no Kurai of the same name. As explained in chapter 15, *suigetsu* means "moon's reflection in water," but is also the common term for the solar plexus. This play on words aptly describes the nature of this technique in which Shikata begins a thrust to Uchikata's solar plexus (one meaning of *suigetsu*), but redirects that attack into *kirioroshi* when Uchikata deflects the thrust, revealing that the intended target was never Uchikata's solar plexus, but was instead—like the moon's reflection on water (the other meaning of *suigetsu*)—somewhere else entirely.

The partners again face each other about eight paces apart during *kiyomeri kokyū* (fig. 171.1), then—with Shikata reacting to Uchikata's movements—both Shikata and Uchikata draw their *bokken*, stepping forward with their right feet into *seigan no kamae* (fig. 171.2). As Uchikata next takes a step forward with his left foot, Shikata takes a step back with his right foot to maintain their separation, both assuming *jōdan no kamae* (fig. 171.3).

As in Ganseki Otoshi, the partners dash toward each other in *jōdan no kamae*, but as they near *kirima* (cutting distance), Shikata lowers his sword to *seigan no kamae* while alighting on his left foot (fig. 171.4), and on the next step thrusts his *kissaki* toward Uchikata's solar plexus, as depicted in figure 171.5. This forces Uchikata to cut down onto Shikata's *mine* to deflect the thrust (fig. 171.6). As Shikata steps slightly to his left, he uses the force of Uchikata's strike to propel his sword in a circular path into *kirioroshi* to Uchikata's *shōmen* (fig. 171.7).

Uchikata and Shikata step back from this position into *ai-seigan* (fig. 171.8), then maintain *seigan no kamae* while stepping back until they are about eight paces apart (fig. 171.9), perform *yoko-chiburi* (fig. 171.10), Chūden *nōtō* (figs. 171.11–12), and lower their hands to their sides, as shown in figure 171.13.

Figures 171.1–8. Tsumeai no Kurai: Suigetsutō

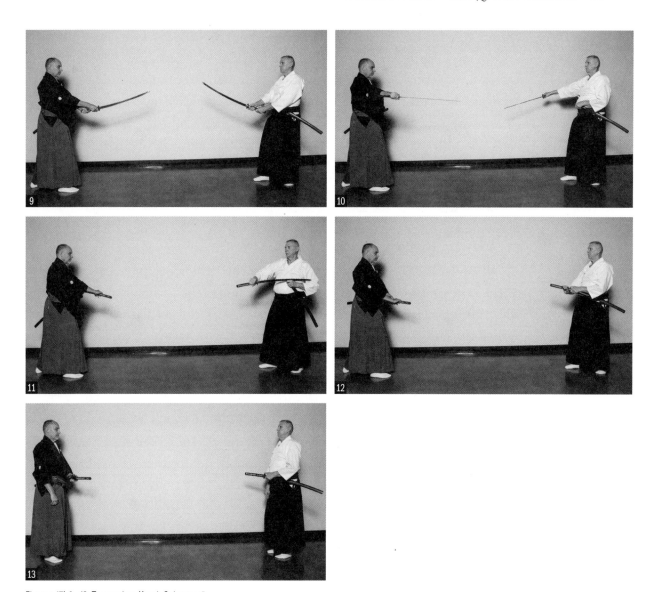

Figures 17I.9–13. Tsumeai no Kurai: Suigetsutō

## 17J: KASUMI KEN

Kasumi Ken (Blurred Sword) is the tenth and last *katachi* in the Tsumeai no Kurai. *Kasumi* means "haze," "mist," or "a blur," and *ken* means "sword." The name of this *katachi* underscores the concept that its core technique must be performed with sufficient speed and suddenness that it cannot be observed in time to defend against it.

Kasumi Ken begins in a manner similar to Ganseki Otoshi, with both partners facing each other about eight paces apart during *kiyomeri kokyū* (fig. 17J.1), then—with

Shikata reacting to Uchikata's movements—both Shikata and Uchikata draw their *bokken*, stepping forward with their right feet into *seigan no kamae* (fig. 17J.2). As Uchikata next takes a step forward with his left foot, Shikata takes a step back with his right foot to maintain their separation, both assuming *jōdan no kamae* (fig. 17J.3).

With Shikata following Uchikata's lead by only a fraction of a second, both partners dash forward and execute *yokomen-giri* to the other's left temple, resulting in their swords intercepting each other just above head height and driving each other's cut offline (fig. 17J.4). If both partners are highly skilled and experienced, *kirioroshi* can be substituted for the safer *yokomen-giri* demonstrated here. The momentum of their running attacks propels them into *tsubazeria* (fig. 17J.5), where the Shikata and Uchikata contend for dominance.

When neither is able to gain an advantage over the other, it appears they have reached the same impasse that occurs in Uchikomi in the Tachiuchi no Kurai, from which they must seek a safe means of withdrawal. Uchikata slackens his pressure against Shikata's sword very slightly to gauge if Shikata will do the same, which he does. In this matter, cautiously sensing each other's sword pressure for indications of the other's intentions, both partners gradually reduce the pressure against each other's swords. When the pressure and counter-pressure are minimal, both partners *yori-ashi* (shuffle-step) slightly back (fig. 17J.6), each ready to reengage in *tsubazeria* at the slightest provocation by the other. Then they shuffle back once more, so that only about one-third of their respective swords are crossed, as shown in figure 17J.7. As Uchikata begins to shuffle back a third time, Shikata dips his *kissaki* beneath Uchikata's sword and sweeps it down and to Shikata's right (fig. 17J.8), continuing this motion in a circular path that ends with *kirioroshi* to Uchikata's *shōmen* (fig. 17J.9).

The partners step back from this position into *ai-seigan* (fig. 17H.10), then maintain *ai-seigan* while stepping back until they are about eight paces apart (fig. 17H.11), perform *yoko-chiburi* (fig. 17H.12), Chūden *nōtō* (figs. 17H.13–14), and lower their hands to their sides, as shown in figure 17H.15.

The primary skill to develop in Kasumi Ken is sensitivity to the energy in the opponent's sword and the ability to detect an opponent's intentions from that energy—particularly sensing when the opponent has provided an opportunity for an effective counterattack. This ability to sense the opponent's actions and intentions through the sword contact provided in *ai-seigan* is an essential skill in *iaijutsu* and *kenjutsu*, described in chapter 15, and should be practiced diligently.

Figures 17J.1–8. Tsumeai no Kurai: Kasumi Ken

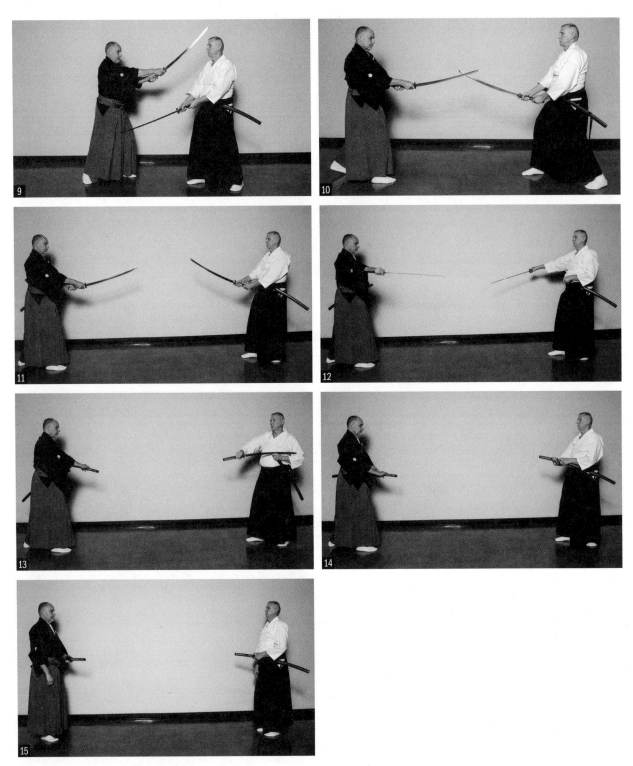

Figures 17J.9–15. Tsumeai no Kurai: Kasumi Ken

# CONCLUSION

The Tsumeai no Kurai present a greater challenge to the *iaidōka* than the Tachiuchi no Kurai, particularly with regard to timing, *maai* (distance control), *seme* (pressuring the opponent), aggressiveness, speed of reaction to opponent's movements, and sensitivity to the opponent's intentions. The six Tsumeai no Kurai performed from *tatehiza* require that the training partners react quickly and decisively to sudden attacks from close proximity. Successful execution of these techniques often depends on Shikata cutting so quickly and powerfully that Uchikata is literally beaten back or beaten down by their ferocity in the true spirit of a samurai. The *katachi* performed with one or both partners running at each other also presents situations of greater speed, aggressiveness, and the closer proximity at the moment of first contact created by that speed and aggressiveness. Hopefully, we have made obvious to the reader the dangers of attempting these techniques without sufficient prior training to develop a high level of skill, precision, and reactivity.

Perhaps because the Tsumeai no Kurai are intended to be taught to intermediate and advanced students, there are also more variations of each of these *katachi* than are typically shown for the Tachiuchi no Kurai taught earlier in the curriculum. For example, Tsubamegaeshi can be performed moving either to the left, as presented in this chapter, or to the right, and with at least two variations of the cutting techniques employed to either side. Here, we have presented only one variation of each of the Tsumeai no Kurai to serve as a general guideline and to encourage readers to join a *dōjō* in which to receive instruction and training in the others.

Chapter 18

# Okuden Kumitachi

**Deep Level Kumitachi**

There are three sets of *okuden kumitachi* in the Eishin-Ryū curriculum: Daishō Zume, Daishō Tachizume, and Daiken Dori. Their exact origins are no longer known, but they, or at least forms of *kumitachi* from which they may have been derived, have doubtless been an integral part of the Eishin-Ryū training system for centuries— perhaps from the earliest of times.

Like all other partner exercises in the Eishin-Ryū curriculum, the *okuden kumitachi* promote the practice of key principles of samurai swordsmanship under controlled conditions based upon reasonably realistic attack-and-defense scenarios, but the *okuden kumitachi* do so in a much different way than the Tachiuchi no Kurai, Tachiuchi no Kata, and Tsumeai no Kurai. Instead of focusing on the techniques of the *katana* itself, these three sets of training exercises employ methods of countering various attempts by one opponent to prevent another's *katana* from being drawn and used. Thus, the key characteristic of the *okuden kumitachi* described in this chapter is that they incorporate techniques one might expect to find in a *jūdō* or *jūjutsu* class. Although they are essentially grappling rather than sword-fighting techniques, it is important to recognize that they are as vital to the practice of *iaijutsu* as any other component of the art.

Perhaps because they focus on grappling more than swordsmanship, these *kumitachi* sets are rarely taught to anyone below the rank of *rokudan* (sixth *dan*), and apparently are not taught at all in some lineages of Eishin-Ryū. They were not included in the first two editions of *Flashing Steel*, primarily because Shimabukuro Hanshi had no students at that time the first two editions went to press who were advanced enough in their training to learn them. The other major reason is that most of these techniques rely on the precise application of coordinated pressure point *(kyūsho* or *itaden)* and joint manipulation (*kansetsu waza*) techniques that are impossible to learn from written descriptions, but can only be taught through hands-on instruction.

We have repeatedly cautioned against trying to learn any aspect of *iaijutsu* exclusively from this or any other book, and this admonition is especially applicable to the *okuden kumitachi* presented in this chapter. The descriptions presented here are deliberately general for that very reason. To describe them in sufficient detail to be learned thoroughly would require an entire book; not merely a chapter. Since the Daishō Zume, Daishō Tachizume, and Daiken Dori are too complex and subtle in nature to be learned from photographs and descriptions—or even videos—alone, the information presented in this chapter is intended only to serve as a means of refreshing the memory of those who have been taught these exercises by a qualified instructor.

In addition, it should be noted that each of the *okuden kumitachi* has more than one variation in order to address the several ways a given attack can be initiated by Uchikata. For example, when Uchikata grasps Shikata's *tsuka* in a given scenario, it could be with the right hand or the left hand, with the hand palm up or the hand palm down, left foot forward or right foot forward, pulling on the *tsuka* or pushing on the *tsuka*, lifting the *tsuka* or pressing it downward, and so forth. Each of those variations in attack requires some degree of adjustment to the defensive method employed, producing a variation in the technique. In the descriptions in this chapter, we have included only one variation for each of the exercises, typically either the most commonly taught variation or the one most easily learned.

# DAISHŌ ZUME

The term Daishō Zume can best be interpreted as "long and short (swords) in close quarters." The eight exercises in this set involve Shikata armed with a *daitō* (long sword) and Uchikata bearing a *shōtō* (short sword), commonly called a *wakizashi*. Once again, in the photographs that follow, we have used *iaitō* in order to better portray the angles and positions of the participants' swords, but during training—in order to endure the contact involved—*bokken* should be used. The names and sequence of the Daishō Zume drills are:

1. Dakizume

2. Koppō

3. Tsuka Dome

4. Kote Dome

5. Mune Dori

**6.** Migi Fuse

**7.** Hidari Fuse

**8.** Yamagata Zume

Prior to performing the Daishō Zume, you should perform *sahō* and *reihō* just as if you were preparing for any other aspect of *iaijutsu* training. Treat your *bokken* just as you would treat an *iaitō* or *shinken*, by performing *tōrei* as you take up your *bokken*. Be sure to observe the appropriate formalities in bowing to your partner. These aspects of training are just as important as performing the *katachi*.

In a formal setting, the highest level of sincerity and respect is shown by performing your preparation and etiquette in a *seiza* position, facing your partner. In the description of each *katachi*, we are assuming that the partners have already performed these rituals of proper etiquette, so our narrative covers only the techniques in the *katachi* itself.

In each *katachi*, one partner practices a key principle of *iaijutsu*, and the other partner provides the appropriate attack to facilitate this training. As with all other Eishin-Ryū *kumitachi*, the partner who practices the principle intrinsic to the *katachi* is called Shikata (User) and the partner assisting is called Uchikata (Striker). As always, although Shikata is the one practicing the key technique of each *katachi*, it is equally important to develop proficiency in the role of Uchikata.

If you don't have a *saya* for your *bokken*, use your left hand to simulate the *koiguchi*, and slide the *bokken* through the opening of the hand as if sheathing it. It is permissible, though not required, to slide the *bokken* through your *obi* to simulate it being in the *saya*.

As with all previous *kumitachi*, a powerful *kiai* should accompany each attacking technique in the *katachi*.

Our final word of caution is that many of the techniques in the Daishō Zume involve pressure to, or twisting of, Uchikata's joints—actions that, if carelessly or excessively performed, can also produce serious injury or even death. It is therefore imperative that the Daishō Zume be practiced with the utmost caution and concern for safety, and—as we have repeatedly admonished—only under the supervision of a qualified instructor.

# 18A: DAKIZUME

The first *katachi*, Dakizume (Close Embrace), is a defense against an opponent's sudden attempt to disarm you by grabbing and drawing your sword from its scabbard.

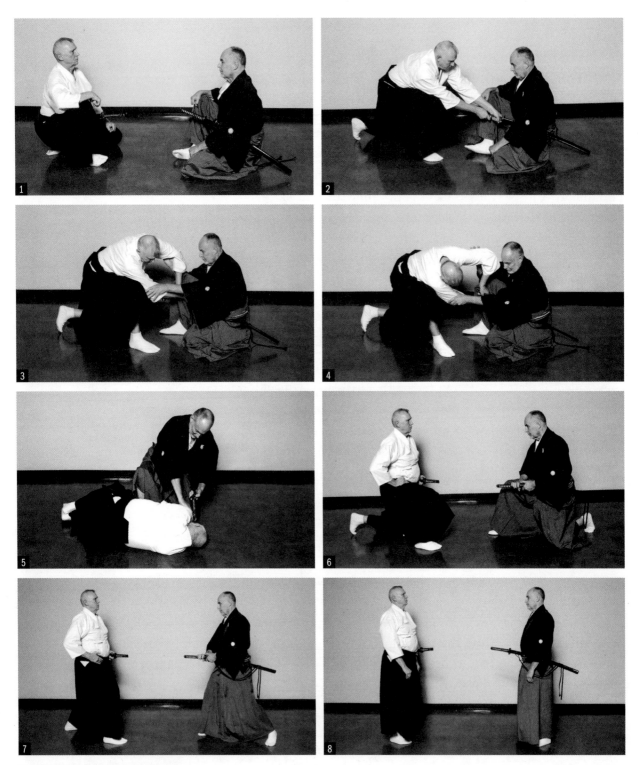

Figures 18A.1–8. Daishō Zume: Dakizume

It begins with the participants seated in *tatehiza* just out of arm's reach from each other (see fig. 18A.1). Both partners perform *kiyomeri kokyū*, at the completion of which Uchikata (on the left) lunges right foot forward, kneeling, and grasps the *tsuka* of Shikata's sword with both hands, as shown in figure 18A.2. Before Uchikata can draw his sword, Shikata grabs Uchikata's arms, gripping Uchikata's right arm just below the elbow and his left arm just above the elbow (fig. 18A.3). While pressing on Uchikata's pressure points and forcing Uchikata's arms to bend at the elbows for leverage, Shikata rises onto one knee, right foot forward, and throws Uchikata to the left side (fig. 18A.4). Shikata then pins Uchikata's left arm across his chest and right arm, and with a counterclockwise motion strikes Uchikata in the face with the side of the *tsuka*, as depicted in figure 18A.5. Shikata shuffles back, still kneeling, and grasps his *tsuka*, ready to perform *koiguchi no kirikata* (fig. 18A.6).

In defeat, Uchikata warily rises to one knee, right foot forward, and moves back to his original position. Note that, as illustrated by Figure 18A.7, Shikata remains ready to draw his sword if Uchikata makes a threatening move, but Uchikata keeps his right hand at his side to avoid any appearance of such a threat. Shikata should maintain *zanshin* and the attitude that, if Uchikata made the slightest move toward his sword, Shikata would instantly attack.

Once the training partners have returned to their original positions, they either sit in *tatehiza* in preparation for the next *katachi*, or stand up if they will be performing a different activity next.

# 18B: KOPPŌ

The second *katachi*, Koppō (Bone Protection) provides another method of preventing an opponent from disarming you by grabbing and drawing your sword from its scabbard.

Begin facing each other seated in *tatehiza* just out of arm's reach (see fig. 18B.1). Both partners perform *kiyomeri kokyū*, at the completion of which Uchikata (at left) rises and to one knee and lunges, right foot forward, grasping the *tsuka* of Shikata's sword with both hands, as depicted in figure 18B.2. Before Uchikata can draw the sword, Shikata grabs Uchikata's right arm just above the elbow and pulls it toward himself while striking Uchikata in the face or throat with his right hand (fig. 18A.3), then rises, right foot forward, kneeling to drive Uchikata backward and off-balance, as shown in figure 18A.4. Shikata then forces the *tsuka* to the floor with his right hand (fig. 18B.5) and uses his right foot to push Uchikata's left hand free of the *tsuka* (fig. 18B.6) and pin it to the floor.

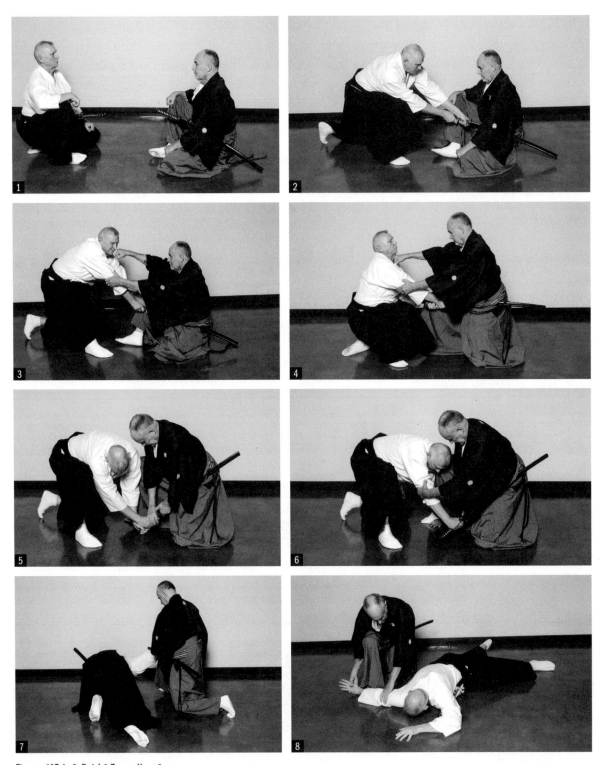

Figures 18B.1–8. Daishō Zume: Koppō

Figures 18B.9–11. Daishō Zume: Koppō

With a clockwise circular motion of the *tsuka* against Uchikata's right forearm and pressure at Uchikata's elbow with his left hand, Shikata drives Uchikata to the floor at Shikata's right side (fig. 18B.7). Once again, the application of pressure from the *tsuka* and Shikata's left hand to specific nerve points on Uchikata's arm are necessary to ensure success of this technique.

Figure 18B.8 shows the relative positions of Shikata and Uchikata from the reverse angle of figure 18B.7 to reveal the manner in which Uchikata is pinned to the floor.

Defeated, Uchikata rises to one knee, right foot forward, and moves back to his original position. As before, Shikata remains ready to draw his sword (fig. 18B.9) if Uchikata makes a threatening move, but Uchikata keeps his right hand at his side to avoid any hint of such a threat. Shikata should maintain *zanshin* and the attitude that, if Uchikata made the slightest move toward his sword, Shikata would instantly attack. Once the training partners have returned to their original positions, they either sit in *tatehiza* in preparation for the next *katachi*, or stand up if they will be performing a different activity next.

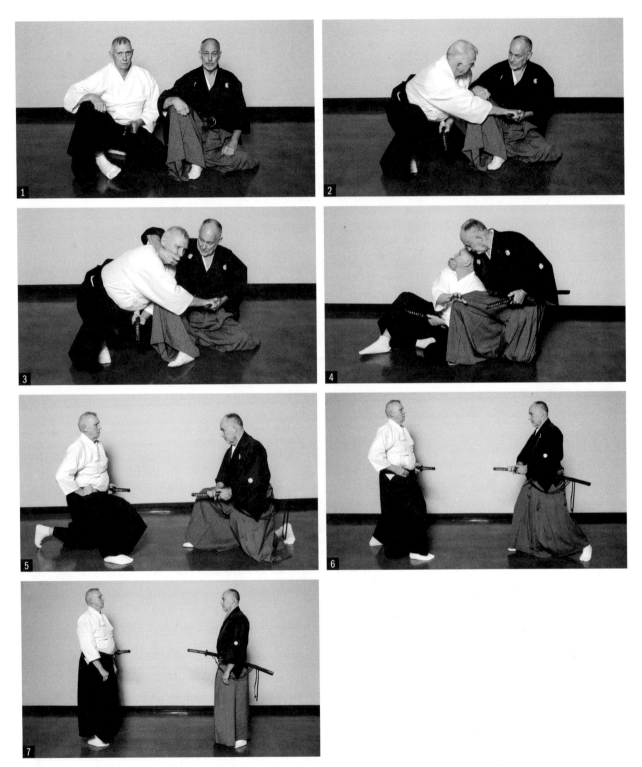

Figures 18C.1–7. Daishō Zume: Tsuka Dome

# 18C: TSUKA DOME

The technique embodied in Tsuka Dome (Handle Barrier) is yet another defense against an opponent's attempt to prevent Shikata from drawing his or her sword. In this case, however, the two opponents are sitting side-by-side, rather than facing each other.

The training partners begin seated in *tatehiza*, facing in the same direction, with Uchikata at Shikata's right side, as they perform *kiyomeri kokyū* (see fig. 18C.1). As they are inhaling their third breath, Uchikata reaches across Shikata with his left hand and grabs the *tsuka* of Shikata's sword (fig. 18C.2). Shikata remains in *tatehiza* while reaching behind Shikata and grasping Shikata's chin with his right hand, as shown in figure 18C.3, then, while rising to one knee, twists Uchikata's neck sharply to the right (fig. 18C.4), possibly breaking it as Uchikata is thrown to the floor.

*Warning:* This is an extremely dangerous technique, and it must be practiced with great caution to avoid injury to Uchikata. During training, Uchikata is not actually thrown to the ground with this technique. Instead, Shikata only turns Uchikata's head about an inch to the right to represent the technique being applied.

Shikata then rises, right foot forward, into a kneeling position, hands ready to draw his *katana*, while Uchikata assumes the equivalent posture facing Shikata, but with his right hand at his hip, as in figure 18C.5. From this position, they either sit in *tatehiza* in preparation for the next *katachi*, or stand up if they will be performing a different activity next.

# 18D: KOTE DOME

In Kote Dome (Wrist Barrier), the technique performed is one that prevents the opponent from drawing his or her sword at close range by blocking the movement of Uchikata's wrist, as the name of this technique explicitly describes.

In Kote Dome, the training partners begin seated in *tatehiza* facing in the same direction, with Uchikata at Shikata's left side, as they perform *kiyomeri kokyū* (see fig. 18D.1). As they are inhaling their third breath, Uchikata turns abruptly to the right, rising to a kneeling position, right foot leading, and performs *koiguchi no kirikata* in preparation to draw his sword, as shown in figure 18D.2. Shikata rises, right foot forward, into a kneeling position and grasps Uchikata's right wrist while taking hold of his own sword at the *tsuba* with his left hand, using his body weight and forward moment to prevent Uchikata from drawing. Then Shikata pushes Uchikata's right hand sharply downward while striking Uchikata in the face with his *tsukagashira* (a strike called *tsuka-ate*), as shown in figure 18D.3.

Figures 18D.1–4. Daishō Zume: Kote Dome

Shikata then shuffles back, still kneeling, right foot forward, hands ready to draw his *katana*, while Uchikata assumes a similar posture facing Shikata (fig. 18D.4), but with his right hand at his hip, signifying defeat. From this position, they either sit in *tatehiza* in preparation for the next *katachi*, or stand up if they will be performing a different activity next.

## 18E: MUNE TORI

The fifth Daishō Zume, Mune Tori (Seize the Chest), presents the first of three defenses against an opponent who grabs your chest or the lapel of your *uwagi*.

The training partners begin facing each other just beyond arm's reach in *tatehiza* while performing *kiyomeri kokyū* (see fig. 18E.1), while inhaling his third breath Uchikata (on the right) rises, right foot leading, to a kneeling position, and grabs Shikata's left lapel with his right hand (fig. 18E.2), pushing Shikata back. Using his right hand to brace himself, Shikata strikes Uchikata in the armpit with a left-handed *tsuka-ate* (fig. 18E.3) and rises to a right-foot-forward kneeling position, pushing Uchikata backward with the *tsukagashira*. Shikata raises the *tsuka* (fig. 18E.4)—which in actual combat would strike Uchikata in the throat, chin, or face—then uses his left elbow to drive Uchikata's right arm downward while drawing his the sword in an upward arc, cutting down into the right side of Uchikata's neck (fig. 18E.5). As Uchikata continues to collapse rearward, Shikata performs *soetezuki* to Uchikata's throat, finishing as indicated in figure 18E.6.

Shikata shuffles back into kneeling *seigan no kamae* right foot leading (fig. 18E.7) while Uchikata kneels, right foot leading, with his left hand controlling the *tsuba* and his right hand at his right hip. Uchikata maintains this position while Shikata performs *yoko-chiburi* (fig. 18E.8), then Okuden *nōtō* (fig. 18E.9). From this position, they either sit in *tatehiza* in preparation for the next *katachi*, or stand up if they will be performing a different activity next.

Figures 18E.1–6. Daishō Zume: Mune Tori

Figures 18E.7–9. Daishō Zume: Mune Tori

## 18F: MIGI FUSE

Migi Fuse (Right Prone) is the sixth Daishō Zume, and is another method of defending against an attacker who grabs your lapel, this time while seated beside you.

In Migi Fuse, the training partners begin seated in *tatehiza* with Uchikata on Shikata's right (fig. 18F.1). When they finish *kiyomeri kokyū*, Uchikata rises to one knee, right foot leading, turns toward Shikata, and grabs Shikata's right lapel with his left hand (fig. 18F.2). Shikata grasps the back of Uchikata's left hand with his left hand and Uchikata's left elbow with his right hand, rises to one knee, right foot forward (fig. 18F.3), then—while applying pressure to nerve points in Uchikata's hand and upper arm—with a rowing motion that sweeps to Shikata's left, forces Uchikata face-down on the floor and pins Uchikata's arm there (fig. 18F.4).

Once Uchikata is subdued, Shikata shuffles rearward, releasing Uchikata's arm and preparing to draw his sword, if necessary (fig. 18F.5). Uchikata rises and moves into a similar posture facing Shikata, (fig. 18F.6), but with his right hand at his hip, acknowledging defeat. As before, they then either sit in *tatehiza* in preparation for the next *katachi*, or stand up if they will be performing a different activity next.

Figures 18F.1–6. Daishō Zume: Migi Fuse

# 18G: HIDARI FUSE

The seventh *katachi* in the Daishō Zume, set is Hidari Fuse (Left Prone), which is practically the mirror image of Migi Fuse as yet another method of defending against an attacker who grabs your lapel while seated beside you.

In Hidari Fuse, the training partners begin seated in *tatehiza* with Uchikata on Shikata's left (fig. 18G.1). When they finish *kiyomeri kokyū*, Uchikata rises to one knee, right foot leading, turns toward Shikata, and grabs Shikata's left lapel with his right hand (fig. 18G.2). Shikata grasps the back of Uchikata's right hand with his left hand and Uchikata's right elbow with his left hand, rises to one knee, right foot forward (fig. 18G.3), then—while applying pressure to nerve points in Uchikata's hand and upper arm—with a rowing motion that sweeps to Shikata's right, forces Uchikata face-down on the floor and pins Uchikata's arm there (fig. 18G.4).

Once Uchikata is subdued, Shikata shuffles rearward, releasing Uchikata's arm and preparing to draw his sword, if necessary (fig. 18G.5). Uchikata rises and moves into a similar posture facing Shikata, (fig. 18G.6), but with his right hand at his hip, acknowledging defeat. As before, they then either sit in *tatehiza* in preparation for the next *katachi*, or stand up if they will be performing a different activity next.

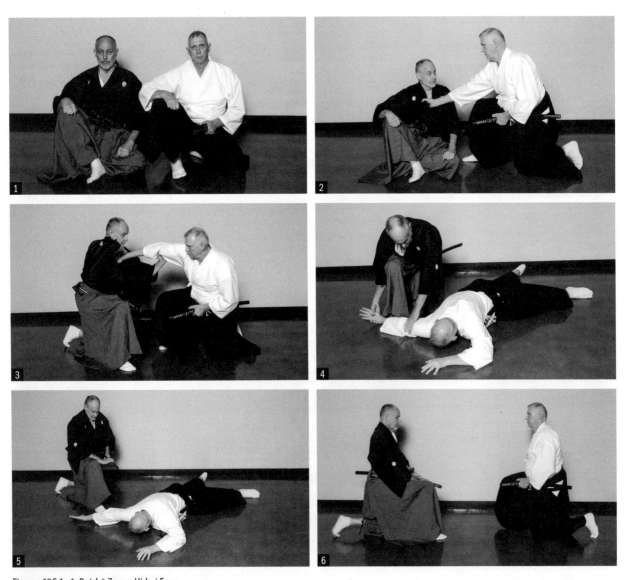

Figures 18G.1–6. Daishō Zume: Hidari Fuse

# 18H: YAMAGATA ZUME

The last *kumitachi* in the Daishō Zume series is Yamagata Zume (Mountain-Shaped Proximity), which is a defense against a rear "bear hug" by an opponent attempting to prevent Shikata from rising from *tatehiza* or drawing his or her sword to defend against one or more additional attackers.

In Yamagata Zume, the training partners begin seated in *tatehiza* with Uchikata directly behind Shikata at about arm's length (fig. 18H.1). When they finish *kiyomeri kokyū*, Uchikata rises to one knee, right foot leading, and wraps his arms around Shikata's shoulders and upper arms (fig. 18H.2). Shikata grasps his *tsuba* and strikes Uchikata in the face with the back of his head (fig. 18H.3). Driving his right leg forward, Shikata uses the power of his hips and shoulders to break Uchikata's grip while drawing his sword (fig. 18H.4).

Figures 18H.1–10. Daishō Zume: Yamagata Zume

Turning his hips and shoulders still farther to the left, Shikata performs *saya-banari* followed by a rearward thrust into Uchikata's chest, as depicted in figure 18H.5. Shikata then pivots to his left 180 degrees and away from Uchikata into kneeling *seigan no kamae* with his right foot leading, while Uchikata assumes a similar posture, but with his right hand as his hip in submission (fig. 18H.6).

Maintaining their relative positions, Shikata performs *yoko-chiburi* (fig. 18H.7) and Okuden *nōtō* (fig. 18H.8). Since this is the last Daishō Zume, both partners rise to a standing position (fig. 18H.9) and return to the positions in which they began the Daishō Zume exercises (fig. 18H.10). With the activity completed, they then perform the customary *reihō* formalities.

## DAISHŌ TACHIZUME

The term Daishō Tachizume can best be interpreted as "long and short (swords) standing in close quarters." The seven exercises in this series involve Shikata armed with a *daitō* (long sword) and Uchikata bearing a *shōtō* (short sword). The Daishō Tachizume are identical in nature to the Daishō Zume, with the exception that they are performed standing, rather than from *tatehiza* and kneeling positions.

As with the preceding Daishō Zume, we have used *iaitō* in the photographs accompanying the descriptions in order to better display the angles and positions of the participants' swords, but during training—in order to withstand the contact involved—*bokken* should be used. In fact, since they involve Uchikata being thrown to the floor with considerable force, we recommend that Sode Surigaeshi, Tombo Gaeshi, and Utsuri be practiced with Uchikata not wearing a sword at all to avoid injury when first learning the Daishō Tachizume.

The names and sequence of the Daishō Tachizume exercises are:

1. Shime Tori
2. Sode Surigaeshi
3. Tsuba Uchikaeshi
4. Koppō Gaeshi
5. Tombo Gaeshi
6. Ran Kyoku
7. Utsuri

Prior to performing the Daishō Tachizume, the participants should perform *sahō* and *reihō* just as if they were preparing for any other aspect of *iaijutsu* training. Treat the *bokken* just as if it was an *iaitō* or *shinken*, by performing *tōrei* as it is taken. Be sure to observe the appropriate formalities and etiquette, as these aspects of training are just as important as performing the *katachi*. In a formal situation, the highest level of sincerity and respect is always demonstrated by performing *sahō* and *reihō* in a *seiza* position with the participants facing each other. In the description of each *katachi*, we are assuming that the partners have already performed these rituals of proper etiquette, so our narrative covers only the techniques in the *katachi* itself.

In each *katachi* one partner practices a key principle of *iaijutsu*, and the other partner provides the appropriate attack to facilitate this training. As with all other Eishin-Ryū *kumitachi*, the partner who practices the principle intrinsic to the *katachi* is called Shikata (User) and the partner assisting is called Uchikata (Striker). As always, although Shikata is the one practicing the key technique of each *katachi*, it is equally important to develop proficiency in the role of Uchikata.

As with all previous *kumitachi*, a powerful *kiai* should accompany each attacking technique in the *katachi*. It is also important than ever to treat the situation as if it was real combat with *shinken*, not only to train your mind under the most realistic conditions possible, but also for safety.

Our final word of caution is that several of the techniques in the Daishō Tachizume involve the twisting or simulated dislocation of Uchikata's joints, strikes capable of fracturing bones, and throws from a standing position—actions that, if carelessly or excessively performed, can produce serious injury. It is therefore imperative that the Daishō Tachizume be practiced with the utmost caution and concern for the safety of both participants.

# SHIMETORI

The first Daishō Tachizume, Shimetori (Gather and Capture), is a defense against an opponent's sudden attempt to disarm you by grabbing and drawing your sword from its scabbard. *Shimetori* means to gather together and hold or capture, a term that accurately describes the nature of this *katachi*.

It begins with the participants standing face-to-face just out of arm's reach from each other (see fig. 181.1). Both partners perform *kiyomeri kokyū*, at the completion of which Uchikata (at left) lunges, right foot forward, and grasps the *tsuka* of Shikata's sword with both hands, as shown in figure 181.2. Before Uchikata can draw the sword, Shikata steps right foot forward and wraps both arms around Uchikata's arms at the elbows, pinning the *tsuka* and Uchikata's hands against his body and lifting upward (fig. 181.3). In actual combat, this would be done with Shikata using a powerful drive of his legs and hips to dislocate both of Uchikata's elbows, rendering him helpless, so in training it must be performed with sensitivity to ensure that Uchikata is not injured. With the technique now complete, Shikata releases Uchikata, and both step back to their starting positions, as shown in figure 18I.4.

Figures 18I.1–4. Daishō Tachizume: Shimetori

# 18J: SODE SURIGAESHI

The next *katachi*, Sode Surigaeshi, is a defense against an opponent who grabs your *tsuka* from the side. The name, Sode Surigaeshi, means "brushing sleeves" and may refer to both the initial position in which the partners are side-by-side with their sleeves nearly brushing or to the technique itself, since Shikata's right sleeve and forearm brush against Uchikata's jaw and throat while executing the throw that is central to this *katachi*.

It begins with both participants facing forward in a standing position, with Uchikata situated on Shikata's right (fig. 18J.1). Uchikata abruptly turns toward Shikata and grabs Shikata's *tsuka* with his left hand (fig. 18J.2). Before Uchikata can draw the sword, disarming him, Shikata grasps his *tsuba* with his left hand, turns to the right with his right foot positioned by Uchikata's left foot, and strikes Uchikata in the jaw or throat with his right elbow, as shown in figure 18J.3. By pressing his right knee against Uchikata's left knee, Shikata unbalances Uchikata while straightening his arm across Uchikata's throat and pushing him rearward (fig. 18J.4), and positioning his *tsuka* at the back of Uchikata's right knee (fig. 18J.5), then using hip rotation Shikata lifts Uchikata's left leg while sweeping Uchikata backward with his right arm, throwing Uchikata to the floor (fig. 18J.6). Turning toward Uchikata, Shikata remains ready to draw his sword (fig. 18J.7) as Uchikata rises and returns to his original position, facing Shikata (fig. 18J.8).

Figures 18J.1–8. Daishō Tachizume: Sode Surigaeshi

# 18K: TSUBA UCHIKAESHI

The third *katachi* of the Daishō Tachizume set is Tsuba Uchikaeshi, a defense against an opponent who grabs your wrist to prevent you drawing your sword. *Tsuba Uchikaeshi* means "*tsuba* reversing strike," which describes the swiveling strike employed in this drill to release Uchikata's grip on Shikata's wrist.

It begins with both participants facing each other in a standing position about an arm's length apart (fig. 18K.1). As Shikata reaches to draw his sword (fig. 18K.2), Uchikata lunges, right foot forward, and grabs Shikata's right wrist with his right hand (fig. 18K.3). Shikata releases his right hand from the *tsuka* and, with a powerful clockwise motion, strikes down onto Uchikata's right wrist with the *tsuba*, as shown in figure 18K.4. Obviously, in real combat this would fracture one or both bones in *Uchikata's* wrist, so it is vital to execute this movement with care and control. The partners then step back to their starting positions (fig. 18K.5).

Figures 18K.1–5. Daishō Tachizume: Tsuba Uchikaeshi

## 18L: KOPPŌ GAESHI

Koppō Gaeshi (Reversing Bone Defense) is the fourth in the Daishō Tachizume series. It is another defense against an opponent who grabs your *tsuka* to prevent you from drawing your sword. This technique utilizes painful pressure against the bones in Uchikata's forearms plus torsion in Uchikata's wrists for the leverage needed to overcome Uchikata's strength.

It begins with both participants facing each other in a standing position about an arm's length apart (fig. 18L.1). Uchikata lunges, right foot forward, and grabs Shikata's *tsuka* with his both hands (fig. 18L.2). Shikata grasps the *tsuka* with both hands, stepping rearward with his left foot, and bears down on the *tsuka* with his body weight to force the *tsuka* down and draw Uchikata off balance (fig. 18L.3), then twists the *tsuka* in a clockwise direction while turning to his right, which brings the *tsuka* into contact with Uchikata's right forearm, as shown in figure 18L.4. Driving with his legs, Shikata continues turning his body to the right, pulling his hands toward his right shoulder to release Uchikata's grip (fig. 18L.5). Figure 18L.6 shows this position from the reverse angle.

With the *tsuka* now free, Shikata turns toward Uchikata, ready to deploy his sword if necessary (fig. 18L.7). Obviously, in real combat this technique would not only be painful to Uchikata, but if executed with sufficient speed and force, would sprain Uchikata's right wrist, so it is vital to execute this movement with care and control to avoid these injuries. The partners then step back to their starting positions (fig. 18L.8).

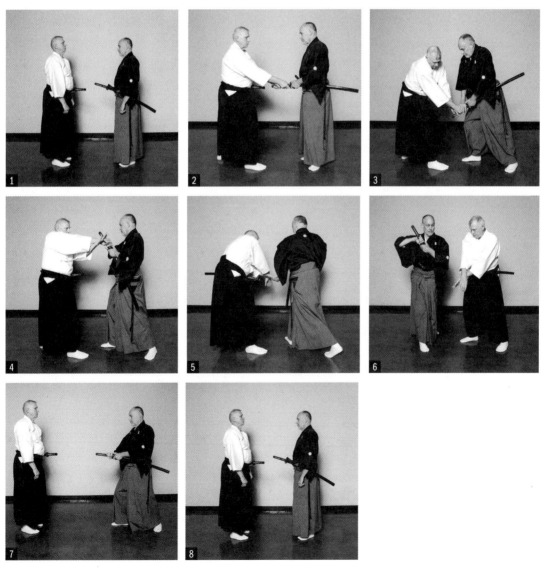

Figures 18L.1–8. Daishō Tachizume: Koppō Gaeshi

## 18M: TOMBO GAESHI

Tombo Gaeshi (Reversing Dragonfly), fifth in the Daishō Tachizume set, is a defense against an opponent who grabs both your *tsuka* and your *saya*. At first glance, this might seem an awkward and marginally effective way to attack a samurai, but it provides the attacker with leverage to push, pull, or turn you while at the same time preventing you from drawing your sword.

This *katachi* begins with Uchikata standing about two paces behind and to the right of Shikata. As Uchikata approaches, Shikata becomes aware of the movement and grasps his *tsuka* in preparation for the attack. With his right foot leading, Uchikata grabs Shikata's *tsuka* with his right hand and the *saya* with his left hand (fig. 18M.1). Shikata now grasps the *tsuka* with both hands and begins twisting powerfully to his right, pulling the *tsuka* to his right hip (fig. 18M.2). Shikata continues to turn, stepping around with his left foot while pushing the *tsuka* downward, simultaneously raising Uchikata's left hand and lowering his right hand (fig. 18M.3). As Shikata finishes stepping to the rear with his left foot, he twists his hips and shoulders powerfully to the right while twisting the *tsuka* in a clockwise motion to his right shoulder (fig. 18M.4), then reverses direction, stepping forward with his right foot and winding the *tsuka* in a clockwise direction to his left shoulder, which dislodges Uchikata's right hand from the *tsuka* while the *saya* twists free of Uchikata's left hand.

Figures 18M.1–6. Daishō Tachizume: Tombo Gaeshi

Note: if done with sufficient speed and force, Uchikata may be thrown to the floor, so this technique should be performed at moderate speed, merely breaking free of Uchikata's grasp, unless mats are available for Uchikata to take *ukemi* (break fall).

With his sword now free, Shikata turns to his left, facing Uchikata, right foot forward, prepared to draw his sword (fig. 18M.5). Uchikata rises if necessary, careful not to show aggressiveness, and the partners face each other at the completion of the technique (fig. 18M.6).

The name Tombo Gaeshi is derived from the figure-8 movement used to release Uchikata's grip. The clockwise movements of the *tsuka* while Shikata is reversing (*gaeshi*) direction form a lateral figure 8 (∞) with both the *tsuka* and *kojiri* that is reminiscent of the wings of a dragonfly (*tombo*).

# RANKYOKU

The sixth *katachi* in the Daishō Tachizume series, Rankyoku (Chaos), is a defense against an opponent who grabs your *saya* from behind to interfere with your ability to draw your sword.

Figures 18N.1–6. Daishō Tachizume: Rankyoku

The name, Rankyoku, can be translated several ways. The customary meaning of *ran* is "rebellion," "uprising," or "disorder." In everyday use, *kyoku* is usually translated as "song," "composition," or "music," but in certain contexts it can also refer to something that is bent, misshapen, or distorted. Given the nature of the technique employed in Rankyoku, it would appear to be used in this latter sense to describe a counterattack that is unpredictable and chaotic.

It begins with Uchikata standing one or two paces directly behind Shikata, as pictured in figure 18N.1. Uchikata suddenly grabs the *kojiri* of Shikata's *saya* with his right hand (fig. 18N.2). Shikata immediately steps back with his left foot and pushes down on the *saya* with his left hand, forcing Uchikata's hand up and rearward, as depicted in figure 18N.3. Shikata then pivots sharply to his left on his left foot while sweeping the *tsuka* in a counterclockwise arc (fig. 18N.4), and steps rearward with his right foot, which either wrenches the *saya* from Uchikata's grasp or, if Uchikata tries to hold on tightly, forces him to the floor. Shikata then turns to face Uchikata, ready to draw his sword (fig. 18N.5). Uchikata rises if necessary, and the partners face each other at the completion of the technique (fig. 18N.6).

## 180: UTSURI

Last in the Daishō Tachizume set is Utsuri (Transition), is a defense against an opponent who grabs you from behind in a "bear hug" to prevent you from deploying your sword. While a bear hug may seem an odd way to attack a samurai, in context it would be a way of rendering him temporarily defenseless while other allies attack him.

Note: For clarity, the sequence of photographs below were taken at a 45-degree angle, rather than head-on as the *katachi* is normally performed.

It begins with Uchikata standing a pace or two directly behind Shikata, as shown in figure 18O.1. Uchikata suddenly wraps his arms around Shikata's upper arms and torso in a bear hug (fig. 18O.2). Shikata grasps Uchikata's right upper arm and left forearm as depicted in figure 18O.3, then drops into a wide-spread stance similar to the *karate-dō* stance, *shikodachi*, pulling Uchikata off-balance and forward, with Shikata's suddenly lowered weight. By forcing his hips rearward, Shikata then levers Uchikata off his feet and throws him over Shikata's right shoulder (fig. 18O.5). After completing the throw, Shikata steps back with his left foot, ready to draw if Uchikata shows intent to pursue any further attack. Uchikata rises, and the partners face each other at the completion of the technique (fig. 18O.6).

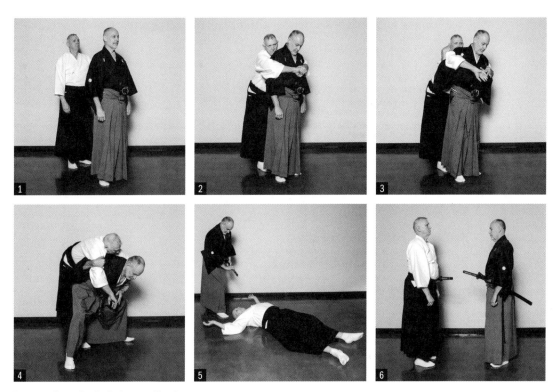

Figures 180.1–6. Daishō Tachizume: Utsuri

# DAIKEN DORI

The term *Daiken Dori* means "large sword capture," and they are another set of *okuden kumitachi* that utilize techniques closely resembling those typically found in *jūdō* and *jūjutsu*. There are ten exercises in the Daiken Dori series. In some, Shikata is armed with a *daitō* (long sword) and Uchikata wears a *shōtō* (short sword), while in others both are equipped with *daitō*. It has been a long-standing tradition that the Daiken Dori are taught only to high ranking *iaidōka*, and then only in hands-on instruction. While there are no "secret techniques" in Eishin-Ryū per se, the Daiken Dori have been treated as *kuden*—techniques only taught personally and orally—for most or all of the twentieth and twenty-first centuries.

After lengthy consideration and reflection, it was decided to uphold this tradition and not to include any descriptions of the Daiken Dori in this edition of *Flashing Steel*, but instead only to list them as a way of making *iaidōka* aware that they are part of the Masaoka-Ha curriculum and may be taught to those who earn that privilege through long and diligent training.

The names and customary sequence of the Daiken Dori exercises are:

1. Muken (Without Sword)
2. Suiseki (Water Rock)
3. Gaiseki (Outer Rock)
4. Tesseki (Iron Rock)
5. Eigan (Glorious Eyes)
6. Eigetsu (Glorious Moon)
7. Yamakaze (Mountain Wind)
8. Sorihashi (Sled Bridge)
9. Raiden (Thunder and Lightning)
10. Suigetsu (Water Moon)

Hopefully, by including mention of the Daiken Dori in this edition, serious *iaidōka* will be encouraged to affiliate with, and train diligently with, a qualified *sensei* of the Masaoka-Ha line to ensure that these and all *okuden kumitachi* sets are preserved and passed on to future generations.

## CONCLUSION

The Okuden Kumitachi are a departure from what most people would consider *iaijutsu*. In most of them, neither Shikata's nor Uchikata's sword is actually drawn. While this may not seem to be swordsmanship, in some ways the Okuden Kumitachi reflect the true nature of *okuden* (deep learning) *iaijutsu*, because Shikata's expertise with the sword is assumed, and therefore Uchikata's actions are intended to prevent Shikata from using that ability. In that context, no *iaidōka* can really be considered an expert unless he or she can defend against actions that would render his or her skills useless.

# Chapter 19
# *Seitei Iai Kata*
## Standardized Kata

These Seitei Kata (Standard Practice Patterns) are presented separately in this book because they are not technically part of the Eishin-Ryū system. They were originally a development of the Zen Nippon Kendō Renmei (All-Japan Kendō Federation) for use by its members. For this reason, we usually refer to this series of techniques as the Seitei Kata (standard patterns) to clearly distinguish them from the orthodox Eishin-Ryū *waza*. Since we perform them in a manner consistent with the *kihon* and principles of Eishin-Ryū, rather than as prescribed by the Zen Nippon Kendō Renmei, we now refer to them simply as the Seitei Iai Kata or as the Eishin-Ryū Seitei Iai Kata. Some historical background on the Seitei Kata will help you understand why we make these distinctions, yet still include descriptions of these *kata* in *Flashing Steel*.

The Zen Nippon Kendō Renmei Seitei Iai Kata were first formulated around 1968 to provide a series of *iaidō* techniques for practice by *kendō* students. The Zen Nippon Kendō Renmei invited the acknowledged heads of each of the major styles of *iaidō*, including Musō Jikiden Eishin-Ryū, Hōki-Ryū, Eishin-Ryū, Tamiya-Ryū, Katori Shinden-Ryū, and Musō Shinden-Ryū, to devise a set of standard techniques for practice by *kendō* students. These representatives selected seven techniques that represented their respective styles to form the Seitei Kata. Representing Musō Jikiden Eishin-Ryū at this meeting was its eighteenth *sōshihan*, Masaoka Kazumi Shihan. In fact, it was Masaoka Sōshihan who was appointed as the chairperson of the committee that formulated the Seitei Kata for the Kendō Renmei. After about a decade of use, around 1980, three more techniques were added to the Seitei Kata, then another two in 2000, bringing their total to the twelve currently in use. In addition to practice by *kendō* students, the Seitei Kata are frequently taught to students of martial arts with an interest in samurai swordsmanship, such as *aikidō*, and even occasionally in *karate* schools, as well many styles of *iaidō*.

The techniques used in the Seitei Kata are not always performed exactly as they are practiced in the system from which they were borrowed. In several cases, substantial modifications were made for purposes of standardization, or to adapt an underlying principle to a different posture or situation. For this reason, they are usually referred to as *kata* (forms or patterns) to distinguish them from the *waza* (techniques) of their respective styles from which they were derived.

The Zen Nippon Kendō Renmei has changed their performance and grading standards for Seitei Iaidō several times over the years, whereas in Masaoka-Ha Eishin-Ryū we have always performed the Seitei Kata in the same manner—that being consistent with the methods and principles of Eishin-Ryū. This affords the Eishin-Ryū Seitei Kata a measure of stability not present in the KenRen versions.

As students of Eishin-Ryū, our principle reason for practicing the Seitei Kata is not for their training value or their principles of attack and defense. In fact, we recommend against training in them for those reasons, because the principles of body movement are not uniform and are sometimes at variance with the theories and practice of Eishin-Ryū. Instead, they are included in the Eishin-Ryū curriculum—and this book—primarily because they are so widely recognized and used frequently in martial arts tournaments in which *iaidō* events are included. Secondarily, since Masaoka Sōshihan was instrumental in the creation of the Seitei Kata, it seems entirely appropriate to preserve them in *Flashing Steel* as part of his legacy. We therefore recommend that students of Eishin-Ryū become familiar with the Seitei Kata, since they are so widely practiced throughout the world and therefore provide a common ground of performance and understanding with *iaidōka* from nearly every style and background. The Seitei Kata can also serve as an introduction to the art of *iaijutsu* for students who train primarily in unrelated arts, such as *karate-dō, jūdō, kendō, aikidō, taekwondo,* MMA, or even boxing or wrestling, as well as anyone who is not committed to learning a complete system as vast and complex as Eishin-Ryū.

With each category of Eishin-Ryū *waza*, we included a description of elements that characterize each series. However, due to their nature—as a collection of techniques from a variety of styles—there are few such characteristics with the Seitei Kata. The principle characteristic of the Seitei Kata, in fact, is probably that they have no singular characteristic! For instance, there is no characteristic method of performing *nōtō* in the Seitei kata.

Since the Seitei Kata were drawn from several different styles, each having a different method of *nōtō*, it is generally held that *nōtō* should be performed in the manner usually followed in the style with which you are most familiar. For Eishin-Ryū students, this usually means using Shoden *nōtō* while performing the Seitei Kata. It is not uncommon, however, to see advanced Eishin-Ryū practitioners using Shoden *nōtō* for the *seiza kata* and Okuden *nōtō* for the *tachiwaza* of Seitei Kata.

As we introduce each of these *kata*, we will explain its origin and the key feature or principle to be practiced.

## 19A: SEIZA MAE

The first *waza*, Mae (Front) or Seiza Mae, also sometimes called Seiza Shōmen (Facing Forward), was derived from the Musō Jikiden Eishin-Ryū Shoden *waza* of the same name. As with its Eishin-Ryū namesake, the purpose for including Mae is for practice of the major elements of *kihon* in their most basic form. This *kata* is performed identically to its Shoden counterpart, with the exception of the footwork involved in *ō-chiburi*.

Mae begins facing straight ahead in *seiza* posture during *kiyomeri kokyū*. As you finish inhaling the third breath, perform *nukitsuke* while rising to one knee, right foot forward. *Furikaburi* and *kirioroshi* are also performed identically to the Eishin-Ryū version of Mae. Ōmori-Ryū (Wet Umbrella) *chiburi* follows, but unlike Eishin-Ryū's Mae, your rear foot does not slide up to meet your front foot as you rise. Instead, you rise straight up, keeping your feet in place. For this reason, in the Seitei version of Mae, you should attempt to reach full standing posture (in *iaigoshi*, of course) at the same moment the sword snaps downward. Usually, the sword completes *chiburi* just a moment before you fully rise. While maintaining *zanshin*, slide your left foot slowly and steadily forward until it is even with your right foot, then, with no noticeable shift in balance side-to-side, slide your right foot back so that only your relative foot positions have changed from figure 19A.15 to figure 19A.17. From this point the *kata* concludes in the same manner as its Ōmori-Ryū counterpart described in chapter 8.

The *ōyō* (practical application) of Mae is defense against a single opponent who is attacking from directly in front of you. Sensing the opponent's intention to attack, you use *nukitsuke* to slice across the opponent's eyes, blinding the attacker to provide the split second needed to safely perform *furikaburi* and *kirioroshi*.

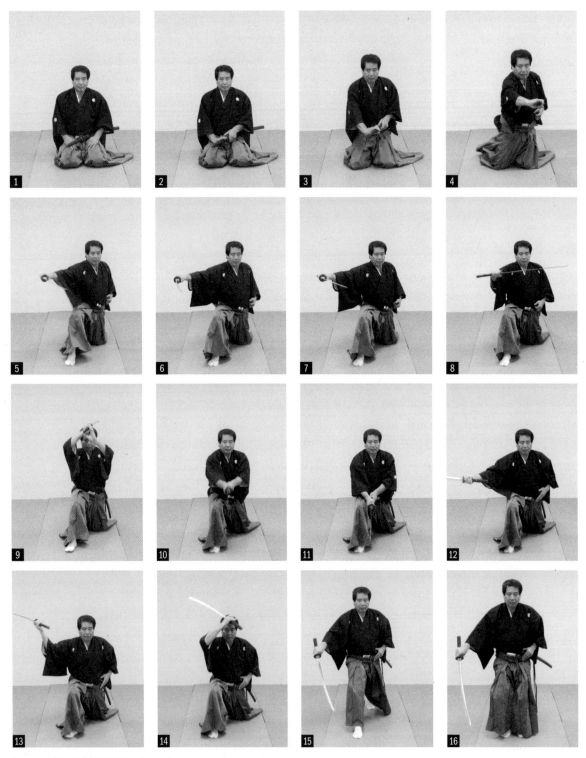

Figures 19A.1–16. Seitei Iai Kata: Seiza Mae

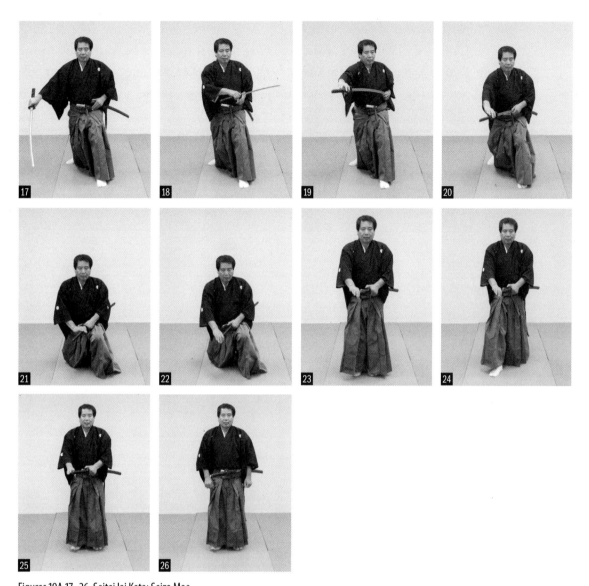

Figures 19A.17–26. Seitei Iai Kata: Seiza Mae

## 19B: SEIZA USHIRO

Like Mae, Seiza Ushiro (Rear) was derived from the Musō Jikiden Eishin-Ryū *waza* of the same name and, like Mae, the only difference between the Seitei and Shoden versions is the footwork accompanying *chiburi*.

Perform *kiyomeri kokyū*, then begin *nukitsuke*. As you rise, pivot 180 degrees to your left and step forward with your left foot while performing *nukitsuke*. Follow with *furikaburi* and *kirioroshi*, just as in Mae, except with the left foot leading. Use an Ōmori-Ryū *chiburi*, but do not bring the feet together as you would in the Eishin-Ryū version of Ushiro. Instead, the feet should remain apart as you rise during *chiburi* (fig. 19B.15). Complete the *kata* with *nōtō*, rise, and return to your starting point.

The *ōyō* of Ushiro is defense against a single opponent who attacks from your rear while you are seated in a formal setting.

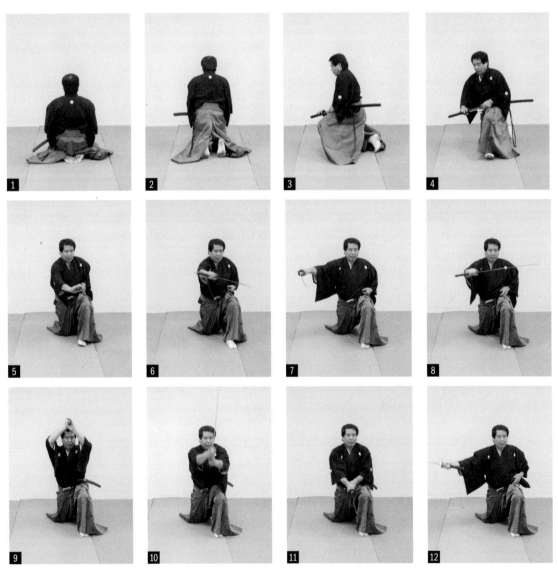

Figures 19B.1–12. Seitei Iai Kata: Ushiro

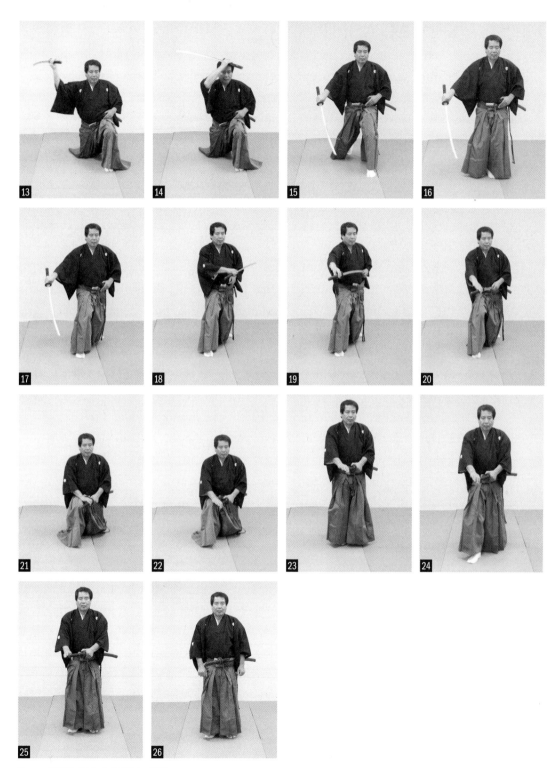

Figures 19B.13–26. Seitei Iai Kata: Ushiro

# 19C: UKENAGASHI

The principle technique practiced in Ukenagashi—the "Flowing Block" from which it takes its name—is common to *waza* from several styles, including Musō Shinden-Ryū, Hōki-Ryū, and Eishin-Ryū. It is perhaps for this reason that there are more noticeable differences between the Seitei and Shoden versions.

The Seitei variation of Ukenagashi begins in *seiza*, facing 90 degrees to the right, rather than 45 degrees, as in the Eishin-Ryū *shoden* version. As you finish *kiyomeri kokyū*, look to your left, then perform *koiguchi no kirikata*. Begin to rise for *nukitsuke*, stepping forward with your left foot as you draw about one-third to one-half of the sword (fig. 19C.2). Rise to a standing position (with *iaigoshi*) as you complete *nukitsuke*, drawing the sword overhead as you turn your body about 45 degrees to your left, with the *kissaki* angled downward to your left as shown in figure 19C.4. In a continuously flowing movement, twist your body another 90 degrees to your left as you grasp the *tsuka* with your left hand and perform *furikaburi*, then perform *kesagiri* (downward right-to-left angular cut) at a 45-degree angle, gaining momentum by stepping back with your left foot into a wide, low stance (similar to a side stance), so that your direction has now turned 135 degrees from your original *seiza* orientation (fig. 19C.7).

With *zanshin*, maintain this stance as you tilt the sword down and to the right at about a 45-degree angle until the *mine* rests against the top of your right thigh, just above the knee, as shown in figure 19C.8. Hold this "drip" *chiburi* steady while reversing the grip of your right hand on the *tsuka*. Release your left hand, still holding the sword in place with your right hand, and grasp the *saya* at the *koiguchi*. Swing the sword in a wide arc to your left side and place it edge up on top of your left forearm to begin *gyakute nōtō*. Lower to one knee as you complete *nōtō*, then rise and return to your starting position.

*Ōyō* for Ukenagashi is essentially the same as for the Shoden version. Your attacker's sword is already drawn and ready, so there is no chance to beat him to the draw. Instead, by appearing vulnerable to attack as you begin to draw, you lure the opponent into a premature attack, then rise with the Flowing Block for which the technique is named. By stepping to the side and allowing the opponent's strike to slide obliquely down your angled sword, his balance is momentarily lost, allowing you to finish him with the *kirioroshi* into which the block flows.

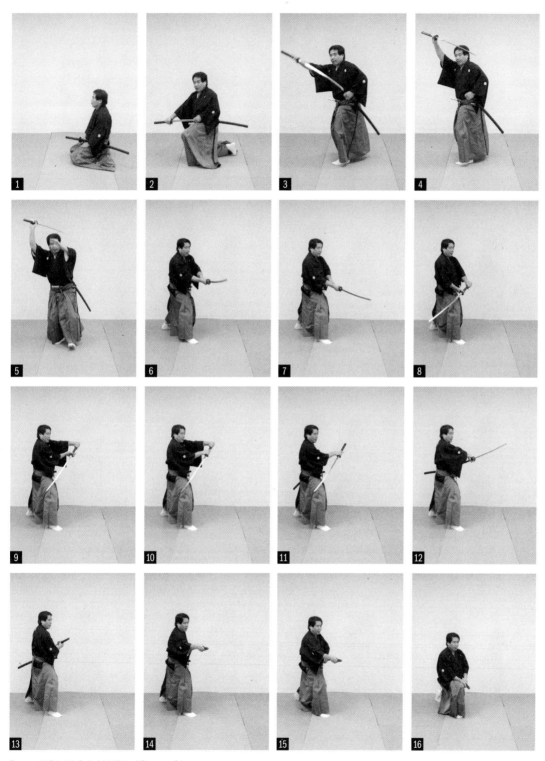

Figures 19C.1–16. Seitei Iai Kata: Ukenagashi

Figures 19C.17–21. Seitei Iai Kata: Ukenagashi

## 19D: TSUKA-ATE

Tsuka-ate (Handle-Strike) is a derivation of a Tatehiza *waza* from Hasegawa Eishin-Ryū (not Musō Jikiden Eishin-Ryū), but it bears some similarities to Towaki in our Okuden Suwariwaza. Tsuka-ate is the only Seitei Kata performed from the *tatehiza* posture. It gets its name from the first defensive technique, which occurs even before *nukitsuke*.

In Tsuka-ate, you begin facing straight ahead in *tatehiza* (see fig. 19D.1).

As you inhale the third cleansing breath, grasp the *tsuka* with both hands, rise to one knee as you step forward with your right foot, circle the *tsuka* clockwise, and strike at face level with the *tsuka-gashira*, as shown in figure 19D.4.

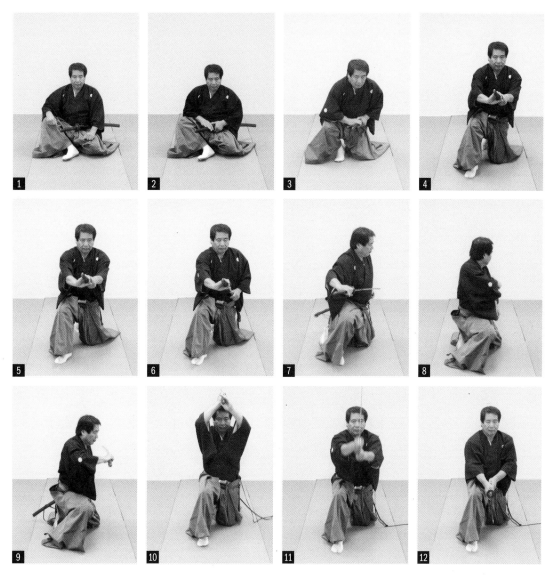

Figures 19D.1–12. Seitei Iai Kata: Tsuka-ate

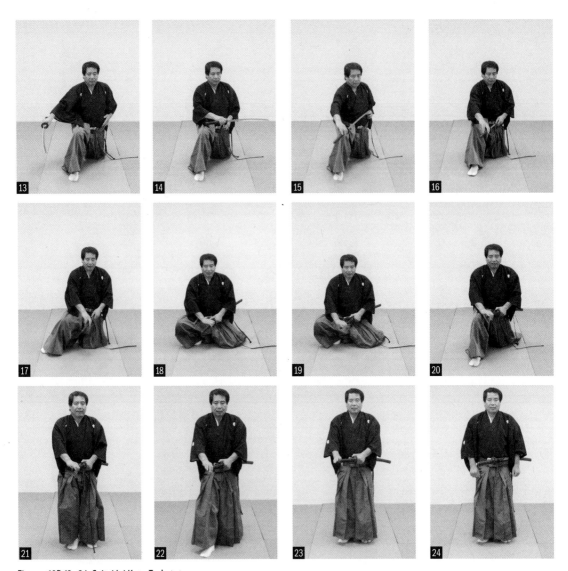

Figures 19D.13–24. Seitei Iai Kata: Tsuka-ate

Perform *koiguchi no kirikata*, then *nukitsuke* by drawing the *saya* back with your left hand, turning your hip and shoulder to the left to draw the *kissaki* from the *koiguchi*, and—with a slight scoot to the rear—thrust one-handed past your left shoulder behind you (see fig. 19D.8).

Use the turn of your upper body to draw your *katana* slightly forward and raise it to *furikaburi*, grasping the *tsuka* now with both hands, then shuffle-step forward with *kirioroshi*, with your right foot front. Follow *kirioroshi* with Eishin-Ryū (*yoko*) *chiburi* and *nōtō*, sliding your right foot back and circling it beneath yourself as you resheath the sword. Rise to standing position, maintaining *iaigoshi*, then step back to your starting point, and return your hands to your sides.

# 19E: TSUKA-ATE (SIDE VIEW)

Details of Tsuka-ate, particularly how the hip-turn is used to complete the draw, and the positioning of the forearm in the rearward thrust, are better portrayed in side view, below:

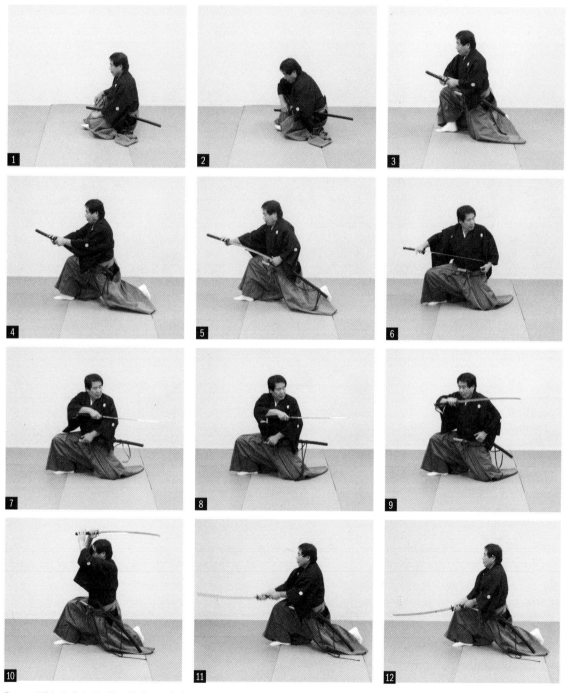

Figures 19E.1–12. Seitei Iai Kata: Tsuka-ate (side view)

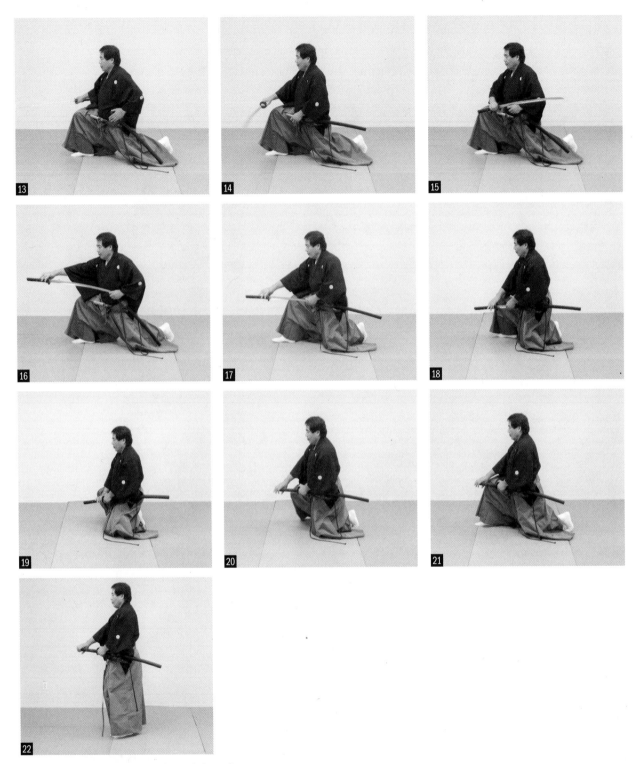

Figures 19E.13–22. Seitei Iai Kata: Tsuka-ate (side view)

The *ōyō* for Tsuka-ate should be somewhat familiar. You have opponents at both your front and rear. The one in front attempts to grab your *tsuka* in order to render you defenseless against the enemy attacking from behind. However, with the clockwise movement of the *tsuka*, you either evade the opponent's grasp or wrench the *tsuka* free, and pummel him in the face. With the sword in striking position, you need only pull the *saya* back and it is instantly drawn, allowing you to pierce the attacker behind you without delay. Then, before the enemy in front of you can recover from the stunning blow to his face, you finish him with *kirioroshi*.

# 19F: KESAGIRI

Kesagiri (Diagonal Cut) is a derivative of a similar technique found in Hōki-Ryū. It is the first of the Seitei Tachikata, or standing techniques. A *kesa* is the traditional robe of a Japanese monk, which covers only the left shoulder and arm. The lapel of the left shoulder runs diagonally across the chest from the left collarbone to the right hip. Kesagiri takes its name from the fact that the angle of its finishing cut follows the line of a *kesa's* lapel—cutting from the left shoulder to the right hip.

As you finish inhaling the third time, take your first step forward with your right foot. During your second step (left foot), raise your hands to the *tsuka* and perform *koiguchi no kirikata*. During your third step, as your sword is nearing *saya-banari*, twist the *tsuka* and *saya* almost a half-turn counterclockwise as you prepare to draw.

*Nukitsuke* swings up and to your right *(kiriage)* at about a 45 degree angle, finishing with the *kissaki* pointing out and away from your body at about 45 degrees, as depicted in figure 19F.6. Twist your right wrist 180 degrees clockwise to point the *kissaki* rearward, then bend your right wrist, performing a modified *furikaburi* over your right shoulder as you take a *yori-ashi* shuffle-step (right foot, then left foot) forward, grasp the *tsuka* with your left hand and perform a diagonal cut angled down and to your left at about a 45-degree angle, ending in the position shown in figure 19F.10.

Step back with your right foot and raise the sword to *hassō no kamae*. Step back with your left foot as you swing the sword past your head, slightly to the left side, and perform a modified Ōmori-Ryū *chiburi*.

After *nōtō*, draw your left foot forward to meet your right foot (maintaining *iai-goshi*), then step back to your starting position.

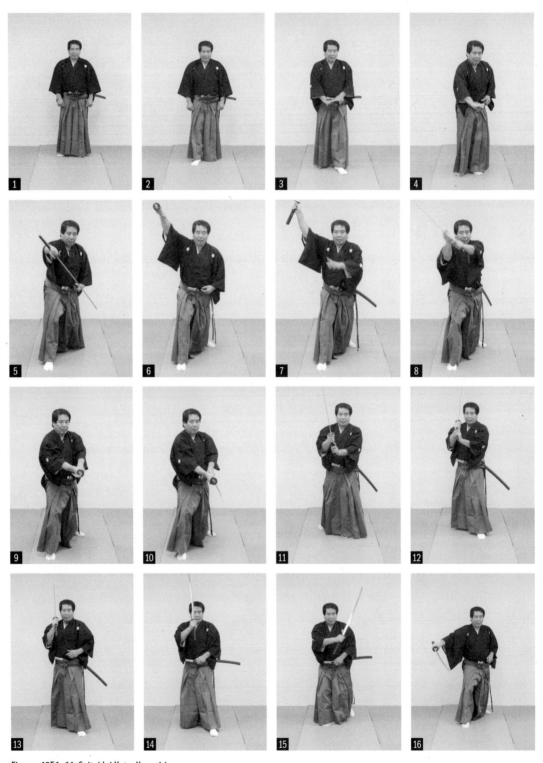

Figures 19F.1–16. Seitei Iai Kata: Kesagiri

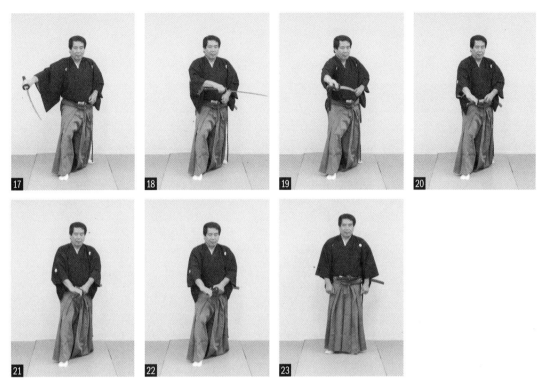

Figures 19F.17–23. Seitei Iai Kata: Kesagiri

*Ōyō* for Kesagiri involves a confrontation with a single opponent whose sword is already drawn. As the opponent attacks with *kirioroshi*, your rising *nukitsuke* slashes one or both of his arms as they reach full extension. Your *kesa-giri* is then used to finish him. By stepping back into *hassō no kamae*, you are on guard in case he is not quite finished or has accomplices nearby. If your opponent is still struggling for life, your tall, overwhelming posture and *zanshin* will serve to crush his resolve and break his spirit, thereby helping him expire and lessening his suffering.

# 19G: MOROTEZUKI

Morotezuki (Two-Handed Thrust) is based upon a common *kendō* technique, but its key principles can also be found in various *iaidō* styles, although normally practiced in a different manner.

As you complete *kiyomeri kokyū*, take your first step forward with your right foot. During your second step (left foot), perform *koiguchi no kirikata*. On your third step, twist the *tsuka* and *saya* 45 degrees counterclockwise and perform *nukitsuke* as an angular downward cut at temple height (fig. 19G.7).

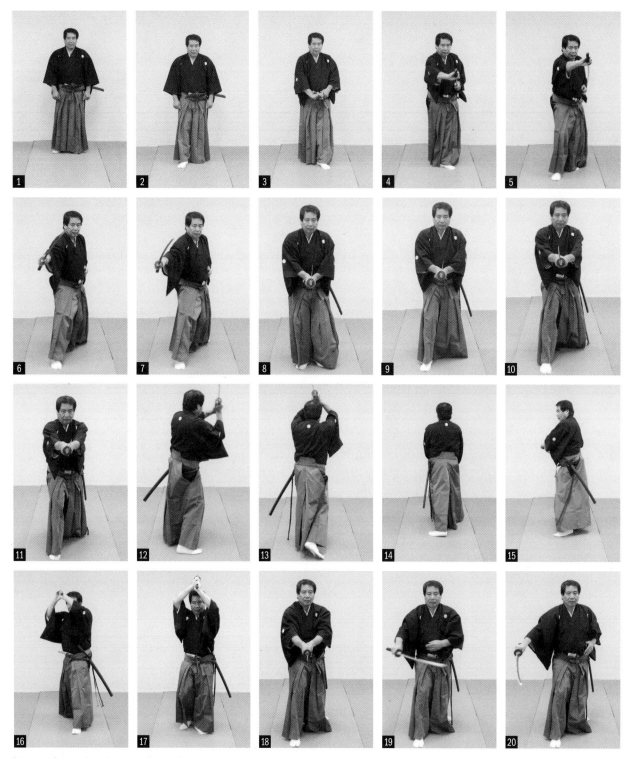

Figures 19G.1–20. Seitei Iai Kata: Morotezuki

Figures 19G.21–29. Seitei Iai Kata: Morotezuki

Pull the *tsuka* back toward your navel and grip it with your left hand, then take a small shuffle-step (*yori-ashi*) forward and make a two-handed thrust to the solar plexus. Simultaneously pull the sword free and turn, pivoting on the balls of both feet without changing their relative positions, performing *furikaburi* as a natural by-product. Step forward with your right foot and perform *kirioroshi* to the rear opponent. Again pivot on the balls of both feet while raising the sword in *furikaburi*. Step forward with your right foot and perform *kirioroshi* to the front opponent. While maintaining *zanshin*, use Eishin-Ryū *chiburi*, followed by *nōtō*, then step back to your original starting position.

## 19H: MOROTEZUKI (SIDE VIEW)

Much of the coordination of footwork with the techniques is better viewed from the side.

Morotezuki is normally considered to be a defense against three attackers: two to your front (one behind the other) and one to your rear. *Nukitsuke* and *morotezuki* are used to first disable, then finish the first opponent in front of you, before turning and finishing the opponent to your rear with *kirioroshi*, then returning to the second frontal attacker with another *kirioroshi*.

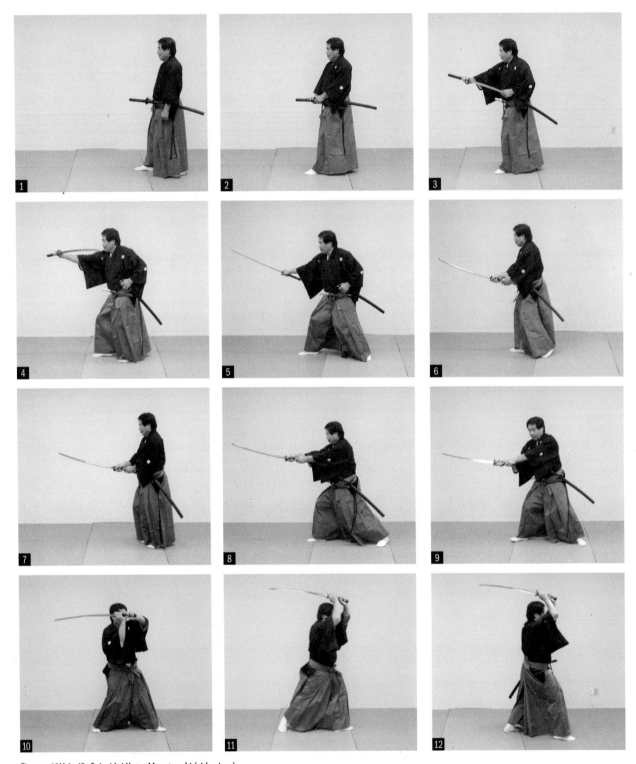

Figures 19H.1–12. Seitei Iai Kata: Morotezuki (side view)

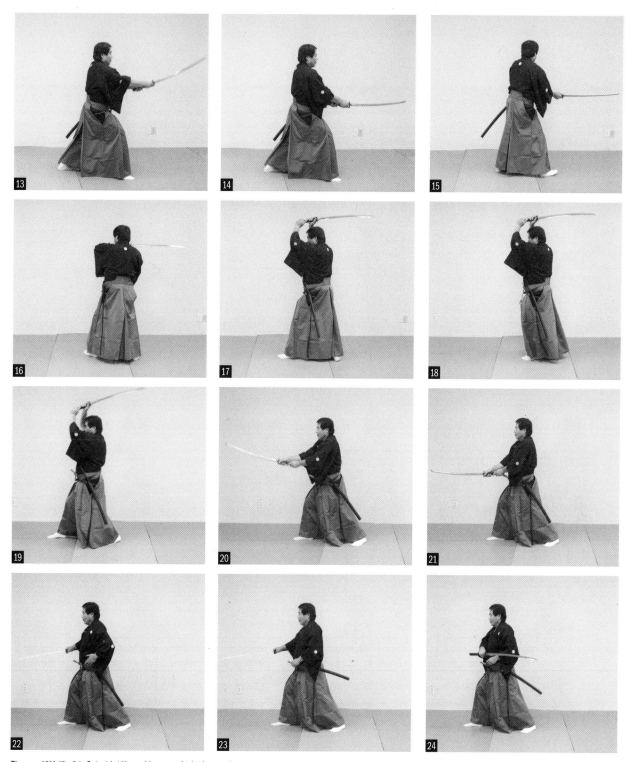

Figures 19H.13–24. Seitei Iai Kata: Morotezuki (side view)

Figures 19H.25–32. Seitei Iai Kata: Morotezuki (side view)

## 19I: SANPŌGIRI

Sanpōgiri (Three-Way Cut) is found in various formats in numerous styles of *iaidō*. It is a defense against three attackers, coming at you from the front and each side.

At the completion of *kiyomeri kokyū*, take your first step forward with your right foot. During your second step (left foot), perform *koiguchi no kirikata*, then your third step is 90 degrees to your right, using *nukitsuke* as a downward cut to the top of the head (*kiritsuke*), stopping with the blade angled upward at about a 45-degree angle (fig. 19I.8).

Figures 19I.1–20. Seitei Iai Kata: Sanpōgiri

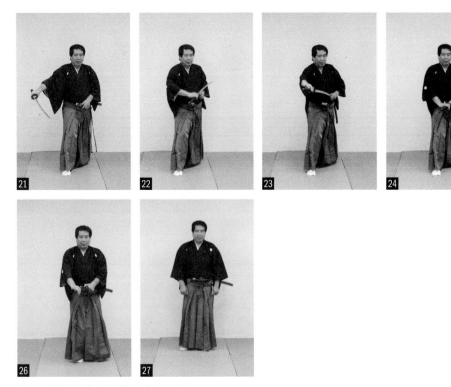

Figures 191.21–27. Seitei Iai Kata: Sanpōgiri

Without changing the position of your feet, pivot 180 degrees to your left on the balls of both feet while raising the sword in *furikaburi*, completing your turn with *kirioroshi* to your left side. Turn 90 degrees to your right, raising the sword in *furikaburi*, then step forward with your right foot and perform *kirioroshi*. Step back with your right foot into *jōdan no kamae*. After a moderate pause, step back with your left foot as you swing the sword slightly to the left side of your head in a modified *ō-chiburi*, then *nōtō*.

*Ōyō* for Sanpōgiri is fairly straightforward: *nukitsuke* is used to dispatch the opponent to your most vulnerable side (right), turning almost instantly with *kirioroshi* to the opponent on your left. The opponent to your front is kept in view at all times, until you turn and finish him with *kirioroshi* as well.

# 19J: GANMEN-ATE

Ganmen-ate (Face Strike) is based on techniques used in Yukichigai and Moniri in the Musō Jikiden Eishin-Ryū *waza*.

As you finish inhaling the third *kiyomeri kokyū* breath, take your first step forward with your right foot. During your second step (left foot), perform *koiguchi no kirikata*. As you take your third step (right foot), thrust the *tsuka* and *saya* forward to face height, striking with the *tsuka-gashira*, as shown in figure 19J.6. Pull the *saya* back with your left hand, then pivot on the balls of both feet, using the rotation of your hips to complete *nukitsuke*, holding the sword at waist level with your right hand, as illustrated in figure 19J.9. Step forward with your right foot and make a one-handed thrust to the solar plexus, using the underside of your right forearm to reinforce the *tsuka* to steady the blade. Note that the blade is turned flat, so its edge is facing outward, as shown in figure 19J.10.

Pull the *tsuka* back toward your navel with your right hand to withdraw it, turning your hand one-quarter turn clockwise, so the *mine* is upward. Then pivot on the balls of both feet, and continue the motion of your hand, raising the sword into *furikaburi* as you grip it with your left hand, then step forward with your right foot, finishing with *kirioroshi*. Maintain *zanshin* during Eishin-Ryū *chiburi* and *nōtō*, then draw your left foot even with your right foot and step back to your starting position before lowering your hands to your sides.

*Ōyō* for Ganmen-ate is usually shown against two opponents: one each at your front and rear. Since both are attacking simultaneously, you must use the *ganmen-ate* strike to the face to temporarily disable the enemy in front of you in order to have time to turn and impale the foe behind you. Before the first opponent can recover from the blow to his face, you must turn again and finish him with *kirioroshi*.

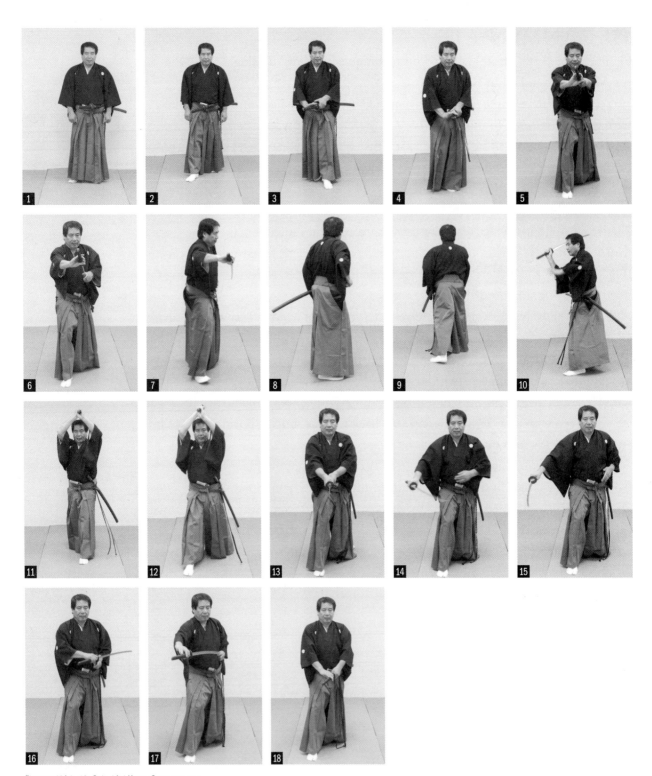

Figures 19J.1–18. Seitei Iai Kata: Ganmen-ate

# 19K: GANMEN-ATE (SIDE VIEW)

Several aspects of Ganmen-ate, particularly the *soetezuki* (one-handed reinforced thrust), are more clearly visible in the side view.

Figures 19K.1–15. Ganmen-ate (side view)

Figures 19K.16–25. Ganmen-ate (side view)

## 19L: SOETEZUKI

Soetezuki (Reinforced Thrust) is derived from one of the best-known techniques found in Hōki-Ryū, containing precise and difficult footwork and movement.

As you finish inhaling the third time, take your first step forward with your right foot. During your second step (left foot), perform *koiguchi no kirikata*. As you begin your third step, twist your right foot inward, preparing to turn 90 degrees to your left, as shown in figure 19L.3. Twist your body to the left as you begin *nukitsuke* (fig. 19L.4). Step back with your left foot into a side-on stance as you complete *nukitsuke* as a downward arcing cut at about a 45-degree angle, as illustrated in figure 19L.7. Pull the *tsuka* back to your right hip, allowing your right foot to slide back about a half-step as you turn your body to the right, and align your left hand along the *mine*, with your thumb on top and fingers parallel to the blade, as depicted in figure 19L.10–12.

Step forward with your left foot and make a reinforced thrust, guiding the travel of the blade with your left hand, letting the *mine* slide along the groove between your thumb and forefinger (see fig. 19L.8). Without moving your feet, raise and extend your right arm, pinching the *mine* between the thumb and index finger of your left hand as you tilt the blade at a 45-degree angle down to your left (fig. 19L.14). Step back with your left foot as you flick the blade forward into an Eishin-Ryū *chiburi*, and follow this with *nōtō*. Bring your left foot even with your right foot, turn 90 degrees to your right, then step back to your starting position.

Soetezuki is normally practiced as a defense against a single opponent attacking from your left as you are walking. The feeling should be that the enemy is waiting in ambush at the corner of a fence, building, or similar structure that hides him from view as you approach. You turn and step back, cutting to the enemy's temple or neck, then thrust through the solar plexus to finish him. An alternative *bunkai* is against two opponents, both attacking from the side. *Nukitsuke* is then used to cut the first opponent's neck, and the reinforced thrust from which Soetezuki gets its name finishes his accomplice.

Figures 19L.1–10. Seitei Iai Kata: Soetezuki

Figures 19L.11–22. Seitei Iai Kata: Soetezuki

# 19M: SOETEZUKI (SIDE VIEW)

Some aspects of Soetezuki can be seen better in the side view.

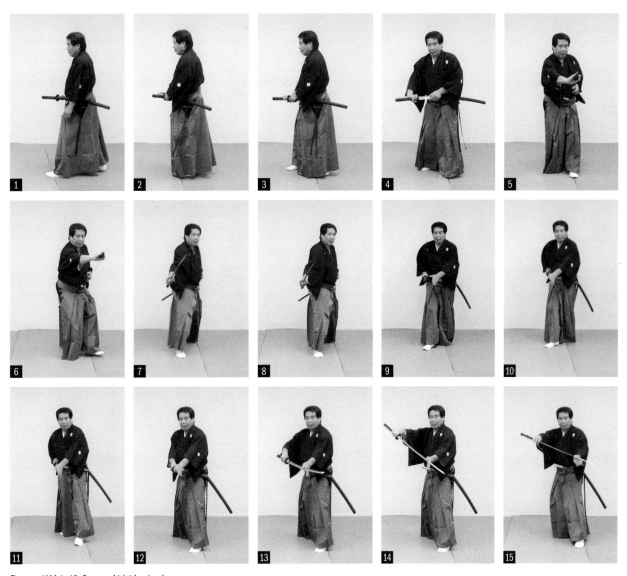

Figures 19M.1–15. Soetezuki (side view)

Figures 19M.16–21. Soetezuki (side view)

# 19N: SHIHŌGIRI

Shihōgiri (Four-Way Cut) is a *tachikata* (standing) version of similar *suwariwaza* (half-kneeling) techniques common to both Musō Jikiden Eishin-Ryū and Hōki-Ryū. Unlike its Eishin-Ryū Suwariwaza counterpart, the *ōyō* for Seitei Shihōgiri is identical to the way it is practiced.

Figures 19N.1–20. Seitei Iai Kata: Shihōgiri

Figures 19N.21–34. Seitei Iai Kata: Shihōgiri

In Shihōgiri, you are surrounded by four attackers—one to each corner. As you complete your third cleansing breath, take your first step forward with your right foot. During your second step (left foot), perform *koiguchi no kirikata*. Turn 45 degrees to your right on the third step. Twist the *tsuka* and *saya* 45 degrees counterclockwise as you strike downward with the side of the *tsuka*, as shown in figure 19N.5. This strike to the wrist of the opponent to your front-right breaks his grip on his *tsuka*, giving you time to pull the *saya* back with your left hand (*saya-biki*) and, with a shuffle-step to your left-rear, perform a thrust to the rear past your left shoulder with the *tsuka* braced against the underside of your right forearm. Raise the sword and grasp the *tsuka* with your left hand in *furikaburi* as you face back toward your right-front. Step forward with your left foot and use *kirioroshi* to finish the opponent whose wrist you first struck. Turn 90 degrees to your right during *furikaburi* and step forward with your right foot as you employ *kirioroshi* against the opponent to your right-rear. Pivot on the balls of both feet 180 degrees to your left, transitioning through *waki no kamae* while preparing your hands for *furikaburi*, and step forward while performing *furikaburi* and land, right foot forward, with *kirioroshi* to the remaining attacker. Step back with your right foot, raising your sword to *jōdan no kamae*. Use the menace of your posture and the strength of your *zanshin* to suppress any remaining spirit in your fallen opponents. Then, step back with your left foot as you swing the sword just to the left of your head in a modified *ō-chiburi*, followed by *nōtō*. Slide your left foot even with your right foot, turn 45 degrees to your right while still in *iaigoshi*, and step back to your starting point.

# 190: SŌGIRI

Sōgiri (Many Cuts) is patterned after Sōmakuri in the Musō Jikiden Eishin-Ryū *waza*.

At the third cleansing breath, step forward with the right foot. Perform *koiguchi no kirikata* on the second step and begin *nukitsuke* on the third step, but push back with the right foot as *nukitsuke* is nearing completion and perform *furikaburi*. Notice in figure 19O.5 and figure 19P.5 that the blade leaves the scabbard at an angle toward the left-rear, serving to protect the head during *furikaburi* in a manner similar to an *ukenagashi* block. Step forward with the right foot into *yokomen-giri* to the left side of the opponent's head, cutting from the temple to the jaw line. Perform *furikaburi*, then shuffle forward with *yokomen-giri* to the neck on the opposite side as in Sōmakuri. Again perform *furikaburi* and move forward with a diagonal cut to the ribs on the opposite side using the same footwork. Then swing the blade overhead and rearward on your left side (figs. 19O.14–17) and lunge forward with *yoko ichimonji*, cutting laterally across the midsection, flowing immediately into *furikaburi* and shuffling-forward *kirioroshi*. All cuts in this *kata* are performed with the right foot forward. Conclude with Eishin-Ryū *chiburi* and *nōtō*, then return to your starting point.

*Ōyō* for Sōgiri is essentially the same as for Sōmakuri: an onslaught by multiple attackers from the front. As with Sōmakuri, Sōgiri should be performed with the attitude that there could be an endless number of attackers whom you could continue defeating indefinitely with this sequence of cuts.

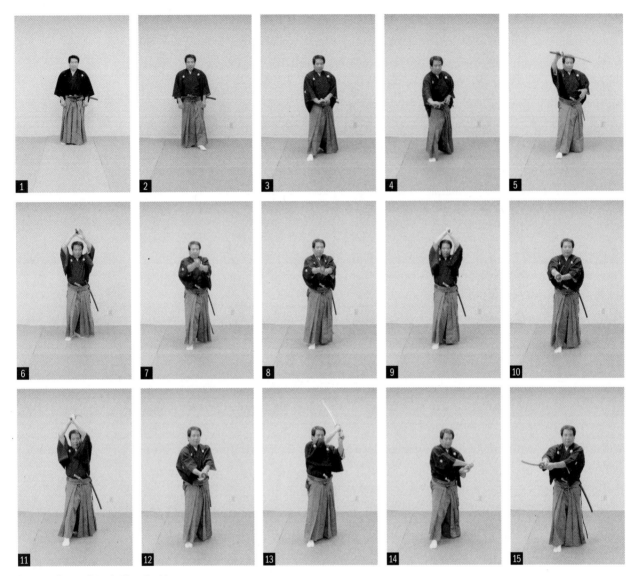

Figures 190.1–15. Seitei Iai Kata: Sōgiri

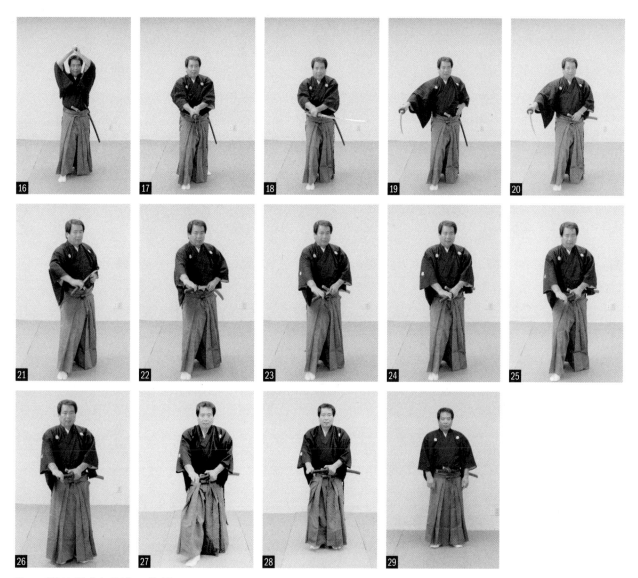

Figures 190.16–29. Seitei Iai Kata: Sōgiri

# 19P: SŌGIRI (SIDE VIEW)

Many aspects of Sōgiri can be best observed in the side view:

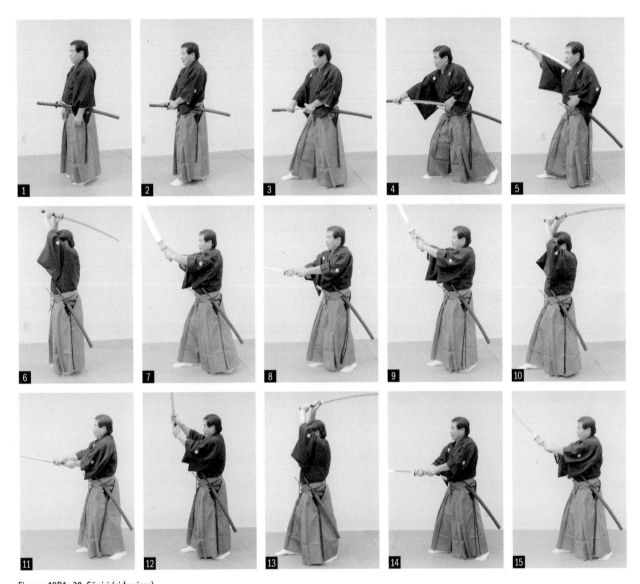

Figures 19P.1–20. Sōgiri (side view)

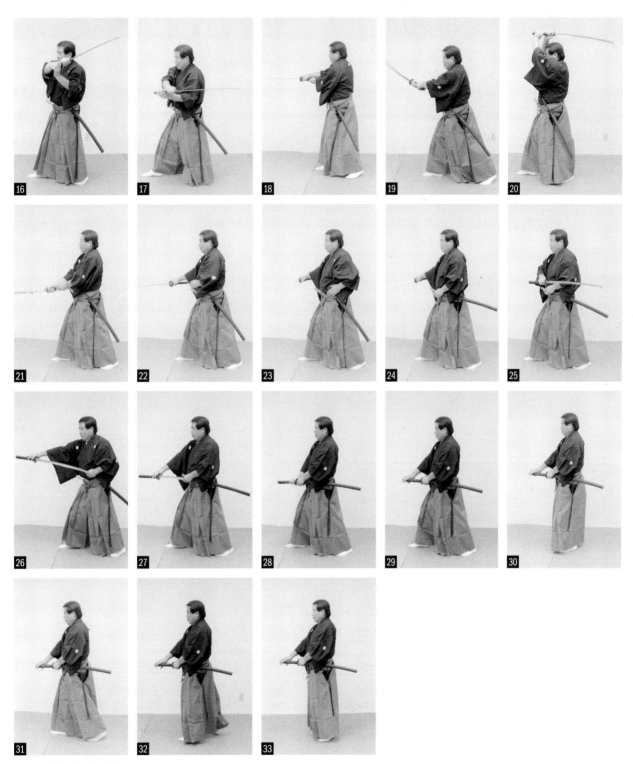

Figures 19P.21–33. Sōgiri (side view)

# 19Q: NUKIUCHI

Nukiuchi (Sudden Attack) is a *tachikata* version of the Musō Jikiden Eishin-Ryū *waza* of the same name.

Holding the third breath of *kiyomeri kokyū,* step backward with the left foot and perform *koiguchi no kirikata* while completing *nukitsuke* vertically as an *ukenagashi* deflection, directly into *furikaburi* (figs. 19Q.2–7) as a single evasive action that also draws the right foot rearward, then lunge, right foot forward, with *kirioroshi,* as shown in figures 19Q.8 and 19Q.9. Step back with the right foot during Eishin-Ryū *chiburi,* then complete the *kata* with *nōtō* and return to the starting point.

The *ōyō* for this *tachikata* version of Nukiuchi appears different from the shoden version, but it remains a *jōiuchi* (orders from above) situation, in which you are either attempting to arrest or ordered to execute an enemy. In either event, the opponent realizes the purpose for which you have been sent and launches a preemptive attack with *kirioroshi* as you begin *nukitsuke.* You evade his cut by drawing back out of reach during *nukitsuke* and *furikaburi,* then complete your mission with *kirioroshi* before the opponent can recover from his missed cut.

Figures 19Q.1–17. Seitei Iai Kata: Nukiuchi

# 19R: NUKIUCHI (SIDE VIEW)

The footwork and sword angles for *nukitsuke, furikaburi,* and *kirioroshi* can be more clearly seen in the side view of the key movements of Nukiuchi.

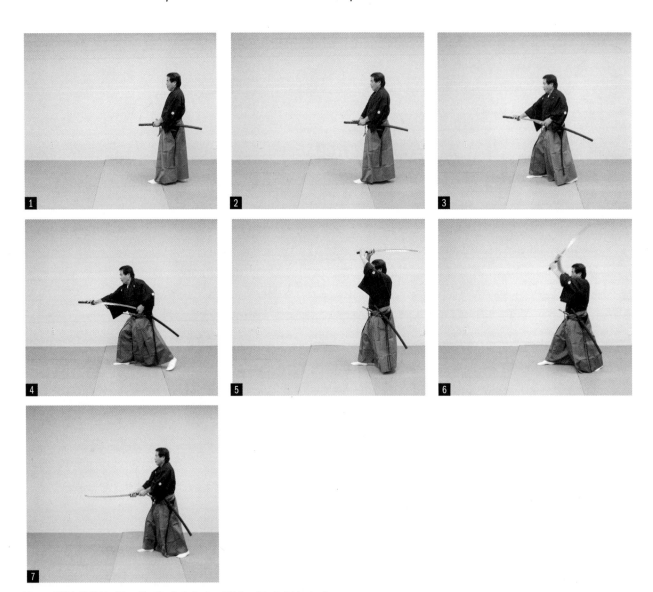

Figures 19R.1–7. Nukiuchi: *nukitsuke, furikaburi,* and *kirioroshi* only (side view)

Chapter 20

# Tameshigiri (Shizan)

## Test Cutting

*Iaijutsu* training has three major components: *waza* (techniques), *kumitachi* (choreographed combat exercises), and *tameshigiri* (test cutting). Together these three elements provide a balanced training program for the physical skills of *iaijutsu* in much the same way that *kata* (forms), *kumite* (sparring), and *tameshiwari* (breaking) promote well-rounded training in *karate-dō*.

The *waza* practice in *iaijutsu* develops the knowledge of appropriate techniques for the various types of attacks a samurai might encounter. It also trains the practitioner to block and cut with correct *kamae* (posture and stance), balance, mental focus, and technique.

However, *waza* practice must be augmented with *kumitachi* (partner exercises), such as the Tachiuchi no Kurai and Tsumeai no Kurai, in order for the student to develop proper timing, distance, and footwork in their practical application. Awareness of, and sensitivity to, an opponent's intentions is another key aspect of *iaijutsu* that can only be developed by training consistently with partners who act and react in a realistic manner.

The third training component, Tameshigiri, is essentially a means of determining if the student can apply the lessons learned in *waza* and *kumitachi* practice to the use of a live sword (*shinken*). In order to cut the target material, you must apply correct swinging technique, together with proper cutting distance (*kirima*) and blade alignment (*hasuji*). If these elements are combined correctly, a clean test cut is the result. If any one or more is faulty, the areas requiring further training are immediately revealed.

The term *tameshigiri* means "test cutting," and it is occasionally misinterpreted as testing the sword's ability to cut. Any sharpened sword of moderate quality will cut. *Tameshigiri* is not a test of the sword, but of the *iaidōka*'s proficiency in the fundamentals (*kihon*), which is why is it a component of training that must not be ignored.

The *kanji* (characters) that form the word *tameshigiri* can also be pronounced as "*shizan*," and for many *iaidōka*, *shizan* is the preferable pronunciation. Another frequently used term is *suemono-giri* (stationary object cutting), which reflects the facts that the targets are stationary and may be composed of a variety of materials (*goza*, bamboo, paper, and so on).

In the past, *tameshigiri* was depicted by some as a practice of such extreme difficulty that only masters should engage in it. While it certainly does require intense concentration and a degree of proficiency, it is by no means a mysterious or inordinately difficult achievement when included in a well-balanced training regimen.

A *shinken* (sharpened sword) is, after all, designed and crafted to cut! The curvature, tempering, and balance of the blade are the product of centuries of experimentation that produced swords capable of cutting almost effortlessly if swung correctly. Proper repeated practice of *waza*, the Happō Giri exercise (described in chapter 7), and *suburi* (practice swinging) will develop the correct cutting stroke, and consistent training in *kumitachi* will develop the necessary footwork, *kamae* (body structure, posture, and stance), balance, and *maai* (distance control) to successfully cut a stationary target.

Before explaining how to use a *shinken*, it is important to define what a *shinken* is. A *shinken* is something more than merely a sharpened sword. The word *shinken* literally means "true sword," yet in English we typically use the term "live sword." Both of these terms apply to a *shinken*.

Consider what makes a sword "true." To be true in the sense a carpenter or machinist would use that word means that it must be straight and pure—made of unadulterated materials. It must be authentic, meaning true to the design, construction, and functionality of the historical *katana* of the samurai, which in turn means it must also be sharp. In addition, it must be properly forged and tempered or it will not withstand the rigors of battle. But, beyond its internal qualities and outward appearances, it must also be wielded by someone who is equally true—someone whose character, purpose, and intentions in using that sword are as pure and true as the sword itself—a person who has, like the sword, been forged and tempered by training to withstand the rigors of battle. This is one of the meanings of the well-known Japanese axiom: *Kokoro tadashi karazareba, ken mata tadashi karazu*, which means "If your heart is not true (pure), your sword will also not be true."

Now consider what makes a sword "live." Its metal is certainly not live. Even holding it in your hands does not bring it to life. It is just a piece of metal with some fittings (*koshirae*) attached to it. It is not "live" until *you* put life into it, meaning that you must energize the sword with your *ki* (energy and spirit) by unifying yourself with it (see *ken-shin ichi nyo* in chapter 3) through the process of consistent and dedicated training that makes the sword an extension of your body, mind, and spirit. When your heart is true and you are one with your sword, then and only then are you wielding a *shinken*.

Since a *shinken* is a *true* sword, the first thing to do when you pick up your sword in preparation for *tameshigiri* is *tōrei*. We perform *tōrei* to our *iaitō* and *bokken*, which are only representations of a *shinken*, so we must assuredly perform *tōrei* to our *shinken*.

Next: **check the *mekugi!***

As important as it is to check the *mekugi*, the bamboo peg that holds the *tsuka* (handle) on the *nakago* (tang), on an *iaito*, it is even more important to check the *mekugi* on a *shinken* before **every** use. If the *mekugi* shows signs of wear or cracking, do not use the sword before replacing it.

The major elements on which to focus for a proper cutting stroke are *te no uchi* (grip and use of the hands), *hasuji o tōsu* (alignment of the cutting edge with the path of the blade), and *enshin ryoku* (centripetal force). The key components that produce balance and *maai* are a stable stance and posture (*kamae*), use of the legs and hips, a large circular cutting path, and making contact with the *monouchi*.

The *monouchi*, you may recall, is the portion of the blade, roughly ten inches in length, that begins four to five inches from the kissaki, as shown in figure 20A.1. This is the section of the blade with the optimal balance of reach, tensile strength, and curvature needed to produce a cut. The *monouchi* is close enough to the *kissaki* to have the power of *enshin ryoku*, and since it is forward of the center of the blade, its curvature produces the natural slicing action for which the *katana* was designed—neither too close to the *kissaki*, where the narrower blade might break on impact, nor too close to the *tsuka*, where it would lack *enshin ryoku* and would chop rather than slice.

Figure 20A.1. *Monouchi*

Correct technique is more important than muscle strength. If you have developed solid *kihon* (fundamentals), you should have little difficulty cutting when the time comes. In fact, women and children can often perform *tameshigiri* earlier in their training than men, because rather than relying on physical strength, they tend to simply let the sword do what it was designed to do. Just before attempting *tameshigiri*, it may prove helpful to silently remind yourself:

The **sword** cuts; not you!

A large circular cutting motion, as described in detail in chapter 7, is the key to *tameshigiri*. Once you are consistently making this kind of swing during *kirioroshi* (downward cut) and *kesagiri* (diagonal cut), successful *tameshigiri* is merely a matter of applying that proper swing to the target. The illustrations that follow diagram the relative positions and angles of the blade and target for *tameshigiri*, and show the most basic cutting technique used: *kesagiri*, the downward diagonal cut that follows the line of a monk's *kesa* (single-sleeved robe).

Generally, *kesagiri* should be made along the line shown in figure 20A.2.

Figure 20A.2. *Kesagiri* (diagonal cut)

The correct path of the sword through the target is shown from a top-down view in figures 20A.3–5. As these diagrams illustrate, a natural swing of the blade in which the arms reach full extension prior to the *monouchi* making contact with the target, combined with the curvature of the blade, will cause the blade to automatically slice from back to front as the blade passes through the material.

Figures 20A.3–5. Correct cutting path of the sword

Conversely, if the sword attempts to move laterally or front to back as it passes through the target, it will wedge into the material, and the cut will be incomplete. This is most often caused by a "baseball swing" in which the arms and wrists are still bent at the moment of impact and the hands are leading the sword, producing a striking or clubbing action rather than a slice. The relative positions of the sword and target under these circumstances is shown in figure 20A.6.

Figure 20A.6. Incorrect (chopping) path of the sword

Figures 20A.7–8 further illustrate the correct alignment of the hands, body, sword, and target for successful *tameshigiri*. Note that in figure 20A.7, the hands and *tsuka* are still slightly behind (to the left in the photo) the *monouchi* as it makes contact with the target, and the arms and wrists are fully extended prior to impact. This will produce a slicing motion as the blade passes through the *goza*. Conversely, in figure 20A.8, the hands and *tsuka* are ahead of the *monouchi*, already past the center of the target, and neither the elbows nor wrists are fully extended at the moment of impact. This will produce a chopping action that wedges the blade in the *goza*.

In addition to fully extending the arms and wrists just prior to impact and properly aligning the hands, *tsuka*, and body to ensure a slicing motion, the other key factor involved in *tameshigiri* is ensuring that the blade itself is aligned with the direction in which it is moving *(hasuji o tōsu)*. As shown in figure 20A.9, if the angle of the sword precisely matches the angle at which it is swinging toward the target, a perfectly straight cut will be the result.

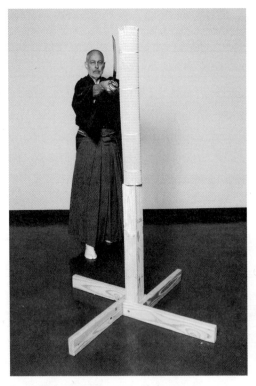 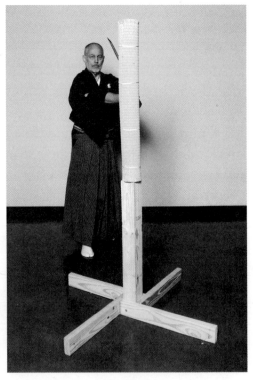

Figure 20A.7. Correct alignment with the target    Figure 20A.8. Incorrect alignment with the target

However, if the angle of the blade, as represented in the cross-sections below, is either shallower or steeper than the angle at which the blade is traveling (as represented by the dashed lines), then a concave or convex cut will occur, as shown in figures 20A.10–11.

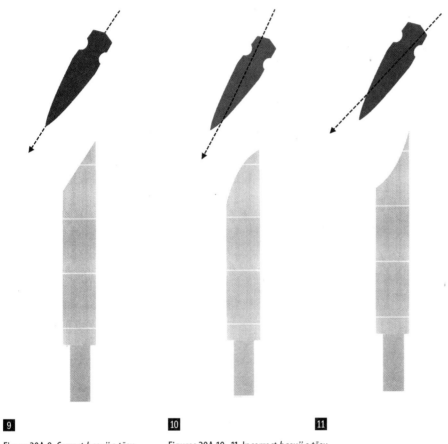

**9**

Figure 20A.9. Correct *hasuji o tōsu*

**10**　　　　**11**

Figures 20A.10–11. Incorrect *hasuji o tōsu*

To assist in *hasuji o tōsu* (maintaining blade alignment), align the sword with the intended path of the cut during *furikaburi*. For *kirioroshi*, this means holding the sword with the *hasaki* (edge) vertical during *kirioroshi* as depicted in figures 20A.12a (front view) and 20A.12b (rear view). When the sword is swung straight down in *kirioroshi*, the *hasaki* will be perfectly aligned with the direction of travel for a straight cut.

Figure 20A.12. *Hasuji* (alignment) for *kirioroshi* (front and rear views)

For *kesagiri* (right-to-left downward diagonal cut), turn the *tsuka* about 45 degrees clockwise to the "1:30" position overhead while in *furikaburi*, as shown in figures 20A.13a–b. This will align the *hasaki* with the line of the *kesagiri* for a straight cut. A common mistake is to swing the *kissaki* to the left side of the body in the mistaken belief that this aligns the sword with the *kesagiri* path. Instead, it causes the blade to move laterally during the cutting motion and usually results in a concave or failed cut. Instead, the *kissaki* should point straight behind you, just as in the position for *kirioroshi*.

Figure 20A.13. *Hasuji* (alignment) for *kesagiri* (front and rear views)

For *gyaku-kesagiri* (left-to-right downward diagonal cut), turn the *tsuka* about 45 degrees counterclockwise to the "10:30" position overhead while in *furikaburi*, as shown in figures 20A.14a–b. This will align the *hasaki* with the line of the *gyaku-kesagiri* for a straight cut. As with *kesagiri*, the *kissaki* should point directly behind you, in the position it would be for *kirioroshi*.

Figure 20A.14. *Hasuji* (alignment) for *gyaku-kesagiri* (front and rear views)

A common error that results from either trying to exert too much muscle power or overrotating the hips during *tameshigiri* is turning or tilting the upper body. The *seichūsen* (center line) of the body should remain aligned with the *seichūsen* of the target throughout the cutting motion, as depicted in figure 20A.15 (*furikaburi*) and figure 20A.16 (*kesagiri*).

Figures 20A.15–16. Proper alignment of the body during *kesagiri*

Particularly when performing an angular cut like *kesagiri*, there is a tendency to turn the hips or body in the direction of the cut, which then causes the blade to move laterally as it passes through the target material, forming a curved, rather than straight, cut. Similarly, either overrotating the hips or leaning forward in an effort to generate more power will also cause the sword to move laterally and produce a curved or failed cut. Figures 20A.17–18 show how actions of this kind place the upper body out of position and result in a poor cut.

Figures 20A.17–18. Improper alignment of the body during *kesagiri*

The most common *suemono* (materials) used for *shizan* (*tameshigiri*) are *goza* (straw mats) and bamboo. *Goza* is a common term used for *tatami-omote* (*tatami* covers) made of rice straw. To be used for *tameshigiri*, *goza* must be rolled tightly, secured with twine or strong elastic bands, then immersed in water and soaked for a minimum of twelve hours (overnight) and up to a full day. Once thoroughly saturated, rolled *tatami-omote* have the consistency of human tissue, making them a realistic material for *shizan*. For beginners we recommend rolling and preparing a single *goza* in this manner, which produces a target that is the rough equivalent of severing a human arm. Once you are adept at cutting single *goza*, then you can roll bundles of two or three *tatami-omote* together to create targets that approximate severing a thigh or torso.

Targets prepared in this manner are then affixed with a ¾-inch to 1-inch wooden dowel to a cutting stand like the one shown in figure 20A.2. Up to six cuts may then be safely made in a single roll of *goza*.

*Tatami-omote* are no longer inexpensive to acquire, so quite a few substitutes have become popular: bamboo stalks (fresh, not dried) between two and six inches in diameter; plastic water or soft-drink bottles filled with water; and a variety of fruits and vegetables, like watermelons, pumpkins, squash, apples, potatoes, and cucumbers. The possibilities are limited only to the imagination of those seeking an inexpensive target. However, many such targets provide little training value, and some may actually damage your sword.

The problem with firm or rinded fruit, for example, is that their rigidity makes them easy to cut, even with poor technique. The purpose of *shizan* is to test the efficacy of your technique, not simply to chop things up. If the target material is not soft enough to reveal errors in your technique, it has no training value and should not be used.

One worthwhile exception to this is newspaper. Miura Sōshihan gained considerable notoriety for his practice of cutting newspaper rolled into cylinders. The paper is lightweight and easily crushed, so it requires nearly perfect technique for a successful cut. It is also inexpensive, costing less than a penny per sheet, plus a little tape to secure it once it has been formed into a cylinder. It is an inexpensive way to practice *shizan*, but also a frustrating one, as it will require several hundred failed cuts to develop the skill to make a single successful one.

During an interview for a magazine article in the mid-1990s, Miura Sōshihan was asked what "trick" he used to make these seemingly impossible newspaper cuts—a special sword, a certain grip on the *tsuka*, or doing something to make paper easier to cut? His answer revealed the one and only secret to proficiency in *iaijutsu*: "The 'trick' is perfect technique."

Figure 20A.19. Miura Sōshihan newspaper cut with *nukitsuke*

As spectacular as it may seem to cut in half nine cylinders of newspaper that are balanced atop nine more cylinders of newspaper with a one-handed *yoko ichimonji nukitsuke*, without toppling the cylinders on which they rested, we want to caution the overzealous *iaidōka* against turning his or her skills into a circus sideshow for the sake of ego gratification or fame. Miura Sōshihan performed such feats for small groups of his own students in order to inspire them to seek higher levels of personal proficiency, not for fame or even to attract new students to his *dōjō*.

*Shizan* is not showmanship; it is training. It should not even be attempted until you have trained sufficiently to perform *kirioroshi* and *kesagiri* correctly and consistently, and even then it should be undertaken as a means of assessing the effectiveness of your technique.

A final word of caution is that *tameshigiri* involves swinging a live sword powerfully and with potentially lethal effect. We therefore strongly urge the reader never to attempt *tameshigiri* except under the supervision of a qualified instructor.

Chapter 21

# Eishin-Ryū no Yōten

## Summary of the Eishin-Ryū System

The preceding chapters have detailed the fifty-eight *waza* and fifty-two *kumitachi* of Musō Jikiden Eishin-Ryū Iaijutsu, together with the twelve Zen Nippon Kendō Renmei Seitei Iai Kata, totaling 122 training drills.

To help you picture the entire Eishin-Ryū system and better understand the progression from *shoden* to *chūden* to *okuden*, we have prepared a chart listing all of the techniques in each level.

When instructing students in Western countries, we normally teach the Seitei Kata and Tachiuchi no Kurai first. This allows them to learn a variety of techniques early in their training and immediately begin practicing distance and footwork with a partner. While Japanese students are already accustomed to the *seiza* posture, and can spend long periods training exclusively in the Shoden *waza*, most Westerners find that practicing the Seitei Kata first helps them gradually become comfortable sitting in *seiza* position and later progress to *tatehiza* with reduced discomfort. For those students desiring to enter tournament competition (see chapter 23), the Seitei Kata provide both variety of technique and relatively uniform recognition by tournament judges.

**Eishin-Ryū Iaijutsu Waza**

SHODEN ŌMORI-RYŪ SEIZA *WAZA* (SHODEN *WAZA* OR SEIZA *WAZA*)

1. Mae

2. Migi

3. Hidari

4. Ushiro

5. Yaegaki

    a. Omote

    b. Ura

6. Ukenagashi

7. Kaishaku

8. Tsukekomi

9. Tsukikage

10. Oikaze

11. Nukiuchi

CHŪDEN TATEHIZA *WAZA* (TATEHIZA *WAZA*)

1. Yokogumo

2. Tora no Issoku

3. Inazuma

4. Ukigumo

5. Yamaoroshi

6. Iwanami

7. Urokogaeshi

8. Namigaeshi

9. Takiotoshi

10. Makkō

OKUDEN TACHIWAZA

1. Yukizure

2. Tsuredachi

3. Sōmakuri

**Eishin-Ryū Iaijutsu Waza** *(continued)*

4. Sōdome

5. Shinobu

6. Yukichigai

7. Sode Surigaeshi

8. Moniri

9. Kabezoe

10. Ukenagashi

OKUDEN ITOMAGOI *WAZA*

1. Itomagoi Ichi

2. Itomagoi Ni

3. Itomagoi San

OKUDEN SUWARIWAZA

1. Kasumi

2. Sunegakoi

3. Shihōgiri

4. Tozume

5. Towaki

6. Tanashita

7. Ryōzume

8. Torabashiri

EISHIN-RYŪ BATTŌ-HŌ

1. Juntō Sono Ichi

2. Juntō Sono Ni

3. Tsuigekitō

4. Shatō

5. Shihōtō Sono Ichi

6. Shihōtō Sono Ni

7. Zantotsutō

8. Zenteki Gyakutō Sono Ichi

**Eishin-Ryū Iaijutsu Waza** *(continued)*

9. Zenteki Gyakutō Sono Ni

10. Tatekitō

11. Koteki Gyakutō

12. Koteki Nukiuchi

BANGAI NO BU

1. Hayanami

2. Raiden

3. Jinrai

4. Akuma Barai

TACHIUCHI NO KURAI

1. Deai

2. Tsukekomi

3. Ukenagashi

4. Ukekomi

5. Tsukikage

6. Suigetsutō

7. Zetsumyōken

8. Dokumyōken

9. Shinmyōken

10. Uchikomi

TACHIUCHI NO KATA

1. Deai

2. Kobushi Dori

3. Zetsumyōken

4. Dokumyōken

5. Tsuba Dome

6. Ukenagashi

7. Mappō

TSUMEAI NO KURAI

**Eishin-Ryū Iaijutsu Waza** *(continued)*

1. Hassō

2. Kobushi Dori

3. Namigaeshi

4. Yaegaki

5. Uroko Gaeshi

6. Kurai Yurumi

7. Tsubame Gaeshi

8. Ganseki Otoshi

9. Suigetsutō

10. Kasumi Ken

DAISHŌ ZUME

1. Dakizume

2. Koppō

3. Tsuka Dome

4. Kote Dome

5. Mune Tori

6. Migi Fuse

7. Hidari Fuse

8. Yamagata Zume

DAISHŌ TACHIZUME

1. Shimetori

2. Sode Surigaeshi

3. Tsuba Uchikaeshi

4. Koppō Gaeshi

5. Tombo Gaeshi

6. Rankyoku

7. Utsuri

DAIKEN DORI

1. Muken

**Eishin-Ryū Iaijutsu Waza**   *(continued)*

2. Suiseki

3. Gaiseki

4. Tesseki

5. Eigan

6. Eigetsu

7. Yama Kaze

8. Sorihashi

9. Raiden

10. Suigetsu

## EISHIN-RYŪ SEITEI IAI KATA* (SEITEI KATA)

*Note: A final reminder that, in the truest sense, the Seitei Kata are not technically part of the Eishin-Ryū system, but are included here because they are were developed under the direction of the progenitor of Masaoka-Ha, Masaoka Katsutane, are widely practiced throughout the world, recognized in most competitive and demonstration settings, and are often taught in Eishin-Ryū *dōjō*.

1. Seiza Mae

2. Seiza Ushiro

3. Ukenagashi

4. Tsuka-ate

5. Kesagiri

6. Morotezuki

7. Sanpōgiri

8. Ganmen-ate

9. Soetezuki

10. Shihōgiri

11. Sōgiri

12. Nukiuchi

# SUGGESTED TRAINING SEQUENCE

To best foster a student's progress in Eishin-Ryū, we recommend training in the following general sequence:

SHODEN (BEGINNING) LEVEL: Ōmori-Ryū Seiza *waza* (12 *waza*), Eishin-Ryū Battō-Hō (7 Shoden *waza*), and Tachiuchi no Kurai (10 *katachi*). As an option, students may wish to include the Seitei Iai Kata (12 *kata*) at the *shoden* level as well.

CHŪDEN (INTERMEDIATE) LEVEL: Chūden *waza* (10 *waza*), Eishin-Ryū Battō-Hō (5 Okuden *waza*), and Tsumeai no Kurai (10 *katachi*). After gaining proficiency in the Tsumeai no Kurai, *chūden* level students may also wish to include the Tachiuchi no Kata (7 *kata*).

OKUDEN (DEEP) LEVEL: Okuden Tachiwaza (10 *waza*), Itomagoi *waza* (3 *waza*), Okuden Suwariwaza (8 *waza*), Bangai no Bu (3 *waza*), Tachiuchi no Kata (7 *kata*) if not done at the *chūden* level, Daishō Zume (8 *katachi*), Daishō Tachizume (7 *katachi*), and Daiken Dori (10 *katachi*).

The Shoden Level curriculum outlined above should be the focus of training up to the rank of *shodan* (first *dan*), equivalent to black belt. The Chūden Level curriculum should be the focus from *nidan* (second *dan*) to *godan* (fifth *dan*). And the Okuden Level curriculum should be the focus from *godan* and above. Naturally, the specific requirements for those rankings and the particular order in which the various components of the curriculum are taught to a given student are up to that student's instructor to determine.

Chapter 22 審
査

# *Shinsa ni Tsuite*

## Promotion Guidelines

Masaoka-Ha Musō Jikiden Eishin-Ryū Iaijutsu awards *kyū* and *dan* ranking in a similar manner to most popular forms of *budō*. A key difference is that in *iaijutsu* these ranks are not designated by colored belts, as is common in *karate-dō* or *jūdō*.

In addition to the *dan* (equivalent to black belt) and *kyū* (below black belt) rankings, Masaoka-Ha Eishin-Ryū also recognizes, and where appropriate awards, five highly coveted *shōgō* (honorary titles): Dōshi, Renshi, Kyōshi, Tasshi, and Hanshi. The exact meaning of these titles is difficult to adequately translate into English. Literally, they translate roughly as: "Mentoring Warrior," "Training Warrior," "Warrior Instructor," "Master Warrior," and "Exemplary Warrior," respectively. However, to convey the nuance of these titles, the terms Master (Dōshi), Senior Master (Renshi), Advanced Master (Kyōshi), Consummate Master (Tasshi), and Grandmaster (Hanshi) convey the relative degree of status and respect accorded to those to whom they have been bestowed. These titles are typically awarded by the governing organization of the style, such as the Kokusai Nippon Budō Kai or the Dai Nippon Butoku-Kai, in recognition of outstanding martial arts achievement and service to that organization or the art of *iaijutsu*.

The unofficial titles of *sensei* (teacher) and *shihan* (master) are generally used as a matter of respect and are not specifically bestowed by an organization. Instead, those *yūdansha* (black belts) who give instruction on a regular basis are typically referred to as *sensei*, and *yūdansha* who are high ranking, have been teaching for a long time, or are deserving of special recognition are referred to as *shihan*. In a smaller *dōjō* with only one instructor, he or she would usually be called *sensei*, unless they are particularly high ranking or widely regarded. In a larger *dōjō*, several instructors might be *sensei*, while the chief instructor would probably be called *shihan*.

Each governing organization, such as the Kokusai Nippon Budō Kai, has specific requirements to be met for each successive promotion. In addition to specified elements to be performed (*waza* and *katachi*), there may be certain aspects of historical, technical, and philosophical knowledge (*gakka*) that must be demonstrated, as well as the instructor's ongoing evaluation of the student's respect and spirit during training.

Since these requirements vary according to the governing organization, they are not detailed here. However, when observing the student's performance of *waza* and *katachi*, promotion examiners typically evaluate the student's *kihon* (fundamentals) by the following criteria:

1. Nukitsuke

   *Koiguchi no kirikata, nukidashi* (draw), *saya-biki* (pulling the *saya* back), *saya-banari* (releasing the *kissaki* from the *saya*), footwork precision, angle of the blade, posture, and spirit.

2. Furikaburi

   Level movement of the blade, position of the *tsuba*, exposure of the arm, and coordination of the hands with the sword.

3. Kirioroshi

   *Hasuji o tōsu* (straightness of the cut), height of the *kissaki* at finish, footwork, *tsuba* position, *tsuka no nigiri kata, enshin ryoku*, and spirit.

4. Chiburi

   Position of the sword hand, angle of blade, timing of *chiburi* to footwork, and *iaigoshi*.

5. Nōtō

   Hand position at *koiguchi*, speed and timing, coordination of *nōtō* with footwork, and *zanshin*.

The examiners will usually also make general assessment of the student's *jitsugi*, his overall presentation and demeanor, looking for the following key elements:

1. *Kibikibi to shita dosa*: sharp, precise, spirited movement.

2. *Reigi to shisei*: sincerity of respect showing from within.

3. *Katana no atsukai kata*: method of handling the sword, showing familiarity, respect, and technical correctness.

Prior to advancement to their first *kyū* rank, students are generally referred to as *shoshinsha* (beginners). The first promotion is usually to a rank between *kyūkyū* (ninth *kyū*) and *rokkyū* (sixth *kyū*). After promotion to *shodan* (first *dan*), practitioners must show increasing knowledge of the Eishin-Ryū system and continuing refinement of technique. With higher ranks, examiners increasingly look for evidence of the Dai-Kyō- Soku-Kei progression (see chapter 5) and exhibition of "personality" in the techniques performed during testing. They also place increasing emphasis on genuine, sincere respect and *heijōshin* being evident in a practitioner's performance as he rises in *dan* rank. Another key factor examiners look for in *yūdansha* is *fūkaku* (depth or strength) in such areas as *chakugan, kokyū, maai, kihaku,* and *zanshin.* Each of these elements most show the advanced student's deeper insight and application.

As a student progresses through stages of Shu ▪ Ha ▪ Ri, his technique passes through equivalent stages called Jutsu-Waza-Ryaku, and the promotion examiners will be watching for these progressive levels of expertise.

*Jutsu* is the most basic level of technique. The term *jutsu* refers to "technique" in almost a mechanical sense. It is purely the method of performance, devoid of personality and predominantly physical in nature.

*Waza* is a higher level of technical expertise, more akin to "skill." At the Ha stage of development, the practitioner should now be exhibiting a degree of finesse in his performance. His techniques should be a blend of both the physical and mental aspects of the art.

*Ryaku* is the highest level of technique. Here, the refinement of physical ability, mental prowess, and the infusion of the personality of a master at the Ri stage of development elevates every technique performed to the level of "art." *Ryaku* can be literally translated as "abridgement," an apt term for a stage at which all of the principles of the art are synopsized into each individual technique performed by a master of this caliber.

In addition to the improved skills and attitude needed for promotion after *shodan,* most governing bodies prescribe minimum age and training time requirements for each subsequent advancement. Training times that are fairly typical in *iaijutsu* are shown in the table below.

### *Dan* Promotion Timing Guidelines

| RANK SOUGHT | MINIMUM TRAINING TIME | AGE | CUMULATIVE |
|---|---|---|---|
| *shodan* (1st *dan*) | 6 months at *shodan-ho* | 13 | 1½ years |
| *nidan* (2nd *dan*) | 1 year at *shodan* | 16 | 2½ years |
| *sandan* (3rd *dan*) | 2 years at *nidan* | 18 | 4½ years |
| *yondan* (4th *dan*) | 3 years at *sandan* | 18 | 7½ years |
| *godan* (5th *dan*) | 4 years at *yondan* | 18 | 11½ years |
| *rokudan* (6th *dan*) | 5 years at *godan* | 18 | 16½ years |

It may seem odd that the minimum age for *yondan, godan,* and *rokudan* remains eighteen, rather than rising to twenty-one, twenty-five, and thirty, respectively. However, there are cases in which a young student has reached *shodan-ho* at the age of eight or nine and subsequently risen no higher than *nidan* due to his or her age. Upon reaching adulthood, such a student would be promoted to the rank, hypothetically as high as *godan,* warranted by his or her skill, knowledge, and years of training.

Similar minimum age and training times normally apply to the titles which may be bestowed upon deserving *kōdansha:*

| TITLE | MINIMUM TRAINING TIME | MINIMUM AGE |
|---|---|---|
| Renshi | 3 years after *godan* | 24 |
| Kyōshi | 7 years after Renshi | 31 |
| Hanshi | 20 years after Kyōshi | 55 |

While it is beneficial to students to have a means of measuring their progress and to feel a sense of accomplishment at their promotion to higher ranks, we should point out that there is also a danger inherent in the ranking system.

Occasionally, students become overly focused on advancing from rank to rank. Worse yet, some become fixated on outranking students they perceive as rivals in their quest for higher rank. For these students, rank becomes the objective of their training rather than perfection of their character and improvement of their skills. In most cases, this selfish ambition becomes apparent and is taken into account when considering students for promotion and can delay their promotion to higher ranks, so obsession with rank can actually work against itself.

While high rank does carry with it a certain degree of status, it is critically important to understand and accept the ranking system for what it is: a tool, a simple means to measure your progress toward your goal. It is probably beneficial to most *iaidōka* that there are no outward indications of rank in *iaijutsu*—no colored belts or insignia that display your rank to others. Thus, in the *dōjō,* all students generally treat each other as equals, or more correctly they treat all others as *sempai* (seniors), with appropriate respect and decorum.

Having said all that, we certainly do not want to minimize the importance of rank nor discourage anyone from seeking advancement. However, the knowledge, skill, and improved lifestyle should be the goals of your training, not merely your rank. Rank is best viewed simply as one barometer of the progress you are making toward your real goal of a victorious life.

Chapter 23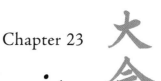

# *Taikai ni Tsuite*

## Tournament Participation

One of the first activities organized by the Dai Nippon Yaegaki-Kai after World War II was an *iaidō* tournament. Not long after establishing their Seitei Iaidō curriculum, the Zen Nippon Kendō Renmei (ZNKR) also began holding *iaidō* tournaments and holding *iaidō* competitions and demonstrations at *kendō* tournaments. But, until late in the twentieth century, there were few tournaments outside Japan featuring *iaidō*. As *iaidō* has steadily increased in popularity outside Japan, *iaidō* tournaments have become increasingly common. In addition, *iaidō* is becoming an increasingly common category in *kobudō* events and other martial arts tournaments.

To help ensure uniform standards of judging, the Amateur Athletic Union of the United States (AAU) established judging criteria for use in those AAU karate tournaments in which *iaidō* is now a sanctioned event. The AAU requested Shimabukuro Hanshi to establish these criteria, which soon became the basis for many, if not most, *iaidō* tournament rules. However, in the years following Hanshi's death, AAU competition in *iaidō*, other than in a few specific locations like Southern California, has been dwindling. Since the specific rules and judging criteria are subject to change, the current tournament rules should be obtained from the AAU website or from the printed rules provided at local tournaments.

Tournament competition offers a number of potential training benefits to the *iaidōka*. Four hundred years ago, a samurai's motivation to train diligently and intently was quite clear: there might be a battle tomorrow in which his life would be at stake. We no longer benefit from such a powerful incentive to train, but an upcoming tournament offers an incentive with several parallels to a battle.

Likewise, life-or-death combat demonstrated with finality whether a samurai was able to apply the lessons learned in the *dōjō* while under intense pressure. Without risking life or serious injury, tournaments now give *iaidōka* the opportunity to test

501

their skills, and their *heijōshin*, under the pressures of competition, providing some realistic and helpful feedback on their training progress.

For these reasons, we encourage students of *iaijutsu* to occasionally participate in the *iaidō* competitions that are well supervised and judged. Tournaments can afford *iaidōka* a variety of venues in which to compete: individual *waza* (or "*kata*"), team synchronized *waza*, *katachi*, and *tameshigiri*. Each of these provides valuable training opportunities. For example, individual *waza* events offer the challenge of perfecting two or three *waza* for presentation under intense, nerve-wracking conditions. Team synchronized *waza* add the factor of coordinating movements with those of teammates, which is an excellent way of practicing *zanshin* under tense and distracting circumstances. Likewise, performing *katachi* or *tameshigiri* under the scrutiny of judges and spectators provides an excellent environment for learning to maintain *heijōshin*.

While it is not appropriate to list detailed rules of competition here, there are some basic criteria for performance that apply in nearly all competitive situations.

Competitors should be required to either perform the Seitei Kata (another reason to learn them), or to be a student of a style of Japanese swordsmanship—whether it is called *iaidō*, *iaijutsu*, *iai heihō*, *battō-hō*, *battō jutsu*, or *kenjutsu*—that is recognized as authentic by a legitimate governing body in Japan, such as the Dai Nippon Butoku Kai. In representing such a style, competitors should be required to perform only techniques that are part of the curriculum of that style. Competitors should also be required to wear the uniform prescribed by the style they are representing, which would typically be a *hakama* and *keikogi* (top) or *montsuki* (jacket bearing a Japanese family crest), either with or without *tabi* (split-toed socks). These requirements eliminate flamboyant clothing and nonstandard techniques that might impair impartial judging of the competitors' performances.

Prior to commencement of any competition all equipment—*iaitō*, *bokken*, *shinken*, etc.—should receive a safety inspection by one or more judges qualified to assess its condition. This inspection ensures that *tsuka* are secure, *mekugi* are sound, blades lack any cracks, chips, or deformations that could lead to breakage in use, and *saya* are in sound condition. All equipment used in competition should be required to be traditional, meaning that *iaitō* and *shinken* have only traditional *koshirae* (fittings), and *bokken* be of sturdy, unpainted hardwood (preferably oak or maple) of standard length for the competitor (*daitō* for adults and *chūtō* for children). For safety, *shinken* (sharpened swords) should not be allowed for use other than *tameshigiri* without the specific permission of the judges or tournament director.

The demeanor and conduct of competitors should at all times be appropriate for a samurai, and any breach of etiquette or respect for judges, staff, or fellow competitors should result in an appropriate penalty, if minor, or immediate disqualification, if major.

## TYPES OF COMPETITIVE EVENTS

Events in an *iaidō* tournament will generally fall into the categories of *waza* (or *kata*), team synchronized *waza* or *kata*, choreographed *kumitachi* (Tachiuchi no Kurai, etc.), and *tameshigiri*.

Since the *waza* in most traditional styles of *iaidō* are brief, a *waza* (*kata*) competition will typically consist of performing three or five *waza* (*kata*) in succession, along with all appropriate *reihō* before and after, in order to afford the judges ample opportunities to evaluate the performances of the competitors. Another method is to allot each competitor a specific time limit of one to two minutes in which to complete a series of *waza* (*kata*) of the competitor's choosing. Either way, the objective is to maintain the pace of the tournament while providing the judges an adequate sampling from which to assess the performances.

In team synchronized *waza* (called *dantai embu*), teams customarily comprising three competitors perform a predetermined number of *waza* or *kata* (usually between three and five) and are judged on their ability to perform them correctly and in synchronization with each other without using any type of signaling.

*Kumitachi* competition is a form of team competition in which two competitors perform between one and three traditional *kumitachi*, such as the Tachiuchi no Kurai or Tsumeai no Kurai. They are judged on their correct performance of the *katachi* (pattern), timing, *maai* (distance control), *kamae*, dignity, and *bushi damashii* (samurai spirit).

*Tameshigiri* can include both individual and team events. Judging criteria include the attitude and demeanor of the competitors, attention to safety factors, straightness of cuts, and number and difficulty of the cuts performed. A separate event for cutting with *wakizashi* can be included, as can *dōdan*, cutting multiple targets (usually *goza*) either stacked vertically or bundled horizontally, with the winner being the one who cuts the largest number of targets.

In each of these events, scoring can either be by a point system in which the competitor accumulating the highest score wins the event, or by single elimination, in which two competitors or teams perform simultaneously head-to-head at each stage of the competition, and the winner determined by direct comparison.

The single elimination format mimics ancient combat, since only one competitor "survives" each encounter to face another opponent. This format is strongly recommended for *yūdansha* (the equivalent of black belts) since it simulates an ancient *musha shugyō* (training journey) in which a samurai traveled the land testing his skills directly against worthy opponents in single combat that often resulted in the death of one. A *musha shugyō* of that kind is no longer practical, so a single elimination tournament is the closest approximation available in the modern world.

Single elimination scoring is also easier for the judges and it probably results in a more equitable outcome. When trying to assign numeric scores to performances, it is difficult to compare a competitor who performed early in the competition to one performing much later. A mediocre performance early in a match might garner a much higher score than the same performance would receive later after judges have viewed several better ones. Conversely, when two competitors perform side by side, the better of the two performances is usually evident, so the single elimination format usually results in the two best competitors meeting in the deciding match.

## GENERAL PRINCIPLES OF JUDGING

It is recommended that each event in a tournament be supervised and decided by a panel of either three or five judges to prevent ties in the scoring. In head-to-head competitions, each competitor or team member should be affixed with a red (*ko*) or white (*haku*) ribbon for ease of identification. At the conclusion of their performance, each judge raises either a red or white flag to indicate the competitor whose performance they considered superior. The competitor signaled in this manner by the majority of the judges wins that match and continues to the next round. A draw or dual disqualification is indicated by crossing the two flags.

1. Individual *waza* (*kata*) should generally be judged by:

    a. Sincerity and correctness of *reigi* (etiquette).

    b. The spirit, demeanor, and personality of the participant during performance.

    c. Technical merits, especially precision of technique, focus, posture, eye contact, breathing, and straight travel of the sword.

    d. Correct performance of the *waza* or *kata* selected or assigned.

2. Synchronized *waza* should be judged by:

    a. Synchronization of movement with other team members.

    b. The judging elements of individual *waza* listed above.

   **3.** *Kumitachi* should be judged by:

     **a.** Spirit of attack and defense

     **b.** Focus and intensity

     **c.** Maintaining proper attack and defense distance with opponent

     **d.** Unity of timing with opponent

     **e.** Precision of technique

     **f.** Coordination of attack and defense with "opponent" (partner)

   **4.** *Tameshigiri* will generally be judged by:

     **a.** The straightness of each cut (deducting for degree of convexity or concavity of each cut)

     **b.** The difficulty of the cut (type and thickness of material, direction of cut, etc.)

     **c.** The angle of each cut (45 degrees for kesagiri, kiriage, and *gyaku-kesagiri*; level for *yoko ichimonji* or *suihei-giri*)

     **d.** Completeness of each cut (not leaving a "skin" or portion still connected)

     **e.** "Cleanness" of each cut (not causing the stand to wobble or topple)

For safety, the *tameshigiri* rules should require that cuts from the competitor's right to left should be made with the right foot forward, and cuts from the competitor's left to right be made with the left foot forward, to reduce the possibility of competitors cutting their own leg with a missed or deflected attempt.

A *tameshigiri* competitor should be immediately disqualified for missing the target entirely, allowing the sword to strike the floor on follow-through, striking the peg holding the target on its stand, losing control of or dropping the sword, making a cut that is less than 75 percent complete, toppling the stand, bending the sword to the extent that it cannot be sheathed, or performing any other action that injures or endangers himself or others present.

# CLASSIFICATION OF COMPETITORS

An important aspect of tournament management is classification of competitors to provide them with fair competition. At a minimum there should be at least three major divisions by experience and ability level for each event: *yūkyūsha* (below black belt), *shodan* through *sandan,* and *yondan* and above. This provides competitors with an opportunity to compete only against those of similar experience and ability. If there are a sufficient number of *yūkyūsha* competitors, they should be further divided into at least two more groups: those with less than a year of training and those with a year or more of training. If there are a sufficient number of competitors, it is also desirable to categorize them by age to prevent children from competing against adults where feasible.

As a general rule it is inadvisable to have fewer competitors in any division than there are awards for that division. Similarly, it can be discouraging if there are more than twice as many competitors in a division than the number of available awards. A well-managed tournament attempts to strike a balance between awarding everyone a trophy, medal, ribbon, or certificate and awarding so few trophies, medals, ribbons, or certificates that competitors become discouraged from participating. The goal should be that competitors arrive at the tournament believing they have a reasonable chance of earning an award with a good performance, and leave believing that every award made—whether they received one or not—was justly deserved.

## TOURNAMENT ETIQUETTE

Tournament organizers must insist on strict etiquette during the competition. Breaches of etiquette, particularly anything potentially hazardous, such as careless handling of a sword, should result in disqualification or even expulsion from the premises.

This is another prime reason to periodically compete in tournaments. It provides a setting and appropriate circumstances in which to practice the highest levels of *sahō* and *reihō*. By placing yourself in these circumstances, you have a reason and opportunity to heighten your awareness of the effects and impression your behavior makes on others. Here are just a few examples to consider:

The respect you have for yourself and others is manifest in part by the care you take in preparing and dressing appropriately (in *hakama* and *keikogi* or *montsuki*) for the event. Ensuring that your hakama is clean and neatly pressed demonstrates the degree of respect you have for yourself, other competitors, judges, spectators, and your own property.

Removing your shoes upon entering the venue and wearing your *tabi* in the competition area similarly display your respect for the tournament organizers, staff, participants, and spectators. Likewise, wearing your shoes anytime you leave the venue keeps your tabi clean and demonstrates your respect for the venue and all present.

Of course, always exhibiting a respectful attitude toward the judges and officials is a basic expectation at an *iaidō* tournament. Even a questioning glance directed at a judge should be considered an act of disrespect, and in a well-managed tournament will get you penalized or disqualified. Judges and referees are human too, and they will invariably make an occasional erroneous call or ruling. An *iaidōka* realizes that this is inevitable and, in the great scheme of life, immaterial. In the long run, the erroneous calls made against you will be offset by an equal number made in your favor. So, you gain nothing by risking offending the judge by questioning something as trivial as a tournament ruling.

If we, as *iaidōka*, train ourselves to put our own lives at risk to perform *kirioroshi* in order to give a mortal enemy a merciful and dignified death in battle, we should certainly be willing to set aside our momentarily wounded pride in order to preserve the dignity of a tournament judge who errs while trying to rule equitably.

Other simple ways of exhibiting respect include: remaining aware of how the tournament is progressing and when you are scheduled to compete rather than disturbing staff or officials to find out; remaining still and quiet when you are not competing so as not to distract competitors, officials, or spectators; staying clear of doorways, walkways, and registration tables so others can easily pass.

In short, an *iaidō* tournament is an excellent opportunity to gain many of the benefits of a *musha shugyō*, not only putting your skills to the test under the duress of competition, but to put into practice many aspects of the philosophy of *iaijutsu*, especially by placing the needs and interests of others ahead of your own for a few hours as an act of respect and compassion.

Chapter 24

# *Shōri e no Michi*

## The Way to Victorious Life

*Kantan na michi o susumeba, jinsei wa muzukashii;*
*muzukashii michi o susumeba, jinsei wa kantan desu.*

*If you take the easy path, life is difficult;*
*if you take the difficult path, life is easy.*

This book contains enough instruction for several lifetimes. It will take a dozen years of training to become adept at the physical techniques alone, and decades more to master them and imprint them with your own personality and spirit. The philosophy contained in this book is condensed from the lives of many of Japan's greatest warriors, and it would be the height of arrogance for any of us to presume that we could assimilate all of it in a single lifetime. Bear in mind also that we have only presented the major tenets of samurai philosophy in this volume. An authoritative and exhaustive study on the philosophy of samurai swordsmanship would require a work of encyclopedic proportions.

This manual can serve you for a lifetime of training, enjoyment, and personal enrichment, and can then be passed on to your children and their children in much the same way the art of *iaijutsu* itself has been passed from generation to generation. We want to close by providing some practical ways to apply this book to your everyday life; to help you achieve true victory over the circumstances and adversities we all face in our family lives, jobs, and ambitions, and to bring you and those around you greater joy.

To begin with, here are twenty-one precepts distilled from ancient samurai philosophy:

武士の心得

## SAMURAI NO KOKORO-E
### Precepts of the Samurai

1. Know yourself. (*Jikō o shiru koto*)

   The foundation of all personal growth is to truly know yourself—that which seems both good and bad in yourself. To understand your faults as well as your virtues allows you to begin working to remedy your faults, strengthen your virtues, and find ways to work around those aspects of your personality and character that you may be unable to change.

2. Always follow through on commitments. (*Jibun no kimeta koto wa saigo made jikkō suru koto*)

   A commitment is essentially a promise you make to yourself. Commitments can be as shallow and short-lived as going on a diet or as deep and lasting as marriage; the marriage vow is the promise you make to your spouse; the marriage commitment is the promise you make to yourself. Each unfulfilled commitment is a personal failure that can be deeply disappointing and damaging to your self-esteem. Think carefully before you make any commitment. Make only those commitments that are truly valuable to you. And don't overburden yourself with so many commitments that you are doomed to failure from the start.

3. Respect everyone. (*Ikanaru hito demo sonke suru koto*)

   If you have gained nothing else from this book, the concept of respect should be indelibly etched into your mind. The true samurai, as we have often stated, respected even his enemies. Respect for others—for their ideas, beliefs, culture, and human rights—is the bridge to mutual understanding and ultimately to peaceful coexistence with others.

   Respecting someone is not the same as admiring them. You can respect someone else's basic humanity—their right to hold different ideas and perspectives from yours—without agreeing with them. Remember, a samurai even respects his sworn enemies.

**4.** Hold strong convictions that cannot be altered by your circumstances. (*Kankyō ni sayu sarenai tsuyoi shinnen o motsu koto*)

It's one thing to develop strong convictions; it's quite another to hold to those convictions even when it appears foolish in the eyes of the world to do so. We now live in an era in which welfare and insurance fraud are commonplace roads to financial success, where TV and movies have glamorized promiscuity to an extent that sexually transmitted diseases are epidemic, where the majority of premature deaths are the direct result of lifestyle choices, where easy money is more highly revered than hard work, and where commitment to family and religious values is publicly ridiculed.

Incredible strength of conviction is necessary to withstand such social and economic pressures—pressures that have led our present generation into a malaise of alcohol and drug abuse, immorality, greed, laziness, and self-indulgence that is out of control and bringing the entire world to ruin.

**5.** Don't make an enemy of yourself. (*Mizu kara teki o tsukuranai koto*)

Don't be your own worst enemy! Jealousy, greed, and self-pity will ensure that you have plenty of enemies if you try to accomplish something worthwhile with your life. If you treat people with respect and compassion, you won't add to the number of your opponents by your own attitude.

**6.** Live without regrets. (*Koto ni oite kōkaisezu*)

This is a double-edged admonition. First, don't wallow in regret over your past mistakes. Take responsibility for them and learn from them—and then put them behind you. Accept the fact that the past cannot be undone, find something of value (such as a lesson learned) in your mistakes, and go forward with the knowledge that you have taken another step toward perfection of character.

Second, if you know—or even suspect—that you will regret an action you are considering, don't do it! Heed the warning of your conscience in advance. As you strive toward improving yourself and grow in compassion and self-awareness, you will find that your conscience allows you to make fewer and fewer regrettable decisions.

**7.** Be certain to make a good first impression. (*Hito to no deai o taisetsu ni suru koto*)

As the old saying goes, "First impressions are lasting impressions." A good first impression is a barometer of the kind of life you are leading. If you consistently leave good impressions on those you meet, it is likely that you are living a more fulfilling and positive life than someone who consistently leaves a poor first impression.

**8.** Don't cling to the past. (*Miren o motanai koto*)

This is more than simply not regretting the past; it means to let go of both the good and the bad. All too often we meet people who sacrifice their own present or future because they are still mired in the past. Their stories of "the good old days" are a telltale sign that nothing of import is occurring in their lives now.

Our past is a good history lesson, and it is as valuable as a road map to our future. But in order to move ahead, we must let go of past glories as well as past failures.

**9.** Never break a promise. (*Yakusoku o yaburanai koto*)

To be a person of character, you must say what you mean and mean what you say. It is really that simple. Don't make promises you can't or won't keep, and if you do make a promise, do whatever is necessary to keep it. Remember: the disappointment and distrust caused by only one broken promise can undo ten years of kept promises.

**10.** Don't depend on other people. (*Hito ni tayoranai koto*)

This precept is a bit paradoxical. We cannot succeed in life without the help of others. We cannot have fulfilling relationships with other people without allowing them to become deeply involved in our lives. Yet, we must not depend on them!

What this really means is that we must take personal responsibility for our lives. Children depend on their parents, but adults must be responsible for themselves. We cannot rely on family, friends, or the government to take care of us, direct us, or make us happy. With realistic expectations of others, we will feel genuine gratitude for their contributions and we will avoid anger and disappointment if others let us down.

**11.** Don't speak ill of others. (*Hito o onshitsu shinai koto*)

If you have a grievance with someone, the respectful and proper way to deal with it is to speak directly with that person, not about that person to others. Compassionate confrontation is the core of good relationships. It is easy to compliment people, but it takes real courage and true friendship to openly discuss with others the things that bother you. Yet we can only have deep friendships if we are willing to take the emotional risks of raising difficult issues and settling them. If we do, then both people benefit. If we don't, both will suffer.

**12.** Don't be afraid of anything. (*Ikanaku koto ni oite mo osorenai koto*)

Fear robs you of *heijōshin* and prevents you from thinking clearly and reacting naturally. It ignites the "fight or flight" reaction, yet often neither fighting nor fleeing is the most beneficial response. This is especially true of the flight response, since our avoidance of all but physical danger usually takes the form of emotional barriers or escapism into drug and alcohol use or submission to cult behavior.

It is always preferable to face your problems, whether they are physical dangers or the everyday obstacles and challenges of life. After all, as a samurai, you have already conquered the fear of death, and are instead pursuing a noble death (see chapter 2). So, since you do not fear death, why should you fear anything that life might throw your way?

**13.** Respect the opinions of others. (*Hito no iken o soncho suru koto*)

The opinions of others have been shaped by a lifetime of experience and thought, just as yours have. It is important not to preconceive different opinions or ideas as "wrong." The other person's opinion may be just as well substantiated as your own—perhaps even more so. If you can set aside your desire to be "right" and focus only on the opinion that has the most value, you will find your attitude encourages others to share their ideas freely, which will in turn provide you with greater insight and more options from which to choose.

Don't forget the lesson of Takeda Shingen, who encouraged and rewarded dissent among his subordinates. It was that very trait that made him one of the greatest leaders in history!

**14.** Have compassion and understanding for everyone. (*Hito ni taishite omoiyari o motsu koto*)

True compassion cannot be achieved without deep understanding of human nature and motivations, so this precept implies the need to really know people. This is especially crucial for leaders, and it can be seen in such examples as Takeda Shingen, Abraham Lincoln, and countless others. Those who take a genuine interest in people inspire great loyalty, dedication, and desire to succeed. There is great truth in the axiom: "People don't care how much you know until they know how much you care."

Compassion is the key to discovering what motivates people. If you sincerely care, you will be interested enough to learn their deepest desires, hopes, and fears and eventually grow to understand them. Compassion is also the key to developing healthy and harmonious relationships with family, friends, and your spouse, the key to appreciating and validating the points of view and feelings of others, even if they differ from yours.

15. Don't be impetuous. (*Karuhazumi ni koto o okosanai koto*)

The samurai of old were bound by a strict code of honor and lived in a society in which the slightest insult could result in a duel to the death. In addition, *iaijutsu* was founded during a tumultuous period of civil wars in which loyalties were constantly changing with the tides of shifting power among warlords and their vassals. In such times, the implications of every action had to be carefully considered beforehand. The slightest mistake could cost you your life and bring about the ruination of your family.

Even though the consequences are not as severe, it is not so different today. Rash decisions or words can cost a new job or a promotion; impulsive financial decisions can throw your family into bankruptcy. If you maintain *heijōshin* and do not allow your emotions and impulses to dictate your decisions, you will enjoy greater abundance in all aspects of life.

16. Even little things must be attended to. (*Chiisa na koto demo taisetsu ni suru koto*)

There is a common saying, "Take care of the little things, and the big things will take care of themselves." There is a great deal of truth in this dictum. If unattended, the little things in life soon compound into big things. Just as small physical tasks, such as personal and financial details, can add up into serious problems if not taken care of, a series of seemingly insignificant emotional hurts will quickly escalate into major conflicts.

It is not always necessary to personally perform the little tasks; it is only important to see that they get done. If your lifestyle requires you to concentrate on major issues, then you must delegate the small tasks and ensure that they are done.

17. Never forget to be appreciative. (*Kansha no kimochi o wasurenai koto*)

A sincere word of thanks is often better than payment for a favor done. Most of us enjoy helping others and gain a sense of satisfaction in knowing that we have done something unselfish, but we also quickly grow tired of doing things for people who do not show any appreciation for our efforts. If we show genuine appreciation for the assistance of others, there will always be friends willing to help us through difficult times. But if we fail to show our appreciation, we will quickly become known as a "taker," and our acquaintances will lose all respect for us.

This is also a prime example of taking care of the little things. Just the simple courtesy of a "thank you" to a friend or loved one, if left unsaid, can build up into great anger and discontent with time and repetition. But that same simple courtesy, if never forgotten, will keep our friends and family steadfast by our side even through the darkest of times.

**18.** Be first to seize the opportunity. (*Hito yori sossenshi kōdō suru koto*)

We must not act impetuously. But once we have reached a well-considered decision we must act quickly and precipitously. As the old saying goes, "Opportunity knocks but once." We usually get only one chance, and that chance only lasts for a limited time.

This is a lesson we practice often in *iaijutsu*. Our opponent will give us few opportunities to win the encounter, and those opportunities will last only moments at best. So we must seize an opportunity the instant it arises. The same holds true in business and other areas of life. True opportunities will be rare and short-lived, so we must be prepared for them and act swiftly when they are presented.

**19.** Make a desperate effort. (*Isshō kenmei monogoto o suru koto*)

Here is another lesson direct from *iaijutsu* training. In important matters, a "strong" effort usually results in only mediocre results. Whenever we are attempting anything truly worthwhile, our effort must be as if our life is at stake, just as if we were under physical attack. It is this extraordinary effort—an effort that drives us beyond what we thought we were capable of—that ensures victory in battle and success in life's endeavors.

**20.** Have a plan for your life. (*Jinsei no mokuhyō o sadameru koto*)

If you don't know where you are going, how will you know when you get there? To have a plan for your life is such an obvious admonition that it almost seems ludicrous to mention it here. Yet sadly, fewer than 10 percent of us have a clear, written plan for our lives. And of those who do have some kind of plan, fewer than 10 percent have planned for anything other than just the financial aspects. The average person spends more time planning a holiday weekend than in planning their whole life.

While financial matters are an important part of an overall life plan, it is equally—if not more—important to set goals for all the other areas of your life. The necessities of life keep economic matters at the forefront of our thoughts, so having specific goals for the other areas of our life helps prevent financial matters from crowding everything else out. Your life plan should also be written, so that you can use it as a road map to your achievements and to help keep you accountable for staying on track.

However, a good life plan does not have to be highly detailed. An outline is usually sufficient. At a minimum, it should include specific goals and timetables for achieving them, in the following areas:

1. Family goals: This broad category concerns such issues as family relationships, marriage, children, where you will live, and most other lifestyle decisions.

2. Social involvement: Your social life can include clubs, social status, political involvement, and will often affect such areas as recreation, charitable activities, and the like.

3. Personal accomplishments: These are your "trophies," how you want to leave your mark on the world, what you will be remembered by.

4. Financial objectives: This area should focus primarily on the income and expenses you generate. The things you purchase and own (cars, home, etc.) are planned under other categories. Your financial plan outlines how you will obtain the money needed to acquire those things that you have planned for elsewhere.

5. Intellectual development: This should include goals for both formal education (high school, college, advanced degrees, etc.) and informal areas (topics you might study—even become expert in—outside academic institutions).

6. Emotional maturity: Just as it helps to have definite, measurable objectives in financial areas, you should plan for your emotional maturation. How will you ensure that you continue to mature and improve your character? Will you attend courses, read self-help books, or join organizations that promote this? How will you establish an underlying philosophy or ethical basis by which to guide your behavior?

7. Spiritual growth: You will not be a whole person until you have resolved your quest for meaning in life. You must deal with the issues that most of us consider "religious": Is there a God? How does the existence or nonexistence

of God affect my life and behavior? Is there a hereafter? What will become of my soul when my body dies? Do I need to make spiritual preparations for the afterlife? What is my role in the universe? Why am I here? Is there a purpose to life beyond mere carnal pleasures? Are there moral absolutes? By what spiritual path can I find these answers? These questions require deep soul-searching and careful investigation. You must be careful to seek truth, rather than what is popular, self-serving, or convenient to believe. And your quest for the answers to such crucial spiritual questions should be at least as well-planned as your family vacation!

To help you focus on what is truly important to you, as opposed to those things that would merely be nice to accomplish if you had a chance, just ask yourself this question: "If I died at the end of this (day, week, month, year, etc.), what accomplishments would leave me with absolutely no regrets?"

Ask this question for your long-term (five-, ten-, and twenty-year) goals, medium-term (one- to three-year) goals, and short-term (weekly, monthly, quarterly) plans. Then, use the answers to set your truly important objectives for each of these planning periods.

This is truly a samurai's perspective—the perspective of a warrior who routinely faced the real possibility of untimely death. If you knew with certainty that you would die exactly one week from today, just think what you would really do during those final seven days. You would make sure that all your personal and financial affairs were as orderly as possible, so as not to inconvenience your heirs. Petty squabbles and hurt feelings would suddenly seem inconsequential, and you would spend hours cherishing the company of your closest friends and loved ones. And you would probably take the time to do one or two really important things that you always wished you had done. Those are precisely the types of things your short-term objectives should concentrate on.

On the other hand, if you knew you would die in exactly three years, you would plan more types of activities and goals. You would set aside money for events planned months ahead. You might schedule a dream vacation to some distant land, or devote several months to working for a cause you believe in deeply. These are appropriate medium-range goals.

Lastly, if you know you would die in exactly ten or perhaps twenty years, you would make other, more far-reaching plans and prioritize them differently. You might plan a dream home to share with your family for the last ten of those twenty years, or establish a fund for your children's college education, or set aside time to research and write a book, or plan a change of careers.

This is truly the secret of living without regrets. If you lived each day as if you were scheduled to die at midnight that night, you would make sure you spent every waking hour accomplishing only the most important things in life, and you would devote the most time possible to the people who mean the most to you. At the end of such a day, you would have no regrets.

Regardless of whether the goals you set are lofty or simple, once you have established a plan for your life, your next step is to begin applying the other principles in this book to accomplishing that plan. Chief among these is always follow through on commitments. Having made a commitment to achieve your written goals, don't stop working toward them, especially when you encounter setbacks.

Not everything you try in life will succeed. The more you try to accomplish, the more failures you will experience. The most successful people in the world are the ones who have failed the most often, because they have tried more things! You cannot allow failures, obstacles, and setbacks to affect your confidence and desire to succeed. Remember: the only people who never fail are the ones who never try.

In *iaijutsu* there is no such thing as a draw. In every battle, you either win or lose, and to lose is to die. The same is essentially true for your ambitions in life. There is no middle ground: you either succeed or fail.

You can think of your life plan like a marathon race: you must complete all twenty-six miles. If you don't cross the finish line, it doesn't matter if you ran only ten or all but the last ten feet, you still didn't *finish*—you didn't run a marathon. A 10K run is still a major accomplishment, but it isn't a marathon. And when you are running a marathon, the judges don't hand out 10K medals to the ones who don't finish.

So, treat your life plan like *iaijutsu*—don't accept anything less than winning. In this way you will be sure you achieve your goals.

This also means you must plan thoughtfully. Set realistic goals, and know what you really want to accomplish. Also, set only those goals that you are willing to sacrifice everything that isn't one of your goals to achieve. If you are really willing to settle for completing a 10K run instead of a marathon, then make a 10K run your life goal. Don't have "marathon" in your plan and think it will be all right to fall back to a 10K. It won't be. At your very core, you will think of yourself as a failure if you do not accomplish what you set out to do. It is much better, in every way, to have a 10K goal and push on to run a marathon than to have a marathon goal and fall short with a 10K. Conversely, if a marathon is really what you have your heart set on achieving, then make it your goal, and then make a desperate effort to finish the race!

21. Never lose your "beginner's spirit." (*Shoshin o wasurubekarazaru koto*)

    This admonition is much deeper than it seems at first. On the surface it means to maintain the freshness and excitement that you bring to any new endeavor as a beginner. Don't lose your eagerness to improve and learn and experience. And don't lose a beginner's humility and openness to instruction. But it also means to never lose touch with the basics in any area of life.

    It is so easy to find ourselves caught up in the complexities of modern living that we lose track of the basics—those elements that bring true meaning and joy to life—love and friendship, an appreciation of nature, gratitude for all the blessings we enjoy, and enjoyment of the simple things of life itself.

    In times of stress, difficulty, and setbacks, keeping your beginner's spirit means to go back to the fundamentals to find the solutions to your problems. The answers are seldom found in the complexities. Our hardships and failures are usually the result of losing touch with the basic principles of life, not the intricacies and minor details.

When adversities arise, you can actually use these twenty-one precepts as a diagnostic tool to find the area of life in which you may have gotten off track. Just start at the top and start asking yourself the questions: Do I truly know myself? Have I followed through on all my commitments? Have I been disrespectful to someone? As you work your way down the list, if you are honest with yourself, you will probably find the cause of your difficulties.

## LIFE'S LABORATORY

The precepts of Samurai no Kokoro-e apply as aptly to life in general as to *iaijutsu* specifically, from knowing yourself to keeping your beginner's spirit. One of the major benefits of *iaijutsu* training, then, is the opportunity to use the *dōjō* as a laboratory in which to experiment with, test, and perfect these principles under controlled circumstances. Once refined, you can then apply them in your own life.

Every day we can improve our character and experience the value of these concepts in the microcosm of the *dōjō*. We can learn by trial and error under the caring, corrective eye of our *sensei* and in the company of understanding and compassionate fellow students who share our struggle with the same lessons—before attempting to apply them in the broader world of daily life.

## RISE ABOVE THE ORDINARY

Animals live only day by day or even hour by hour, driven by instinct and reaction to their environment, and satisfied with whatever outcome befalls them. Only humans have freedom of choice, the ability to set goals, to establish principles and ideals by which to live, and to strive for an improved life despite the obstacles and circumstances of their environment. It is this very ability that creates stress, worry, fear, and uncertainty, but it is also this ability that allows us to persevere and overcome the trials of life and experience true victory and joy.

Those who have neither hope nor ideals to live by are living only on the level of brute animals. Your first step in rising above a primitive existence is to establish strong convictions that will form the basis for an enriched and rewarding life and give you the emotional stamina to endure its hardships and trials.

A person of high ideals and character appreciates the laws of nature and the fundamental laws and mores of his or her society. Even if you disagree with how some of these laws are enforced or applied, such principles give you a foundation for exercising sound judgment, even in complex and difficult circumstances. If you really know yourself and have compassion for yourself (as well as others), then every action or decision you make will polish your character—even those that turn out adversely—because you will accept responsibility and continue to strive for improvement.

It is this strength of character and commitment to continual improvement that will set you apart from the ordinary and mundane, and allow you to remain unaffected by your environment and circumstances. With a spirit of purpose and a dedication to continual self-improvement, you will learn to benefit almost equally from adversity as from success. When you can do this, you will no longer find your emotions rising and falling with your changing fortunes. You will know and experience *heijōshin*.

# DON'T BE A CIRCUS ELEPHANT

Nearly all of us have seen a circus live, or at least watched one on television. Although the trapeze and high-wire acts are more daring and the acrobats more amazing, there is a magnificent, quiet power to the performance of the circus elephants. It is remarkable that they can raise and balance their enormous weight in a handstand. And for all their size and strength, they are so gentle and obedient with their handlers.

But one of the most interesting aspects of elephant behavior occurs when their performance is over. If you walk outside the Big Top when their act is finished, you will see the trainers tether the elephants by slender chains to foot-long stakes driven into the ground. What is amazing about this is that, with almost no effort at all, these mighty creatures could snap those inadequate shackles or uproot them from the ground, yet they remain leashed in place as if helpless. Why?

It is a result of conditioning. When the elephants were babies, they were kept tethered with heavy-gauge chains lashed to stout, immovable posts. Their attempts to pull free only chafed their ankles raw. After so many weeks and months of this, the baby elephants learned to avoid the pain by not tugging at their shackles. Once they were conditioned in this fashion, only a slender chain was necessary to keep them from trying to roam about.

People are conditioned in the same way by their experiences in life. We all develop ways in which we are physically or emotionally restrained by the pain or humiliation of previous mishaps. Sometimes the result is obvious, like the wallflowers who are afraid to ask someone to dance because someone previously turned them down. But many of our conditioned behavior patterns are invisible to casual observation, such as the ways in which many of us mask parts of our identity with humor or bravado or deft conversation.

To perfect our character, to fulfill our purpose in life, to live up to our fullest potential, we must not allow ourselves to be held back by imaginary restraints. We must always be willing to try. And be willing to try again! We cannot allow a previous setback, failure, or humiliation condition us not to try again. How many wallflowers have missed out on a "Yes" from the person of their dreams only because they first got a "No" from another, and were never willing to risk another minor humiliation?

To become all that you are capable of being, you must be willing to risk all that you already are.

Saigo no Hito Koto

A Closing Thought

*Yu wa yasuku, okonai wa muzukashii.*
*Okonai wa yasuku, satoru koto muzukashii.*
*Talk is easy; action is difficult. But action is easy; true understanding is difficult!*

The meaning of this proverb is fairly obvious. But, like all of *iaijutsu* philosophy, it has deeper and more subtle shadings of meaning the more it is contemplated. At the obvious level, it tells you to get busy right now with your *iaijutsu* training. Thinking or talking about it are worthless unless you *do* something about it. So begin and persist in your training. Take action!

As you do so, the truth of the second half of the saying will become apparent. Compared to motivating yourself to action, the herculean task of acquiring true understanding of *iaijutsu* will prove to be a lifelong endeavor.

If you are diligent in your training and attempt to practice *iaijutsu* philosophy in daily life, you will soon discover a subtler truth: that knowing *iaijutsu* philosophy and being able to explain it ("talk") is simple compared to applying it consistently in every-day life. Likewise, as you begin to apply *iaijutsu* philosophy on a daily basis, you will find that a true understanding of its limitless depth and applicability is a monumental but worthy undertaking.

Your journey will be fraught with difficulty, frustrations, adversities, and setbacks—bruises, blisters, aches, and painful nicks on the body as well as the soul—but liberally seasoned with incomparable joys and triumphs. It is a journey of self-discovery, self-enrichment, and the discovery and enrichment of others.

Come join us on this journey of victorious living!

# *Atogaki*

## The Making of *Flashing Steel*

Shimabukuro Hanshi was always certain that *Flashing Steel* would have a powerful impact on the martial arts world. I was skeptical at first, despite my excitement over the opportunity to help write the book. But, looking back twenty-five years later with the benefit of hindsight—and considerably more insight into both myself and our world—I am no longer surprised by the reception this book has received. Shima was always the visionary. I am merely the scribe.

The making of *Flashing Steel* began in late 1993 or early 1994. Shima Sensei—he was still *sensei* back then, not having received any formal titles yet—had just returned from one of his frequent visits to the Eishin-Ryū *hombu dōjō* in Ōsaka and had asked me to meet him at our usual place: the Jack in the Box restaurant near his dry-cleaning shop in Chula Vista, California.

At this point, I had been training with Shima Sensei since late 1988 in the arts of *iaijutsu*, *jōjutsu*, and Shitō-Ryū *karate-dō*, and I had been assisting him from time to time with the marketing efforts of the Jikishin-Kai International division, having designed its logo, letterhead, and flyers, as well as occasionally answering correspondence. I had also served as his *uke* several times, performing demonstrations of *iaijutsu* and *jōjutsu* at major *karate* tournaments in the southwestern United States. So, I arrived expecting to be informed of an upcoming event or a new marketing task for which he wanted my help.

Instead, beaming with excitement, he told me of a conversation he had had with Miura Hanshi during his recent visit to *hombu dōjō*, in which he had mentioned to Miura Hanshi that, while there were many books on Eishin-Ryū written in Japanese, there were none yet in the English language. He had suggested to Miura Hanshi that such a book would help greatly with the promotion of Eishin-Ryū to the English-speaking world, and Miura Hanshi had authorized him to write one.

I remember that moment as clearly as yesterday, down to the corner booth in which we were seated and the beads of condensation on my Diet Coke. Sensei leaned forward, holding my gaze, and with a grin, asked, "So, do you want to write a book, Len *san?*"

I had already written four action-adventure novels that had been resoundingly rejected by more than fifty agents and publishers, so naturally I said, "Yes!" Somehow that made sense to me at the time.

So began what would become one of the most challenging and fulfilling endeavors I have ever undertaken. It was clear from the outset that Shima Sensei, as his students all knew him, carried a burdensome sense of responsibility for the project. Miura Hanshi had expressly authorized the project, and it was now up to Shima Sensei to produce a book that would faithfully explain the culture, traditions, philosophy, and technical curriculum that Hanshi had imparted to him in the preceding eighteen years. He was resolved to ensure that the book would reflect favorably on Miura Hanshi, the style of Eishin-Ryū, and the art of *iaijutsu* as a whole. If it was to be the vehicle that carried Eishin-Ryū worldwide, then it could be nothing less than world-class.

We began meeting every Thursday around 10 a.m. to discuss the book, take notes, and review the previous week's work. Sensei would explain his ideas to me in Japanglish and I would repeat them back to him in Eihongo to be sure I had understood him correctly, all the while manically scribbling notes in a spiral-bound notebook. This worked well, since Sensei had a solid, but heavily accented, command of English, and I had both a basic grasp of Japanese and an extensive library of Japanese dictionaries, travel guides, and history books at home. Following each two- to four-hour session, I would return to my office and compose the information on my word processor.

It's hard to believe now that the internet was practically nonexistent in 1994. It had been launched in 1991, but in 1994 still had only a few thousand users, most of whom connected by 9,600-baud (bits per second) dial-up modems—not megabits or gigabits, as we measure data transfer speeds today; just *bits*. As a government contractor who communicated frequently with the Pentagon, I was using a state-of-the-art 28.8 kbps modem. For reference, my current fiber-optic internet connection is more than three thousand times faster. Nevertheless, any research needed had to be done at the public library, because there was nothing about *iaijutsu* or any other *koryū budō* on the Web at that time.

I spent several hours every day fact-checking and double-checking information for the book before writing. In one of our meetings, Shima Sensei might say something like, "*Shinnen* means 'very strong determination of mind,' but you can check dictionary for better explanation." Afterward, I would sift through my *kanji* dictionaries and Japanese-English dictionaries in search of a word or phrase that would properly convey the meaning of the term to an audience we assumed knew little or nothing of the Japanese language and culture. The most dog-eared and weather-beaten book in my house is my copy of the 1969 edition of *The Modern Reader's Japanese-English Character Dictionary* by Andrew Nelson.

To create manuscripts, I was still using an Intel 80386-based personal computer, preparing drafts in Word Perfect 5.0, and printing them out for Shima Sensei (who did not own a computer yet) on a dot-matrix printer. The files were all stored on 1.4-megabyte 3½-inch floppy disks. By today's standards, that was Stone Age technology. Each page of the manuscript took almost a minute to print, so I would start printing a chapter for Sensei to review, then take my lunch break and come back, hoping to find it finished. With a freshly printed chapter or two in hand, I would return to Jack in the Box the following week to present a new or updated draft for Sensei's review.

So it went, week after week, chapter after chapter, writing and rewriting. It was unquestionably the most arduous project I have ever undertaken—not because of its innate difficulty or scope, but because of our mutual commitment to creating a book of lasting value and importance. Each draft was carefully scrutinized, not just by Shima Sensei, but by some of his other students, to be certain we were expressing our thoughts in a way readers would understand. It is no exaggeration to say that each chapter was significantly revised at least five times before we submitted it for publication. Some chapters were discarded outright and rewritten from scratch. Eighteen chapters, more than six months of composition, review, and revision before we had a completed manuscript to submit: 66,000 words on 270 pages.

Now that we had a book, who would publish it? One of Sensei's students, who was in the publishing business but did not handle nonfiction, suggested that we contact North Atlantic Books in Berkeley, California. At that time, North Atlantic was best known as a publisher of works on poetry, literature, and alternative medicine. They had one or two books on tai chi in their catalog, but they took a chance on us and accepted the manuscript for publication. That's when the fun began.

First, there was the question of a title. Several suggestions were tossed around: *Iaijutsu: The Way of the Samurai; Life or Death: The Essence of Eishin-Ryū;* and *Living on the Edge: The Art of Iaijutsu* were among the early contenders. I argued strongly for a title that better reflected the Japanese origins and dignified nature of *iaijutsu*, such as *Iaijutsu Kyōhan: The Art of Samurai Swordsmanship*. At least twenty different titles were discussed, but Sensei was not satisfied with any of them. We tabled the discussion when the time came to shoot the photographs for the book, and focused our attention on that.

We scheduled an appointment with a professional photographer I had known personally for several years, Larry Hoagland. He had done the photography for a large number of national and international advertising campaigns for major corporations like McDonald's, and I knew he would create a great cover for the book. We arrived at his studio in downtown San Diego, and he first asked what the title of the book was going to be. When we told him we hadn't decided yet, he asked us to tell him about the nature of *iaijutsu* and the goal or purpose of the book. We began explaining some of the key philosophical and spiritual concepts of *iaijutsu*, like *kokoro* (heart), *shisei* (sincerity), *shinnen* (total conviction), and living a meaningful life for a cause, but he stopped us short.

"I get it," he said. "It's all about making you a better person and living a more fulfilling life. That's what you explain *inside* the book after they've joined your *dōjō*. But what's on the *outside* of the book should be what someone would see if they peeked in the window at your *dōjō*. Show me one of the techniques you teach."

Shima Sensei performed the Seitei Kata *kesagiri* for him.

"Wow," Larry said. "What I saw just now was a really scary piece of steel flash by right in front of me!"

"Flashing steel," Sensei exclaimed. "Len *san*, that's the name of the book: *Flashing Steel*."

At that point Larry brought in his business partner, Dick Van Patton, to discuss how to shoot a cover that would portray the concept of steel flashing through the air. This was before photo-enhancing software, so they had to devise a way to capture the blade sweeping downward without computer effects. It was Dick Van Patton who devised a way to capture the movement of the sword using a long exposure and precisely angled lighting to produce the photograph used for the original cover of Sensei performing a *kesagiri* cut.

While the book was being edited, we began filming a set of seven instructional videos with Panther Productions that would complement *Flashing Steel* and provide students with access to both written and visual instruction in the performance of Eishin-Ryū *waza*. Filming these videos gave Sensei and I a fascinating glimpse behind the scenes of movie and video production. At that time, Panther was the world's largest producer of martial arts instructional videos. They had an enormous studio in San Clemente, California, in which they performed their filming and editing. Many of their staff were Hollywood professionals—directors, camera operators, gaffers, grips, and editors—who moonlighted with Panther when not working in television or on a feature film. The director for our videos was one who had worked as an assistant director on more than fifty major movies.

Based on their long experience with similar productions, we were scheduled for a full week of filming. We arrived promptly at 9 a.m. Monday morning in order to change into our *iaidōgi*, have any needed make-up applied, hair arranged, and be wired with microphones so that filming could start on time at 10 a.m. The first thing the director requested is that Sensei make several *kirioroshi* (full downward cuts) next to a microphone on a boom, so they could use the *tachikaze* (the swish of the sword) as a sound effect during editing.

"No need," Sensei told him. "You hear real *tachikaze* just fine when I cut."

The director insisted that the microphones on the sound stage would not pick up the *tachikaze*, so Sensei relented and performed several cuts. Of course, not a single one of those sound effects was used in the final production because the actual *tachikaze* on set was loud enough.

Next, they blocked out the first shot, which was Sensei performing Mae in the Shoden *waza*, and filmed him performing the *waza* from a front view and side view. After another setup to accommodate both of us at a 45-degree angle to the main camera, they filmed us demonstrating the *ōyō* (practical application) of the *waza*. Sensei's *kirioroshi* streaked down at me with a loud *tachikaze*, stopping about a quarter inch above my head, close enough that I could feel the edge brushing my hair. The B-camera operator screamed the name of a major religious figure and toppled over, dragging his camera to the floor with him and disconnecting the cable that synchronized the two cameras.

The director yelled, "Cut!" and demanded to know what had happened.

"I thought he was going to get killed," the cameraman told him, visibly shaking. "I thought I was about to see his skull get split in half, and it scared the ___ out of me."

The director looked at him in disgust. "And you call yourself a professional." Then he turned to Sensei and I and winked.

That was the only scene for which we had to do a second take all day Monday. By the time we left the building late that afternoon, we had completed filming of the first three videos in the series. We returned Tuesday morning, and filming went just as smoothly. When craft services arrived with lunch, the film crew gathered around Sensei as he was making his sandwich.

"Sir," the director said, "Do you mind if we ask you a question?"

"Please."

"We noticed that you and your student never rehearse before a shot. You just take your positions, hit your marks, and get it right the first time. Every time."

"Yes, of course," Sensei said, "But that's not a question."

"Well, you see, we've worked with some of the best actors in Hollywood. Some of them rehearse for months and still don't get it right on the first take. So we were wondering how long you had to rehearse back in San Diego to be able nail all your scenes in one take."

"Rehearse? We no rehearse. This not play-acting. This is real *budō*. Use for real life, not movie. We're samurai. If samurai not do perfect first time, no second chance because *dead*."

After the four men backed away, nodding and speaking to each other in hushed voices, Shima Sensei turned to me and said, "Len *san*, I think they actually believe that BS I just told them."

Before filming was completed Wednesday morning, we did have to reshoot four or five more scenes, but two of those were because the microphones picked up the sound of police vehicles and helicopters pursuing a suspect outside. Panther was so impressed by our performance, precision, and work ethic that they signed us to return in 1995 to film a set of videos on *jōjutsu* without even asking what the content would be.

On April 7, 1995, North Atlantic published *Flashing Steel* as the first book released under their newly formed imprint, Frog Ltd. At the time, we joked that they did this to be able to disassociate the good name and reputation of North Atlantic from the book if it was a dismal failure. Just the opposite proved true.

Within months, Shima Sensei was receiving letters from all over the world expressing appreciation for *Flashing Steel*. The praise was effusive and deeply satisfying. People consistently said that they had never read such a comprehensive treatise on both the philosophy and performance of any form of *budō*. Many said that it had improved their outlook on life and helped them find greater meaning and purpose. In other words, we had accomplished our goal.

There is one other factor that merits mentioning here. In July 1995, a little company based in Seattle opened for business, calling itself "Earth's Biggest Bookstore." It certainly wasn't. Despite massive funding from its initial public stock offering, Amazon generated only $1 million in sales that year. But, the following year it grew to $16 million, then $148 million in 1997, and over $600 million in 1998. In 1999 North Atlantic began distributing *Flashing Steel* on Amazon, helping drive Amazon's sales to more than $1.6 *billion*. That is to say, Amazon's remarkable sales growth in 1999 included the revenue from selling several copies of *Flashing Steel*.

Obviously, sales of *Flashing Steel* had little actual effect on Amazon's staggering growth, but Amazon's emergence as a major global online retailer meant that *budōka* all over the world now had the ability to purchase *Flashing Steel* online, and this resulted in Shima Sensei's reputation and influence spreading across the entire international *budō* community. *Flashing Steel* received rave reviews from readers in Western Europe, Eastern Europe, the Mediterranean, India, Australia, and South America. And the Jikishin-Kai International began receiving requests for affiliation from students and *dōjō* all over the world.

It is no exaggeration to say that *Flashing Steel* is greatly responsible for the worldwide recognition, prestige, and acclaim that Shimabukuro Hanshi and Eishin-Ryū now enjoy. In 1995 there were only one or two *dōjō* in the entire western hemisphere teaching authentic *iaidō* or *iaijutsu*. Twenty-five years later, thanks in no small part to *Flashing Steel*, *dōjō* teaching Eishin-Ryū can be found in every U.S. state, every Canadian province, many parts of Mexico, and every nation in Central and South America. The same can be said of continental Europe and much of the Middle East. Of course, many factors and individuals combined to create this massive worldwide popularization of Eishin-Ryū and *iaijutsu*, but is has been extremely gratifying to have played one of the significant roles in that growth.

But the story does not end with the publication and growing popularity of *Flashing Steel*. As it turned out, that was only the first act of a three-act play.

Life can take us in unexpected directions. It took me to Aurora, Colorado, shortly after the galley proofs of *Flashing Steel* were approved, then brought me back to San Diego in 1996, where I decided to go back to school and get my MBA. I was then forty-five years old, and when applying for jobs and promotions, I was being passed over for less experienced, less qualified, but younger candidates, so my plan was to update my academic credentials and hopefully regain an edge in the employment market.

Instead, a week after receiving my diploma as a newly minted master of business administration, I was in a college classroom teaching quantitative analysis to juniors and seniors. And so began the academic phase of my life. Two years later, I was on a jet to Indiana, where I would spend the next dozen years managing the online graduate business degree programs for a major Midwestern university and growing their enrollment from fewer than two hundred students to more than six thousand.

That was great for my academic career, but I was now living over two thousand miles from Shima Sensei, which not only made it difficult to train with him as often as I would have liked, but it also meant an entirely different approach to producing the second edition of *Flashing Steel*, which was released in 2008.

It had been a challenge back in 1994 to meet with Shima Sensei once a week, face to face, to discuss the current draft and make revisions to the original edition, but attempting the same process for the updated, revised, and expanded second edition long-distance was exasperating for both of us. Japanglish and Eihongo work well face-to-face, where they can be embellished with gestures or actual performance of the techniques being discussed. But by phone and email, communication was much more difficult. Compounding the problem was the fact that we were trying to respond to some of the criticisms we received from readers of the first edition.

There were two major issues raised by readers of *Flashing Steel:* the first that the text was not accompanied by enough photographs for them to easily follow our descriptions of the techniques, and the second was that we had used Aimee Shimabukuro and Jennifer Soto as the models for the Tachiuchi no Kurai.

Both of these had been carefully considered decisions on our part, and we debated at length whether or not to change either of these features of the book. In the first edition, we deliberately kept the photographs to a minimum, because we did not want students attempting to learn the *waza* from the book alone. Our goal was to provide just enough description and illustration to jog the memory of students who had been taught the *waza* by a qualified instructor, but not enough for someone to learn the details of the *waza* solely from the book.

We had used Aimee and Jennifer as models for the *katachi* because we wanted to broaden the appeal of *iaijutsu* to women. When we began work on *Flashing Steel* in 1994, only a handful of women worldwide were training in *iaijutsu*, and we wanted the book to be instrumental in attracting more women to the art. Aimee and Jennifer were both training in *iaijutsu*, but both were novices at the time we took the photographs, and their lack of expertise was evident in their poses.

After much discussion, we decided to reshoot all of the photographs, except the decorative ones, for the second edition and to use an experienced *iaidōka* (Jason Mizuno) as a model for the Tachiuchi no Kurai, so his poses would reflect a higher level of knowledge and expertise. Had I been living in San Diego, that would not have presented a problem, but 1,753 new photographs presented a bit of a challenge. At a megabyte or more each, they were too large to email back and forth, so Shima Sensei mailed them to me on several data CDs. Even then, the time to locate them on the CD and describe them in the text was enormous. And I was taking a full course load for a PhD, so time was a scarce commodity. It amazes me to this day that I got fewer than a dozen of those photos out of place while preparing the text.

The second edition of *Flashing Steel*, now 78,000 words and more than 1,750 photographs and diagrams, went on sale in January 2008, and it appears we made the right decisions regarding the additional photographs, content revisions, and models.

The reviews were, for the most part, exceptionally glowing, and the majority of readers commented on how much the additional photographs had improved the book.

I finished my doctoral course work in 2009, and Shima Sensei and I decided that our next project would be a second book on *karate-dō*, tentatively to be titled *The Art of Killing*. We had completed about two-thirds of the first draft when Sensei called to inform me that he had been diagnosed with cancer of the gall bladder. We were again working long distance, and our progress soon ground to a halt as he underwent chemo and radiation therapy, while still traveling the globe teaching *iaijutsu*.

I flew out to San Diego to meet with Sensei and do some training in November 2011. He was showing signs of his illness, but was in excellent spirits and confident that he would beat the disease. He told me to keep working on *The Art of Killing* by myself, and that he would review my progress when his treatments were over. In March 2012 he underwent surgery for the removal of his gall bladder and some of the surrounding tissues that had been invaded by the cancer. He called a couple weeks later to tell me that the cancer had spread to his liver, but he assured me that he was strong and was not going to succumb to the disease. "Just give me a couple months to regain my strength, then we'll get back to work on the book," he told me in late March.

The next time he called was in late May or early June to tell me he only had a month or two left to live. The cancer was continuing to spread, and nothing his doctors could do was slowing its progress. "Sorry, Len *san*. You'll have to finish the book yourself."

On September 7, 2012, Shimabukuro Hanshi passed from this life to whatever lies beyond, having taught a seminar on *iaijutsu* in Los Angeles only days earlier. With his passing I lost my *sensei*, my mentor, and my closest friend, leaving a hole in my life that can probably never be filled, and the curtain closed on Act Two of the making of *Flashing Steel*.

I lost the will to complete *The Art of Killing*. It was *our* book, not just mine, and so far I have not found the will to pick up where we left off.

Years passed and brought new adventures: more grandchildren, a move to San Antonio, a new *dōjō*, and world travels. All the while, in the back of my mind I could hear the clock ticking. Not just ticking away the time remaining in my life, but ticking toward an idea that germinated sometime around 2015: a third and final edition of *Flashing Steel*. An edition that would bring the saga—and Sensei's legacy—to a conclusion. An edition that would include the materials we had consciously omitted from the first two editions.

When the notion of a third edition first came to me, I had no idea what a massive undertaking it would become. Had I known, I might have abandoned the thought as madness. In the process of trying to complete the work that Hanshi and I began back in 1994, I have added nearly 50,000 words to the manuscript and over 650 new photos. That's nearly double the size of the first edition. But in so doing, I hope and trust that I have now completed what he and I would both consider to be his master work. Shima Sensei was truly the sage. I am merely the scribe.

As the scribe, my goal with this edition was to create a lasting tribute to the life, work, teachings, and memory of Shimabukuro Hanshi—a work truly worthy of him. As I write these final passages, it is with a sense that I could and should have done more. That he deserves better than what I am able to produce, but that I have done my best, and that he would be pleased with the result.

The feudal system was officially abolished in 1871, and in 1876 the former samurai were forbidden to carry swords any longer. In 1877, the last significant samurai rebellion was crushed by the modern Japanese army. Accordingly, there are those who hold that the samurai no longer exist.

While that may be true in a purely technical sense, I know that samurai can and do live on today. I know because I walked alongside a samurai for more than twenty years, training with him, dining with him, traveling with him, facing some of life's greatest challenges and difficulties with him, laughing with him, rejoicing with him, and occasionally crying with him.

Such men still do walk the earth, and if you encounter one, it will change your life forever, as it has mine.

*LEONARD J. PELLMAN*
*November 19, 2019*

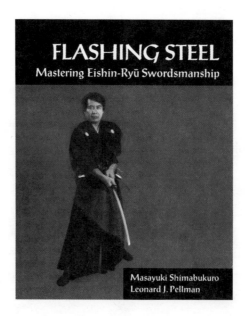

# *Samurai no Kokoro-e*

## Precepts of the Samurai

Since the Samurai no Kokoro-e is a solid foundation for developing samurai spirit and applying *iaijutsu* principles to everyday life, we have prepared this quick reference sheet of these basic principles, which can be copied, posted, and easily reviewed on a daily basis.

1. Know yourself. (*Jikō o shiru koto*)

2. Always follow through on commitments. (*Jibun no kimeta koto wa saigo made jikkō suru koto*)

3. Respect everyone. (*Ikanaru hito demo sonke suru koto*)

4. Hold strong convictions that cannot be altered by your circumstances. (*Kankyō ni sayu sarenai tsuyoi shinnen o motsu koto*)

5. Don't make an enemy of yourself. (*Mizu kara teki o tsukuranai koto*)

6. Live without regrets. (*Koto ni oite kōkaisezu*)

7. Be certain to make a good first impression. (*Hito to no deai o taisetsu ni suru koto*)

8. Don't cling to the past. (*Miren o motanai koto*)

9. Never break a promise. (*Yakusoku o yaburanai koto*)

10. Don't depend on other people. (*Hito ni tayoranai koto*)

11. Don't speak ill of others. (*Hito o onshitsu shinai koto*)

12. Don't be afraid of anything. (*Ikanaku koto ni oite mo osorenai koto*)

13. Respect the opinions of others. (*Hito no iken o soncho suru koto*)

14. Have compassion and understanding for everyone. (*Hito ni taishite omoiyari o motsu koto*)

15. Don't be impetuous. (*Karuhazumi ni koto o okosanai koto*)

16. Even little things must be attended to. (*Chiisa na koto demo taisetsu ni suru koto*)

17. Never forget to be appreciative. (*Kansha no kimochi o wasurenai koto*)

18. Be first to seize the opportunity. (*Hito yori sossenshi kōdō suru koto*)

19. Make a desperate effort. (*Isshō kenmei monogoto o suru koto*)

20. Have a plan for your life. (*Jinsei no mokuhyō o sadameru koto*)

21. Never lose your beginner's spirit. (*Shoshin o wasurubekarazaru koto*)

# SAIGO NO HITO KOTO
## Closing Thoughts

*Yu wa yasuku, okonai wa muzukashii. Okonai wa yasuku, satoru koto muzukashii.*
*Kokoro tadashi karazareba, ken mata tadashi karazu.*
*Talk is easy; action is difficult. But, action is easy; true understanding is difficult!*
*If your heart is not true, your sword also will not be true.*

# *Yōgoshū*

## Glossary of Common Terms Used in Iaijutsu

用
語
集

For the pronunciation of Japanese terms, see "Pronunciation Guide" at the end of the Introduction.

| JAPANESE Term (*rōmaji*) | Japanese | ENGLISH Equivalent |
|---|---|---|
| *agura* | 胡坐 | sit cross-legged |
| *age* | 上げ | upward, rising, lifting |
| *aiki* | 合気 | blending/uniting with opponent's energy |
| *aisatsu* | 挨拶 | courteous (formal) greetings |
| *aite* | 相手 | other person, training partner ("companion hand") |
| *aiuchi* | 合い打ち | simultaneous strike(s), mutual kill |
| *aka(i)* | 赤(い) | red |
| *aka(i)* | 紅(い) | dark red |
| *ashi* | 足 | foot, feet |
| *ashigaru* | 足軽 | peasant foot soldier ("plain feet") |
| *ashikubi* | 足首 | ankle, ankles |
| *ashi-sabaki* | 足捌き | footwork |
| *ashi* | 脚 | leg |
| *atama* | 頭 | head |
| *ato de* | 後で | after, afterward |

| JAPANESE Term (rōmaji) | Japanese | ENGLISH Equivalent |
|---|---|---|
| bōgu | 防具 | protective equipment |
| bōgyo waza | 防禦技 | defensive technique(s) |
| bokken | 木剣 | wooden sword |
| bokutō | 木刀 | wooden sword |
| bōshi | 帽子 | temper line (hamon) on the fukura of a katana |
| bōzu | 坊主 | priest, monk |
| bushi | 武士 | peacemaker, protector |
| bushidō | 武士道 | way of the peacemaker |
| chambara | ちゃんばら | swordplay, sword-fighting sport |
| chiburi | 血振り | blood-flinging |
| chinugui | 血拭い | blood wiping (on a cloth or opponent's hakama) |
| choku | 直 | straight, direct |
| choku-tō | 直刀 | straight sword (sword with straight, uncurved blade) |
| chūdan | 中段 | middle level, mid-height |
| chūdan no kamae | 中段の構え | mid-level posture (sword pointing at opponent's solar plexus) |
| chūden | 中伝 | intermediate teachings |
| chūtō | 中刀 | medium-length sword (usually for children) |
| daimyō | 大名 | Japanese feudal lord ("big name") |
| daishō | 大小 | large-and-small (a daitō-shotō sword pair) |
| daitō | 大刀 | large sword (same as odachi) |
| dan | 段 | level, step |
| danketsu | 団結 | unity, togetherness |
| dantai | 団体 | group, team, together |
| dattō | 出っ刀 | remove sword (from belt) |
| dō | 道 | way, path, the way |

| JAPANESE Term (*rōmaji*) | Japanese | ENGLISH Equivalent |
|---|---|---|
| *dō* | 胴 | torso |
| *dōbarai* | 胴払い | sweep across torso (lateral cut or strike) |
| *dōbarai giri* | 胴払い切り | lateral (sweeping) cut to torso |
| *dōbarai uchi* | 胴払い打ち | lateral (sweeping) strike to torso |
| *dōjō* | 道場 | training place |
| *embu* | 演武 | performance of *bujutsu* |
| *embusen* | 演舞線 | line, direction, or sequence of performance |
| *enshin ryoku* | 遠心力 | centripetal force |
| *enzan no metsuke* | 遠山の目付 | distant gaze ("eyes fixed on distant mountains") |
| *fuchigane* | 縁金 | metal sword fitting between *tsuba* and *tsuka* |
| *fukura* | 脹 | curved tip ("bulge") of a *katana* |
| *furikaburi* | 振り被り | raise (swing) sword overhead |
| *furu* | 降る | swing, fling (verb) |
| *fudoshin* | 不動心 | immovable or indomitable spirit |
| *fundoshi* | 褌 | loincloth (underwear) |
| *futari* | 二人 | two people |
| *futari geiko* | 二人稽古 | training with a partner |
| *gasshuku* | 合宿 | training camp |
| *gedan* | 下段 | low-level |
| *gedan no kamae* | 下段の構え | low-level (sword lowered) posture/stance |
| *geta* | 下駄 | Japanese wooden clogs (for rainy, muddy conditions) |
| *gi* | 着 | clothing, uniform (generic term) |
| *go* | 後 | after, later (implies reacting to opponent) |
| *goshin* | 護身 | self defense |
| *goshin jutsu* | 護身術 | self-defense technique(s) |
| *guntō* | 軍刀 | "army sword" (sword made in World War II era) |

| JAPANESE Term (*rōmaji*) | Japanese | ENGLISH Equivalent |
|---|---|---|
| *gyaku* | 逆 | reverse, opposite direction |
| *gyaku-hassō (no kamae)* | 逆八相(の構え) | reverse-*hassō* posture |
| *gyaku-te* | 逆手 | reversed hand(s) |
| *gyaku-te mochi* | 逆手持ち | reversed-hand grip |
| *ha* | 刃 | blade |
| *habaki* | 鎺 | brass collar fitting on blade |
| *hai* | はい | yes |
| *hairei* | 拝礼 | venerating bow (to founder, dojo emblem, dignitaries, etc.) |
| *hajime* | 始め | begin, start, first time |
| *hakama* | 袴 | samurai trousers |
| *hakama sabaki* | 袴捌き | handling the *hakama* (especially during *seiza* or *tatehiza*) |
| *hamachi* | 刃褌 | point where *nakago* and *ha* meet |
| *hamon* | 刃紋 | tempering pattern on blade |
| *han* | 半 | half, halfway |
| *han* | 藩 | the territory controlled by a *daimyō* (similar to a county) |
| *hambun* | 半分 | one-half (a piece) |
| *hanmi* | 半身 | angled (half-turned) body |
| *hantai* | 反対 | switch (hands, feet, places, etc.) |
| *hanza-handachi* | 半座半立 | "half-sitting, half-standing" (another term for *tatehiza*) |
| *hara* | 腹 | abdomen |
| *harakiri* | 腹切り | belly-cutting (crude term) |
| *hasaki* | 刃先 | edge of the blade |
| *hassō (no kamae)* | 八相 (の構え) | eight-phase (posture) |
| *hasuji* | 刃筋 | angle ("line") of the blade |
| *hasuji o tōsu* | 刃筋を通す | "maintain blade alignment" while cutting |

| JAPANESE | | ENGLISH |
| --- | --- | --- |
| Term (*rōmaji*) | Japanese | Equivalent |
| *heikō* | 平行 | parallel |
| *heisoku* | 平足 | feet side by side |
| *heihō* | 兵法 | military methods (martial arts) |
| *henka* | 変化 | variation, alteration |
| *hi* | 樋 | groove in a sword blade |
| *hidari* | 左 | left, leftward |
| *hiji* | 肘 | elbow |
| *hiki* | 引き | pulling |
| *hikite* | 引き手 | pulling hand |
| *hikiwake* | 引き分け | drawn match, tie game |
| *hiku* | 引く | to pull |
| *himo* | 紐 | string(s), strap(s) |
| *hira* | 平 | flat, level, even |
| *hiraji* | 平地 | side of blade between *shinogi* and *hamon* |
| *hiraki ashi* | 開き足 | sidestep, sidestepping |
| *hiza* | 膝 | knee |
| *hō* | 法 | method, technique |
| *honte* | 本手 | normal hands |
| *honte mochi* | 本手持ち | normal grip (on a weapon) |
| *iai* | 居合 | face-to-face |
| *iaidō* | 居合道 | the way of *iai* |
| *iaigoshi* | 居合腰 | *iai* hips (flexed ankles, knees, and hips) |
| *iaijutsu* | 居合術 | the art of *iai* |
| *iaitō* | 居合刀 | *iai* sword (unsharpened practice sword) |
| *ichi* | 一 | one |
| *ichimonji* | 一文字 | the character *ichi* (lateral cut) |
| *ii* | いい | good |

| JAPANESE Term (*rōmaji*) | Japanese | ENGLISH Equivalent |
|---|---|---|
| *iie* | いいえ | no (said rarely) |
| *ippon* | 一本 | one point |
| *itadaku* | 頂く | to receive (a gift, etc.) |
| *itai* | 痛い | painful |
| *ito* | 糸 | thread |
| *jaken* | 邪剣 | evil sword (a sword used unjustly) |
| *jibun* | 自分 | self, by oneself, alone |
| *jigane* | 地金 | area of blade between *hamon* and *shinogi* ("earth metal") |
| *jikiden* | 直伝 | direct heritage (personal legacy) |
| *jikishin* | 直心 | pure heart, mind, and spirit |
| *jiko* | 自己 | self, oneself |
| *jitsu* | 実 | truth, fact(s) |
| *jitsu* | 術 | art (alternate pronunciation of *jutsu*) |
| *jō* | 杖 | stick (50.2-inch staff) |
| *jōdō* | 杖道 | way of the *jō* |
| *jōjutsu* | 杖術 | art of the *jō* |
| *jōdan* | 上段 | upper level |
| *jōdan no kamae* | 上段の構え | high-level posture (sword raised overhead) |
| *jōzu* | 上手 | skillful |
| *jūban* | 襦袢 | *samurai* undershirt |
| *jūdō* | 柔道 | way of yielding |
| *jūji* | 十字 | the character *jū* (十) |
| *jūji-dome* | 十字止め | cross-shaped (十) block |
| *jūjutsu* | 柔術 | art of yielding |
| *jutsu* | 術 | art |
| *jutte* | 十手 | steel police weapon ("ten hands") |
| *kachi* | 勝 | victory |

| JAPANESE Term (*rōmaji*) | Japanese | ENGLISH Equivalent |
|---|---|---|
| *kagami* | 鏡 | mirror |
| *kaishaku* | 介錯 | assist (behead) someone committing *seppuku* |
| *kami* | 神 | god, deity, gods |
| *kamiza* | 上座 | "upper seat" (a place of honor for symbols of a *dōjō*) |
| *kamon* | 家紋 | family symbol, family crest |
| *kansetsu* | 関節 | joint |
| *kashira-gane* | 頭金 | metal cap on a sword handle |
| *kashiwa* | 柏 | Japanese white oak |
| *kata* | 肩 | shoulder |
| *kata* | 型 | pattern of techniques |
| *katachi* | 形 | pattern of movements |
| *katana* | 刀 | sword |
| *katate* | 片手 | one-handed |
| *katsu* | 勝つ | to win (verb) |
| *katsu* | 活 | live, life, alive, living |
| *katsujin ken* | 活人剣 | life-giving (lifesaving) sword |
| *keiko* | 稽古 | training |
| *keikogi* | 稽古着 | training clothes, uniform |
| *ken* | 剣 | sword |
| *ken* | 拳 | fist |
| *kendō* | 剣道 | sport based on *kenjutsu* |
| *kenjutsu* | 剣術 | art of samurai sword combat |
| *kesa* | 袈裟 | a monk's tunic covering only one shoulder |
| *kesagiri* | 袈裟切り | a cut that follows the lapel of a *kesa* |
| *ki* | 気 | spirit |
| *kigurai* | 気位 | poise, dignity, bearing |
| *kihaku* | 気迫 | intense spirit |

| JAPANESE Term (*rōmaji*) | Japanese | ENGLISH Equivalent |
|---|---|---|
| *kihon* | 基本 | fundamentals, basics, foundation |
| *kime* | 決め | focus, precision |
| *kimaru* | 決まる | inevitable, inevitability |
| *kimono* | 着物 | clothing (general term) |
| *kiriage* | 切り上げ | upward cut |
| *kirikaeshi* | 切り返し | returning cut |
| *kirioroshi* | 切り落ろし | downward cut |
| *kiriotoshi* | 切り落とし | downward cut (alternate pronunciation) |
| *kiritsu* | 起立 | stand up, standing |
| *kiritsuke* | 切り付け | shortened downward cut ("sticking cut") |
| *kiru* | 切る | to cut (verb) |
| *kiru* | 斬る | to kill (verb) |
| *kissaki* | 切先 | point, tip |
| *kiza* | 跪座 | sit like *seiza*, but on the balls of the feet |
| *kobushi* | 拳 | fist |
| *kodachi* | 小太刀 | small sword (a.k.a. *wakizashi* or *shōtō*) |
| *kōhai* | 後輩 | junior student |
| *kōhaku* | 赤白 | red-and-white (red versus white match) |
| *koiguchi* | 鯉口 | hand wrapped around mouth of *saya* ("carp's mouth") |
| *koiguchi no kirikata* | 鯉口の切り方 | loosening the sword in the *saya* ("cutting the carp's mouth") |
| *kojiri* | 小尻 | closed end (butt) of the *saya* |
| *kokoro* | 心 | heart |
| *kokoro-e* | 心得 | principles, precepts, ideals |
| *koshi* | 腰 | hip(s) |
| *koshi-ita* | 腰板 | stiff back-piece of a *hakama* ("hip board") |

| JAPANESE | | ENGLISH |
|---|---|---|
| Term (*rōmaji*) | Japanese | Equivalent |
| *koshirae* | 拵え | sword fittings/mountings (everything attached to the blade) |
| *kotō* | 古刀 | "old sword" (made before AD 1600) |
| *koryū* | 古流 | old style, old school, ancient ways |
| *kōsa* | 交叉 | crossed (wrists, legs, arms, fingers, etc.) |
| *kote* | 小手 | forearm |
| *kuchi* | 口 | mouth |
| *kumitachi* | 組み太刀 | partner training drills ("crossing swords") |
| *kurikata* | 栗形 | fitting on *saya* to which *sageo* are tied |
| *ma* | 間 | distance, interval |
| *maai* | 間合い | distance control |
| *mae* | 前 | front, frontward |
| *mae ni* | 前に | in front of |
| *maki dome* | 巻き止め | place where *tsukamaki* ends at *tsuka gashira* |
| *me* | 目 | eye(s) |
| *mekugi* | 目釘 | wooden peg(s) that hold the *tsuka* in place |
| *mekugi ana* | 目釘穴 | hole(s) in the tang (*nakago*) for the *mekugi* |
| *men* | 面 | face |
| *menuki* | 目貫 | metal decorations on the *tsuka* |
| *metsubushi* | 目潰し | "destroy the eyes" (blind or obstruct opponent's view) |
| *metsuke* | 目付 | eye contact ("affix the eyes") |
| *migi* | 右 | right, rightward |
| *mimi* | 耳 | ear(s) |
| *mine* | 峰 | spine, center of the back |
| *minemachi* | 峰区 | notch separating *nakago* from *mine* |
| *mitori geiko* | 見取り稽古 | learn by observation ("train by capturing with the eyes") |

| JAPANESE Term (*rōmaji*) | Japanese | ENGLISH Equivalent |
|---|---|---|
| *mokusō* | 黙想 | focusing the mind ("silent thought") |
| *mon* | 紋 | emblem, symbol, crest, logo |
| *monouchi* | 物打 | ideal cutting or striking portion of a weapon |
| *montsuki* | 紋付 | jacket with family crest imprinted or embroidered |
| *mune* | 刀背 | back (dull side) of sword blade |
| *mune* | 棟 | ridge (dull side) of sword blade |
| *mune* | 胸 | chest, bosom, breast |
| *munemachi* | 棟区 | notch separating *nakago* from *mune* |
| *musha* | 武者 | a peacemaker, a *budōka* |
| *musha shugyō* | 武者修行 | training journey |
| *musō* | 夢想 | dream, vision |
| *musō* | 無双 | unequaled, unbeatable |
| *mushin* | 無心 | empty mind (limitless mental capacity) |
| *naka* | 中 | center, middle, inside, within |
| *nakago* | 茎 | tang of a sword |
| *nōtō* | 納刀 | resheathing the sword |
| *nukitsuke* | 抜き付け | initial (drawing) cut |
| *o-* | お | honorific (extra polite) |
| *ō-* | 大 | big, large, great |
| *obi* | 帯 | belt, sash |
| *ō-chiburi* | 大血ぶり | large *chiburi* (*shoden*, wet umbrella style) |
| *ōdachi* | 大太刀 | large sword (same as *daitō*) |
| *okuri ashi* | 送り足 | front foot leads moving forward; rear foot leads moving backward |
| *onore* | 己 | self, oneself |
| *otagai ni* | お互いに | face toward, facing toward |
| *rei* | 礼 | respect |

| JAPANESE | | ENGLISH |
|---|---|---|
| Term (*rōmaji*) | Japanese | Equivalent |
| *reigi* | 礼儀 | respectfulness, politeness |
| *reihō* | 礼法 | acts of respect |
| *reishiki* | 礼式 | formal etiquette |
| *renshū* | 練習 | training for mastery ("polishing") |
| *riron* | 理論 | principles, concepts |
| *ritsurei* | 立礼 | standing bow |
| *ryaku* | 略 | fusion of technique |
| *ryoku* | 力 | power |
| *ryōte* | 両手 | (using) both hands |
| *ryū* | 流 | style, school, system, teachings, ("flow") |
| *ryū-ha* | 流派 | schools, styles, branches, and divisions (as a whole) |
| *sageo* | 下げ緒 | cords on a *saya* |
| *sahō* | 作法 | preparation (mental, physical, and spiritual) |
| *saki* | 先 | edge |
| *same* | 鮫 | shark |
| *samegawa* | 鮫皮 | sharkskin (covering for a *tsuka*) |
| *satsujinken* | 殺人剣 | murdering sword (sword used to harm others) |
| *saya* | 鞘 | scabbard, sheath |
| *saya-banari* | 鞘離り | "*saya* separation" (the moment the *kissaki* exits the *saya*) |
| *saya-biki* | 鞘引き | pulling the *saya* rearward |
| *sayaguchi* | 鞘口 | mouth (opening) of the *saya* |
| *seichūsen* | 正中線 | center line |
| *seimei* | 生命 | life, living, being alive |
| *seiretsu* | 整列 | line up ("adjust alignment") |
| *seishin* | 正心 | pure, true, righteous heart |

| JAPANESE Term (rōmaji) | Japanese | ENGLISH Equivalent |
|---|---|---|
| seito | 生徒 | student, pupil |
| seitō | 正統 | traditional, authentic, classic |
| seiza | 正座 | sit on heels with feet flat ("true sit") |
| seme | 攻め | maintain pressure on opponent ("attack") |
| sen | 先 | before, prior (implies initiative or preemption) |
| sempai | 先輩 | senior student |
| sensei | 先生 | teacher, instructor ("previously born") |
| seppa | 切羽 | thin washer between *habaki* and *tsuba* ("split wings") |
| seppuku | 切腹 | cutting the abdomen (ritual suicide by a samurai, polite term) |
| setsudo | 節度 | discipline |
| shiai | 試合 | match, contest, tournament |
| shikata | 仕方 | user (person using technique being practiced) |
| shin | 心 | heart, mind, spirit |
| shinken | 真剣 | sharpened sword ("true sword") |
| shinobi | 忍 | stealth (also a term for *ninja*) |
| shinobu | 忍ぶ | move stealthily (verb) |
| shinogi | 鎬 | ridge on the side of a sword blade |
| shinogi ji | 鎬地 | area between the *mine* and *shinogi* |
| shinsa | 審査 | test, examination (for rank promotion) |
| shintō | 新刀 | "new sword" (made between 1600 and 1870) |
| shintō | 神道 | native Japanese religion |
| shiro(i) | 白(い) | white |
| shisei | 姿勢 | posture, bearing |
| shisei | 至誠 | sincerity, integrity |
| shitachi | 仕太刀 | using sword (sword applying attack being practiced) |

| JAPANESE Term (*rōmaji*) | Japanese | ENGLISH Equivalent |
|---|---|---|
| *shitodo-me* | しとど目 | decorative insert in the *kurikata* |
| *shizan* | 試切 | test cutting (polite) |
| *shizentai* | 自然体 | natural stance, posture ("natural body") |
| *shōbu* | 勝負 | a match, bout, or round in a contest ("victory-defeat") |
| *shōmen* | 正面 | center of the face ("true face") |
| *soete* | 添えて | reinforced, reinforcing, supported, stabilized |
| *soetezuki* | 添えて付き | reinforced thrust (with sword) |
| *sori* | 反り | amount of curvature in a sword blade |
| *suigetsu* | 水月 | the moon's reflection in water ("water moon"); solar plexus, abdominal nerve center |
| *suishin* | 水心 | mental agility ("water mind") |
| *suri-ashi* | 摺り足 | move by sliding feet on the floor |
| *suwari* | 座り | sitting, seated |
| *suwariwaza* | 座り技 | seated techniques (*waza* that begin in *seiza* or *tatehiza*) |
| *suwatte* | 座って | sit down, be seated (command) |
| *tabi* | 足袋 | split-toed stockings worn with *waraji*, *zōri*, or *geta* |
| *tabi* | 旅 | a journey, travels, wandering |
| *tachi* | 太刀 | sword ("large sword") |
| *tachi* | 立ち | stance, standing, upright |
| *tachirei* | 立ち礼 | standing bow |
| Tachiuchi no Kurai | 太刀打ちの位 | *kumitachi* drills for *iaijutsu* |
| *taikai* | 大会 | convention, tournament ("large meeting") |
| *taitō* | 帯刀 | insert(ing) sword(s) in belt |
| *tameshigiri* | 試し切り | test cutting (common use) |
| *tanden* | 丹田 | lower abdomen |
| *tanren* | 鍛錬 | hard training ("tempering" or "forging") |

| JAPANESE Term (*rōmaji*) | Japanese | ENGLISH Equivalent |
|---|---|---|
| *tatehiza* | 立膝 | sitting with one knee raised ("upright knee") |
| *te* | 手 | hand(s) |
| *te no uchi* | 手の内 | within the hands (fine points of gripping a sword) |
| *tenugui* | 手拭い | hand towel, wash cloth (used under *kendō* headgear) |
| *teitō* | 剃刀 | holding/carrying the sword (in left hand) |
| *teki* | 的 | enemy, opponent |
| *tō* | 刀 | sword (alternate pronunciation of *katana*) |
| *tōrei* | 刀礼 | bow(ing) to the sword |
| *tōshin* | 刀身 | "body of the sword" (bare sword without *koshirae* or *saya*) |
| *tsuba* | 鍔 | guard, shield |
| *tsuba-wari* | 鍔割 | split(ting) the *tsuba* (also a weapon by that name) |
| *tsubazeria* | 鍔迫り合 | clashing *tsuba* to *tsuba* with opponent |
| *tsugi-ashi* | 次足 | another term for *yori ashi* |
| *tsuji-giri* | 辻斬り | murdering peasants to test a new or repolished blade |
| *tsuka* | 柄 | handle |
| *tsukagashira* | 柄頭 | butt-cap of the *tsuka* |
| *tsuka-ito* | 柄糸 | string(s) for wrapping the *tsuka* |
| *tsuka-maki* | 柄巻 | wrapping a *tsuka*, or *tsuka* wrappings (in place) |
| *tsukazeria* | 柄迫り合 | clashing *tsuka* to *tsuka* with opponent |
| *tsukekomi* | 付け込み | seize the opportunity/initiative |
| *tsukeru* | 付ける | to affix, stick to, connect (verb) |
| *tsuki* | 突き | thrust |
| *tsukidashi* | 突き出し | run through |

| JAPANESE Term (*rōmaji*) | Japanese | ENGLISH Equivalent |
|---|---|---|
| uchi | 打ち | to strike, to hit |
| uchikata | 受ち方 | receiver (person receiving technique being practiced) |
| uchikata | 打ち方 | striker (person receiving technique being practiced) |
| uchitachi | 受ち太刀 | receiving sword (sword receiving technique being practiced) |
| uchitachi | 打ち太刀 | striking sword (sword receiving technique being practiced) |
| ue | 上 | up, upward |
| uke | 受け | block, intercept, deflect |
| ukemi | 受身 | controlled falling ("receiving body") |
| ukenagashi | 受け流し | flowing deflection ("flowing reception") of an attack |
| ukekomi | 受け込み | deflect and suppress |
| ushiro | 後ろ | rear, rearward, backward |
| uwagi | 上着 | *gi* jacket ("upper clothing") |
| wa | 和 | peace, harmony (also nickname for Japan) |
| wa | 輪 | ring, ring-shaped |
| waka musha | 若武者 | young *bushi* |
| waki | 脇 | side, beside |
| wakigamae | 脇構え | posture with sword held at the side |
| wakizashi | 脇差 | another word for *kodachi* ("side carry") |
| waza | 技 | technique |
| ya | 矢 | arrow |
| yama | 山 | mountain |
| yamabushi | 山伏 | hermit priest(s) |
| yamaoroshi | 山嵐 | wind sweeping up a mountainside (name of a technique) |

| JAPANESE Term (*rōmaji*) | Japanese | ENGLISH Equivalent |
|---|---|---|
| *yamato* | 大和 | a nickname for Japan |
| *yame* | 止め | stop (command) |
| *yasunde* | 休んで | rest, relax (command) |
| *yoko* | 横 | sideways, sideward |
| *yoko chiburi* | 横血振り | sideways *chiburi* (*chūden chiburi*) |
| *yoko ichimonji* | 横一文字 | sideways cutting technique |
| *yokomen* | 横面 | side of the face (usually temple) |
| *yokote* | 横手 | line demarking the *fukura* from the rest of a sword blade |
| *yūdansha* | 有段者 | a person holding *dan* rank |
| *yūkata* | 浴衣 | an evening-wear *kimono* |
| *yūkyūsha* | 有級者 | a person holding *kyū* grade |
| *zanshin* | 残心 | "leave mind" (awareness of surroundings) |
| *zōri* | 草履 | Japanese thong-sandals |

Appendix C

# Contact Information and Supplemental Materials

## KOKUSAI NIPPON BUDŌ KAI

c/o Sakura Budōkan

390 Tioga Avenue

Kingston, PA 18704

USA

Carl E. Long, *kaichō* (chairman)

📞 (570) 288-7865

🌐 www.knbk.org

**f** http://facebook.com/KokusaiNipponBudoKyokai

## NIPPON BUDŌ SEISHIN-KAN

PO Box 8684

San Antonio, TX 78208

USA

Leonard J. Pellman, Kanchō (managing director)

📞 (210) 591-7551

🌐 kancho@seishin-kan.org

🌐 www.seishin-kan.org

**f** http://facebook.com/NipponBudoSeishinKan

# SUPPLEMENTAL MATERIALS

The Kokusai Nippon Budō Kai (KNBK) and the Nippon Budō Seishin-Kan are continually creating and updating supplemental materials that are available either on their websites or in other published formats, so you are encouraged to visit the websites to acquire additional training resources, as well as the location and contact information for a member *dōjō* near you.

For more detailed descriptions of the Eishin-Ryū Battō-Hō and additional training exercises, we particularly recommend the book *Samurai Swordsmanship: The Battō, Kenjutsu, and Tameshigiri of Eishin-Ryū* (2011) by Masayuki Shimabukuro and Carl E. Long, as well as the DVDs *Samurai Swordsmanship*, volumes 1, 2, and 3, by Masayuki Shimabukuro, and the three-volume *Advanced Samurai Swordsmanship* DVD set by Masayuki Shimabukuro and Carl E. Long.

These resources are available through the Kokusai Nippon Budō Kai (KNBK) and many online retailers.

# Sakuin 索引

## Index

*italic* page numbers indicate figures

# *Hissha Shōkai*

筆者紹介

## About the Authors

### Shimabukuro Masayuki Hanshi and Ko-Sōshihan

The life and achievements of Masayuki Shimabukuro have been previously described in sufficient detail that it would be superfluous to repeat them here.

He was born on March 27, 1948, in Ōsaka, and followed his lifelong passion for traditional Japanese *budō* right up to his untimely death on September 7, 2012. He devoted himself to the mastery and promotion of *budō*, and eventually became one of the most highly respected authorities on *budō* in the world—of his or any other time.

More than his many awards and accomplishments, his life was a testimony to his resolute effort to live the life of a samurai—a life lived for the purpose of serving and benefiting others. His warm smile, his gracious and caring attitude, his love of *budō*, and his zeal to see *budō* reach the largest possible audience and improve the world are the things for which he should be remembered. The high rankings, titles, and accolades he received in life, and his posthumous induction into the Dai Nippon Butoku-Kai, are merely the tangible evidence of the impact he had on the people who knew him and trained with him.

It should be enough to say that people of his stature and influence are precious and all too rare, and it was a privilege to have walked by his side for a time.

## Leonard J. Pellman Shihan

Leonard Pellman was introduced to martial arts at the age of fourteen when, in 1966, after years of suffering persistent bullying in school, his parents enrolled him in a *jūdō* program in San Diego. He continued his *jūdō* training and was introduced to *kendō* while an exchange student to Japan in 1968. His fascination with *iaijutsu* began in 1973, when he returned to Japan to visit the family with whom he had stayed as an exchange student five years earlier. At the wedding of his exchange student "sister" in Toyohashi, Japan, her uncle, a fifth *dan* at the time, performed an *iaidō* demonstration (common at traditional Japanese weddings), which kept Pellman Shihan spellbound with its elegance, artistry, and intense focus and precision. Despite his keen interest, he was unable to find a qualified *iaijutsu* instructor until he was introduced to Shimabukuro Hanshi in late 1988.

As one of the Shimabukuro Hanshi's earliest and longest-standing students, Pellman Shihan was also one of the first members of the Jikishin-Kai International, serving as a director from its inception until moving to Indiana in 2001, and its successor organization the Kokusai Nippon Budō Kai.

Pellman Shihan established his own *dōjō*, the Nippon Budō Seishin-Kan, in 1989, and continues to serve as its *dōjō-chō* (chief instructor), teaching *iaijutsu*, *jōjutsu*, *kenjutsu*, and *aiki-jūjutsu*, in addition to *karate-dō* and Okinawa *kobujutsu*. As one of the first *budōka* to create a website (the Web-Dojo) in 1996, Pellman Shihan continues to maintain an extensive internet and social media presence promoting traditional Japanese *budō*.

# About North Atlantic Books

North Atlantic Books (NAB) is an independent, nonprofit publisher committed to a bold exploration of the relationships between mind, body, spirit, and nature. Founded in 1974, NAB aims to nurture a holistic view of the arts, sciences, humanities, and healing. To make a donation or to learn more about our books, authors, events, and newsletter, please visit www.northatlanticbooks.com.

North Atlantic Books is the publishing arm of the Society for the Study of Native Arts and Sciences, a 501(c)(3) nonprofit educational organization that promotes cross-cultural perspectives linking scientific, social, and artistic fields. To learn how you can support us, please visit our website.